Religion and Legitimation of Power

Anderson

Religion and Legitimation of Power in Sri Lanka

Edited by Bardwell L. Smith

South and Southeast Asia Studies by

ANIMA Books

Library of Congress Cataloging in Publication Data

Main entry under title:

Religion and legitimation of power in Sri Lanka.

Bibliography: p.
1. Buddhism and state—Sri Lanka—Addresses, essays, lectures.
2. Buddhism and politics—Addresses, essays, lectures. 3. Buddhism—Sri Lanka—History—Addresses, essays, lectures.
I. Smith, Bardwell L., 1925-
BQ359.R44 294.3'3'77095493 77-7449
ISBN 0-89012-008-0

South and Southeast Asia Studies
by ANIMA Books

ANIMA Books are published by Conococheague Associates, Inc., 1053 Wilson Avenue, Chambersburg PA 17201.

LC Number 77-7449
ISBN 0-89012-008-0

Foreword*

Bardwell L. Smith

This volume is one of three collections of essays on the theme of religion and the legitimation of power in South and Southeast Asia. As a whole, they examine various aspects of Islam, the Hindu tradition and Theravada Buddhism in relationship to the social and political order in several cultural and historical contexts. The present volume deals principally with Sri Lanka, though it includes consideration of Ceylon's long-term relationship with South India. The second volume is entitled *Religion and Political Power in Thailand, Laos and Burma*; it deals mainly with Burma and Thailand, especially the latter, though two of its essays devote attention to the Laotian context. A third volume, entitled *Religion and the Legitimation of Power in South Asia* and published by E. J. Brill (Leiden, 1978), deals principally with India, though it contains an essay on Pakistan and another on Sri Lanka. Originally, it was to have included ones on Bangladesh and on Nepal, but these essays were not completed as planned.

In 1973, when the idea for a set of essays on this topic was first considered, the plan called for a single volume, with essentially one chapter on most countries in South Asia and mainland Southeast Asia. At the 1975 annual meetings of the Canadian Association for South Asian Studies and the American Academy of Religion two symposia were held at which the larger share of the essays appearing in these three collections were first read. Both because it did not prove possible to obtain essays on certain countries and because several excellent ones were submitted on the same country (covering different historical periods and diverse aspects of the basic theme), the original plan was modified and the material fell into three groupings rather than one. Subsequent to the 1975 meetings of those two professional associations other papers were solicited from persons known to be working on comparable material, and it was also decided to reprint a few previously published articles, in most cases from journals not well known in this country.

In any collection of essays by several contributors it almost goes without saying, though no reviewer worth his or her salt fails to point this out, that certain chapters are of more enduring value than others and that the

---

*Essentially the same Foreword serves to introduce each of these volumes. Following the lead of A. L. Basham, editor, *A Cultural History of India* (Oxford: Clarendon Press, 1975), a simplified transliteration system is used in these essays. For the most part, only five letters with diacritical marks appear here (*ā*, *ī*, *ū*, *ṅ*, and *ś*), except in quotations and in the Index (where the standard system used by Indologists is employed). Also, those terms which have become familiar ones in the West (e.g., Theravāda, Mahāyāna, Brāhamanism, etc.) are used without long marks. Likewise, Sri Lanka (Śrī Laṅkā) is transliterated without diacritic marks.

volume as a whole does not possess the same cohesiveness a single first-rate scholar could bring to the subject. Certainly, in these collections, there are not only important lacunae, but there is no systematic attempt to relate ideas in one chapter to those in another, let alone to relate one volume to either or both of the others. The attempt here is more modest. It is simply to present together several reflections on a common theme, with breadth of scope and diversity of analysis compensating in part for lack of cohesiveness. Such is the editor's *apologia pro libro suo* in each of these three cases. It is necessary, however, to say something about the theme itself and to indicate how the concept was presented to those who wrote expressly for one or another of these volumes.

On a very general level the theme served to help the contributors focus their attention on how political leaders or a politicized group within a specific religious tradition and its membership (*or* an ideological tradition, for example, Marxism, civil religion in its modern guises, secularism, etc.) made use of "religious" beliefs, practices and institutions to provide cohesiveness to the realm and legitimacy to the holding of power. Examples of this, of course, abound in history. Some of the more famous ones include Constantine in the fourth century A.D., Aśoka in the third century B.C., and Han Wu-ti in the early Han dynasty of the second century B.C.

In the examination of any particular context one needs to consider a number of factors. Obviously, in any short essay only a few considerations can be explored in depth, though one can allude to others which could be examined in a longer treatment. The following factors were suggested to each contributor, though they were not intended to be exhaustive. In fact, part of each symposium's intent was to go beyond the merely descriptive approach to the subject and to help sharpen theoretical tools, i.e., to perceive new ways of analyzing the ongoing relationship between various kinds of ideology and political, social and economic power.

First, some attention must be given to the context itself in an essentially chronological manner. What factors, events, circumstances give rise to a situation in which it becomes possible and/or important for political power to align itself with and make use of a specific ideology or tradition in order to gain credibility and empower its sanctions? One need not begin with this descriptive analysis, but some attention is obviously in order.

Second, beyond the particulars which evolve over time to create a new social context, analysis includes examination of factors of social change, social contact and conflict, forms of cultural and political pluralism, and other aspects of an essentially dynamic picture which prompt different approaches to the organizing and enhancing of power.

Third, other pertinent considerations are the process and forms of legitimation which take place as power seeks to authenticate itself in the minds of potential supporters. Except in circumstances where "naked" or autocratic power is used, one finds a whole spectrum of subtle manifestations of legitimation, e.g., patronage of the arts, the granting of political patronage, direct or indirect support to certain religious groups, etc. Part of the picture here includes exploring how legitimation is nurtured, both within the body politic and within religious communities themselves.

Fourth, in the process of this evolution what happens to the religious tradition (or the ideology) when used in these ways? What happens to the political process, its structures and its goals? One needs to consider the dangers of communalism and the effect upon social, ethnic and religious minorities within the society. Does one find an inevitable corruption of religious tradition and ideology, or may reform and the seeds of a genuine renaissance emerge from these sorts of circumstances? What forms of syncretism emerge and how are these continuous or discontinuous with past forms?

Fifth, part of any such analysis may reveal challenges to the very process of legitimation itself from other forces within the society when threatened by such a development and by members of the political or religious hierarchy who perceive this process as inimical to a healthy social order and/or a given religious tradition. Examining these kinds of factors highlight the complexities of any situation and question univocal interpretations of what may otherwise appear as clearcut and self-evident forces at work.

As implied above, the intent of this endeavor was not to discover one set of criteria by which to examine the relationship between social power and ideological legitimacy, but to open up the investigation in fresh ways. This entails examining critically and with intensity an immense variety of common factors which, while present in most situations of these kinds, assume different forms and possess their own unique dynamics. To identify as many common factors as possible was thus one purpose, but to perceive their idiosyncratic combinations was no less important.

The present collection deals with several periods of Ceylonese history. The first five chapters focus mainly on the Anurādhapura period, which covered more than twelve centuries and ended toward the close of the tenth century A.D. The next five chapters examine developments from the tenth to the eighteenth centuries, though several of these essays also discuss earlier elements of mythology which came to fruition in later periods. The last three chapters deal mainly with the present stage of history. While the volume as a whole does not attempt to treat the theme of religion and the legitimation of power in Sri Lanka in all its aspects, the coverage is extensive and the essays have considerable cohesiveness.

Finally, the editor wishes to thank Professors A. L. Basham, Heinz Bechert and A. K. Ramanujan for the critical reading they gave to some of these essays. Needless to say, they are in no way responsible for the content of any essay, nor for the collection as a whole. Also, I am personally indebted to several persons who read my own bibliographical essay on the Polonnaruva period in its draft form. Besides A. L. Basham and Heinz Bechert, these included H. A. I. Goonetileke, R. A. L. H. Gunawardana, Sirima Kiribamune, Gananath Obeyesekere, and Frank E. Reynolds. The suggestions of Professor Bechert especially were extensive.

Contents

The Beginnings of Buddhist Historiography: *Mahāvaṃsa* and Political Thinking

Heinz Bechert

SRI LANKA (Ceylon) is universally known as occupying a unique position in the development of historical literature in the world of Indian and Buddhist culture: it is the only South Asian country where a historiographic tradition was started in a very early period and continued to the modern period without interruption. On the other hand, it is well-known that in mainland India there has been no historical literature in the strict sense of the word prior to the period of the first Muslim invasions. The explanation of the non-existence of early Indian historical literature has caused considerable difficulties for modern writers of Indian history. Besides that, it strikingly contrasts with the existence of an uninterrupted transmission of religious literature in India. In fact, no other culture except that of India can be proud of an unbroken tradition of religious texts for such a long period as that from the *Ṛgveda* to Hinduism in our days. Other branches of literary activity have likewise developed since early times. Even political science (*arthaśāstra*) was cultivated as a highly specialized branch of studies in ancient India.

The systematic study of the chronicles of Ceylon was one of the first subjects of modern Indological research. As early as 1833 a first (but uncritical) translation of the *Mahāvaṃsa* was published by Edward Upham in London, and in 1837 the Pāli text of the *Mahāvaṃsa* was edited along with a translation by George Turnour in Ceylon. Since that time, scholars were occupied with determining the reliability of the Ceylonese chronicles as sources of history, with the search for the source books from which the chronicles have drawn, and with the determination of the date of the *Sīhala-Aṭṭhakathā-Mahāvaṃsa*, which is considered as the main source used by the authors of the *Dīpavaṃsa* and of the ancient *Mahāvaṃsa.* The earlier research on the topic was summed up by G. C. Mendis in 1946 (see Mendis, 1946: 1-24) and by Frank Perera in 1974 (Perera, 1974: 8-29). Hermann Oldenberg has provided us with a critical edition and translation of the *Dīpavaṃsa* (*Dīpavaṃsa*, 1879) which should be made use of even today, because B. C. Law's recent edition and translation of this chronicle (*Dīpavaṃsa*, 1959) is unreliable and faulty. For the *Mahāvaṃsa*, Wilhelm Geiger's editions and translations (*Mahāvaṃsa*, 1908-30) serve as the basis of all further studies. The standard work on the history and development of the Ceylonese chronicles is Wilhelm Geiger's monograph on the subject (Geiger, 1905). Methodically, an important step forward was done in Erich Frauwallner's short paper on the historicity of Aśoka's Buddhist mission to Suvaṇṇabhūmi (Frauwallner, 1952 b) and this scholar's discussion of the beginnings of Buddhist literature in his book on the earliest Vinaya (Frauwallner, 1956). In 1961, I undertook a study of Aśoka's *sāsana* reform by a comparative analysis of the inscription and the relevant passages of the chronicles (Bechert, 1961). While working on this, I was forced to admit that the description of this event in the chronicles, though derived from a tradition based on facts, has been influenced by a particular tendency which resulted in giving a quite different representation of the events than the one we get from Aśoka's inscription. For a historian, there can be no question which of these sources must be considered as the more reliable source of history. I should add that I then still failed to evaluate the fact that the chronicles do not refer to the bureaucracy in control of religious affairs which was installed by Aśoka. In the so-called "schism edict," the function of this bureaucracy to control the observance of monastic rules is clearly described (Bechert, 1961: 24-27). There must be some reason why this important aspect of the reform has not been referred to in the chronicles.

It was as a result of work in a seemingly quite different field that I came to understand better the intentions of the redactors of the ancient chronicles, viz. in connection with a study of the history, the structures and the ideology of contemporary Theravada Buddhism (Bechert, 1966-73). Here, I was confronted with the problem of continuity and discontinuity in the interpretation of political thinking in Buddhist societies. Some of the results of this re-consideration have been published in a contribution "Zum Ursprung der Geschichtsschreibung im indischen Kulturbereich" in the Proceedings of the Academy of Sciences in Göttingen (Bechert, 1969). This paper has, however, hardly been noticed beyond the boundaries of Germany due to the lack of knowledge of German by a number of Ceylon specialists, which has prevented scholars like Gananath Obeyesekere from using my publications (see his remark in Obeyesekere, 1972: 58 note 1). Moreover, several aspects can be more precisely understood and formulated now than six years ago.*

At that time there existed two different approaches to the understanding of the chronicles. On the one hand, we find them interpreted as works written out of a purely religious motivation, and the holders of this view tended to ascribe the emergence of the so-called Sinhala-Buddhist nationalism along with most of the other features of Buddhist resurgence to the period towards the end of nineteenth century. On the other hand, there were the writings of the authors representing the Buddhist resurgence movement. These works served mainly as primary sources for the study of contemporary Buddhism, showing the ideology of the movement of political Buddhism. I need not elaborate here on this use of history which is being made in all types of apologetic writing and quite naturally in this branch of modern Buddhist writing as well.

When I read the early parts of the *Mahāvaṃsa* again after having been preoccupied with these studies on modern Buddhism for some years, I was struck by being continuously reminded of some of the ideological positions occupied by Buddhist "modernists" as far as the interrelations of religion, religious institutions, state, and society are concerned. The theory on the beginnings of Buddhist historiography presented here has resulted from this observation. I should, however, add that it would be an inadmissable simplification to say that the political aspect of the chronicles discussed here is the only important

*A paper on some related points was sent several years ago to the editor, *Journal of the Bihar Research Society*. I was informed recently that it was published there, but I have not seen proofs nor a copy yet. In any case, I thank the editor of the *Journal of the Bihar Research Society* for having no objection to my using parts of the text of the article sent to him in the present contribution.

aspect of these works. The Ceylonese chronicles are documents of the religious history of the island not less than of the emergence of political ideas, but I propose to single out this aspect which, in my opinion, contributed to the origination of Buddhist historiography more than any other single factor. I refer readers for other aspects of the chronicles to the relevant work done by Wilhelm Geiger on the historical value of the material (see Geiger, 1905; and Geiger, 1973: 284-307), by Bardwell L. Smith on the ideal social order as portrayed in the chronicles of Ceylon (Smith, 1972: 31-57), and others (see also Perera, 1974: 8-29 for an assessment of modern studies on the chronicles).

To make my point clear, I again recall here the well-known fact that historical works do not exist in the earlier Indian literary tradition, a fact which has been a riddle to scholars for a long time. In general, there was a tendency to attribute the lack of interest in handing down historical information to the ways of Hindu thinking. Some scholars like Hermann Goetz have proposed the theory that a considerable number of early historical sources which had existed in ancient India are lost to us (Goetz, 1924).

The theory proposed by H. Goetz, however, does not stand a critical examination. Admittedly, inscriptions, references in the records of Chinese travellers, and so on, point to the existence of "court-chronicles" in the first millennium A.D., but these cannot be considered historical writings in the strict sense of the word. Such records were kept for the particular needs of a royal court, and they were similar to genealogies and other traditions of a more personal or local character. Such documents did not form part of the national literature of India, and their loss was quite natural after the respective dynasties had ceased to rule. Some Indian scholars have also put forward the view that some sections of the Purāṇas should be looked upon as historical writing. Undoubtedly, there are historical traditions contained in Purāṇas and in a number of other Sanskrit texts, but we are concerned here only with historical writing in the true sense of the word. The transformation of these collections of historical material into historiography has never taken place in Purāṇa texts.

The non-existence of historical literature in ancient India is confirmed by the negative evidence of the fairly large recent finds of ancient Indian manuscripts (Gilgit manuscripts, Turfan manuscripts, manuscripts discovered and photographed by Rāhula Saṃskṛtyāyana in Tibet, etc.). It becomes quite clear from these discoveries that historical works were not included in the Indian libraries of the respective periods. Surprisingly, this fully applies to the literature of Indian Buddhism, though we would expect that the need to authenticate the uninterrupted tradition of a valid monastic ordination (*upasampadā*) prescribed by Buddhist ecclesiastical law should have resulted in the development of literary activities in the field of historical writing. But what do we meet with in Indian Buddhist literature? Some more or less isolated records of important events of the history of the Buddhist church and some short historical chapters in hagiographical texts are the only historical sections of Indian Buddhist literature. Some of these records have originated in connection with the controversies of the Buddhist sects, but not even these were developed into coherent works of ecclesiastical history.

Thus, it cannot be doubted that the only early historical literature within the realm of South Asian culture which ever has existed is that of Ceylon, and that historical writing in the strict sense of the word was started in the Indian sub-continent only after the first Muslim invasions had disturbed the traditionally established order of Indian life and culture.

Therefore, I dare to propose a new approach to the problem of the beginnings of South Asian historiography, viz. to reverse the way of examination and to search for the motivation of the earliest historiographers instead of trying to explain the non-existence of an early Indian historical literature. This way of examination is justified by a comparison with the beginnings of historical literature in non-Indian cultures. It shows us that the composition of historical works has never been a quasi-automatic process in the course of cultural history, but always depended on a particular motivation, e.g., the self-assurance of Greek culture against Persian influence in the case of the earliest Greek historical writers.

For the historian, the answer to the question of the motivational background of the earliest historical writers of South Asia in Ceylon is of utmost importance. Answering this question helps judging the value of the tradition of the Ceylonese chronicles as historical sources from a new point of view and deciding the old controversy in which famous scholars like Rudolf Otto Franke and Wilhelm Geiger had occupied antithetic positions. (For a discussion of details of this controversy, see Mendis, 1946: 1-14). Naturally, the relative importance of epigraphical material, literary evidence, and other sources too, can be correctly evaluated only if the motivation of the authors of the documents is understood.

For this purpose, some general observations on the relation between Ceylon and the sub-continent are helpful. The question "India and Ceylon" has been dealt with in many books and papers, but these studies almost invariably concentrate on the material aspects of this relation, thereby limiting the scope of research to problems like these: Where did the population of Ceylon come from? When and how did Ceylonese tradition take over certain elements of Indian culture? What was the contribution of the Ceylonese people to the development of South Asian culture in general? Answers to these and similar questions have been proposed, and a considerable amount of knowledge relative to the Indo-Ceylonese political and cultural relations has been collected, though many of the results of these studies are still questionable. However, a typological comparison has not been undertaken so far.

Selecting an example which can be dealt with from my point of view, I may quote here a striking peculiarity of Sinhalese culture as compared with that of India and of Southeast Asia, viz. the non-existence of the *Rāmāyaṇa* tradition in the higher strata of traditional Sinhalese literary culture. The subject of the *Rāmāyaṇa* constitutes a main element in the literary tradition of every country influenced by Indian culture, whether Hindu or Buddhist, with the exception of Ceylon. In Indonesia the story of the *Rāmāyaṇa* has lost nothing of its popularity even after the conversion of the country to Islam. The absence of the *Rāmāyaṇa* in Ceylon is all the more surprising if we consider the fact that Lanka is the scene of the epic. The existence of some popular ballads based on a distorted form of *Rāmāyaṇa* in later Sinhalese folk-literature and the existence of the mediaeval Sanskrit kāvya *Jānakīharaṇa*, which was based on the *Rāmāyaṇa* story and composed (but not handed down) in Ceylon, cannot be accepted as valid arguments to disprove the general statement that this epic has not become a part of Sinhalese culture in the way it has become an integral part of that of other Buddhist peoples, e.g., of the Khmer and Thai.

(Details of the *Rāmāyaṇa* versions in Sinhalese popular literature clearly show the comparatively recent introduction of these stories to the island; cf. Bechert, 1977, s.v. Mala rāja and s.v. Rāma). The only available explanation for this fact is based on some passages in the classical Pāli commentaries where the Sanskrit epics are criticized from a Buddhist point of view (see Malalasekera, 1960: 2, 1155). Considering that there are many non-Buddhist elements in Sinhalese mythology and that the cult of the gods forms an integral part of the culture of Buddhist Ceylon, this explanation is completely unacceptable. We shall discuss this problem later.

In the religious field, Buddhism as the religion of the Sinhalese is entirely different from South Indian Hinduism. The language of the Sinhalese is historically not related to the Dravidian languages of South India. Even the cult of the popular gods of Ceylon widely differs from South Indian religious traditions. Whereas Viṣṇu is the main god of Sinhalese popular religion, Śiva is the highest god of Tamil Hinduism.

The development of these and other differences between Ceylon and India can be traced back to the vicissitudes of history. Buddhism came from North India to Ceylon as well as to South India, but it has totally disappeared in South India before the end of the fifteenth century. The cult of the gods of the Sinhalese, though it is very different from South Indian religion in our days, still reflects many characteristics of early South Indian religion (see Bechert, 1968/9; Lohuizen, 1971). The same applies to the social system of the Sinhalese which bears similarities to ancient forms of South Indian social structure, in particular in its matrilocal elements (see Bechert, 1963).

From a comparative study of Indian and Ceylonese culture and from a number of other observations we can derive the conclusion that a particular form of a conservative tendency is characteristic of the culture of the Sinhalese. A study of Sanskrit literature in Ceylon yielded similar results (see Bechert, 1960). Generally, certain texts of literature and of science have been taken over and faithfully transmitted, but there was not much impetus to change the once accepted tradition. As an obvious example, the grammatical literature of Ceylon may be quoted. Here the Pāli grammarians have adopted one of the systems of Sanskrit grammar without basic change (see Franke, 1902: 14-19). The use of the formal categories of Sanskrit grammar to describe the Pāli language has resulted in a number of inconsistencies. The insufficient description of Pāli in the works of traditional Pāli grammar which contrasts to the very exact informations contained in classical Sanskrit grammars can thus be explained as a result of the rigorous imitation of Sanskrit grammar and, therefore, as a consequence of a conservative tendency.

In the field of politics, the nearly uninterrupted political independence of the Island from the political powers of mainland India is most remarkable. Periods of South Indian predominance were invariably ended by liberation movements. Even the British administration soon separated Ceylon from the colonial possessions in India and thereby opened the way for final independence.

In the history of Ceylon Buddhism, the conservatism is evident at first sight. The influence of Mahayana was systematically combatted by the orthodox bhikkhus of Theravada tradition. Though certain elements of Mahayana doctrine have influenced the development of Buddhism in Ceylon, e.g., the conception of *prāpti* and the current understanding of *anumodanā* (see Bechert, 1964: 534 f.), Mahayana Buddhism as a distinct form of religion was never accepted by the main stream of Sinhalese tradition. (For details, see Bechert, 1976.)

The conservatism of Sinhalese culture is closely connected to the self-consciousness of the Sinhalese, and it was combined with a remarkable capacity to adjust elements taken over from other cultures, thereby restoring the unity of national culture if it was endangered. In this context, the assimilation of South Indian immigrants in the coastal areas to the Sinhalese during the early modern period should be mentioned. That conservatism does by no means prevent the evolution of creativity is evident to all who have studied the development of fine art as well as of dancing in Ceylon. The transformative power of Sinhalese culture is also evident from many aspects of popular religion and ritual. As one out of many examples, the famous tradition of the Sanni demons which originated in South India, but has been completely "Sinhalized" in the course of time may be mentioned (see Obeyesekere, 1969: 198 ff.; other examples from Sinhalese mythology, see Bechert, 1977, passim). This transformation can be observed also with the well-known eighteen Vannam of Kandyan dancing, which are originally derived from South Indian dance. We may also refer to the fact that the Sinhalese were almost the only South Asian people not to pass over from Prakrit to Sanskrit as the language of epigraphical records in the early mediaeval period. Retaining the use of the local language, an expression of a conservative attitude, was at the same time the cause of an important innovation, viz. the formation of the Sinhalese literary language, and an act of self-assurance of the Sinhalese nation as well.

Thus it is no longer surprising for us to trace the beginnings of historiography in South Asia from this very culture which we have characterized as inclined towards conservatism. An examination of the records of Asoka's period in the Ceylon chronicles will help us to go one step further in understanding this development. Traditionally, the installation of Buddhism as a religion of state is traced back to Aśoka (Pāli, Asoka). Devānaṁpiyatissa is believed to have followed Aśoka's example when he made Buddhism the state religion of Ceylon in the particular orthodox form of Theravada (Rahula, 1956: 62). Some scholars have recently tried to establish the reliability of the record of the chronicles on Aśoka's sangha reform as a historical record by a comparison of these accounts with the pertinent inscriptions of Aśoka (Alsdorf, 1959; and Jayawickrama, 1959). The so-called Third Buddhist Council at Pātaliputra – which actually was the Fourth Council, as Erich Frauwallner has proved (Frauwallner, 1952a: 256-259) – is, however, not recorded in the inscriptions. Besides, the similarities of the account in the chronicle and in the inscriptions can easily be explained by the fact that both make use of the same terminology of vinaya. Thus, the inscription does prove that a sāsana reform was enacted by Aśoka and that it was implemented in a way by which the principles of vinaya were observed. Therefore, it is not probable that Aśoka was partial towards any section of the sangha, as suggested by the authors of the chronicles. Such a partiality would not have been justified by the rules of vinaya. I have given a detailed analysis of the sources elsewhere which need not to be repeated here (Bechert, 1961). It is, therefore, evident that Aśoka has not been a follower of a particular *nikāya*, as suggested by the chroniclers.

The Ceylonese record of Aśoka's sāsana reform shows traces of a conscious redaction of the tradition, the aim of which becomes clear to readers of the record of the establishment of Buddhism in Ceylon in the *Mahāvaṃsa* (Chapter XV). Here, the ideology of state-sangha relations is quite different from the way of thinking found in Aśoka's inscriptions. Not a dharma conception generally acceptable in a multi-religious society, but the conception of a particularly Buddhist state is proposed in the *Mahāvaṃsa* record. Therefore, we must distinguish the Aśokan ideology as testified in the inscriptions and the Aśokan ideology as recorded in the literary sources. It was, of course, not the tolerant Aśoka and his non-denominational dharma that influenced the thinking of later periods. Aśoka's inscriptions had long been forgotten when they were rediscovered and read in the nineteenth and twentieth centuries. Buddhists in Theravada countries knew Aśoka only as depicted in Pāli commentaries and chronicles, i.e., in their particular transformation of the historical tradition. By this transformation the basis was laid for the ideology of state-sangha relations in Theravada countries which proved historically relevant. In this way, history was made by historians in early Ceylon through the development of a particular way of thinking.

Another element of early Ceylon historiography which must be referred to in this connection is the record of the origins of the Sinhalese nation. The chronicles make mention of personal visits of the Buddha in the island and of a prophecy that Ceylon would be the *dhammadīpa* ("island of the [Buddha's] teaching") and the descendants of Vijaya and his followers would become the preservers of the Buddhist religion in the future. These traditions, which I need not quote here in detail, because they are too well-known, must be understood in the context of the ideology of state-sangha relations. By this way a complete system of political thinking is provided in the early Ceylonese chronicles, not in a systematic way, but in the form of examples from the past. The basic idea of this ideology was that of the unity of nation and religion. The culminating point of the chronicler's account is at the same time the most evident exemplification of the principle of this unity of Sinhalese nation and Buddhist religion, the so-called epic of Duṭṭhagāmaṇī. The record in the 25th chapter of the *Mahāvaṃsa* shows that even the basic principles of Buddhist religion were made subordinate to this leading notion.

Once we have correctly understood the motivation of the chronicler, we have arrived at the answer to the question asked at the beginning of this paper. The origination of a historical literature in Ceylon in the existing form was an intentional act of political relevance. Its object was the propagation of a concept of national identity closely connected with a religious tradition, i.e., the identity of the Sinhalese Buddhists. This idea has shaped the history of Ceylon from the days of the earliest chroniclers to the present day in its particular way. Without the impact of this idea, the remarkable continuity of the cultural as well as of the political traditions in spite of the vicissitudes in the history of the island would have been impossible. Its impact has, at the same time, entirely changed the Aśokan ideology. For Aśoka, the idea of a non-denominational welfare-state was born from the inner conflict of the king resulting from his repentance of the war he had made before his conversion to the Buddhist religion. For the author of the *Mahāvaṃsa*, on the other hand, the war of Duṭṭhagāmaṇī against the Tamil invaders was by no means a problem of religion and morality, but it was a justified act of national politics.

The existence of non-historical elements in the contents of the Ceylon chronicles, which are similar to motifs in Purāṇa traditions, may not be quoted against my argument. These traditions mostly refer to the description of the period prior to the introduction of Buddhism in Ceylon, which is based on Purāṇa-style traditions which were handed down orally. The authors of the chronicles accepted them without questioning their trustworthiness. In our context it is important to notice how the authors of the chronicles have made use of such popular traditions and myths for the explication and exemplification of their views on the early history of the island.

The impact of ancient Indian political science on the authors of the chronicles cannot be denied either. In the latter continuation of the *Mahāvaṃsa*, which was composed by Dhammakitti, we can trace the direct influence of the *Kauṭalīya-Arthaśāstra* as Wilhelm Geiger has shown in his study of the culture of mediaeval Ceylon (Geiger, 1960: XXI, 54, 68, 148). But there remains a basic difference between Indian political science and the ideology of the chronicles of the Sinhalese. The *Kauṭalīya-Arthaśāstra* provides its readers with political instructions which were universally practicable, whereas the Ceylon chronicles gave political lessons from the past applicable only to the particular situation of the Sinhalese nation. In this way, a form of nationalism originated in ancient Ceylon which was rather close to modern nationalism with its conceptions of a united nation with common linguistic, cultural and religious traditions. The chronicles served as educational works to cultivate this consciousness of national identity. They were works of "*nīti* literature" with this particular object.

The authors of the chronicles were Buddhist monks. It is surprising at first sight that bhikkhus should have been the propagators of a state ideology, when we recall the rules of the Order. We know, however, that religious ideas always have occupied an important place in the traditional state ideology of a Theravada Buddhist kingdom. The king was customarily described as a *cakravartin*, i.e., as a universal monarch as described in canonical Buddhist works. He was also identified as a *bodhisattva*, i.e., a Buddha-to-be, and his Buddhist legitimation was bound to his function as a promoter and protector of orthodox Theravada Buddhism. All these elements were essential in building up a charismatic appeal of the ruler, but not for practical politics. For the practice of political power Indian tradition provided a system of politics free from religious ideology, viz. the political science of *arthaśāstra.* Thus, Indian culture offered the conception of religious legitimation of kingship, but at the same time it provided a tradition of purely secular state craft which made the ruler free from all eventual restrictions resulting from religious traditions – a dualism which must be considered in order to understand state-sangha relations.

In this context it is clear that the integration of the sangha into the political system was worked out within the tradition of rational politics, but it had to be justified in terms of religious ideology. This was done by emphasizing the need to protect the sangha from decay, i.e., from meddling in "mundane" activities, the sangha being an institution with purely religious or "supramundane" (*lokuttara*) aims. Protection of the sangha, therefore, included, at the same time, the need of preventing it from taking part in "mundane" activities which was forbidden by the rules of vinaya, and, at the same time, by reason of state. The kings regularly carried out reforms of the sangha (see Bechert, 1974).

This delimitation of the spheres of state and sangha did not, however, conflict with the contribution of the sangha towards the development of the political ideology. On the contrary, it furthered this development by effectively preventing a state-sangha rivalry. Pahamunē Śrī Sumangala, Mahānāyaka of Malvatta from 1927-1945, thus has correctly understood the lessons of Ceylon history when he called attention to the importance of the sangha as a guide of the nation and of the kings in social and political as well as in religious matters (see his contribution in Vijayavardhana, 1953: 15-20). This political function of the sangha proved effective by its contribution to the ideology which was formulated in the historical literature of the Sinhalese, and this literature was composed by bhikkhus. The inseparable connection of national identity and Buddhist religion resulted in a feeling of responsibility towards nation and state and thus in the continuous preservation of a particular political entity, i.e., the state of the Sinhalese, throughout the centuries. Historiography thus effected long-term political results.

We can derive conclusions for dating the earliest historical writings of Ceylon from these findings. The date of the existing Pāli chronicles is fairly well-known. According to S. Paranavitana's study on Mahānāma, the author of the *Mahāvaṃsa*, this work was composed shortly before A.D. 518 (Paranavitana, 1962). The *Dīpavaṃsa* can be dated between the beginning of the fourth and the first half of the fifth century A.D. (Geiger, 1905: 46 f.). Whereas the *Mahāvaṃsa* presents a well-arranged account, the *Dīpavaṃsa* is a somewhat confused collection of rather unconnected records. A number of events in the history of the sangha and parts of the history of Ceylon are found in two or even three versions in the *Dīpavaṃsa.* An analysis of this work shows that it is nothing else but a collection of excerpts consisting of *ākhyāna* verses and memorial verses drawn from three different sources. There cannot be much doubt that Erich Frauwallner is correct in describing two of these sources as the monastic chronicles of the two main vihāras in Anurādhapura, viz. Mahāvihāra and Abhayagirivihāra (Frauwallner, 1952b: 192-194).

Mahānāma refers to the *Dīpavaṃsa* in his introductory verses as the "*Mahāvaṃsa* composed by the Old." The later tradition, including the author of the commentary of the *Mahāvaṃsa*, has misunderstood this phrase, because they mistook it as a reference to his main source, which was the *Sīhalaṭṭhakathā-Mahāvaṃsa* or *Aṭṭhakathā-Mahāvaṃsa* (see Geiger, 1973: 435). This earlier work is lost to us; it was the same monastic chronicle consisting of verses in Pāli and prose-text in Old Sinhalese which had been made use of by the author of the *Dīpavaṃsa.*

We may safely suppose that the main contents of the accounts in both chronicles are derived from the source books and therefore the main characteristics of Sinhalese historiography must already have applied to the source-books. The philological analysis of the *Mahāvaṃsa* and the *Dīpavaṃsa* has proved that the *Aṭṭhakathā-Mahāvaṃsa* must be considered as the first historical work in this tradition, its sources being Purāṇa-style geneologies, lists of the heads of the sāsana, and short accounts of events in the sāsana history. The transformation of these elements into historical writing took place when they were arranged under the point of view of one concept, viz. the concept which we have discussed before. It is probable that this transformation occurred when there was a particular situation which caused the rise of a national feeling. Such a situation arose twice in the course of the early history of the Sinhalese, viz. when Duṭṭhagāmaṇī and when Vaṭṭagāmaṇī liberated the island from foreign domination. It is rather evident that the source-book underlying the *Dīpavaṃsa* cannot have been composed in connection with Vaṭṭagāmaṇī's successful liberation of Lanka from Tamil domination. During Vaṭṭagāmaṇī's reign the first schism in the sangha of Ceylon took place. The monastic chronicles of the Mahāvihāra and the Abhayagirivihāra – i.e., the two main sources of the *Dīpavaṃsa* – are clearly derived from one original chronicle which, therefore, must be dated earlier than the first schism. In this way, we are led to the conclusion that the origin of the earliest Sinhalese historiography must be dated before Vaṭṭagāmaṇī. Its date can be determined in the period shortly after the reign of the national hero of the Sinhalese, King Duṭṭhagāmaṇī. This date exactly agrees with the date which Frauwallner inferred from absolutely different considerations (Frauwallner, 1952b: 193).

The period of Vaṭṭagāmaṇī has, however, played a very important role in the emergence of the ideology of Sinhalese-Buddhist nationalism. By comparing the reconstructed contents of the source-book and the *Dīpavaṃsa* on the one hand and Mahānāma's *Mahāvaṃsa* on the other hand, we observe that Duṭṭhagāmaṇī's performances and reign are rather shortly dealt with in the earlier sources (see *Dīpavaṃsa* 18.53-19.23), whereas it has become one of the main topics of the *Mahāvaṃsa* (22.1-32.84). The so-called "epic of Duṭṭhagāmaṇī" (see Geiger, 1905: 20-27) probably was elaborated in connection with events of the Tamil occupation which was ended by Vaṭṭagāmaṇī's war of liberation. It marks the final and decisive step in the emergence of the ideology of Sinhala-Buddhist nationalism. (Vaṭṭagāmaṇī's role for the emergence of Sinhalese historiography was first discussed by Perera, 1974:111 f.).

By this understanding of the ideological background of Buddhist historiography in Ceylon the above-discussed non-existence of the *Rāmāyaṇa* tradition in the main stream of Sinhalese culture also becomes intelligible. There was, in principle, no restriction in the assimilation of Indian cultural influence in Sinhalese culture, but there was a strict limit if such influences would cause a conflict with the basic concepts of the historical and religious mission of Sri Lanka. The tradition laid down in the chronicles and in other Buddhist literary works was the only acceptable way to describe the early history of the island for the Sinhalese literates. Therefore, we can conclude that the absence of the *Rāmāyaṇa* tradition was by no means a kind of gap or deficiency; on the contrary, it was the consequence of a conscious decision of the Sinhalese authors to prevent the spread of contradictory ideas concerning the historical mission of Lanka.

There are many other developments leading into the same direction. I may refer here to the importance which the palladium of Sinhala royalty, viz. the sacred Tooth Relic, gained in the mediaeval period. By its symbolic value this relic has greatly contributed to establishing the concept of legality in the political life of mediaeval Ceylon. It would lead too far to comment on this and related questions here, but it seems that the points mentioned in my paper may be sufficient to enter into a discussion of the origins of historiography of Lanka.

References

1. Alsdorf, Ludwig
   1959 "Aśokas Schismen-Edikt und das dritte Konzil," *Indo-Iranian Journal,* III (1959), 161-174.
2. Bechert, Heinz
   1960 "Sanskritliteratur bei den Singhalesen," *Indologen-Tagung*, 1959, ed. by E. Waldschmidt, Göttingen 1960, 225-231.
   1961 "Aśokas 'Schismenedikt' und der Begriff Sanghabheda," *Wiener Zeitschrift für die Kunde Süd-und Ostasiens*, V (1961), 18-52.
   1963 "Mother Right and Succession to the Throne in Malabar and Ceylon," *The Ceylon Journal of Historical and Social Studies*, VI (1963), 25-40.
   1964 "Zur Frühgeschichte des Mahāyāna-Buddhismus," *Zeitschrift der Deutschen Morgenländischen Gesellschaft*, CXIII (1964), 530-535.
   1966-73 *Buddhismus, Staat und Gesellschaft in den Ländern des Theravāda-Buddhismus*, 3 vols., Frankfurt: A. Metzner (vol. 1) and Wiesbaden: O. Harrassowitz (vols. 2-3). (Schriften des Instituts für Asienkunde in Hamburg, XVII/1-3).
   1968-69 "Eine alte Gottheit in Ceylon und Südindien," *Beiträge zur Geistesgeschichte Indiens, Festschrift für Erich Frauwallner, Wiener Zeitschrift für die Künde Süd-und Ostasiens*, 12/13 (1968/69), 33-42.
   1969 "Zum Ursprung der Geschichtsschreibung im indischen Kulturberich," Nachrichten der Akademie der Wissenschaften in Göttingen, *Philologisch-historische Klasse*, 1969, No. 2, 35-58.
   1974 "Sāsana-Reform im Theravāda-Buddhismus," *50 Jahre Buddhistisches Haus,* ed. by Sri Gnanavimala Maha Thera, G. Auster, R. Leu, Berlin-Frohnau, 1974, 19-34.
   1976 "Buddha-Feld und Verdienslübertragung: Mahāyāna-Ideen im Theravāda-Buddhismus Ceylons," Acadámie Royale de Belgique, *Bulletin de la Classe des Lettres et des Sciences Morales et Politiques*, 1976, 27-51.
   1977 "Die Mythologie der singhalesischen Volksreligion," *Wörterbuch der Mythologie*, ed. by H. W. Haussig, 15. Lieferung, Stuttgart.
3. *Dīpavaṃsa*
   1879 *The Dīpavaṃsa, An Ancient Buddhist Historical Record*, ed. and trans. by Hermann Oldenberg. London: Williams and Norgate.
   1959 *The Chronicle of the Island of Ceylon or the Dipavaṃsa*, ed. by Bimala Churn Law, *The Ceylon Historical Journal*, VII (1957/58), Dehiwala 1959.
4. Franke, Rudolf Otto
   1902 *Geschichte und Kritik der einheimischen Pāli-Grammatik und -Lexicographie.* Strassburg: K. J. Trübner.
5. Frauwallner, Erich
   1952a "Die buddhistischen Konzile," *Zeitschrift der Deutschen Morgenländischen Gesellschaft*, CII (1952), 240-261.
   1952b "Die ceylonesischen Chroniken und die erste buddhistische Mission nach Hinterindien," *Actes du IVe Congrès International des Sciences Anthropologiques et Ethnologiques*, Vienne 1952, t.2: *Ethnologica*, 1, Wien 1955, 192-197.
   1956 "The Earliest Vinaya and the Beginnings of Buddhist Literature," Roma: Is.M.E.O. (*Serie Orientale Roma*, VIII).
6. Geiger, Wilhelm
   1905 *Dīpavaṃsa und Mahāvaṃsa und die geschichtliche Überlieferung in Ceylon*, Leipzig: A. Deichert'sche Verlagsbuchhandlung.
   1960 *Culture of Ceylon in Mediaeval Times*, ed. by Heinz Bechert. Wiesbaden: O. Harrassowitz.
   1973 *Kleine Schriften zur Indologie und Buddhismuskunde*, ed. by Heinz Bechert. Wiesbaden: F. Steiner. (Glasenapp-Stiftung, VI).
7. Goetz, Hermann
   1924 *Die Stellung der indischen Chroniken im Rahmen der indischen Geschichte.*

München-Neubiberg: O. Schloss (Untersuchungen zur Geschichte des Buddhismus, XI).

8. Jayawickrama, N. A.
   1959 "A Reference to the Third Council in Aśoka's Edicts?", *University of Ceylon Review*, XVII (1959), pp. 61-72.
9. Lohuizen-de Leeuw, J. E. van
   1971 "Aiyanār, An Aspect of Hindu Influence in Ceylon," Paper read at: Symposium on Religion in South Asia, School of Oriental and African Studies, London 1971.
10. *Mahāvaṃsa*
   1908-1930 *The Mahāvaṃsa*, ed. by Wilhelm Geiger, London: Pāli Text Society, 1908; *Cūlavaṃsa, being the more recent part of the Mahāvaṃsa*, ed. by Wilhelm Geiger, 2 vols., London: Pāli Text Society, 1925-27; *The Mahāvaṃsa or The Great Chronicle of Ceylon*, transl. by Wilhelm Geiger, London: Pāli Text Society, 1912 (4th ed., Colombo: Ceylon Government Information Department 1960); *Cūlavaṃsa being the more recent part of the Mahāvaṃsa*, transl. by Wilhelm Geiger, 2 vols., London: Pāli Text Society, 1929-30.
11. Malalasekera, G. P.
   1960 *Dictionary of Pāli Proper Names*, 2 vols., 2nd ed., London: Pali Text Society, 1960.
12. Mendis, G. C.
   1946 "The Pāli Chronicles of Ceylon, An Examination of the Opinions expressed about them since 1879," *University of Ceylon Review*, IV (1946), 1-24.
13. Obeyesekere, Gananath
   1969 "The Ritual Drama of the Sanni Demons: Collective Representations of Disease in Ceylon," *Comparative Studies in Society and History*, II (1969), 174-216.
   1972 "Religious Symbolism and Political Change in Ceylon," *The Two Wheels of Dhamma: Essays on Theravada Tradition in India and Ceylon*, ed. by Bardwell L. Smith, AAR Studies in Religion, No. 3, Chambersburg, Pa., 58-78.
14. Paranavitana, Senerat
   1962 "Mahānāma, The Author of Mahāvaṃsa," *University of Ceylon Review*, XX (1962), 269-286.
15. Perera, Frank
   1974 *The Early Buddhist Historiography of Ceylon*, unpublished doctoral dissertation. Georg-August-Universität, Göttingen.
16. Rahula, Walpola
   1956 *History of Buddhism in Ceylon, The Anurādhapura Period.* Colombo: M.D. Gunasena, 2nd edition, 1966.
17. Smith, Bardwell L.
   1972 "The Ideal Order as Portrayed in the Chronicles of Ceylon," *The Two Wheels of Dhamma: Essays on the Theravada Tradition in India and Ceylon*, ed. by Bardwell L. Smith, AAR Studies in Religion, No. 3, Chambersburg, Pa., 31-57.
18. Vijayavardhana, D. C.
   1953 *Dharma-Vijaya (Triumph of Righteousness)*, or *The Revolt in the Temple.* Colombo: Sinha Publications.

The Relic on the Spear: Historiography and the Saga of Duṭṭhagāmaṇī

Alice Greenwald

AS EVIDENCED IN the early historical chronicles of Ceylon, the portrait of the celebrated Buddhist warrior-king Duṭṭhagāmaṇī (r. 161-137 B.C.) provides a rich context for investigating the functional implications of the historiographical genre.* Deemed by Walpola Rahula to be "undoubtedly the greatest national hero of early Buddhist Ceylon," who can "justly be regarded as the originator of religio-nationalism which has persisted through the whole history of Ceylon,"[1] Duṭṭhagāmaṇī is yet a most complex character whose actions, especially in war, would seem an outright affront to the Buddhist sensibility. To remark categorically, as does Rahula, that "Duṭṭhagāmaṇī seems to have exploited to the utmost all the religious and national sentiments of the masses in order to unite the people and to rid his motherland of foreign rule,"[2] is to understate the issue and, moreover, to account insufficiently for whatever motivational logic may have legitimated such exploitation. This study will explore how historiography both mediates and justifies the contradiction inherent in a Buddhist king who would go so far as to place a relic of the Buddha in his battle lance and call for a company of 500 monks to escort his troops to war.

Prior to an investigation of the interplay of discrepancy and exemplar in Duṭṭhagāmaṇī's character, it is imperative to understand the nature of the chronicles which relate his saga. The *Dīpavaṃsa (Dpv.)*, the *Mahāvaṃsa (Mhv.)*, and the *Thūpavaṃsa (Tpv.)* – ranging in date of composition respectively from the fourth century A.D. to the late fifth to the thirteenth century – represent a genre of narrative which cannot rightfully be termed "objective" history. The effort of monks, they epitomize what Bardwell L. Smith has variously termed "history written with a motive," *"Heilsgeschichte,"* "the sacred history of a people," "interpreted history."[3]

> Reluctance is expressed in some quarters to regard the *Mhv.* as history. If the *Mhv.* is not a history of Ceylon, it is decidedly the history of Buddhism in Ceylon, and the history of Buddhism in Ceylon covers the major part of the Island's history. Both the *Dīpavaṃsa* and the *Mahāvaṃsa* are histories of Buddhism. In them secular history is subservient to religious history.[4]

These are texts which construct a historical narrative around certain archetypal personages or events which, whether founded in historical fact or, more likely,

*It should be stated at the outset that as a means of gaining access to an understanding of how the genre of religio-historiography functions, we are constructing a polemic which, in reality, does not exist. The texts under consideration will be measured against the ideals of canonical Buddhism in the effort at determining ostensible discrepancy with "orthodoxy."

However, this is not to suggest that we presume an existent canonical Buddhism. Rather, canon is understood in terms of its etymological meaning, as a standard or "rule" against which one can measure one's activities. This should be clearly understood before proceeding to the body of the paper.

extrapolated from history, constitute a charter-like sanction for the historical existence of Buddhist Ceylon. Charter is conceived of in the Malinowskian sense as that which, through the medium of myth (or, in this case, religious historiography), both engenders and substantiates a cultural self-consciousness:

> Myth serves principally to establish a sociological charter. . . . Myth, as a statement of primeval reality which still lives in present-day life and as *a justification by precedent*, supplies *a retrospective pattern* of moral values, sociological order, and magical belief . . . . The function of myth, briefly, is to strengthen tradition and endow it with a greater value and prestige by *tracing it back to a higher, better, more supernatural reality of initial events.*[5]

The intent of the historiographical texts under consideration is expressly to locate and affirm an irrefutable interconnection between Buddhism and Ceylon. In the effort to realize this intent, the texts comprise, within the context of a chronological account, a patchwork of reflective typologies, sequence parallels, and pivotal moments of temporal/historical intersection which testify to the Buddhist penetration into the Sinhalese historical reality. In this regard, it is notable that both the *Dīpavaṃsa* and the *Mahāvaṃsa* begin their accounts with an event unrecorded in the Pāli Canon, but essential to a "sacred" history of Lanka (Ceylon): the three visits of the Buddha to the Island during the early years of his enlightenment. One is reminded of the earliest histories of Britain, those composed by Nennius or Geoffrey of Monmouth, which trace the history of their island to the arrival of Joseph of Arimathea upon the shores of Cornwall. A connection both to Jesus and the Roman Empire was thereby established, British ancestry afforded a sacred and prestigious origin, and historical chronicle transformed at the outset into religious historiography. Likewise, the history of a nation in which "the Buddha Sasana (the system, i.e., Buddhism) and ethnic culture (would become) identified together,"[6] could only begin at that point when the Buddha himself makes Lanka "a fit dwelling place for men" (*Mhv.* 1:43), when the gods are invoked to insure protection for the island where "his doctrine should (thereafter) shine in glory" (*Mhv.* 1:20). As Mark began his gospel not with a birth story or a lengthy genealogy but with the baptism that marked Jesus' sacred birth, so the history of Lanka opens at the moment of its sacred inception. It is a moment of intersection, fossilized in the footprint allegedly (*Mhv.* 1:77) left by the Buddha on "Adam's Peak" (Mt. Sumanakūṭa), a "scar" which serves both to locate the destiny of the Island within the Buddha's realm of influence, and to testify continually to that connection, as do the "tracks" of the ancestors for the Australian aborigines. Though, indeed, "the Buddha, so far as is known, never visited Ceylon,"[7] it is a fact wholly irrelevant to the purposes of Sinhalese historiography. For it becomes the imperative of the historiographer to stress the transformation of the religio-philosophical "impression made upon the small southern island by the culture of its great continental neighbor,"[8] into a physical imprint, the immediate and material testimony of interconnection.

As the chronicles commence with a statement of religio-national authentication rooted in acts of the Buddha himself, so the whole history proceeds in the manner of self-conscious self-appraisal in the light of archetypal Buddhist precedents. Vijaya, supposedly descended from a lion (the "king of beasts"; *Mhv.* 6:2), and the conquering colonizer of Lanka from whose ancestry is derived both the name and the race, Sinhalese ("people of the lion race"[9]), is said to have landed in Ceylon on the very day of the Buddha's *parinibbāna* (*Mhv.* 7).

Clearly, this temporal synchronicity further associates the nation with the "faith," and notably the date itself – the full-moon day of the month Vesākha (April/May), which is also recorded as the date of the Buddha's birth and according to *Mhv.* 1:12, his enlightenment – recurs consistently throughout the chronicles at moments of significant occurrences.

Where Buddhist Ceylon was prefigured in the visits of Gotama Buddha, it was actualized, according to the chronicles, through the efforts of the paradigmatic Buddhist king, Asoka (Skt., Aśoka). According to Bardwell Smith, "one finds in Asoka the *locus classicus* of kingly prudence and virtue."[10] Consequently, in linking Asoka to the formal introduction of Buddhism into Ceylon, the chronicles once again presume and affirm a prestigious religio-national origin. By means of this introduction, Lanka is afforded both imperial legitimation and ecclesiastical organization. Devānaṃpiya-Tissa, the Sinhalese king whose initial authority was guaranteed by an indigenous ceremony of consecration (which was inferentially reminiscent of certain archetypes of Buddhist kingship[11]), is sent by Asoka all the material paraphernalia "that was needful for consecrating a king" (*Mhv.* 11:32). He is consecrated yet a second time with this message from his exemplary patron:

> I have taken refuge in the Buddha, his Doctrine, and his Order, I have declared myself a lay-disciple in the religion of the Sakya son; seek then even Thou, O best of men, converting thy mind with believing heart, refuge in these best of gems! (*Mhv.* 11:34 ff; c.f., *Tpv.* p. 60)

Not only does Asoka extend to Lanka the proper form of coronation suitable for a Buddhist king, but, according to Rahula, it is probable that Asoka as well conferred upon Tissa the honorific title, *Devānaṃpiya* ("beloved of the gods," not previously used as a kingly epithet in Ceylon) as "a mark of imperial recognition."[12] Thus, through Asoka, Sinhalese kingship is given political stature and deemed implicitly Buddhist. It is a fact confirmed and authenticated in the second consecration of Tissa, a gesture of initiation into "proper" imperial posture, which characteristically takes place on that pivotal date saturated with spiritual overtones, the full-moon day of Vesākha (*Mhv.* 11:42).

Buddhism, in its doctrinal form and ecclesiastical structure, is brought to Lanka in the mid-third century B.C. by Mahinda, the alleged son of Asoka, who together with Devānaṃpiya-Tissa convert the Island, and so lay the foundations for a Buddhist state. It was through Mahinda's (and his sister, Saṃghamittā's) entrance into the Order that Asoka became a "kinsman of the religion" (*Mhv.* 5:196). Likewise, it was through Mahinda and Saṃghamittā that Lanka achieved a national kinship with the Dhamma. Devānaṃpiya-Tissa and Mahinda meet, in the manner of historiographical predicability, on the full-moon day of Vesākha,[13] and from that point, Mahinda with the king's full support, sets out to promulgate the teachings and establish a local Sangha. Notably,

> if there had been any known trace of Buddhism existing on the island before this time, the chronicle chose to ignore it, since the visit of Mahinda was an event of such importance for the development of the history and culture of Ceylon that the chronicler whose heart was in these things, gave it the aura of preternatural significance it demanded . . . (In doing so), the Pali chronicle . . . stakes a claim for the special character of the island as a Buddhist realm. To poets and to the ordinary man it was *Dhammadipa* – the island of the *Dhamma.*[14]

During Devānaṃpiya-Tissa's reign, a branch of the Bodhi tree under which the Buddha achieved his Enlightenment is brought to Lanka, and this "king of trees" miraculously roots and sprouts instantaneously in Sinhalese soil. Apart from the obvious symbolic assertion of Buddhist ingrowth in the Sinhalese context which this incident relates, another, perhaps more significant, gesture of rootedness and potential is chronicled by the thera Mahānāma in the fifteenth chapter of his *Mahāvaṃsa.*

According to Mahinda, the "doctrine of the Conqueror," that is, of the Buddha, would not "stand" until "the boundaries (*sīmā*) are established" which demarcate the ceremonial center of an indigenous Buddhist monastery (*vihāra*). Anxious to comply with doctrinal prescription, Devānaṃpiya-Tissa states, "I will abide under the Buddha's command . . . . Therefore, establish the boundaries with all speed, *taking in the city*" (*Mhv.* 15:182ff.; emphasis mine). Not only would boundaries be set for the building of the Mahāvihāra (the monastery at Anurādhapura), but those very boundaries would establish and define the inclusion of the capital city within sacred precincts. "If it be so," advises Mahinda, "then do thou thyself, lord of the earth, mark out the course of the boundary" (*Mhv.* 15:184). The king himself "ploughed a furrow in a circle" (v. 191) and at the completion of the *sīmā*-fixing, the "great earth quaked." With cosmic acknowledgement reminiscent of the earthquakes and thunder which marked the Buddha's death,[15] the kernel of a Buddhist state was given foundational structure.

Though written without reference to our present concern, the following remarks by Robert Heine-Geldern provide a most insightful commentary on Devānaṃpiya-Tissa's actions:

> In Southeast Asia . . . the capital stood for the whole country. It was more than the nation's political and cultural center: it was the magic center of the empire. The circumambulation of the capital formed, and in Siam and Cambodia still forms, one of the most essential parts of the coronation ritual. By this circumambulation the King takes possession not only of the capital city but the whole empire.[16]

Though the act of boundary-setting was decidedly not a gesture of Devānaṃpiya-Tissa's coronation, it may indeed be considered as a "coronation" scenario for Buddhism in Lanka. If the capital stands for the country, and if the capital city is itself located within the bounds of the *sīmā*, then the consequent equation is that the country as a whole exists within the bounds of the *Sāsana.* That Buddhism rules Lanka, that indeed this circumambulation represents a coronation ritual, is corroborated when these chronicles of sacred history record Devānaṃpiya-Tissa's bestowal of kingship upon the Bodhi-branch itself (*Mhv.* 19:43; *Tpv.* p. 72), and so animate the declaration of the *Aṅguttara Nikāya* that the Dhamma is the "ruler of rulers."[17]

Tissa is succeeded by three pious kinsmen whose line of sovereignty is interrupted by the throne-usurping activities of Tamil-speaking Hindus from South India. Though their reigns are not lacking in meritorious deeds, they are not of the line that can trace a prestigious national origin back to the Buddha, and thus they are inherently insufficient as kings of Lanka. It becomes the task and honor of Duṭṭhagāmaṇī – descended from Devānaṃpiya-Tissa's second brother whose royal family settled in the southern part of the Island while the Tamils ruled in Anurādhapura[18] – to restore the purity of the Buddhist state.

Gāmaṇī, considered by Ludowyk to be "the ideal king" of the "chronicle of the great line of kings"[19] and from whom certain contemporary Sinhalese citizens stake a status claim of prestigious descent,[20] is first introduced in both the *Mhv.* and the *Tpv.* at the point of death in his former life. A pious bhikkhu, he gives up his arahantship (i.e., his freedom from re-birth) to be reborn as the son of a previously barren Buddhist queen. Thus entering life with a pre-established record of meritorious action, Gāmaṇī is born in a manner befitting the idealized Buddhist king, the Cakkavatti, as he is "endowed with all auspicious signs" (*Mhv.* 22:63) and his merit calls forth treasures and symbols of state (e.g., the elephant Kandula: *Mhv.* 22:60-63). Notably, his birth into royalty concurs with scriptural pre-requisites as exemplified in the *Saṃyutta Nikāya* which holds that "kingship is generally regarded as a reward for meritorious action performed in past births."[21]

His full potential for kingship, however, is evinced in a gesture precipitated by his father's request that he never fight the Tamils. Enraged and frustrated, the young prince assumed a fetal position, and analogizing himself to the Island, declared: "Over there beyond the Gaṅgā are the Damiḷas, here on this side is the Goṭha-ocean, how can I lie with outstretched limbs?" (*Mhv.* 22:86) An image of the person of the king representing the nation is here expressed; Gāmaṇī's sense of stricture and obligation crystallized, and the popular sentiment which would localize the ideal of religio-nationalism in Duṭṭhagāmaṇī himself is afforded a substantive image.

In a few years, Gāmaṇī's skill as a warrior catches up with his sense of urgency. Declaring his intent to wage war upon the Tamils, he is countered by his father, and with an insulting retort and self-imposed exile, he earns the epithet, *Duṭṭha* (the "enraged one"). From this point, warfare becomes Duṭṭhagāmaṇī's mode of action, as he battles with his brother to gain control of the throne, kills 32 Tamil kings throughout Ceylon, and then vanquishes Eḷāra, the Tamil ruler in Anurādhapura, so to bring Lanka "under one parasol of state" (*Tpv.* p. 87). From this point too, his actions and his saga exhibit a character of ostensible discordance with the Buddhist ideal, which it shall be our present task to examine.

The most evident affront to the Buddhist ideal of statecraft is Duṭṭhagāmaṇī's waging of war. In Buddhist thought, the primary function of kingship is that of order-maintenance.[22] By living a life of contemplation and engaging in meritorious deeds, by setting thereby an exemplary standard, the king serves to inspire the moral transformation of his subjects and so insure an orderly realm. However, if a king acts immorally, his actions effect a sympathetic response in his kingdom, not only in the moral demeanor of his subjects, but in the natural order itself. Interestingly enough, this sentiment is expressed by the Tamil king, Eḷāra (*Mhv.* 21:29), who notes that "a king who observes justice surely obtains rain in due season."

As one means of insuring national order, the sovereign was

> expected to cultivate the virtue of noninjury (*avihimsā*) and rule without the aid of force (*daṇḍa*) and weapons of destruction (*sattha*) . . . . Early Buddhist political thought insists on *the principle of nonviolence and noninjury as the "ideal" basis of statecraft* and hopes to minimize the violence inherent in the power of the state by ordaining that this power be, at all times, restrained by morality.[23]

Inaugurating his reign with double counts of warfare, moving victoriously from sibling struggles to external foes, Duṭṭhagāmaṇī would be, by ideal standards, inviting disorder, and in his manner, ostensibly antithetic to the portrait of that righteous and exemplary king of the *Cakkavatti Sīhanāda Suttanta* who "lived in supremacy over this earth to its ocean bounds having conquered it, *not by the scourge, not by the sword, but by righteousness.*"[24] Though two centuries earlier, Asoka had determined the efficacy of "conquest by righteousness" or the *dharma-vijaya*, it was a lesson which Duṭṭhagāmaṇī chose, from one viewpoint, to ignore, from another, to exploit. For, the very act of placing a symbol of Dhamma (i.e., the Buddha relic) upon a battle lance, itself serving as the royal standard, was indeed to burlesque the king's role as *Dhammarāja* and ultimately to travesty the Asokan model of dharma-vijaya.

As if to prove the dictum of lawless king, lawless country, the Sangha members in Duṭṭhagāmaṇī's kingdom as well acted most peculiarly for Buddhist monks. Allowing 500 ascetics to accompany the king to war (*Mhv.* 25:3ff.), the Brotherhood responded in blatant contradiction to the Buddha's measure (itself an index of his disdain for war), forbidding monks from witnessing army parades and reviews.[25] Not merely do they witness here, but they actually participate in the very activity which prompted the Tathāgata's scorn. Moreover, one of Duṭṭhagāmaṇī's generals, Theraputtābhaya, is portrayed as having been, in fact, a former monk. As Ludowyk rightly asserts, the texts themselves and their ecclesiastical authors are guilty of the same fault, dwelling on the subject of war, that which the Buddha himself denounced as "animal talk," a diversion unfit for a thera.[26]

Clearly, in requesting a company of bhikkhus, even as "blessing and protection" (*Mhv.* 25:3), Duṭṭhagāmaṇī violated "one of the primary duties of (kingship)," which was "to suppress . . . undesirable heretical elements that stained the purity of the Sāsana."[27] But the acquiescence of the Sangha indicates an equal or perhaps more grievous felony. In Ceylon, monks were to be exemplary of dhamma, where

> "merit" was the investment that ensured security in the next world. The Sangha is called *puññak-khetta*, "merit-field," where one could sow seeds of merit and reap a good harvest in the next world. If the field was not fertile, the crop would be poor, and the farmer must naturally be unhappy about it. If the Sangha was impure, the charity bestowed on them would bring poor results, and the donors must naturally be unhappy about it. That was one reason why kings and the people were so anxious about the unblemished purity of the Sangha. There was, of course, another obvious reason for this anxiety: the monks were the teachers and guides of the nation, and if they were corrupt, the whole nation would go astray. If the monks were bad, it would be harmful not only to the monks themselves personally, but also to the whole nation – not only in this world, but in the world to come as well.[28]

The degree of the Sangha's "dhammic" inconsistency becomes evident in its response to Duṭṭhagāmaṇī's post-battle reflections. Blatantly reminiscent of Asoka's remorse after the Kaliṅga massacres, Duṭṭhagāmaṇī, "looking back upon his glorious victory, great though it was, knew no joy, remembering that thereby was wrought the destruction of millions (of beings)" (*Mhv.* 25:105; *Tpv.* p. 88). Recognizing the king's distress through a kind of psychic telepathy, eight arahants arrive in miraculous fashion and comfort the king in an equally "phenomenal" manner, advising:

> From this deed arises no hindrance in thy way to heaven. *Only one and a half human beings* have been slain here by thee, O Lord of men. The one had come unto the (three) refuges, the other had taken on himself the five precepts. Unbelievers and men of evil life were the rest, *not more to be esteemed than beasts.* (*Mhv.* 25:109-111; emphasis mine.)[Ironically, one of the five precepts is "abstention from destruction of life" (Cf., *Mhv.* p. 7, n. 3)]

It is notable that the author of the *Thūpavaṃsa* (who, incidentally, drew all of his material from various prior sources, with the bulk of Duṭṭhagāmaṇī's saga taken from the *Mahāvaṃsa's* account) chose to edit out the specific content of this message of solace, presumably in response to its markedly uncharacteristic suppositions.

That any killing is abhorrent to the Buddhist ideal has been made evident in the Buddha's preference for non-violence. Thus, to justify murder on the grounds of the "bestiality" of one's victims is invalid in terms of classical Buddhist dogma. The *Cakkavatti Sīhanāda Suttanta* holds that the king, being "(himself) a Norm-banner, a Norm signal . . . should provide the right watch, ward, and protection for (his) own folk, for the army, for the nobles . . . for town and country dwellers, for the religious world, and *for beasts and birds*."[29] The *Dhammapada* further asserts that "it is not by hurting creatures/that a man becomes excellent./Only by non-violence/is excellence achieved."[30] Indeed, Asoka's remorse at extensive murder led him to place restrictions on the unnecessary slaughter and abuse of animals as evinced on his Rock Edict I and Pillar Edict V.[31] But, in contradistinction, Duṭṭhagāmaṇī is relieved of any sense of wrong-doing by the remarkable and, so far as we can deduce, novel assertions that one's humanity is a function of one's being Buddhist, and that to kill a non-Buddhist is therefore as of little consequence in terms of blemishing one's record of merit as killing an animal. From a classical standpoint, this logic is convoluted, disturbingly inappropriate for an arahant to suggest, and verges on the scandalous.

Unlike the dictum repeatedly proposed in the Chinese Buddhist saga of *Monkey*[32] that "to save one life is better than building a seven-storeyed pagoda," Duṭṭhagāmaṇī's post-warfare piety resides not in saving lives, but indeed in the construction of buildings for religious purposes. Though the act of building thūpas (mounds which contain relics, originally for burial) and vihāras (loosely, monasteries) is well within the kingly province of providing for the Sangha and his obligation to proliferate the Dhamma, it is Duṭṭhagāmaṇī's sudden turnabout and excessive concern for meritorious action which arouses one's hermeneutical suspicions.

Rahula notes that "the first thing that a (Sinhalese) king did after ascending the throne was to display his interest in religion by giving alms and granting endowments, building or repairing monasteries . . . ."[33] And, indeed, Duṭṭhagāmaṇī's first recorded action after the Tamil victory is that of building the Maricavāṭṭi-vihāra. But, what is of interest here is his motivation for doing so. In light of his prior disregard for Buddhist ethics, his sudden concern for the minutia of meritorious practice would seem a hyperbolic juxtaposition. Once comforted by the arahants as just related, the king discovered what would appear a relatively slight oversight on his part. In the context of the Buddhist ideal of sovereign/Sangha reciprocity,[34] Duṭṭhagāmaṇī had been cautioned "never to take a meal without the Brotherhood." Realizing with great dismay that he had "unthinkingly" eaten a single pepper without sharing it, he resolves to do penance which comes in the form of the Maricavāṭṭi-vihāra, *maricavāṭṭi* meaning, in fact, "the pepper in the pod."[35] Such a gesture, though exemplary of ideal kingship, seems an imbalanced and disproportionate recompense for the misdeed which prompted it. Duṭṭhagāmaṇī, it appears, reacts only in extremes.

One final incident of discrepant behavior comes likewise in the form of an over-reaction. In striving for merit and presumably seeking to actualize the rule of Dhamma, Duṭṭhagāmaṇī felt motivated to disturb the "balance of power" upon which any Buddhist state is founded, and usurp the priestly office, "since . . . a gift (by preaching) of the doctrine is more than a gift of worldly wealth" (*Mhv.* 32:42). However, it is not within the office of the king to do so, and Duṭṭhagāmaṇī is consequently unable to preach the Sutta he had chosen. According to Malalasekera, in his commentary on *The Pāli Literature of Ceylon*, "although (Duṭṭhagāmaṇī) was quite familiar with the Sacred Scriptures, he could not proceed; he descended from the pulpit 'perspiring profusely'; he had realized how difficult was the task of teachers, and his munificence towards them was greater."[36] Though this deed can hardly be called "criminal," it does reinforce an image of a most anarchic Buddhist king, whose actions, despite any admirable intent, convey a persistent disregard for the ideals of Buddhist teachings.

In spite of these ostensible affronts to orthodoxy, Duṭṭhagāmaṇī has been hailed as an exemplary Buddhist king whose "meritorious" life rewards him with the exalted rebirth status of being the first disciple of the coming Buddha Metteyya (*Mhv.* 32:81). The *Dīpavaṃsa*, which has only thirteen short verses on Duṭṭhagāmaṇī, most of which concern his building efforts, notably includes the fact of his killing 32 Tamil kings and his subsequent entrance into the "most venerable" Tushita Heaven (*Dpv.* 18:53; 19:11). As indicated in the *Dīpavaṃsa's* encapsulated history, and thus from the historiographers' points of view, Gāmaṇī's acts of violence hardly negate the prestige he earns; rather, they would seem to encourage it.

The degree of contradiction which Duṭṭhagāmaṇī as king ostensibly represents is implicitly a function of how one chooses to read the texts. Though in light of classical Dhammic teachings Duṭṭhagāmaṇī's saga evinces major points of discordance with respect to the historiographer's "homiletic" goal, the supposed madness would appear to have its method. In reading a text such as the *Mahāvaṃsa*, "compiled for the serene joy and emotion of the pious,"[37] one was to learn from the deeds and foibles of historical personalities, the nature and consequences of meritorious and non-meritorious acts. Moreover, as illustrated earlier, one was to gain a sense of national heritage, one's ecclesiastical and imperial, spiritual and national, racial, in fact, line of descent from the most exalted Buddhist figures, Gotama Buddha in the spiritual realm, King Asoka in the imperial. These texts were, to recapitulate, histories "written with a motive," charters providing a legitimation for Sinhalese national consciousness. Manipulated histories, they would establish a continual, spiritual correspondence to acts in historical time through the application of sacred precedent. Hence, Ludowyk:

> History, as in medieval Europe, is given the justification of a moral sermon, its actors and catastrophes are exempla for the contemplation and self-examination of the devout. Yet the *Mhv.* is more than a sermon which takes the history of a people as its text. It is, not surprisingly, the national epic of the Sinhalese . . . . The poem is characterized by a strong national sentiment which, identifying religion with nation, claims a state of predestinate grace for the people and the island. The emotions which colour a great deal of the poem are those of ***a national fanaticism with strong religious components.***[38]

It is within the context of history as charter, and not history as the dramatic replication of scriptural ideal, that Duṭṭhagāmaṇī's saga becomes both legitimated and exemplary. In adjusting historical fact to the assumptions predicated by his own material, the historiographer designs a text which supplies its own justifications. He works within a genre which could be termed "midrashic" historiography: the application of normative typologies to historical events, giving the history a quality of consistency and internal authenticity. "Midrash" – a rabbinical method of teaching scripture – is the actualization of prior activity in the present; it is

> a reflective method by which events and sayings of the situation narrated are presented in terms drawn from analogous situations in earlier stages of sacred history, precisely for the purpose of showing the continuity of the situations and the fulfillment of the first in the second.[39]

Not unlike the expressed intent of the Buddhist historiographer to stimulate piety through the reading of his text,

> Le but d'exégese midrashique, (c'est) avant tout un but practique, qui est de dégager les leçons de foi et de vie religieuse que la texte . . . recèle.[40]

Very similar to the midrashic style is a mode of literary interpretation described by Erich Auerbach in his classic, *Mimesis*, which may help to clarify what is meant by midrashic historiography. Based on a Christian model of Old Testament exegesis, Auerbach's "figural interpretation"

> establishes a connection between two events or persons in such a way that the first signifies not only itself but also the second, while the second involves or fulfills the first. The two poles of a figure are separated in time, but both, being real events or persons, are within temporality. They are both contained in the flowing stream which is historical life, and only the comprehension, the *intellectus spiritualis*, of their interdependence is a spiritual act.[41]

It is our contention that the Buddhist historiographer Mahānāma, in compiling the *Mahāvaṃsa*, and his ecclesiastical peers in their similar efforts, produced their texts with minds characterized by such an *intellectus spiritualis*, that is to say, conscious of the implicit interrelationship between historical activity and sacro-historical paradigm. Bearing this in mind, we shall now turn to the question of internal logic; how the *Mhv.* and its later historiographical sister, the *Thūpavaṃsa*, themselves resolved, or rather legitimated, primarily within the context of their own assumptions, the ostensible contradictions which we have heretofore outlined.

That Duṭṭhagāmaṇī was a warrior and a man of violence is not as much discrepant with scriptural ideals of, or the historical precedents for Buddhist kingship, as may be thought. As stressed by Gokhale, Reynolds and Gard,[42] one of the roles specifically predicated by the Pāli texts for a Buddhist king was that of the *khattiya* (Skt., *kshatriya*), or "one of the class of nobles and warriors." Presumably as a consequence of the Buddha's having been himself born into the *khattiya* tribe of Sakyas, early Buddhist thought held that the *khattiyas* were "the highest among classes and castes."[43] With this conception as foundation, and given the assumption that kingship was an institution essential to the maintenance of order, a Buddhist king was titled in "three standing phrases," *Mahāsaṃmata* ("chosen by many"), *Khattiya* (the "protector of fields"), and *Rājā* (because he would rule in accordance with the precepts of Dhamma).[44]

Thus, warriorship was intrinsic to rulership, a fact further substantiated in the *kshatriya* image articulated in Hindu notions of kingship, with which the Buddhist model we have described has, what Bardwell Smith calls, "apparent continuity." As Charles Drekmeier notes, the *Shāntiparva* (the twelfth book of the Sanskrit epic *Mahābhārata*)[45] holds that in a crisis the king is

> that man who is able to fulfill the kshatriya function . . . . Those who are charged

> with the preservation of order may be duty-bound to perform acts that are in themselves evil. Occasionally, in the epics, kshatriyas pause on the brink of battle to consider the moral implications of their acts. Yudhishthira, like Arjuna in the *Gita*, is sorely tempted to retreat to the forest and the life of an ascetic. Alas, this is not the kshatriya prerogative . . . . His fate is to die on the battlefield protecting the sacred order of things.[46]

Indeed, if not to die, at least to fight . . . . Drekmeier continues:

> In the faithful and selfless accomplishment of the rajadharma, sin is unavoidable. (It is *the premise of Buddhism, without the conclusion.*)[47]

Drekmeier is a bit severe with Buddhism, for, in fact, a certain realism did emerge alongside what would seem an idealistic standard of non-violence. Though dharma-vijaya is favored, the *Saṃyutta Nikāya* testifies that "the Buddha himself admits the difficulty of ruling without the use of force in any manner and under all circumstances," and, as Gokhale further notes, "nor is it known that the Buddha advised total disarmament by a state."[48] Though Asoka disclaimed the utility of warfare, he chose, after all, *not* to disband his army.[49]

That Duṭṭhagāmaṇī should function as a warrior is then eminently acceptable, if not downright mandatory in terms of the "proper" assumption of Buddhist kingship. In the *Cakkavatti Sīhanāda Suttanta* (75:24), the ideal king is referred to as the "conqueror," and, to be sure, the Buddha is repeatedly called the "Conqueror" in both the *Mhv.* (cf., for instance, 1:19; 3:1) and the *Tpv.* (which refers to all Buddhas as "Conquerors," cf., chapter 1b). By emphasizing Duṭṭhagāmaṇī's activities as the conqueror of the Tamils, by calling him, in fact, the "subduer of foes" (*Mhv.* 31:1), the historiographer succeeds in effecting an ineluctable paratactical association between the Buddha's conquering activities – the Buddha having been called "the victorious over enemies" (*Mhv.* 1:18) – and those of our presumably anarchic king. Disregarding any events which may have occurred between the Buddha's alleged visit to Lanka and Duṭṭhagāmaṇī's accession to the throne, the mere juxtaposition of the two conquerors effected through typological recall, or what Eliade would call "repetition of archetype," "historiographic anamnesis"[50] (recollection; making the present contemporary with primeval time), is sufficient from the vantage-point of historiographic logic to justify Duṭṭhagāmaṇī's warring proclivities.

As a matter of fact, the correspondence between Duṭṭhagāmaṇī's warfare and the Buddha's "vanquishing" of the Yakkhas, the aboriginal inhabitants of Lanka,[51] is made perfectly explicit in the *Thūpavaṃsa* (p. 79), which relates in one paragraph Gāmaṇī's victory over the Tamils, and follows in the next paragraph with a matter of historiographical recall:

> The Exalted One, it is said, came to this Island in the ninth month after his Enlightenment and entering the assembly of Yakkhas in the Mahānāgavana Park . . . and remaining in the sky above them, terrified those Yakkhas with rains and gales and darkness and so forth . . . .

(In great fear, the Yakkhas give the island to the Buddha who then deposits them in another part of the island.) There is no conjunction or statement of transition; the diachronic process which in temporal terms dissociates the two events is here wholly irrelevant. For the author of the *Thūpavaṃsa*, the two deeds of conquest are quite simply typologically equivalent, and so require no intermediary unit of association.

The *Mhv.* relates that "Laṅkā was known to the Conqueror as a place where his doctrine should (thereafter) shine in glory; and (he knew that) from Laṅkā, filled with yakkhas, the yakkhas must (first) be driven forth" (*Mhv.* 1:20). According to Bardwell Smith, the yakkhas represented more than primitive or non-human beings, being symbolic of that primal chaos which it is the sovereign's responsibility to control:

> The threat of anarchy and chaos is ever-present in the chronicler's mind . . . . If aborigines in some sense, (the yakkhas) represent the aboriginal spirit of man which lurks not far beneath the surface . . . . While on one level, the Buddha's coming to Lanka can be interpreted as freeing it from yakkha control, making it ready for the Sinhalese race, on another level, it becomes exorcism of the demonic from man himself . . . . Hypostasized into imaginary figures, the yakkhas may represent tradition's own realistic fear of man's proclivity toward disorder and evil.[52]

The Buddha's conquest over the yakkhas, which makes Lanka "a fit dwelling place for men" (*Mhv.* 1:43), becomes thus the archetypal gesture of Sinhalese kingship. Chaos is overcome, order thereby established, and the equation of Buddhism and humanity definitively asserted. From this point, the history of Lanka would be a chronicle of the perpetual struggle to maintain that order, to battle the elements of chaos which defy or challenge the implicitly Buddhist nature of Ceylon. The Buddha's action represents what Smith has termed, "a foretaste of what must occur throughout time . . . . The confrontation with disorder looms as a permanent vocation."[53] Following the "figura" (to use Auerbach's terminology) of Gotama Buddha, Vijaya – himself the progenitor of the Sinhalese race, who arrives at Lanka in synchronic coincidence with the Buddha's *parinibbāna* – must also conquer the yakkhas, an act of "historiographically justifiable" murder chronicled in Chapter 7 of the *Mhv.* Likewise, Duṭṭhagāmaṇī, responding to the threat of a non-Buddhist Lanka, is motivated to overthrow the Tamil dynasty, where *Tamil* can be understood as a typological equivalent of *yakkhas*. Any element which stands in the way of the fulfillment of the Buddha's intent, that Lanka would be a Buddhist stronghold (cf. *Mhv.* 7:4), is intrinsically representative of chaos and disorder, and so must be eliminated or, at least, controlled. Gāmaṇī, in responding to his *khattiya* obligations, thus recapitulates the prototypical gesture of that other *khattiya*, the Buddha, and so is, contextually speaking, a more "pious" Buddhist king than was his father who did not heed the full implication of Tamil rule in Anurādhapura.

Duṭṭhagāmaṇī's revolt against Eḷāra, despite the latter's reputation for meritorious acts,[54] was thus very much in order. Moreover, by virtue of Devānaṁpiya-Tissa's "boundary-setting" (*Mhv.* 15:182ff.), a precedent had been set for state religion in Lanka. The capital, representative of the entire nation, had been established literally within the bounds of the Mahāvihāra, and metaphorically "within the Buddha's command." From the viewpoint of historiography, the act determined a precedent which could not be contradicted; only a Buddhist, and, in this case, only one descended from the Buddhologically authenticated Sinhalese, had the legitimate right to rule in Anurādhapura, and so govern Ceylon. This conception of legitimate authority would grow so intense that by the tenth century the king of Ceylon was expected to be not only a Buddhist but a Bodhisattva,[55] a sentiment which Duṭṭhagāmaṇī, enjoying rebirth in the Tushita Heaven, tangentially prefigures.

Thus, Duṭṭhagāmaṇī's throne-usurping activities are justified not only by the Buddha's precedent of conquest, but moreover in the *sīmā*-setting ritual of Devānaṁpiya-Tissa, an act which symbolically corroborated the intimate association, established by the Buddha, of Lanka with Buddhism and Buddhist practice. By historiographical standards, Eḷāra was in no way a legitimate sovereign of Lanka; that he must be removed from office was an irrefutable imperative which, ironically, only the most pious would seek to actualize. Though Duṭṭhagāmaṇī's saga antedates a passage from the *Pūjāvaliya*, a Sinhalese prose work of the thirteenth century, we find the expressed sentiment remarkably applicable:

> This island of Lanka belongs to the Buddha himself, it is like a treasury filled with the Three Gems. Therefore, the residence of wrong-believers in this Island will never be permanent, just as the residence of the Yaksas of old was not permanent. Even if a non-Buddhist ruled Ceylon by force a while, it is a particular power of the Buddha that his line will not be established. Therefore, as Lanka is suitable only for Buddhist kings, it is certain that their lines, too, will be established.[56]

As noted, the Buddha's activities on Lanka set the precedent for more than the exemplary scenario of chaos-control. His actions predicated a racial mentality, which the chronicler captured in the notion of "making Laṅkā fit for humankind." To overcome the yakkhas was to contend with the chaotic, with the aboriginal, the less-than-human. In light of this fact, the assertion of racism which the arahants pronounce in comforting Duṭṭhagāmaṇī during his post-battle remorse, appears radically less caustic and irrational. In slaying the Tamils, Duṭṭhagāmaṇī did no more an unpious act than did the Buddha himself in terrifying and ridding the Island of the yakkhas. Though ostensibly the logic seems unsound, within the context of religio-historiographical assumptions, to kill an "animal," so to speak, was a far less heinous crime than permitting the perpetuation of non-human, i.e., non-Buddhist, rule in Lanka. By historiographical predication, those arahants functioned as exemplary of bhikkhu-hood; reinforcing the ideal of sovereign/Sangha interdependence, they offered counsel that reflected – however paradoxically – "orthodox" (if not Buddhist, then Sinhalese Buddhist) concerns.

Duṭṭhagāmaṇī, it may be recalled, marched off to war with the relic in his spear, proclaiming violence in the name of piety, "to make the Dispensation shine forth" (*Tpv.* p. 79). That violence and piety could co-exist without contradiction is a fact further validated by precedents to which the chronicles attest. Vihāramahādevi, pregnant with Gāmaṇī, longs to

> eat the honey that remained when she had given twelve thousand bhikkhus to eat of it, and then she longed to drink (the water) that had served to cleanse the sword with which the head of the first warrior among King Eḷāra's warriors had been struck off, (and she longed to drink it) standing on this very head . . . . (*Mhv.* 17:43-45)[57]

Indeed, this passage reflects more than the outlandish cravings of motherhood. Her exaggerated piety, juxtaposed with bloodthirstiness, prefigures that same duality which would manifest itself in the son she bore. With this as foundation, it comes as no surprise that Gāmaṇī, in the midst of battle, should announce that his "striving (has been) ever to establish the doctrine of the Saṃbuddha" (*Mhv.* 25:17). Likewise, it becomes fully consonant with textual suppositions that the chronicler, oblivious to the ostensible contradiction he implies, would describe our figure as "the wise King, who was hero in battle as in largess, whose pure heart was filled with faith in the Three Gems . . . ." (*Mhv.* 27: 23).

The sequence of elements in this last quotation proves most insightful. That violence and piety can be juxtaposed with impunity within Sinhalese sacred history is of less import for our purposes than that one should precede the other. As Rahula notes:

> Religion was often no deterrent to kings when their political power was endangered. They forgot religion and killed one another, even plundered monasteries as long as

> they were intent on seizing the throne. But immediately, after they ascended they become devoted and religious and begin to perform "meritorious" activities, mainly to evade the evil consequences of their past.[58]

Indeed, this is the pattern of action which Duṭṭhagāmaṇī exhibits, and, according to Rahula, it remained a fairly typical procedure throughout Sinhalese history. The point is simply this: in order to have an "ideal" Buddhist state, that is, one which follows (as closely as possible) the paradigms or standards presented in the classical discourses, it is *first* necessary to secure the very existence of the state. As noted, this is the conception which underlies the Buddha's alleged visits to Lanka. By virtue of these visits, he not only provides Ceylon with a prestigious religio-national origin through physical connection, but he is said to transform the island into a sacred locality, a place suitable for the growth of his Doctrine and so eminently fit for humanity. The state is thus secured before Buddhism as *sāsana* arrives in the person of Mahinda. Likewise, in the case of Duṭṭhagāmaṇī (as always, justified by precedent), he cannot get down to the kingly business of performing meritorious deeds until the prior kingly (*khattiya*) business of securing the state is accomplished. In order to maintain order, a particular "order" must first be defined.

Though dharma-vijaya, the "conquest by righteousness," would be a *preferred* mode of "order-establishment", "conquest by force" was not conceived of as a tragic perpetuation to which the chronicles attest. It is rather the standard and anticipated mode of the Sinhalese chronicles, made exemplary through the Buddha himself. Indeed, the consistency of this mode is captured and encapsulated in the pendular movements of that warrior/monk, Theraputtābhaya. According to a fourteenth century Pāli chronicle based on earlier works, known as the *Rasāvahinī* (II. 94, c.f., *Mhv.* 23:63), Theraputtābhaya (or the "son of the Thera") was a *sāmaṇera* or novice in the Order when he became a warrior, eventually serving under Duṭṭhagāmaṇī. Fighting valiantly against the Tamils, he desires to return to the Sangha post-battle, explaining to the king that "when a single realm is created, what war is there? . . . I will do battle with those rebels, the passions, (battle) wherein victory is hard to win" (*Mhv.* 26:3). With the unification of Lanka "under one parasol of state," a condition of order is achieved which then generates and legitimates a concern for the non-military, non-violent control of personal disorder and chaos, the internal battle, the striving for meritorious deeds. When, however, projected or external chaos (e.g., yakkhas, Tamils) threatens, one must respond as did Theraputtābhaya, in a matter befitting the impetus; with "sanctioned sin,"[59] as in this case, where martial force comprised the proper etiquette of response.

It remains to be said that while Duṭṭhagāmaṇī's actions *can* be read as reflective of a tragic continuance of conquest by violence or as eccentric, exploitative gestures bordering on outright "bad taste," they are, in fact, better understood as a creative synthesis, though we would presume unintentionally, of two complementary conceptions of kingship which emerged out of Indian or Sanskritic philosophies concerning the socio-political order and later Mahayana ideas about the bodhisattva and cosmic sovereignty. The two major Hindu law codes, the *Arthashāstra* of Kauṭilya (ca. 300 B.C.) and the Dharmashāstras, though differing in their respective emphases (the former stressing coercive power; the latter, virtue in those who wield coercion), both take as their symbol for state authority, *daṇḍa*, the sceptre or rod of chastisement. In contrast, Buddhist political thought, most evident in Mahayana tradition though certainly present in the Theravadin texts, epitomizes kingship in the symbol of *cakka*, the wheel.[60] Without drawing the analogy too strictly, this author feels that the contradiction implied by Duṭṭhagāmaṇī's junction of violence and piety – most visibly actualized in his placing a relic of the Buddha on his sceptre – is simply a "visual metaphor" of the "merging of (these) two distinct but overlapping notions of sovereignty."[61] *Daṇḍa*, the socio-political element of coercion and control, is here materialized in the battle lance, whose brutal effect is yet tempered by the religio-cosmological suggestion of cakka (the Wheel of Dhamma), which a relic of the Buddha surely connotes.

As was the case of the Buddha's leaving a footprint on Adam's Peak, Duṭṭhagāmaṇī's gestures always connote more than mere acts. As Bardwell Smith has stressed, the "world" presented in the chronicles is one "in which bare fact was always less important than what the fact signified."[62] The relic on the lance, monks going off to war, quite simply signify more than ostensible disrespect. To be sure, the latter incident signifies more than the expressed textual justification, that the sight of bhikkhus ensured "both blessing and protection," or Rahula's equally insufficient explanation that the act, in insinuating Sangha approval, was a means of assuring public support and sympathy for the campaign.[63] More than wise political moves or strategies, the placing of a relic on the lance and the conscription of bhikkhus are fundamentally symbolic gestures witnessing the conquest of Buddhism over the chaos represented by the Tamil dynasty. Mahinda had declared, eight chapters previous, that to behold the relics is to behold the Conqueror. (*Mhv.* 17:3). It is not Duṭṭhagāmaṇī the king who fights battles, it is rather Duṭṭhagāmaṇī actualizing the "figura" of the Buddha and rubricing this "repetition of archetype" by carrying forth to war the material equivalent of his figura. Without understanding the purpose of historiography, a reader can only perceive these gestures to connote a travesty of dharma-vijaya. But to reiterate emphatically, this is a kind of history which chronicles moments, whether fact or fiction, to which the exponents of the faith trace their roots, which extends to the people a religio-ethnic sensibility, and which establishes a lineage to sacred personae with the consequent obligation to perpetuate that legacy into the future. In the context, then, of *Heilsgeschichte* in which the fanaticism of religio-national self-consciousness supersedes any conception of classical propriety, Duṭṭhagāmaṇī's acts, prefatory to battle, provide a concretization *not* of conquest by Dhamma, but rather the conquest *of* Dhamma over whatever comprises the imminent threat.

With this understanding behind us, it becomes increasingly valid that Duṭṭhagāmaṇī should emerge from the chronicles not only as their pivotal characterization but indeed as an exemplary Buddhist king. It has already become evident that his warring activities fulfill rather than contradict "one of the primary duties" of kingship, which is "to look after the well-being of the *Sāsana*."[64] In this concluding portion of our study it shall be our effort to understand how the historiographical characterization of his post-warfare activities further corroborates and reinforces Duṭṭhagāmaṇī's exemplary status.

As already indicated, with the Buddhist state secured, Duṭṭhagāmaṇī is at last free to exercise his kingly prerogative of performing meritorious deeds. As he had made the conquest of the Buddhist Sāsana visible in wartime, he proceeds with consistency to make visible its peacetime prevalence. It may be recalled that Asoka actualized the rule by Dharma predicated in the *Cakkavatti Sīhanāda*

Suttanta (61:5 – "leaning on the Norm") in his "kingdom of piety" through an imperial institutionalization of Dharma: the *Dharma-mahāmātras*, "ministers of Dharma" whose office it was to spread Dharma through service to both ascetics and householders. Like Asoka, Duṭṭhagāmaṇī moves from warfare to the concerns of piety, but, in partial contradistinction to the former, his mode of actualization takes the form of buildings.

Duṭṭhagāmaṇī as peacetime sovereign is first and foremost a "master-builder," a commissioner of thupas and vihāras. Very much in the Asokan tradition, and, in the *Thūpavaṃsa* consciously expressed as such, Duṭṭhagāmaṇī's buildings represent an institutionalization, a visible testimony to the existence of Buddhism in Ceylon. The Asokan paradigm is implicit, for the *Tpv.* relates that Asoka had built 84,000 cetiyas (thūpas) in parallel to the 84,000 parts of the Dhamma, thus "honouring each unit of the Teaching with a monastery" (*Tpv.*, p. 52). Paul Mus writes in this regard:

> Si le dharmakāya est le Buddha visible dans sa Loi, chaque section de la Loi est un peu du Buddha, et toutes ensemble sont une réplique verbale de sa personne. C'est bien ainsi que l'entendent les chroniques cinghalaises, lorsqu'elles nous parlent 'des quatre-vingt-quatre mille sections de la Loi, qui sont comme l'image du Buddha parfaitement accompli.' Les 84.000 stūpa d'Açoka se présenteraient donc, dans la légende, *comme la matérialisation des 84.000 chapitres du canon* et les deux collections équivalent également au corps du Buddha.[65]

Duṭṭhagāmaṇī's enterprise is that of actualizing or, perhaps, condensing the Sāsana into the form of the thūpa itself. Literally and metaphorically, he builds upon that which the Buddha's visits had prefigured, and so engages in another, a new kind of "*sīmā*-setting" or boundary establishment. "In order to see continuity . . . one must establish distinctions where in reality none exist. The planting of the Bodhi-tree and the bringing of relics" (and we might add, the building of thūpas to enshrine the relics) "are ways of making visible, therefore present, what was never absent, though always invisible."[66]

In the *Tpv.* (pp. 79-80) the first building act of Duṭṭhagāmaṇī occurs, unlike the chronology of the *Mhv.*, during the Tamil confrontation. Arriving at Mahiyaṅgaṇa, the very spot where the Buddha had presumably overcome the yakkhas, Dutthagāmaṇī both wages war and erects the "mantle-thūpa," enlarging thereby an already existing shrine. Apart from the evident construct of historiographic anamnesis previously discussed, the *Tpv.* seems concerned to establish a continuum of Dhammic realization. It becomes the kingly imperative not merely to recall or "repeat" exemplary scenarios but as well to perpetuate their consequences. Thus, the *Tpv.* (pp. 80-81) relates that after the Buddha's *parinibbāna*, an Elder enshrined on this spot within a thūpa the relic of the neck-bone. His act was followed by Devānaṃpiya-Tissa's brother who enlarged the cetiya, and thus did Duṭṭhagāmaṇī in his turn. Duṭṭhagāmaṇī functions then, on a metaphorical level, as a fulfillment of the figura of the Buddha, but on a less figurative level, in the capacity of a perpetuator of – literally one who builds upon – tradition.

However, the buildings themselves are immanently figural. What midrash accomplishes in an interpretative function, Duṭṭhagāmaṇī's structures effect in their very form. They are reflections of paradigm, rubrics of the primeval "tracking," their foundations literally sunk in Buddhist precedent. The Maricavāṭṭi-cetiya, previously mentioned as the atonement for Duṭṭhagāmaṇī's pepper-pod oversight, is built on the spot at which the relic-bearing spear was planted after the Tamil victory. When the spear could not be removed, Duṭṭhagāmaṇī took it as a sign of his commission to build a thūpa around the relic (*Mhv.* 26). Likewise, the Mahāthūpa, or the Great Thūpa, whose construction is inaugurated on that favorite date, the full-moon day of Vesākha, is built at the spot where the Buddha sat during his third visit to Lanka. To build upon that ground is to recall the Buddha's visit, to commemorate and actualize his motions during that visit. We have been forewarned of this inclination towards continuum, for it was written as early as *Mhv.* 1:80 ff., that

> the Great Sage . . . knowing well which places were fit and which unfit . . . seated himself with his disciples at the place, where the Bodhi-tree came afterwards to be, the Master gave himself up to meditation; and likewise there where the Great Thūpa stood (in later days) . . .

What the Buddha's actions prefigure, the later structures reflectively actualize.

Not only serving as monuments to ancestral tracks, Duṭṭhagāmaṇī's buildings, in the manner of most Buddhist temples,[67] actively reflect the cosmology and the Sinhalese social structure. In the Buddhist cosmology, Mt. Meru forms the center of the universe and is surrounded in a concentric pattern by seven mountain ranges, each separated by a body of water. Ascending Mt. Meru and going beyond it, one passes through successive heavenly abodes which increase in prestige the higher one gets. According to Heine-Geldern, Buddhist temples represent microcosms, as "practically every temple in Southeast Asia, whether Hindu or Buddhist, whether built of stone, brick or wood, (is) considered as the image of a mountain, usually though not invariably, of Mt. Meru."[68] As the chronicles concerned do not make explicit this connection (though, indeed, thūpas clearly follow a mountain/Meru motif; e.g., Mus: "Nous entrevoyons ce que devait enfermer la bulle formée par l'architecte cinghalais . . .: ce n'était tout simplement que l'univers entier, autour du mont Meru."),[69] we will pursue it only insofar as it can be clearly deduced from textual implication.

Fulfilling a prophecy of Mahinda (the chronicles always underscoring the backward glance to sacred precedent), Duṭṭhagāmaṇī sets out to build the Lohapāsāda, for the Sangha's use as an uposatha-house.[70] It is built as an exact replica of a "celestial palace" in the heaven of the thirty-three gods, whose blueprint is diligently copied onto linen by eight "cosmo-trotting" arahants. Though not acknowledged outright, the very heaven travelled to is the one which Heine-Geldern locates on the summit of Mt. Meru, and so we may extrapolate from suggestion and understand the structure as an earthly (microcosmic) complement to the divine (macrocosmic) model. Moreover, like Mt. Meru, the building is designed in graded levels so that

> those bhikkhus who were yet simple folk stood on the first story, those learned in the tipiṭaka on the second, but those who had entered on the path of salvation and the others (stood) each on one of the third and higher stories, but the arahants stood on those four stories that were highest of all. (*Mhv.* 27:44ff.; Cf., *Tpv.* p. 93)

In the tradition of actualization, the Lohapāsāda reflects both the religio-social order and the celestial paradigm; serving as visible testimony to the "structure" of Buddhism within Sinhalese experience, it comprises a nexus of spheres of existence.

Duṭṭhagāmaṇī's most celebrated act of building is that of the Mahāthūpa, an account of which forms the major thematic focus of the *Thūpavaṃsa*. In comparison with this structure, the Lohapāsāda seems but a shallow microcosmic model. The very construction of the Mahāthūpa involves all levels of society:

king, gods, and Sangha. ("By the royal wondrous power of the King, the divine wondrous power of the deities, and the truly noble wondrous power of the Noble" – *Tpv.*, p. 122). So as not to tax the energies of the populace, the gods provide the bricks for building, and, in miraculous fashion, all manner of decorative metals and gems appear successively in clockwise fashion at villages located in each of the compass-point directions (from N to NE to E, etc.), with Anurādhapura at the center. Thus, with cosmic cooperation that recalls a title attributed to the exemplary king of the *Cakkavatti Sīhanāda Suttanta*, the "Conqueror of the Four Quarters," Duṭṭhagāmaṇī can proceed with his building.

Work begins, as mentioned, on the day which recalls the Buddha's enlightenment, and, as part of the ceremony of ground consecration, the entire Order "stood (around) like an encircling coral railing . . . leaving an open space for the King in the centre" (*Tpv.*, p. 103). By this gesture, the Sangha coagulates into a "human edifice" which clearly prefigures the symbolic connotation the structure itself will signify. At the laying of the first ceremonial brick, an earthquake resounds in cosmic affirmation, and, with a ceremonial reading of unspecified teachings, 40,000 lay folk are converted, 40,000 attaining "the fruits of Stream-entry," 1,000 the reward of Once-Return, 1,000 non-Return, and 18,000 bhikkhus and 14,000 bhikkhunīs attain to arahantship! (*Tpv.*, p. 106; *Mhv.*, 29:67ff.)

Since the chronicles note the coincidence of the date of the Buddha's enlightenment with the commencement of building, we feel it legitimate to explicate further this instance of historiographic anamnesis. As the Buddha's enlightenment "set rolling the Wheel of the Law" (*Mhv.*, 1:14), so the building of the Mahāthūpa would perpetuate its motion. As the Enlightenment "brought sixty (hearers) to arahantship" (1:14), and so began the building of a Sangha and the architecture of the Sāsana, the building of the Great Thūpa witnessed the sudden conversion and miraculous attainments of innumerable denizens within the Buddhist community, and so confirmed the Sāsana. In its very structure, the Thūpa recapitulates sacred precedent. On Duṭṭhagāmaṇī's orders, the walls of the relic chamber bear portrayals of the major events which occurred after the Buddha's experience under the Bodhi-tree. From the Wheel of the Doctrine newly set in motion to the distribution of the relics (*Mhv.* 30: 78-89), a testimonial is constructed which not merely depicts, but makes present, the life of the Buddha.

In a figurative sense, the Thūpa actually gives new life to the person of the Buddha. The building itself, based on a deifically-ordained plan (the god Vissakamma possesses and speaks through the medium of the architect; *Mhv.* 30:11; *Tpv.* p. 108), is to house Buddha-relics, and we have already noted the equivalence of relics with the Buddha himself. The Thụpa thus represents more than a cosmic microcosm; it is symbolic of the body of the Buddha himself. In overseeing the process of construction, though Duṭṭhagāmaṇī's death precedes its completion, the king functions in a creative capacity; more than just protecting the Sāsana, he insures its renewal.

Indeed, the goal of building the Mahāthūpa was to enshrine and so preserve the relics originally received by Devānaṁpiya-Tissa (including the Alms-Bowl, the right eye-tooth, and the right collar-bone). With Duṭṭhagāmaṇī officiating, they are deposited, as expected, amidst celestial orchestration on the full-moon day of Vesākha, and here the chronicles at last provide explicit correspondence (beyond the mere mention of the date) with that which the date signifies:

> By the wondrous power of the relics the entire world-system became gaily dressed as on the occasions such as the (Bodhisatta's) entry into the mother's womb and the gaining of supreme enlightenment. (*Tpv.*, p. 126)

With the relics thus enshrined, the person of the Buddha is given new form: the Thūpa, within the boundaries of the center of the nation (i.e., Anurādhapura), is itself a visual metaphor of the centricity and implicity of Buddhism in Lanka. "Mettre des reliques dans le stūpa," writes Mus, "image du monde, donc image rituelle du royaume, c'est symboliquement introduire la Loi dans ce royaume."[71]

As if to suggest that the buildings themselves were not enough of a manifestation of the Buddha's authoritative presence in the land, the chronicles move on to what may be considered the pinnacle of Duṭṭhagāmaṇī's kingly career: the bestowal of the kingship of Lanka upon the relics. As if underlining an already italicized word, the historiographer would seem to be making *absolutely* certain that no one misses the point. And so, proceeding within a framework of typological reflection characteristic of the genre in which he has been portrayed, Duṭṭhagāmaṇī invests the relics with sovereignty:

> To the Master of the world, to the Teacher who bears the threefold parasol, the heavenly parasol and the earthly, and the parasol of deliverance, I consecrate three times my kingly rank. (*Mhv.* 31:91-92; *Tpv.* p. 133)

His action recalls Asoka's own bestowal of sovereignty upon the monk Nigrodha[72] (*Mhv.* 5:69) and later upon the bodhi-tree (*Mhv.* 18:35), and, as well, Devānaṁpiya-Tissa's parallel action in respect to the newly transplanted Bodhi-branch (*Mhv.* 19:31). In so doing, each of these kings exhibits a sentiment best phrased by none other than Duṭṭhagāmaṇī:

> Not for the joy of sovereignty is this toil of mine, my striving (has been) ever to establish the doctrine of the Saṃbuddha. (*Mhv.* 25:17)

From the lesson of the chronicles, ideal Sinhalese-Buddhist kingship is characterized by a figure-head position; one rules with Sangha support in proxy for the true ruler, and the foremost obligation of sovereignty thus becomes the perpetuation of that sacred "dynasty."

It has been the effort of this study to define the charter-like function of historiography through an examination of how the genre itself legitimates the traditional glorification of an ostensibly anarchic Sinhalese-Buddhist king. Though the texts may create ostensible discrepancies with orthodoxy, they also supply the resolutions, and, of course, it should by now be evident that these are not charters of Buddhism, but of Buddhism *in Ceylon*. These are charters specifically intended to establish and affirm Sinhalese religio-national consciousness. The actualization of orthodoxy is thus of far less significance than the construct of a radically nationalistic sentiment rooted in historiographically predicated sacred sanctions. For thus writes the author of the *Dīpavaṃsa*:

> Listen to me, I shall relate the Chronicle of the Buddha's coming to the Island, the arrival of the relic and the Bo-tree and the advent of the Buddha's religion in this Island and of the doctrine of the teachers who made the collection as well as of the advent of the chief of men . . . . Listen to the eulogy of the Island, incomparable, *that which deals with the lineage of the best dwellers*, original, unrivalled, and well-narrated, handed down by the elect, described by the noblest and adored by the righteous.[73]

As here illustrated, the chronicles create their own sacred status, which in turn legitimates the prestigious national self-conception which it is the chronicler's objective to articulate. As in a midrashic exercise, "the present is vividly connected with the past, providing both for legitimacy and for remembrance of the tradition's roots."[74]

With this concern as a contextual motivation, it is eminently reasonable that Duṭṭhagāmaṇī emerges as a "real national hero," that the chronicles (the *Tpv.*, more evidently than the *Mhv.*) should comprise works in which all that precedes the saga of Duṭṭhagāmaṇī is but preface – in the form of relevant antecedents – to its celebration, and all that follows, more in the mode of an afterthought.[75] (Out of thirty-seven chapters in the *Mhv.*, eleven are devoted to Duṭṭhagāmaṇī, thus close to a third.) Duṭṭhagāmaṇī is exemplary because he does exactly what a Sinhalese king should do, as predicated within the bounds of historiographical presupposition. As king, he homologizes himself to the Island, follows sacred and imperial precedents, responds to the threat of the hour, insures order, and sets about to actualize the interconnection of Buddhism and the nation in the form of thūpas and other ceremonial buildings. Moreover, his sudden remorse after killing, his pangs of conscience – which, by religio-historiographic logic, is wholly unprovoked – adds yet a quality of humanity to this otherwise hyperbolic and mythicized figure of exemplar.

The dynamic of role-reversal had already proved its esteem-inspiring function in the case of Asoka whose characterization as *Candāśoka* (Asoka the cruel) was transformed into *Dhammāśoka* (Asoka the pious), with his realization of the futility of mass genocide. "The carnage which brought Asoka's conscience into sensitivity was but a ripple in the world's history of slaughter, but the paradigm which his response provided continued to effect Buddhist communities."[76] In the transition from warrior to master-builder, the chronicled portrait of Duṭṭhagāmaṇī not merely recalls the Asokan model, but succeeds in providing the audience with access to a more human and believable Duṭṭhagāmaṇī, and so paves the way for his celebration in national reverence which has persisted to the present day. "In the simplest terms of structure, repetition" – that which we have called historiographic anamnesis – "provides the outlines, while juxtaposition of contrasts makes up the basic colours used."[77]

Notes

1. Walpola , Rahula, *History of Buddhism in Ceylon: The Anurādhapura Period: 3rd Century B.C. - 10th Century A.D.* (Colombo: M. D. Gunasena and Co., Ltd., 1956), pp. 79, 80 note 4. Rahula gives 101-77 B.C. as the reign dates for Duṭṭhagāmaṇī; the *University of Ceylon, History of Ceylon* uses 161-137 B.C. as the dates.
2. *Ibid.*, p. 80.
3. Bardwell L. Smith, "The Ideal Social Order as Portrayed in the Chronicles of Ceylon," in Bardwell L. Smith, (ed.) *The Two Wheels of Dhamma* (Chambersburg, Pa.: American Academy of Religion, 1972), p. 32.

   It should be stated at the outset that the major portion of our material is derived from the *Mhv.*, a later expanded redaction of the earlier, more fragmentary *Dpv.* Both were expressly "histories" or dynastic chronologies of Ceylon. The *Tpv.*, though reflective of sacred history, was less a chronology of Ceylon rulership than of the events leading to the building of the Mahāthūpa during the reign of Duṭṭhagāmaṇī Because it follows in the genre of *Heilsgeschichte* and focuses ultimately on Duṭṭhagāmaṇī's saga, the *Tpv.* is of considerable interest for this study. However, it should be understood that where the *Mhv.* establishes precedents for exemplary kingship, the *Tpv.* stresses rather the religio-historical precedents for thūpa-building. Other texts, not central to our study, which relate Duṭṭhagāmaṇī's saga include the *Mahāvaṃsatīkā* or *Vaṃsatthappakāsinī*, a ninth century commentary on the *Mhv*, and the *Rasāvahinī*, a fourteenth century Pāli prose work.
4. Rahula, *op. cit.*, pp. xxiii-xxiv (introduction).

5. Bronislaw Malinowski, *Magic, Science and Religion, and Other Essays* (Garden City, N.Y.: Doubleday Anchor Books, 1954), pp. 144, 146. Also see M. Robinson, "'The House of the Mighty Hero' or 'The House of Enough Paddy'? Some Implications of a Sinhalese Myth," in E. R. Leach, editor, *Dialectic in Practical Religion* (Cambridge: Cambridge University Press, 1968), pp. 124ff. Emphasis mine.
6. Richard A. Gard, "Buddhism and Political Authority," in Harold W. Lasswell and Harlan F. Cleveland, eds., *The Ethic of Power: The Interplay of Religion, Philosophy and Politics* (New York: Conference on Science, Philosophy and Religion in Their Relation to the Democratic Way of Life, Inc., No. 16, Harper, 1962), p. 46.
7. E. F. C. Ludowyk, *The Footprint of the Buddha* (London: George Allen and Unwin, Ltd., 1958), p. 12.
8. *Ibid.*
9. *Ibid.*
10. Smith, *op. cit.*, p. 83.
11. It is notable that even before the formal bringing of Buddhism to Ceylon, there were overtones of Buddhist ideology written into the "histories." With Devānaṃpiya-Tissa's first consecration as king, his merit calls forth treasures that had been buried deep in the earth (*Mhv.* 11:8ff.), a power reminiscent of that of the Cakkavatti – the "Wheel-turning Universal Monarch" – whose charisma calls forth the wheel which normally rests in the ocean depths. Tissa's natural charisma would indicate his appropriateness in being the first truly Buddhist king in Lanka.
12. Rahula, *op. cit.*, pp. 27-28.
13. Ludowyk, *op. cit.*, p. 84.
14. *Ibid.*, pp. 83, 71.
15. Richard H. Robinson, *The Buddhist Religion: A Historical Introduction* (Belmont, Calif.: Dickenson Publishing Co., Inc., 1970), p. 35.
16. Robert Heine-Geldern, "Conceptions of State and Kingship in Southeast Asia," Southeast Asia Data Paper No. 18 (Ithaca, N.Y.: Cornell University, 1956), pp. 2-3.
17. Reference is made to this passage in Frank Reynolds, "The Two Wheels of Dhamma: A Study of Early Buddhism," in Bardwell L. Smith, ed., *op. cit.*, p. 17, and in Balkrishna G. Gokhale, "Early Buddhist Kingship," in *Journal of Asian Studies*, XXVI, No. 1, Nov., 1966, p. 20.
18. *Mhv.* 23:13. "In Rohaṇa there are still princes who have faith in the Three Gems."
19. Ludowyk, *op. cit.*, pp. 110, 107.
20. Marguerite Robinson, *op. cit.*
21. Gokhale, *op. cit.*, p. 17. Also, Robert Heine-Geldern, *op. cit.*, p. 8: "It is his good karma, his religious merit acquired in previous lives, which makes a man be born a king or makes him acquire kingship during his lifetime, be it even by rebellion and murder."
22. Smith, *op. cit.*, Introduction, p. 2.
23. Gokhale, *op. cit.*, pp. 20-21, drawn from the *Dīgha Nikāya.* Emphasis mine.
24. "Cakkavatti Sīhanāda Suttanta," p. 60, in T. W. Rhys-Davids, ed., *Sacred Books of the Buddhists* (London: Humphrey Milford, 1921), No. 26 of the *Dīgha Nikāya*, Vol. IV. Emphasis mine.
25. Gokhale, *op. cit.*, p. 21.
26. Ludowyk, *op. cit.*, p. 107.
27. Rahula, *op. cit.*, p. 67.
28. *Ibid.*, p. 259. See also Richard A. Gard, *op. cit.*, p. 57.
29. "Cakkavatti Sīhanāda Suttanta," *op. cit.*, p. 62. Emphasis mine.
30. P. Lal, trans., *The Dhammapada* (New York: Farrar, Straus, and Giroux, 1967), p. 129.
31. N. A. Nikam and Richard McKeon, trans. and eds., *The Edicts of Asoka* (Chicago: University of Chicago Press, 1959), pp. 55-57.
32. See, for instance, p. 256 in Arthur Waley, trans., *Monkey: Folk Novel of China by Wu Ch'eng-en* (New York: Grove Press, Inc., 1943).
33. Rahula, *op. cit.*, pp. 70-71.
34. Though unrelated to Duṭṭhagāmaṇī's saga, the *Mhv.* relates a delightful anecdote which

condenses this obligation of reciprocity into a memorable scenario. In Chapter 15, Devānaṃpiya-Tissa is given a magnificent mango-tree, a fruit of which he offers to Mahinda. Mahinda gratefully eats the mango and returns the seed to the king who then plants it. In order "that it might grow," the Thera washes his hands over the kernel whereupon a new shoot sprouts immediately, the full tree evolving shortly thereafter! The "moral" of the tale is clear: the willing and generous interdependence of king and Sangha will nourish and effect vitality, prosperity, and growth.

Ludowyk, *op. cit.*, p. 111.

G. P. Malalasekera, *The Pāli Literature of Ceylon* (London: Royal Asiatic Society of Great Britain and Ireland, 1928), p. 38. Also in Bardwell L. Smith, *op. cit.*, p. 45.

This phrase occurs at the end of every chapter of the *Mhv.*, and may be found occasionally throughout the *Tpv.* Cf., *Tpv.*, p. 68.

Ludowyk, *op. cit.*, pp. 108-109. Emphasis mine.

Richard J. Dillon, "St. Luke's Infancy Account: A Study in the Interrelation of Literary Form and Theological Teaching," in *The Dunwoodie Review*, Jan., 1961, Vol. 1, No. 1, p. 22.

Renee Bloch, "Midrash," in *Supplément au Dictionnaire de la Bible*, Vol. 5, (Paris: Librarie Letouzey et Ane, 1957), p. 1265.

Erich Auerbach, *Mimesis: The Representation of Reality in Western Literature* (Garden City, N.Y.: Doubleday Anchor Books, 1957), p. 64.

Gokhale, *op. cit.*, p. 17; Reynolds, *op. cit.*, pp. 18-19; Gard, *op. cit.*, p. 45.

Gokhale, *ibid.*, p. 17, from the *Saṃyutta Nikāya.*

Cf., Reynolds, *op. cit.*, pp. 18-19; and Gard, *op. cit.*, p. 45.

Charles Drekmeier, *Kingship and Community in Early India* (Stanford: Stanford University Press, 1962), p. 132.

Ibid., pp. 251, 249.

Ibid., p. 139. Emphasis mine.

Gokhale, *op. cit.*, p. 21, from the *Saṃyutta Nikāya.*

Drekmeier, *op. cit.*, p. 266.

See Mircea Eliade, *The Myth of the Eternal Return* (Princeton: Bollingen Series XLVI, Princeton University Press, 1954), Chapter One. Also, *Myth and Reality* (New York: Harper and Row, Publishers, 1963), pp. 134-138.

According to F. D. K. Bosch (*The Golden Germ*; The Hague: Mouton and Co., 1960, p. 193), the word "yaksha" or "yakkha" appeared in early Buddhist literature as a synonym for deva, devatā, and devaputta, names for various gods of high rank, and that yakkhas themselves enjoyed a kind of cult worship, centered on tree symbolism. Though, in the context of the Pāli chronicles under consideration, the yakkhas are most definitely portrayed as the pre-Buddhist and pre-Vijaya indigenous inhabitants of Lanka, it is not beyond the range of possibility, that within the historiographic scenario of the Buddha's vanquishing the yakkhas was a suggestion of the yakkhas' "demythologization." That is, the Buddha's conquest not only rid Lanka of its aboriginal menace, but as well inaugurated a new theistic (or, for want of a better word, cosmological) focus and fulcrum. The Yakkhas were stripped of their divine status, transformed into demons, and perforce had to be annihilated (by Vijaya) before the Buddha's realm could be realized.

Smith, *op. cit.*, p. 41.

Ibid., pp. 41, 42.

Mhv. 21:34, re: Eḷāra: "Only because he freed himself from the guilt of walking in the path of evil did this (monarch), *though he had not put aside false beliefs*, gain such miraculous power; how should not then an understanding man, established in pure belief, renounce here the guilt of walking in the path of evil?" Emphasis mine.

Rahula, *op. cit.*, p. 62.

Passage quoted in Rahula, *ibid.*, p. 63.

See M. Robinson, *op. cit.*, pp. 138 ff., for an interesting structural analysis of this passage, within the context of the binary oppositions of piety and violence in the Duṭṭhagāmaṇi saga.

Rahula, *op. cit.*, p. 256.

59. Drekmeier, *op. cit.*, p. 135.
60. See Gokhale, *op. cit.*, p. 21; Smith, *op. cit.*, p. 55. For an in-depth discussion of *daṇḍa* in Hindu legal conceptions, see Drekmeier, *op. cit.*, chapters 8, 11-13.
61. Smith, *ibid.*, p. 55.
62. *Ibid.* p. 32.
63. Rahula, *op. cit.*, p. 70.
64. *Ibid.*, p. 67.
65. Paul Mus, *Barabaḍur: Esquisse d'une Histoire du Bouddhisme fondée sur la Critique Archaéologique des Textes* (Hanoi: Imprimerie d'Extrême-Orient, 1935), Tome 1 er, part 2, p. 280. Emphasis mine.
66. Smith, *op. cit.*, p. 51.
67. Heine-Geldern, *op. cit.*, pp. 2-4.
68. *Ibid.*, p. 3.
69. Mus, *op. cit.*, p. 111.
70. "Uposatha" is the Buddhist "sabbath" occurring four times per month.
71. Mus, *op. cit.*, p. 286.
72. According to F. D. K. Bosch, p. 70, the Buddha's Bodhi-tree is called "nigrodha" in Pāli literature, and, in fact, the Bodhi-tree of Bodh Gaya was a "nyagrodha" or "banyan tree." Thus, Asoka's bestowal of kingship upon the monk Nigrodha implies a linguistic equivalence to the act of imperializing the bodhi-tree itself.

    Bosch also notes the symbolic structural and spiritual equivalence of thūpas with the bodhi-tree (pp. 172ff.). Since his analysis is quite general and not specifically related to the Sinhalese experience, we feel some hesitation in applying his hypothesis to our material. However we would note that if the thūpa *is* understood as symbolically equivalent to the "great Cosmic Tree," then Duṭṭhagāmaṇī, in building the Mahāthūpa, is once again reiterating spiritual/imperial precedents; for his building the thūpa-tree becomes reflective of and equivalent to Devānaṃpiya-Tissa's planting of the Bodhi-branch in Lanka's soil.
73. *Dpv.*, pp. 129-130; also in Smith, *op. cit.*, p. 31. Emphasis mine.
74. Smith, *ibid.*, p. 36.
75. Ludowyk notes the climactic nature of Duṭṭhagāmaṇī's saga on p. 143 of his work. Likewise, the introduction of the *Tpv.* (p. xxxii ff.): "It is thus patently clear that in spite of all the efforts of the author to conceal the fact, the central figure in Thūp. is Duṭṭhagāmaṇī . . . One would not be far wrong in calling Thūp. the Duṭṭhagāmaṇī-apadāna following the better known Aśokāvadāna." (N. A. Jayawickrama, p. xxxiv)
76. Smith, *op. cit.*, p. 47.
77. Ludowyk, *op. cit.*, p. 143.

Bibliography

1. Auerbach, Erich. *Mimesis: The Representation of Reality in Western Literature.* Garden City, N. Y.: Doubleday Anchor Books, 1957.
2. Bloch, Renee. "Midrash," in *Supplément au Dictionnaire de la Bible.* Paris: Librarie Letouzey et Ane, 1957, Vol. V, pp. 1263-1281.
3. Bosch, F. D. K. *The Golden Germ.* The Hague: Mouton and Co., Inc., 1960.
4. Dillon, Richard J. "St. Luke's Infancy Account: A Study in the Interrelationship of Literary Form and Theological Teaching," in *The Dunwoodie Review*, Jan., 1961, Vol. 1, No. 1.
5. Drekmeier, Charles. *Kingship and Community in Early India.* Stanford: Stanford University Press, 1962.
6. Eliade, Mircea. *Myth and Reality.* New York: Harper and Row, Publishers, 1963.
7. Gard, Richard A. "Buddhism and Political Authority," in Harold W. Laswell and Harlan F. Cleveland, editors, *The Ethic of Power: The Interplay of Religion, Philosophy and Politics.* New York: Conference on Science, Philosophy and Religion in Their Relation to the Democratic Way of Life, Inc., No. 16, Distributed by Harper, 1962.

8. Geiger, Wilhelm, trans., assisted by Mabel Brode. *The Mahāvaṃsa or The Great Chronicle of Ceylon.* London: Henry Frowde, 1912. Pali Text Society Translation Series No. 3.
9. Gokhale, Balkrishna G. "Early Buddhist Kingship," *Journal of Asian Studies,* XXVI, No. 1, Nov., 1966, pp. 15-22.
10. Heine-Geldern, Robert. "Conceptions of State and Kingship in Southeast Asia." Southeast Asia Data Paper No. 18. Ithaca, N.Y.: Cornell University, 1956.
11. Jayawickrama, N. A. *The Chronicle of the Thūpa and the Thūpavaṃsa: Being a Translation and Edition of Vacissaratthera's Thūpavaṃsa.* London: Luzac and Co., Ltd., 1971.
12. Lal, P., trans. *The Dhammapada.* New York: Farrar, Straus, and Giroux, 1967.
13. Ludowyk, E. F. C. *The Footprint of the Buddha.* London: George Allen and Unwin, Ltd., 1958.
14. Malalasekera, G. P. *The Pāli Literature of Ceylon.* London: Royal Asiatic Society of Great Britain and Ireland, 1928.
15. Malinowski, Bronislaw. *Magic, Science and Religion, and Other Essays.* Garden City, N.Y.: Doubleday Anchor Books, 1954.
16. Mus, Paul. *Barabaḍur: Esquisse d'une Histoire du Bouddhisme fondée sur la Critique Archaéologique des Textes.* Hanoi: Imprimerie d'Extrême-Orient, 1935.
17. Nikam, N. A. and McKeon, Richard, trans., eds., *The Edicts of Asoka.* Chicago: University of Chicago Press, 1959.
18. Rahula, Walpola. *History of Buddhism in Ceylon: The Anurādhapura Period: Third Century B.C. - Tenth Century A.C.* Colombo: M. D. Gunasena and Co., Ltd., 1956.
19. Reynolds, Frank. "The Two Wheels of Dhamma: A Study of Early Buddhism." In Bardwell L. Smith, ed. *The Two Wheels of Dhamma: Essays on the Theravada Tradition in India and Ceylon.* AAR Studies in Religion No. 3. Chambersburg, Penna.: American Academy of Religion, 1972, pp. 6-30.
20. Robinson, Marguerite S. " 'The House of the Mighty Hero' or 'The House of Enough Paddy'? Some Implications of a Sinhalese Myth," in Leach, E. R., ed. *Dialectic in Practical Religion.* Cambridge: Cambridge University Press, 1968, pp. 122-152.
21. Robinson, Richard H. *The Buddhist Religion: A Historical Introduction.* Belmont: California: Dickenson Publishing Co., Inc., 1970.
22. Rhys-Davids, T. W., ed. "Dialogues of the Buddha." Volumes II-IV of *Sacred Books of the Buddhists.* London: Humphrey Milford, 1921. Especially Volume IV, No. 26 of *Dīgha Nikāya* III: the "Cakkavatti Sīhanāda Suttanta."
23. Smith, Bardwell L. "The Ideal Social Order as Portrayed in the Chronicles of Ceylon," and "Sinhalese Buddhism and the Dilemmas of Reinterpretation." In Bardwell L. Smith, ed. *The Two Wheels of Dhamma: Essays on the Theravada Tradition in India and Ceylon.* AAR Studies in Religion No. 3, Chambersburg, Penna.: American Academy of Religion, 1972, pp. 31-57; 79-106, the first of which is reprinted in this volume.
24. Waley, Arthur, trans. *Monkey: Folk Novel of China by Wu Ch'eng-en.* New York: Grove Press, Inc., 1943.

The *Dhammadīpa* Tradition of Sri Lanka: Three Models within the Sinhalese Chronicles

Regina T. Clifford

THE TRADITION of *dhammadīpa*, which is traced most extensively and articulately in the three Pāli chronicles of Sri Lanka, comprises the central thread running through the centuries of Sinhalese Buddhism. Indeed, it embodies the uniqueness and vitality of Buddhism in Sri Lanka. While its ramifications are innumerable, the myth itself consists of two main parts: the Buddha's purification and consecration of Lanka in order that the island realize his vision of it as the sanctuary of true (i.e., Theravada) dhamma; and, the exemplification of the means by which dhammadīpa is to be maintained and edified. Each of the three chronicles, the *Dīpavaṃsa, Mahāvaṃsa,* and *Cūlavaṃsa*, however, renders the myth in a manner appropriate to the demands of its respective milieu. It is in reference to this continuity and change that the *tradition* of the myth is emphasized. One perceptive view of tradition describes it as

> something handed on from the past which is made contemporary and transmitted because of its intense contemporaneity. Tradition involves both the giver and the taker, backward in time and forward as well. It imposes a dynamic relationship, a creative tension between the remote past, with its authority based on a myth of revelation . . . and the remote future, with its power vested in the capacity to continue to vivify, or to abandon and thus kill, a received legacy.[1]

Precisely this conception of tradition, as the activity of the myth shaping and being shaped by history, underlies both this investigation and the nature and interrelationships of the chronicles themselves. The *Dīpavaṃsa* relates the earliest version of the myth extant; the *Mahāvaṃsa* transmits a recension of that; and the *Cūlavaṃsa*, a continuation of the *Mahāvaṃsa*, implies still a third interpretation of the myth, although it does not explicitly alter the *Mahāvaṃsa* version. The three chronicles cover a period of approximately 1500 years, and the dhammadīpa myth asserts itself throughout as the matrix of Sinhalese Buddhism. Clearly, it is "something handed on from the past which is made contemporary and transmitted because of its intense contemporaneity."

Ceylonese historiography records sacred history. "It is the sacred history of a people destined with a sacred mission, namely, to maintain the purity of the *Dhamma* in a world of impermanence and self-seeking."[2] Accordingly, the guiding principles of the chroniclers were far less concerned with the historicity of an event than with its significance.

> The point and purpose of tradition are not to pass on historical facts but both to create and to interpret contemporary reality, to intervene in history. The interest in the past arises solely because of its paradigmatic value, not for its authority over the present in some lesser, banal, and factual sense. The past is not dead, is not past, specifically because it is paradigmatic.[3]

The historiography of the chronicles describes a world order that is perfect and, at the same time, because that world order is perfect, provides a framework for comparison and judgement. The biography of the Buddha, which comprises the first section of the texts and also embodies the dhammadīpa myth, sets forth the cosmological and soteriological framework within which Sinhalese history unfolds and from which it derives meaning. As the blueprint for the ordering of Lanka's history, the biography of the Buddha provides the model par excellence to be emulated in order to achieve the ideal world order, or more concretely, to actualize dhammadīpa.

In this respect, the dhammadīpa myth provides the structure of intelligibility by which the writers of the chronicles understand and judge the various kings and the course of history. According to L. S. Perera,

> The emergence of a more defined historiography from this amorphous body of tradition is without doubt due to the emergence of the concept of the *Dhammadipa* which by wedding the history of Buddhism and its destiny to that of the island provided a theme, a purpose, and a framework within which to include such of the data on the past history of the island as they had.[4]

Perera's statement reflects a fairly accurate assessment of the role of the dhammadīpa myth in Ceylonese historiography. However, the adoption of this myth as a framework should not be seen merely as a device by means of which the authors of the *Dīpavaṃsa* and *Mahāvaṃsa* were able to organize all their material. Rather, the dhammadīpa myth renders intelligible "such of the data . . . as they had." This characterization of myth will be elucidated later in the analysis of the *Mahāvaṃsa's* new formulation of the biography and the implications this holds for the description of the ideal king.

The historiographical purpose peculiar to the chronicles is twofold: it is didactic and polemical.[5] While there is often a fine line differentiating the two and while the demarcation is violated frequently in these texts, this distinction is heuristically helpful, if not always precise. With the dhammadīpa myth as the central and binding point of reference, the authors of the chronicles seek to instruct the readers, kings and laity in the proper relations between king and sangha which will preserve the purity of the dhammadīpa. As L. S. Perera observes,

> History had a further use for these monk authors. They could not desist from drawing moral lessons from history and using it for edification. This purpose is implicit in the religious panegyric. . . . Its main purpose is to demonstrate the impermanence of worldly wealth, pomp, and power, and the necessity to shun wickedness and pleasure which lead to heaven or *Nirvana*. A moral judgement is also implicit in the judgement the authors sometimes pronounce on kingship at the end of their reigns. Some are sent to hell, some to heaven, and some just "fall into the jaws of death." The criterion of judgement is meritorious works and the patronage of the sangha.[6]

At the end of each chapter in the chronicles, the authors add a didactic verse, for instance, "the wise king, whose name contains the words 'beloved of the gods,' patronizing the great thera Mahinda, of spotless mind, first built here in Laṅkā this Mahāvihāra."[7] A number of criteria for ideal kingship are revealed here. A king is wise who supports the sangha and edifies the Buddhist order by building vihāras, stūpas, and the like. This action finds its sacred precedent in the biography of the Buddha when, in the second and third visits of the Buddha to Lanka, he is fed by the Nāga kings and presented with gifts including the throne, the royal symbol of sovereignty. In following the teaching of such a sacred precedent, King Devānaṃpiyatissa (250-210 B.C.E.), the king lauded above, attains the status of a Buddhist ideal king, or Cakkavattin, and fully actualizes Lanka as the dhammadīpa.

The *Mahāvaṃsa* is by far the most polemical of the three chronicles. The *Dīpavaṃsa*, being a compilation, does not exhibit the same degree of intentionality, although it is unmistakably a product of the Mahāvihāra sangha. While the *Cūlavaṃsa*, having been written in the thirteenth century, is not quite as concerned with sectarian strife as is the *Mahāvaṃsa*, it also rarely misses an opportunity to distinguish itself from the other sects on points of purity and, of course, authority. But the *Mahāvaṃsa* is a clear polemic against the Abhayagirivihāra, which was ushered into Lanka by King Vaṭṭagāmaṇī-Abhaya in about 25 B.C.E. and received its greatest boon at the expense, literally and figuratively, of the Mahāvihāra from King Mahāsena in about 325 C.E. All of the chronicles, however, expound the viewpoint of the "orthodox" Mahāvihāra sangha, which embraces the pure dhamma and hence the means by which dhammadīpa is to be realized.

Serving the didactic and polemical purposes of the dhammadīpa tradition is a blend of chronology, synchronism, and genealogy. The *Dīpavaṃsa, Mahāvaṃsa,* and *Cūlavaṃsa* record chronologically the succession of kings as well as the occurrences within the sangha. However, the dictates of sacred history ensure that the value ascribed by the sangha to each sovereign determine the length and type of discussion he will receive. So it is also with the use of synchronism and genealogy. For example, the arrival of Vijaya, the founder of the Sinhalese race, is synchronized with the *parinibbāna* of the Buddha thereby signifying that this extraordinary chronology takes up and carries on the destiny of the Buddha's teaching. Similarly, the first Sinhalese king to embrace the dhamma reigns at the same time as the archetypal Buddhist Cakkavattin, Asoka, and receives his title and second coronation from Asoka. Both of these examples of synchronism symbolize the transference of a major aspect of Buddhist religio-political tradition onto the shoulders of Ceylonese sacred history.

Further highlighting and valorizing the lines of chronology is the use of genealogy. Genealogy facilitates certain claims to authority by tracing descent. For instance, the *Dīpavaṃsa* and *Mahāvaṃsa* map the ancestry of the Buddha back through the race of Mahāsaṁmata, the Great Elect, who is the primordial king. The Buddha is thereby posited in a long, illustrious, and pure line of royal descent. (This genealogy also emphasizes the complementary nature of a Buddha and a Cakkavattin, or Buddhist ideal king.) At the same time that genealogy traces history through descent, it also collapses the generations, merges past with present, and describes the structure of things for all times. The present is essentially the same as the past; the power and authority of the origin abide in the present. "Unlike history, 'genealogy' refers to both the past and the present simultaneously. It deals with the past that is wholly present in the offspring."[8] The lineage of the Mahāvihāra sangha which is articulated in the chronicles reveals its importance in the light of this discussion. The claims to orthodoxy advanced by the Mahāvihāra sangha derive from a lineage tracing back through Mahinda (and the inception of Buddhism in Lanka) to the third council of Mogalliputta Tissa which established the Theravadins as the true bearers of the Buddha's teachings and so ultimately to the Buddha himself. Genealogy, chronology and synchronism are powerful tools in the hands of the monk-chroniclers concerned to advance the dhammadīpa tradition.

Considering the pivotal role of the dhammadīpa myth, it is difficult to recognize a methodology which discards myth from its inquiry as anything short of grossly reductive of the tradition. The method employed here assumes the centrality of myth in Ceylonese historiography, and leans heavily upon two characteristics inherent in the texts. First, the biography of the Buddha provides the paradigm for kings; and second, the degree to which a given king actualizes the dhammadīpa is the degree to which he attains to the Cakkavattin ideal. The procedure is a comparison, on the one hand, of the paradigm formulated and operative in each chronicle and, on the other hand, of the king who most fully activates the paradigm. The *Mahāvaṃsa* is an avowed recension of the earlier *Dīpavaṃsa* and covers precisely the same ground. These two texts allow the neatest comparison, for the points at which Mahānāma, the author of the *Mahāvaṃsa*, diverges from the *Dīpavaṃsa* signal the stress points where reinterpretation was necessary to renew the paradigm. The *Cūlavaṃsa*, a continuation of the *Mahāvaṃsa*, ostensibly accepts the paradigm set forth in the biographical section of the *Mahāvaṃsa*, though the king singled out as the ideal operates on a somewhat different model. These comparisons yield three variant conceptions of dhammadīpa and the corresponding proper means of actualizing dhammadīpa. These conceptions are not, of course, explicit, but rather implicit in the biography of the Buddha and actions of the kings. It is necessary, therefore, to deal first with the concrete means by which the myth is actualized and then to induce the understanding which informs the means.

As stated in the opening paragraph of this paper, the myth consists of two main parts: the Buddha's purification and consecration of Lanka so that the island may realize his vision of it as the sanctuary of the true (i.e., Theravada) dhamma; and the exemplification of the means by which dhammadīpa is to be maintained and edified. These two points comprise the focus of the following discussion.

The *Dīpavaṃsa* was completed sometime between the beginning of the fourth century and the first third of the fifth century C.E. Herman Oldenberg believes the text to be the product of one author, attributing the repetitions and radical breaks in style and thrust to the multiple texts from which the author was drawing.[9] Wilhelm Geiger, however, contends that the *Dīpavaṃsa* is the collective effort of several authors and compilers.[10] The evidence clearly favors Geiger's theory. If the *Dīpavaṃsa* were the product of one author, even one compiler, there would be greater continuity, and less repetition and variance of versions. For instance, chapter four describes the first and second councils, and chapter five describes all three. The presence of a single hand is apparent within specific chapters, but no clear intentionality exists throughout, save the general bias toward the Mahāvihāra sangha. This is to be expected, of course, since it is their record.

The *Mahāvaṃsa* is a later text composed in the sixth century C.E. Its greater purposiveness mark it as the product of one author, who drew primarily from the *Dīpavaṃsa*, using it both for text and historical structure. The evidence of the author's, i.e., Mahānāma's, intentionality is reflected in the chronicle's statement of purpose. While both chronicles seek to "awaken serene joy and emotion," the *Mahāvaṃsa* qualifies its goal with the reference to those "*passages* which awaken serene joy and emotion" (italics mine). The implication being, of course, that the *Mahāvaṃsa* recognizes that not all the passages foment such a response. Some passages clearly portray a bleaker picture of the past. This assessment by the *Mahāvaṃsa* is further evidenced by its omission of the *Dīpavaṃsa's* intention to dwell "upon the most excellent successions (of teachers and kings)." The not-so-excellent successions bear upon the *Mahāvaṃsa's* historiography as well. The new thrust of the *Mahāvaṃsa* takes on even deeper significance when considered in conjunction with Mahānāma and his background. He was a monk of the Mahāvihāra sangha in the early sixth century A.D., and, according to the *Cūlavaṃsa*, was commissioned by King Dhātusena to rewrite the *Dīpavaṃsa*.

Given this much information and an understanding of Ceylonese historiography, it is safe to assume that Mahānāma is an author invested with the interests of the Mahāvihāra sangha. From the inception of Buddhism in Lanka, the Mahāvihāra fraternity was the sole orthodox authority on the dhamma and the major beneficiary of the king.[11] However, at the hands of the Buddhist king Mahāsena, the Mahāvihāra met with crisis and destruction. Mahāsena (274-301 A.D.) gave his support to the rival and heterodox Abhayagiri-vihāra and then, further persuaded by the evil monk, Saṃghamitta, destroyed and pillaged the Mahāvihāra, sending its bhikkhus into the hills to escape persecution.

> An adherent of the thera Saṃghamitta, the ruthless minister Soṇa, a favourite servant of the king, and (with him) shameless bhikkhus, destroyed the splendid Lohapāsāda seven stories high, and carried away the (material of the) various buildings from hence to the Abhayagiri (vihāra), and by means of the many buildings that were borne away from the Mahāvihāra the Abhayagiri vihāra became rich in buildings. Holding fast to his evil friend, the thera Saṃghamitta, and to his servant Soṇa, the king wrought many a deed of wrong.[12]

The emergence of the dominant purification theme becomes evident here both in Mahānāma's motive for writing and in his selection of King Duṭṭhagāmaṇi (161-137 B.C.E.) as the ideal. The Mahāvihāra fraternity, as stated above, traces its lineage back to Mahinda, the bhikkhu son of King Asoka, and ultimately to the Buddha through the third council of Mogalliputta Tissa. The fraternity perceives itself as the embodiment of the orthodox, pristine Buddhism which the Buddha foresaw as being preserved and carried on in Lanka. Most importantly, they are the teachers and representatives of the true dhamma, which is identified with Lanka in the myth of the dhammadīpa. The loss of kingly sanction and the destruction and pillaging of this fraternity breaks with the sacred precedent set by the Buddha and the Nāga kings on his second visit to Lanka and actualized in subsequent history by Mahinda and King Devānaṁpiyatissa. Not only is the Mahāvihāra persecuted and dispersed, but the dhammadīpa itself is thereby exiled. The failure to protect the Mahāvihāra represents a rupture with sacred time and space, an obstruction of the Buddha's vision for Lanka. Further, this action implies grave soteriological consequences because with the conversion of King Asoka to Buddhism came a new definition of the state as a soteriological institution.[13] That is, the Buddhist state exists for the protection and promotion of the dhamma, functioning in a way parallel to the sangha in the spiritual realm. Each of the three ideal kings (i.e., the *Dīpavaṃsa's* Devānaṁpiyatissa, the *Mahāvaṃsa's* Duṭṭhagāmaṇī, and the *Cūlavaṃsa's* Parakkamabāhu) ruled Lanka with precisely this crucial understanding of the purpose of the state. It was this purity of mind which channeled their extraordinary powers in a righteous way, setting them apart (in the minds of the authors) from the less illustrious kings.

G. P. Malalasekera does not acknowledge that this crisis had any impact on Mahānāma's recension. As he explains it,

> Mahānāma lived in an age when the clumsy, inartistic diction of the *Dīpavaṃsa*, with its faulty arrangement, would not suffice for the edification of the learned, and he set about to compile a work which was more in keeping with the literary development of his time.
>
> The *Dīpavaṃsa*, like the *Mahāvaṃsa*, finished its record with the death of king Mahāsena. Whether this is due to the *Mahāvaṃsa* having superceded it after that date, or whether, as Oldenberg suggests, the authors stopped at the epoch of Mahāsena's reign, where the past destinies of their spiritual abode, the Mahāvihāra, were divided from the present by the success of a hostile party in obtaining the king's sanction for destroying the Mahāvihāra, we cannot say. I am inclined to the former view.[14]

Malalasekera's theory is not only anticlimactic, but it denies the gravity of Mahāsena's breach of contract. Oldenberg's theory, on the other hand, deserves attention because it does recognize the magnitude of the crisis. Oldenberg's theory also coheres with the didactic and polemical purposes of the chronicles' historiography, and the emergent theme of purity with respect to the fulfillment of dhammadīpa. For these reasons, it is unlikely that the *Mahāvaṃsa* represents a strictly aesthetic effort, but rather demonstrates Mahānāma's attempt to vindicate the Mahāvihāra and to purify the dhammadīpa. Bearing in mind the story behind the story, an analysis of the paradigms in the two texts is instructive.

According to both texts, Lanka is chaotic and overrun with the evil Yakkhas (protean supernatural beings fond of devouring humans), who, because they are too inferior to receive the dhamma, are consequently retarding Lanka's authentication. The Buddha, therefore, visits the island and expels the Yakkhas by calling forth a terrifying chaos in the form of darkness, wind, and rain. The Yakkhas, paralyzed with fear, submit to the Buddha's superior powers. In other words, while the Yakkhas unequivocally symbolize chaos, the Buddha prevails by wreaking even greater chaos. According to the *Dīpavaṃsa*, however, when the Buddha perceives their fear, he is moved to compassion. This is an important emphasis in the *Dīpavaṃsa*, because the Tathāgatha's power is then transformed by his compassion. Consequently, as the narrative goes on to relate, the Buddha caused the resplendent isle of Giridīpa, even more verdant and desirable than Lanka, to draw near. The Yakkhas relocate their abode joyfully and the Buddha has accomplished his goal by compassionate means.

The *Mahāvaṃsa*, on the other hand, narrates only the fear wrought by the Buddha's power, unmitigated by compassion, and the resultant expulsion of the Yakkhas to Giridīpa. The reference to Giridīpa is completely glossed, no longer describing the island as a more than adequate alternative to Lanka. Most significantly, there is not even an allusion to compassionate means employed by the Buddha. Lanka has been purified, but the *Mahāvaṃsa* evinces no concern to temper the means utilized. Rather, it is the goal that is paramount and that transforms the Buddha's power into righteousness. The means become unimportant, unlike the *Dīpavaṃsa* in which it is the means that are paramount and that transform the Buddha's power into righteousness.

The shifting of focus from means to goal reveals an alteration in perception of the paradigm in the *Mahāvaṃsa.* The ramifications of the contrasting paradigms are manifest in contrasting types of Cakkavattins. By definition, the Cakkavattin is one who rules by non-violence. The Buddha sets a precedent in the *Dīpavaṃsa* congruent with this definition, which is later actualized by the non-violent king Devānaṁpiyatissa. The definition is reinterpreted in the *Mahāvaṃsa* where the Buddha actually sets a violent precedent, which is then actualized by the warrior king Duṭṭhagāmaṇī. Although a new twist has been added, the two main points of the dhammadīpa myth remain: the Buddha's purification and consecration of Lanka so that the island may realize his vision of it as the sanctuary of the true (Theravada) dhamma; and the exemplification of the means by which dhammadīpa is to be maintained and edified.

Devānaṁpiyatissa, as the *Dīpavaṃsa's* closest realization of the Buddha, purifies Lanka by plowing the boundaries, *sīmā*, of the Mahāvihāra. He thereby sets the inviolable ground of the vihāra apart from profane society and delineates the inner sanctum of dhammadīpa. He then maintains the order through patronage of the theras and therīs, and by his submission to their authority.[15] The Cakkavattin further edifies the dhamma with gifts such as the Mahāmeghavana park, and with enshrinement of relics, notably the branch from the sacred bo-tree under which the Buddha attained enlightenment. Devānaṁpiyatissa is, above all, characterized by compassion and his reign by peace and prosperity.

In the *Mahāvaṃsa*, while Devānaṁpiyatissa figures prominently, he does not approach the heroism of King Duṭṭhagāmaṇī. This chronicle holds the more politically and militarily dynamic king as its ideal and closest realization of the Buddha. Gāmaṇī is marked as an auspicious figure even before his birth and develops a profound national consciousness at an early age. While Gāmaṇī is a young boy, his father requests that he and his brother promise never to fight Damiḷas (i.e., Tamils, the perennial invaders from South India). To this the boys stoutly refuse. Gāmaṇī thereupon

> went to his bed, and drawing in his hands and feet lay upon his bed. The queen came, and caressing Gāmaṇi spoke thus: "Why dost thou not lie easily upon thy bed with limbs stretched out, my son?" "Over there beyond the Gaṅgā are the Damiḷas, here on this side is the Goṭha-ocean, how can I lie with outstretched limbs?" he answered.[16]

Curiously, the blatant transgression of filial piety by Duṭṭhagāmaṇī poses no problem for sixth century Lanka, nor does it for subsequent generations. In fact, Gāmaṇī comes finally to be known as Duṭṭhagāmaṇī, the angry Gāmaṇī.[17] But it is not only in this instance that Duṭṭhagāmaṇī displays violent traits. When the hero finally does wage war with the Tamil invaders, he purifies Lanka of their presence in a way unmistakably reminiscent of the Buddha's routing of the Yakkhas in the biography section of the *Mahāvaṃsa*. The Tamil king Eḷāra holds the throne at this time. While the chronicle praises the justice of his reign, he is not a national Buddhist, and, therefore, symbolizes the presence of impurity at the heart of the dhammadīpa, breaking with both the paradigm and the subsequent historical precedent of Devānaṁpiyatissa. With Duṭṭhagāmaṇī's victory the dhammadīpa is purified and the boundaries redefined. The king then maintains the reestablished order by providing for the needs of the sangha and submitting his power to their authority. And Duṭṭhagāmaṇī, more than any other Cakkavattin, glorifies the dhamma by the prolific building of thūpas, and the like.

Yet, despite the striking parallel in the *Mahāvaṃsa* between the Buddha and Duṭṭhāgamaṇī, the warrior king is not wholly justified in his actions without some explicit demonstration of compassion and cognizance of the virtue of non-violence. After his battle, he is stricken with remorse that his victory brought with it the destruction of innumerable beings. However, a delegation of arhants reassures him of his innocence, reasoning that

> from this deed arises no hindrance in the way to heaven. Only one and a half human beings have been slain here by thee, O lord of men. The one had come into the three refuges and the other had taken in himself the five precepts. Unbelievers and men of

evil life were the rest, not more to be esteemed than the beasts. But as for thee, thou wilt bring glory to the doctrine of the Buddha in manifold ways; therefore cast away care from thy heart, O ruler of men![18]

A number of intriguing things are going on behind this passage. For instance, the criterion for human status seems to be Buddhism, a rather dogmatic stance. Also the assumption that "unbelievers and men of evil life" are "not to be more esteemed than beasts" is incongruous, since the doctrine of non-violence unquestionably extends to all sentient beings. The concern in this context is first the conflict within Duṭṭhagāmaṇī between piety and violence, and, second, the significance of legitimation by the arhants of the new paradigm.

Although Duṭṭhagāmaṇī's actions are anticipated in the new biography of the Buddha, the vestiges of the previous paradigm of a more compassionate Buddha live on in the person of Devānaṁpiyatissa who does figure influentially in the *Mahāvaṃsa*. Duṭṭhagāmaṇī embodies the two paradigms vying for predominance, although the balance is tipped in favor of the warrior king from the outset. After the achievement of the purity of Lanka, Duṭṭhagāmaṇī serves the sangha with countless good acts, especially profuse building in a pious and generous manner befitting his predecessor, Devānaṁpiyatissa. Violent means appear to be necessary before pious acts of preservation and edification are possible; these two tensions are linked in the conflict Duṭṭhagāmaṇī feels.

The legitimation given Duṭṭhagāmaṇī by the arhants rests on two points: those destroyed by the king were non-Buddhists, and the destruction was wrought for the glorification of the dhamma. The first point indicates a powerful Sinhalese Buddhist nationalism in emergence. Lanka must be free of all culturally heterodox, i.e., impure, elements before the dhamma can flourish. In this regard, the *Mahāvaṃsa* depends heavily upon the identification of the Tamil invaders with the evil Yakkhas. As the Yakkhas symbolize the chaos subjugated by the Buddha, so the Tamils symbolize the chaos subjugated by the Buddhist king. Germinal in this politico-religious parallel is the clear identification of political unity and religious purity which is apparent in the time of Parakkamabāhu.

The second point reflects the justification of the warrior aspect because the performance of all conquests and violent acts is for the sake of the dhamma. Receiving a crucial precedent in the first part of the reinterpreted biography section and then explicit sanction later in the text by the arhants, violence becomes the acknowledged means toward attaining a united Lanka and hence pure dhamma. However, this very significant shift testifies to the recognition on the part of the monk-chroniclers that indeed dhamma is not capable of attaining the conditions of its own existence. The contrast is marked between the means employed by Devānaṁpiyatissa who conforms to the classic Cakkavattin mold of ruler by non-violence and those employed by Duṭṭhagāmaṇī who forges the warrior ideal king mold in Sinhalese history. Dhamma stands no longer as the means of its own attainment, but rather as the goal. In the national arena, dhammic action will not achieve the national unity necessary for its own prosperity; violence is necessary and hence justifiable. The right goal, therefore, is the pivotal factor; this was discerned above as the crucial factor in the new biography as well.

The full-blown institutionalization of the sangha is also reflected in this stance; in keeping with the myth of dhammadīpa, the brotherhood provides the power of the king with legitimate authority. The arhants have the authority to legitimate the full transformation of the paradigm from its emphasis upon piety and its actualization in Duṭṭhagāmaṇī. With the new paradigm the glorification of the dhamma, regardless of the strategy necessary to attain that objective, takes precedence over (the politically and militarily less effective) compassionate means. It is interesting to note at this point that the normative relationship between king and sangha remains consistent in all of the chronicles. This relationship finds its paradigm set forth in the second and third parts of the biography of the Buddha which do not participate in the paradigm shift. It is easy to imagine that the arhants would be less receptive to a paradigm shift that would endanger their position.

As stated above, the *Cūlavaṃsa* does not permit the total parallel comparison of the paradigms set forth in the biographies and the ideal kings eulogized later in the texts. Being a continuation of the *Mahāvaṃsa*, it ostensibly presumes the same biographical section and therefore the same paradigm. However, a comparison of Duṭṭhagāmaṇī, the hero of the *Mahāvaṃsa*, and Parakkamabāhu (1153-1186 C.E.), the hero of the *Cūlavaṃsa*, reveals a third type of Cakkavattin. Parakkamabāhu and Duṭṭhagāmaṇī do not exhibit the radical change in paradigm that occurs with Duṭṭhagāmaṇī and Devanaṁpiyatissa. Rather, it is more accurate to say that Parakkamabāhu is a further development of Duṭṭhagāmaṇī. He portrays rebellious traits similar to those of Gāmanī, though the author of the *Cūlavaṃsa* has been at a loss to appeal to a higher order, that is the purification of Lanka and the glorification of the dhamma, that comprised Duṭṭhagāmaṇī's rationale. As a matter of fact, the author, a monk named Dhammakitti, seems quite enthralled with Parakkamabāhu's prowess. It is not until late in the narrative that Dhammakitti begins to assert his hero's ardent concern with the propagation of Buddhism. A brief digression on the author and his cultural milieu is enlightening here.

Dhammakitti is a monk of the thirteenth century and, as Mahānāma and the compilers of the *Dīpavaṃsa*, a member of the Mahāvihāra fraternity. His viewpoint, therefore, is also that this fraternity embraces the pristine dhamma, although his presentation is less polemical. By the time of Dhammakitti, much of the sectarian strife has been settled and the Mahāvihāra and Abhayagiri sanghas share an advisory capacity to the king. Lanka has also been greatly influenced by Hinduism, which is sustained through the presence of numerous Hindu queens and a large Hindu population. The *nīti* literature of India has also pervaded the Ceylonese courts, especially the *Arthaśāstra*, a Machiavellian-type work on statecraft. The latter two influences are of special import. The purpose of the *Arthaśāstra* is to enumerate efficient means of stabilizing and expanding a kingdom. The concern for such virtues as compassionate means is relegated either to a function of propaganda or forsaken entirely until stability and strength are sufficiently established to entertain such tangential notions. Geiger's translation of the *Cūlavaṃsa*[19] and his *Culture of Ceylon in Medieval Times*[20] carefully note the instances when Dhammakitti models particular actions on sections of the *Arthaśāstra.* The influence of Hindu gods also changes Dhammakitti's model, as is evidenced by the frequent comparisons of kings to Indra. The effect of the *Arthaśāstra* and Indra is an increased emphasis upon power and courage, and Dhammakitti allows this effect full expression in the figure of Parakkamabāhu.

The hero of the *Cūlavaṃsa* conducts a long campaign, begun while still a youth, to win complete sovereignty over Lanka. While initially these acts appear as rebellious exercise of fierce ambition, Dhammakitti is careful to explain Parakkamabāhu's strategy as the necessary course of the law of kamma. Parakkamabāhu's success derives from the accumulated merit of past actions. He is clearly an auspicious prince, destined to be a notable Cakkavattin. But, as the discussion of the *Arthaśāstra* foreshadowed, Parakkamabāhu's techniques are not always laudable. There are numerous instances of deceit and murder perpetrated by Parakkamabāhu for the sake of demonstrating his awesome courage and strength. These character traits have been elevated to the level of virtues despite their manner of expression. In the course of the chronicle, the union of Lanka "under one umbrella" becomes the paramount concern. All of Parakkamabāhu's actions are justified by this goal, which is also the first point in the arhants' speech to Duṭṭhagāmaṇī. Fully identified with this goal is the purity of the dhammadīpa, for if Lanka is united under a Buddhist Cakkavattin the dhamma will flourish.

The significant difference between Parakkamabāhu and Duṭṭhagāmaṇī is the former's total lack of remorse for his actions prior to his unchallenged sovereignty. Apparently, Dhammakitti perceived no paradox in the existence of piety and violence and so imposed no symptoms of conflict on his hero. The goal of uniting Lanka and, thereby, of purifying dhammadīpa, transcends the concern for compassionate means. However, the emphasis on the *Arthaśāstra*, and Dhammakitti's unabashed use of its techniques and pragmatism suggest a further politico-religious identification. The religious means of right action have been identified with the political (i.e., *Arthaśāstra*) means of right action. If this is indeed the case, as it certainly seems, there would be no conflict between piety and violence, since the means are now thoroughly consistent with the goal of unity and purity.

Thus far, the dhammadīpa tradition has been traced from its earliest extant version in the fourth century C.E. *Dīpavaṃsa* through its sixth century C.E. *Mahāvaṃsa* version to its thirteenth century C.E. *Cūlavaṃsa* version. The most significant reinterpretation occurs in the *Mahāvaṃsa* with the recension of the paradigm, and consequently a new perception of both the Buddha and the Sinhalese Cakkavattins. No longer are compassionate means paramount, but rather the establishment of the Buddhist state. The conflict arising from this shift is assuaged by the delegation of arhants who sanction the change and suggest the identification of political and religious goals. This, then, is taken further in the *Cūlavaṃsa* in which there is not only identification of political and religious goals but, in fact, identification of political and religious means.

The complementary relationship of the political and the religious is implicit in the notion of the Buddhist state and is reflected as well in the term dhammadīpa where dhamma indicates the religious aspect and dīpa ("island") the political aspect. But the relationship also inheres in the Buddha himself, whose portrait in the chronicles is the innovation of the Sinhalese Buddhist state. A closer analysis of the concepts of Buddha and Cakkavattin prove instructive with regard to the Buddhist tradition in Ceylon. According to Edward Conze,

> the *cakravartin* is the figure of cosmic significance. He has seven treasures which are his magical insignia, and he is to society what the Buddha is to the world of the spirit his exact counterpart . . . each ruler who supported the *samgha* was viewed as one. . . . So what Buddhism seeks in the social sphere is a *dharma-raja*, a king of *dharma*. The same *dharma* which rules the spiritual should, in other words, also dominate the social sphere.[21]

As Conze has observed, a Buddha and a Cakkavattin are counterparts, yet what occurs in the chronicles is a merging of these two ideals in the prism of Gotama Buddha. Focus is thereby pinpointed on the Buddha as the perfect model for both king and bhikkhu. Through their emulation of the Buddha, king and bhikkhu unite in the consummation of dhammadīpa. As Gotama embodies both Cakkavattin and Tathāgatha, so the dhammadīpa embodies both political state and religious state. The sacred city of Anurādhapura epitomizes just such a center. In the *Dīpavaṃsa*, when Mahinda brought Buddhism to Lanka, King Devānaṃpiyatissa requested that the boundaries of the Mahāvihāra be set within the city limits. Centuries later, when King Mahāsena destroyed the Mahāvihāra and, therefore, destroyed the center of the dhammadīpa, he effected a virtual exile of the homeland in much the same sense that the destruction of the Temple of Jerusalem exiled Israel.[22] Similarly, Parakkamabāhu, although he had essentially brought all of Lanka under his dominion, believed his rule to be illegitimate without the possession of the sacred relics of the Tooth and the Almsbowl, which had become the palladia of the dhammadīpa. So while the manner in which the dhammadīpa was to be realized came increasingly to be defined in political terms, the center and meaning of the dhammadīpa continued to be defined in the conjunction of sovereign and sangha and their complementary emulation of the Buddha. The thrust of this paper is captured in these words:

> Tradition, as a process of handing on and passing forward, thus is dynamic and not static. Its interest is not in what was originally said alone, but in how what was said in the past endows with meaning, imposes sense upon, the issues of the new age. Tradition is killed when handed on unchanged. It is vivified when it goes forward, while not intact, fundamentally unimpaired.[23]

Notes

1. Jacob Neusner, "The Study of Religion as the Study of Tradition," *History of Religions*, XIV (1975): 193.
2. Bardwell Smith, "The Ideal Social Order as Portrayed in the Chronicles of Ceylon," in *The Two Wheels of Dhamma: Essays on the Theravada Tradition in India and Ceylon*, edited by Bardwell Smith (Chambersburg, Pa., 1972), p. 32. Reprinted in this volume.
3. Neusner, pp. 195-196.
4. L. S. Perera, "The Pali Chronicles of Ceylon," in *Historians of India, Pakistan and Ceylon*, edited by C. H. Philips (London, 1961), p. 43.
5. For an alternative view of the purpose of the chronicles, see Smith, p. 32.
6. Perera, p. 39. This pattern seems to prevail in Chinese historiography as well. According to H. L. Borman, "In addition to compiling, however, the traditional historians were also consciously constructing a corpus of precedents designed to guide future generations of Chinese bureaucrats in the theory and practice of public administration as it should be conducted according to Confucian ethical standards. The *lieh-chuan*, or biographies, were thus selected as illustrative examples to illuminate aspects of the main thread of history as recorded in the *pen-chi*, the basic annals. The ultimate purpose of biography was to instruct officials in orthodoxy, not to present rounded portraits of fallible human beings." See H. L. Borman, "The Biographical Approach to Chinese History: A Symposium," *Journal of Asian Studies*, XXI (1962): 453.
7. W. Geiger, tr., *The Mahāvaṃsa, or The Great Chronicle of Ceylon* (London, 1912), p. 113.
8. Judith Shklar, "Subversive Genealogies," in *Myth, Symbol and Culture*, edited by Clifford Geertz (New York, 1971), p. 144.
9. H. Oldenberg, tr., *The Dīpavaṃsa: An Ancient Buddhist Historical Record* (London, 1879), pp. 1-2.
10. *Mahāvaṃsa*, pp. ix-lxiii.

1. See *Mahāvaṃsa,* xxxvii; also see W. M. K. Wijetunga, "The Spread of Heterodox Doctrines in Early Ceylon," in *The Ceylon Historical Journal* XIX (1969-1970): 16-28; E. W. Adikaram, *Early History of Ceylon* (Colombo, 1946); G. P. Malalasekera, *The Pāli Literature of Ceylon* (Colombo, 1928).

2. *Mahāvaṃsa*, p. 268; see *Dīpavaṃsa*, chapter 22.

3. This notion of the Buddhist state is taken from a lecture delivered by Joseph M. Kitagawa on 30 October 1974: see also his article, "The Japanese *Kokutai* (National Community) History and Myth," *History of Religions*, XIII (1974): 209-226.

4. Malalasekera, p. 137; see also *Dīpavaṃsa*, p. 8.

5. For an interesting and provocative discussion of the transformation of symbols of power, see N. Falk, "Wilderness and Kingship in Ancient South Asia," *History of Religions*, XIII (1973): 1-15.

6. *Mahāvaṃsa*, pp. 153-154.

7. *Ibid.*, p. 164, n. 5.

8. *Ibid.*, p. 178.

9. W. Geiger, tr., *Cūlavaṃsa: Being the More Recent Part of the Mahāvaṃsa*, Part I (Colombo, 1953), Part II (London, 1930).

0. W. Geiger, *Culture of Ceylon in Medieval Times*, edited by Heinz Bechert (Wiesbaden, 1960).

1. Edward Conze, "Dharma as a Spiritual, Social, and Cosmic Force," in *The Social Concept of Order*, edited by P. Kuntz (Seattle, 1968).

2. For an excellent discussion of the center and related imagery, see J. Z. Smith, "Earth and Gods," *Journal of Religion*, XLIX (1969): 103-127.

3. Neusner, p. 194.

The Ideal Social Order as Portrayed in the Chronicles of Ceylon

Bardwell L. Smith

> [*Suṇātha me. Suṇātha me.*] Listen to me, I shall relate the Chronicle of the Buddha's coming to the island, the arrival of the relic and the Bo-Tree and the advent of the Buddha's religion in the island and of the doctrine of the teachers who made the collection as well as of the advent of the chief of men . . . . Listen to the eulogy of the island, incomparable, that which deals with the lineage of the best dwellers, original, unrivalled and well-narrated, handed down by the elect, described by the noblest and adored by the righteous.[1]

SO BEGINS THE earliest Pāli chronicle of Ceylon, an authoritative historical poem, written in the late fourth or early fifth century A.D. by an unknown author. It is the attempt of this essay to discern the image or concept of an ideal social order which may be found within the pages of the two primary chronicles of the Sinhalese people, the *Dīpavaṃsa* and the *Mahāvaṃsa*, which together trace the history of Lanka (Ceylon) from the advent of Vijaya in 483 B.C. down to modern times. It must be stressed that this essay is dealing with the image of an *ideal* and not with historical facts in some independent sense. In line with the chronicles themselves, the focus here is upon the classical period of Sinhalese Buddhism from its inception in the third century B.C. to the fall of its early capital Anurādhapura in 1029 A.D. For primary material the essay limits itself to these chronicles, with a few exceptions, though examination of various other sources has helped fill out the picture.[2] These other materials amplify but do not essentially alter the picture found within the Sinhalese chronicles.

Immediately, the question of historiography arises: how is one to treat source material such as the *Dīpavaṃsa* and the *Mahāvaṃsa*, material which is more normative than descriptive, more poetic than the writing of history as we now know it? It is difficult enough knowing how the chroniclers imagined the history of Buddhism, let alone discovering what the facts were during this period. B. C. Law may not be far wrong in saying about the chronicles that "just as the religious motive cannot be divorced from the cultural advancement, so the patriotic motive cannot be separated from the promotion of the general cause of piety."[3] Clearly, this is history written with a motive. It is *Heilsgeschichte.* It is the sacred history of a people destined with a sacred mission, namely, to maintain the purity of the *Dhamma* in a world of impermanence and self-seeking.[4] As one enters the world of these chronicles, one enters a world not unlike that of the Old Testament, a world in which bare fact was always less important than what the fact signified. In any case, this is interpreted history. It is didac-

Originally published in *The Two Wheels of Dhamma: Essays on the Theravada Tradition in India and Ceylon* (Chambersburg, Pa.: American Academy of Religion, 1972), edited by Bardwell L. Smith, AAR Studies in Religion, No. Three, pp. 31-57. Reprinted with permission, in a slightly revised version.

tic by nature, sometimes moralistic. By definition, it is ethnocentric; history itself revolves around the history of this people. At its worst, it becomes fiercely judgmental, condoning savagery if done in the cause of mission. But, in all of this, one is walking upon familiar ground, as no people recording their ancient past (or their present, for that matter) are free of self-justification. As with wisdom literature in general, whether in the Old Testament, the *Jātakas*, or as found within the Sinhalese chronicles, the primary intent is twofold: to provide paradigmatic models for the present and the future and to engage in anamnesis or cultic reawakening of a people to the high points in its past and present destiny.

Any piece of literature can be judged by what it excludes as well as by the bias it reveals. Clearly, the interests of the chroniclers acted as a sieve which ignored much that we would like to know. As Rahula stressed about these writings, "secular history is subservient to religious history."[5] Here is in no sense a history of Ceylon. It is at most source material for the history of Buddhism in Ceylon, especially for the Mahāvihāra bhikkhus, material comprised of myth, fable, legend, and history interpreted through tradition. Law is right, however, in saying that "germs of historical truth" are "buried deep under a mesh of absurd fables and marvellous tales."[6] Or, to put it differently: "The garb in which these fantasies appear says more perhaps of the cultural and social circumstances of a people than its recorded history. To discard legend, and myth, and fairy tale would just as much rob one of one's most valuable sources of information about a people as to reject its art and literature as unimportant."[7]

With this preface in mind the essay proceeds to sketch out the central ingredients of an *ideal social order* as this emerges from the richly varied stories, accounts, and interpretations which comprise the chronicles in question. In the process four categories will be explored: first, the sense of continuity which is present throughout, continuity of Indian tradition with Sinhalese tradition, of earliest Buddhism with later emerging forms, of popular religious expression with the *Buddha-sāsana* itself; second, the awareness of evil and the ever-present sensed threat of disorder, in relationship to which the concept of kingship becomes an ambiguous reality; third, the concept of *Dharma-vijaya* (of conquest through righteousness, not force) as developed originally by Aśoka (Pāli, Asoka) and as reaffirmed by the *Saṅgha* in Ceylon, providing the basis for symbiosis between monarch and Sangha and between monarch and people, establishing the normative pattern for Sinhalese kings from the earliest days; and fourth, the assumed interconnection between what happens in society and what occurs in the cosmos at large, alongside the depiction of an ideal king and the configurations of the City of Righteousness as these in some sense presage, in some sense prepare men for, the ultimate goal of *Nibbāna.*

I. The Sense of Continuity

From start to finish in the chronicles one is kept aware of historic continuities, whether those of royal clans and families, apostolic succession (*ācariya-paramparā*) within the early Sangha, the lineage of the Buddha himself, or whether those stemming from cultural contact and productive of new forms.[8] Only a detailed study could do justice to Ceylon's cultural indebtedness to both Aryan and Dravidian India. The basic social and political institutions, the vast majority of literary and art forms, the gift of the Dharma[9] itself all passed from the subcontinent over centuries to Ceylon. The story is a complex and fascinating one in its own right. Only certain highlights can be touched here.

One thread which provides both meaning and threat to Sinhalese self-consciousness is the ever-recurring pressure of Tamil invasion and occupation. Neither the present scene in Ceylon nor its lengthy history can be understood without a vivid awareness of the ambivalent relationship between these two peoples, now one of alliance and reciprocity, now of embittered hostility. Over the centuries it was essentially the latter which prevailed, reaching epic proportions in the chronicles and draining the economy and manpower seriously at many points in time. The "myth had been cultivated under Duttugemunu [Duṭṭha-Gāmiṇī, 101-77 B.C.] and was writ into Sinhalese political tradition" that the Tamils were Lanka's natural enemy.[10] Whether from the Pāṇḍyans, the Cōḷas, or the Pallavas, the threat never disappeared. By invasion, by infiltration, by being used increasingly as mercenaries, and through intermarriage, the Tamil presence made itself felt until finally in 1325 they had established an independent kingdom in the north of Ceylon.

Far more important for our present subject, however, were the Brahmanic influences upon Sinhalese culture and religion. Following the lead of Aśoka in his tolerance of other religions, Buddhism displayed openness toward many Hindu institutional forms and devotional practices, absorbing or converting them in the process. Wilhelm Geiger rightfully underscores the fallaciousness of separating too radically Buddhism from Brahmanism.[11] The latter was regarded more as preparatory to the former than antagonistic. The Hindu gods, Indra (Sakka) especially, are invoked throughout as guardian and protective figures who further the Buddha's cause in Lanka. As Theravada Buddhists typically indicate, the gods play no role in the attainment of Nibbāna.[12] In the Buddha's words, one must remain a refuge or island unto oneself;[13] no one can cross over for another. If this qualification is maintained, then orthodoxy has no quarrel with divine assistance. In the *Mahāvaṃsa* the Buddha himself speaks to Sakka, prior to entering *parinibbāna*, recording his last will and testament, namely, that Vijaya, his followers, and Lanka be protected by the gods.[14] Throughout the establishing and maintaining of the Dhamma in Ceylon, the path is cleared and facilitated for the Buddha's followers by the heavenly hosts, whether this be in the consecrating of the nation's rulers, the arrival of the relics, the coming of the Bodhi-tree, or the wars against enemies. To put this into perspective with the core of the Buddha's teaching, one may posit a correspondence between this kind of assistance rendered by the gods and that afforded by Sinhalese kings. While different in substance and in degree, ideally both help to create the climate in which the Dhamma may thrive. In essence, then, the gods are converted to the Buddha's cause, revealing the cosmic nature of its scope.

With respect to the Brahmanical influences upon the Sinhalese concept of kingship and the political order, an entire study would be profitable.[15] Suffice it to indicate here the continuity which is apparent, without elaborating upon upon its configurations. Of immense symbolic importance is the fact that Sinhalese kings retained both the central ingredients of the Hindu coronation ceremony (*abhiṣeka*) and the institution of the *purohita* or domestic chaplain to the throne. While partly ceremonial or cultic in form, these provided also a perspective and dimension which conveyed extensive Brahmanical culture in the process. It is possible to make too much of this channel, as discontinuities in the transformation of the caste system and in other areas are important, but the tie with Aryan tradition which this provided is unmistakable. Linguistic, religious, familial, economic, and political elements passed regularly from Indian to Sinhalese soil, in the end inadvertently contributing to a "Sanskritization" of this culture and to an increasing, almost dominant, Hindu influence in the Gupta period and beyond.

One aspect of the purohita-monarch relationship which needs further exploration is the degree to which this helped introduce and institutionalize *Realpolitik* procedures and policies. In what ways, for instance, whether through the king's chaplain directly or not, were policies shaped by the strategems of Kauṭilya's *Arthaśāstra*, the Machiavellian manual of Indian regents? Paul Mus, in commenting upon the Theravada scene as a whole, raises this same question: "Even in ancient history has not State Politics in the area derived its inspiration more from the pragmatic tradition of power developed in neighboring Hindu Kingdoms, than from so aloof and retiring a Church?"[16] While somewhat rhetorical in nature, for he is equally concerned in this essay to show how Buddhism has expressed itself politically, his question suggests the impact Indian statecraft had upon policy-making in Theravadin societies generally, an impact which does not go unnoticed in the Sinhalese chronicles. The teaching of *nīti*, or statecraft, to the future King Dhātusena by his uncle is one case in point.[17] While not at the hands of a royal chaplain, in fact the uncle was a bhikkhu, the explicit mentioning of a ruler's need for such knowledge and training is both symptomatic of the internecine and foreign adversaries each king faced *and* symbolic of the Sangha's recognition that, this side of Metteyya's coming, heads of state do not rule by righteousness alone.

The final continuity to be mentioned is, for our purposes, the most important. It is that which links the Buddha and early Buddhism in India to the advent and confirmation of the Dhamma in Ceylon. The *Dīpavaṃsa* and the *Mahāvaṃsa* both open with an account of the *Tathāgata's* three visits to Lanka in the first eight years of his enlightenment. These events are not recorded in the Pāli Canon but, alongside the Buddha's invoking of divine protection for Lanka, serve to set the stage in Sinhalese self-consciousness for its efforts to preserve uninterruptedly the purity of the Master's doctrine. Even this continuity is set in a Brahmanic context, for it is an astute Brāhmaṇa, the youngest of 108 consulted to interpret the meaning of the thirty-two "distinctive marks" (*lakkhaṇāni*) upon the infant Siddhattha, who predicts he is to become a Buddha, not a Universal Monarch (*Cakkavatti*).[18] And it is a converted Brāhmaṇa, Dāsaka, who inherits the apostolic mantle from Upāli as the chain of succession proceeds from the Buddha, over two centuries, to Mahinda (Asoka's bhikkhu son) and from him to the Sangha as it roots itself in Ceylon. Coupled with the placing of Gotama himself in the lineage of *Mahāsaṃmata*, the Great Sage-King "in the beginning of this age of the world,"[19] one is given a distinct sense of the new doctrine and religion being presented as "a repetition of the ancient archetype."[20] The present is vividly connected with the past, providing both for legitimacy and for remembrance of the tradition's roots. One has the sense also of how the Mahāvihāra chroniclers, writing several centuries later in a time of political and sectarian turmoil, are engaging in the task of recreating their own tradition.[21]

Aside from the cosmic and existential significance of tracing its origins to the Buddha, the key ingredients in the Sangha's authentication of its mission were doctrinal, devotional and political. With respect to *doctrine*, the history of Sinhalese Buddhism could be written from the standpoint of the interplay between the Theravadins and the whole Ācariyavāda (or heterodox) movement with its many sects, beginning with the Vesālī monks at the time of the Second Council and continuing to the present. Early in the chronicles one is exposed to the conciliar movement, arising in Buddhism upon the Tathāgata's passing and reaching its peak at the time of Asoka with the "compilation of the true Dhamma."[22] Throughout the *Mahāvaṃsa* one is aware not only of the obvious tensions existing between the Mahāvihāra bhikkhus and those in various sects co-existing with them in Anurādhapura but also of the subtle influences these sects, especially those affected by Mahayana ideas, had upon the *Theriya Nikāya* or orthodox strain. Some of these influences will be examined later. It only needs indicating here that Buddhism, like all great religious traditions, has dealt with difficulty with the problems of schism, sectarianism, and heresy. While tolerant of other faiths, popular and sophisticated, and while able to incorporate and transform indigenous elements, Sinhalese Buddhism has persistently felt threatened by the specter of heretical movements from within. In the words of G. P. Malalasekera: "To the assaults of open opponents the Buddhist displays the calmest indifference, convinced that in its undiminished strength his faith is firm and inexpungable; his vigilance is only excited by the alarm of internal dissent, and all his passions are aroused to stifle the symptoms of schism."[23]

The *devotional* ingredients continuous with earliest Buddhism likewise play a major part in the chroniclers' saga. If continuity of doctrine can be traced through the councils, the apostolic succession, and the safeguarding of the Dhamma's purity by the Sangha, the sense of wonder released through awareness of the Buddha's gift is enlivened through anamnesis and celebration. While images of the Buddha came only after centuries, his sensed presence was (in the testimony of the chronicles) from the beginning. The words voiced by Mahinda, as he yearns for his homeland and the holy places associated with Gotama, are the words of tradition: "If we behold the relics we behold the Conqueror."[24] As the story of Sinhalese Buddhism could be told through the interplay between orthodoxy and sectarianism, it could be told also by discussion of the Buddhist sense of adoration. Without question, the high points in the reigns of Ceylon's two greatest kings during the Anurādhapura period, which spanned fourteen centuries,[25] were the arrival and enshrinement of relics from India. Kings Devānaṁpiyatissa and Duṭṭhagāmiṇī are remembered as epic figures for many reasons, but the coming of the relics confirmed and consecrated not only their reigns but the nation itself in the judgment of the Sinhalese chronicles. As the planting of the Bodhi-tree symbolized the spreading of the doctrine from its land of origin, the receiving of the relics confirmed the Buddha's authority in the land. With both gifts, the results were seen to be miraculous and enduring; the chronicles spare no words in telling of the wonder: "When the prince [Duṭṭhagāmaṇī] saw the celestial parasol, the celestial perfumes, and the rest, and heard the sound of celestial instruments of music and so forth, albeit he did not see the Brahma-gods he, rejoicing and amazed at the miracle, worshipped the relics, with the offering of a parasol and investing them with the kingship of Laṅkā."[26]

The problem of true authority and kingship leads directly to the third ingredient of continuity established by the Sangha in the doctrine's spread to Ceylon, namely, the *political.* This was preeminently crystallized in the reconsecration of Devānaṁpiyatissa by envoys from Asoka. The *Mahāvaṃsa* records that at the first consecration of King Tissa "many wonders came to pass . . . treasures and jewels that had been buried deep rose to the surface," and that "all this was the effect of Devānaṁpiyatissa's merit."[27] Out of gratitude he sends these treasures to King Asoka, a friend though they had never met. In return, Asoka sends "all that was needful for consecrating a king" and with these the message of his having taken refuge in the Three Jewels (*Triratna*), urging his friend: "Seek then even thou, O best of men converting thy mind with believing heart refuge in these best of gems!"[28] It is a delightful passage, punctuated by directions to his envoys: "Consecrate my friend yet again as king."[29]

In these words and actions are symbolized the line of continuity from the imperial majesty of Asoka to the small island of Lanka *and* from where the doctrine arose to where it was destined to flourish. In time, Anurādhapura became the Sinhalese counterpart of Pātaliputta, the great capital of Asoka. In a sense, when Mahinda came to Ceylon, he brought not simply a religion but "a whole civilization at the height of its glory," its concepts of art and architecture, its language and literature, even its very alphabet.[30] But from the standpoint of establishing Buddhism's legitimacy there could have been no greater safeguard than imperial sanction. As more than one commentator has pointed out and as the chronicles themselves infer with frequency, royal support is a two-edged sword. Established religion is not always, if ever, true religion. In any case, while it cannot be said that the Buddha's doctrine entered Ceylon for the first time with Asoka's envoys or even with Mahinda, it can be dated as a state or court religion with the second consecration of Tissa. At this juncture and in what unfolded with Asoka's follow-up mission through his son Mahinda two lines of succession merged and Sinhalese Buddhism came into being. These lines were those of *rāja-paramparā* and *thera-paramparā*, of royal and ecclesiastical legitimacy. In the process were brought into new relationship two central realities within the Sāsana, both essential historically to Theravada at large, that of the patron-monarch and that of the bhikkhu-sangha.

The image of Asoka loomed larger with time. Legends about the great king were circulated soon after his death (later collected in the Sanskrit *Aśokāvadāna*), but their full impact only hit Ceylon about the time the chronicles were being written.[31] It is evident not only from the prominence given Asoka in the early part of the scenario but, as one reads further, it becomes even clearer that the Sinhalese model for kingship, as well as for the *upāsaka* in general, is based upon the image these legends afford of the great king. A major feature of what is to be sensed in the figure of Asoka is the tradition's superimposing of the two great Kings: the Buddha and the Universal Monarch. This only becomes manifest as one perceives the emergence of the Cakkavatti figure in later centuries. But suggestions of it are apparent in the first part of the *Mahāvaṃsa*, i.e., by the early sixth century. It was this image which, however variously construed, became the paradigm for each king of Lanka. It was the image both of the Universal Monarch (the Cakkavatti) and of the Great Man (the *Mahāpurisa*, the Buddha himself) fused into one.

> It is in this light that the emblem of the sacred footprint should be considered. It could be taken as the symbol of the imprint of the civilization of the mainland on its island neighbor. It is more, it is the token of the Great Man. Incomprehensible

though the devotion shown to it may be, its real value lies in its plain significance too – the veneration Indian civilization has always paid to the great human being, the sage who through his wisdom enables humankind to free itself from ignorance.[32]

II. The Threat of Disorder

If there was a tendency for the image of Asoka to assume Cakkavatti proportions, there was also the constant insistence that this flower had emerged from the mud of human rapacity. Injustice is done to Asoka himself, the tradition insists, if one forgets what preceded his transformation. Indeed, this is central to his appeal as an ideal monarch; it is what makes identification with him by ruler after ruler more potent. It is not simply the majesty of his imperial power which appeals; it is the attraction of power tamed and made righteous. We have here then an *ideal* of righteous and benevolent power in tension with self-seeking power as most men know it. The total image of Asoka contains both; "his cruelty and his piety"[33] must each be seen in order to comprehend his paradigmatic attraction and to discern what Buddhism is saying about man. Asoka, therefore, is cast not only as the Great Man (the Mahāpurisa); he is also Everyman. Asoka, the wicked and cruel (*Candāsoka*), becomes Asoka, the just and righteous (*Dhammāsoka*).[34] In one human life we have the crystallization of two contrasting images, that of classic brutality and that of classic tolerance. As is well known, what unites these two images is the sense of horror and repentance which were said to be Asoka's following the carnage of the Kaliṅgas by his troops. It was this decisive event and its aftermath which, as tradition reports, impelled him toward Dharma-vijaya, conquest through righteousness rather than by force. Here is not the renunciation of power but its transformation. It is this perceived *metanoia* which makes him a compelling model throughout the Theravada world.

That this is seen to be of one piece with the experience of Prince Siddhattha makes the model all the more authentic. The latter's exposure to the existence of suffering was transmuted upon enlightenment into insight regarding its causes. The Buddha's vision of human nature in the grips of self-aggrandizement was profoundly realistic. This insight is intrinsic to Buddhism, sparing it from becoming naive about man's capacity for evil. While the Buddha's teachings added new depth to this vision, it may in retrospect be seen as continuous with the overall Indian analysis of man's plight. This is made graphic in the *Cakkavatti-Sīhanāda Suttanta* within the Pāli Canon which presents two apocalyptic images – of life under the rule of evil, and of life ruled by Dhamma.[35] The one is a picture of injustice, disorder, and confusion; the other portrays liberation and reciprocity. Both are extended images of the human potential, kept in balance as with Asoka. From the Buddhist standpoint, neither one can be fully appreciated except in relationship to the other. It does little good trying to make sense of the Ideal King concept or that of the City of Righteousness (as portrayed in *The Questions of King Milinda*), even of the king-Sangha relationship, unless one takes seriously the note of realism sounded by the tradition. This note is repeatedly implicit within the Sinhalese chronicles.

The opening words of the *Mahāvaṃsa*, in fact, state the chronicler's intent throughout, namely, that these passages awaken in the reader "serene joy and emotion" (*pasāda* and *saṃvega*): joy, blissfulness and satisfaction in the doctrine of the Buddha; and emotion, horror, and recoil from the world and its misery.[36] Similarly, each chapter ends with the same refrain, "compiled for the serene joy and emotion of the pious." If one is encouraged toward ecstatic euphoria by some passages and events, one is brought into sharp confrontation with more somber reality by others. Sobriety alternates with the sense of wonder in powerful juxtaposition. One is never led too far in either direction. If tempted to place evil outside one's community, it springs up in one's midst. Though stylized and moralistic at times, the language of the chronicles does not romanticize the human predicament. Sinhalese man, like man in the Old Testament, is portrayed with candor. At the very times one expects the picture to leave out the darker hues they suddenly appear. Indeed, profane history portrayed in this manner becomes a subject for meditation (*kammaṭṭhāna*), showing not only life's impermanence but man's anxiety in the face of it.[37] In the words of one commentator: "What better theme for meditation than the crimes and follies of mankind. If history had no other lesson to teach, scanning its pages or rather hearing its sad stories of the death of its kings, was to fortify oneself anew in the knowledge of the transiency of all things, and to savour, by contrast, the joy of the mind directed towards the Four Noble Truths."[38]

Basic to the Buddhist understanding of evil is apprehension about the consequences of disorder. The threat of anarchy and chaos is ever-present in the chronicler's mind. While the identity of the *yakkhas* has often been debated, whether demons or non-human tutelary deities or ancestors of the present *Vaddās*, it is more probable that tradition has invested them with even profounder symbolism. If aborigines in some sense, they represent the aboriginal spirit of man which lurks not far beneath the surface, the protean fount of fear and self-enslavement which, unless stilled, infects all his acts and colors every throught. While on one level the Buddha's coming to Lanka can be interpreted as freeing it from yakkha control, making it ready for the Sinhalese race, on another level it becomes exorcism of the demonic from man himself. As with the Marcan account in the New Testament of the Gerasene demoniac, one senses here the removal of that which can be lodged in any man.[39] When confronted by the Buddha, the yakkhas, "overwhelmed by fear," beseech "the fearless Vanquisher to release them from terrors."[40] Hypostasized into imaginary figures the yakkhas may represent tradition's own realistic fear of man's proclivity toward disorder and evil. In any case, sensitivity toward the demonic remains a permanent ingredient of Sinhalese consciousness. Though the yakkhas are released from their distress and are converted to the Buddha's cause, the chronicles record the on-going turmoil within and between men. Three centuries after the Master's visit, Mahinda, in the *Dīpavaṃsa* account, reflects about his own mission to Lanka in conversation with Sakka (the lord of the gods) and makes a statement which history proves to be double-edged: "Tambapaṇṇi [Ceylon] is covered and closed with the overclouding darkness of ignorance and of worldly existence, it is destroyed by jealousy and selfishness . . . . It has obtained the wrong path, it has gone astray, it is entangled like a ball of string and covered with blight."[41] Such a statement can be double-edged, for to Sinhalese nationalism the liberation from fear and ignorance can seem to be a *fait accompli*, an unrepeatable act making Lanka for all time "fit for human habitation,"[42] while to more honest self-reflection it may appear as but a foretaste of what must occur throughout time.

The evidence is overwhelming in the chronicles that the latter appraisal is more basic. Consistent with the tension found in the image of Asoka, the image of the island kingdom presented in these pages is twofold: as the archetype of delusion and as the paragon of enlightenment. What one finds here is a mixture of both in the nation's history. If the forces of evil are stilled in some, they are rampant in others. In all, however, they are realities acknowledged and underscored. As Vijaya, forebear of the race, was wild in his conduct before taming, so each man needs separation from ignorance and self-possession. The centuries of Sinhalese history, like that of each people, are written in blood. Intrigue follows intrigue. Parricides appear *seriatim*. Subversion, treason, infamy, and unrest unfold with ritualistic regularity. The threat of disorder is constant, stayed only by strong monarchs who contain their adversaries. Whether viewed on the level of society or in the realm of man's spirit, the confrontation with disorder looms as a permanent vocation. On both levels the final destiny is soteriological; it is ultimate freedom. The stabilizing of order by the king and the exorcism of the demonic by religious incantation[43] are both requisite to the ultimate goal of Nibbāna. The establishment of the sacred boundaries (*sīmā*) of the Sangha as coterminous with the sacred city of Anurādhapura by Mahinda Thera and King Devānaṁpiyatissa symbolizes the inclusion of social and political order within the larger order of the Dhamma, which is the source of freedom from disorder itself. The symbiotic ideal which this suggests is seen to have repercussions which incorporate not only society, but all nature and the cosmos at large. It is in this perspective that one can comprehend the urgency to maintain both the purity of the doctrine and the unity of the Sangha. With the continuum between the "secular" and the "sacred" so conceived, any threat to order in the latter was automatically construed as disruptive of the former. It is to the politically relevant dimensions of Dhamma that we must now turn.

III. The Monarchy-Sangha Relationship

In the long history of Sinhalese Buddhism there is no relationship more complex or more crucial than that existing between the monarchy and the Sangha. Of all the pithy sayings concluding each chapter of the *Mahāvaṃsa* none perhaps is more telling in this respect than the following: "Thus, reflecting that sovereignty, being the source of manifold works of merit, is at the same time the source of many an injustice, a man of pious heart will never enjoy it as if it were sweet food mixed with poison."[44] The Sangha's historic dependence upon the monarchy for support, protection, and confirmation of the faith has not been an unmixed blessing. At the core of the issue is the understanding of Dhamma and the role each institution had in its furtherance. Not unrelated are the problems caused by a religion's becoming established, problems which can be devastating for the religion as for the society in general, raising the very question of what the "establishment" of Buddhism (or of any religious faith) means.

The most extreme instance of fanatical religious and national sentiment occurring in Sinhalese history was in the kingship of its classical hero, Duṭṭhagāmaṇī, who, after the pattern of Asoka, lamented the carnage his victories had wrought.[45] While similar in outward form, resemblance to the Asokan ideal stops there. In the vanguard of a crusade, Duṭṭhagāmaṇī, with a relic in his spear and accompanied by five hundred bhikkhus, marches into battle with the Tamils, declaring solemnly: "Not for the joy of sovereignty is this toil of mine, my striving (has been) ever to establish the doctrine of the Sambuddha."[46] And even his remorse following the slaughter is short-lived, for the Sangha, knowing his thoughts, send eight arahants to comfort him: "From this deed arises no hindrance in thy way to heaven. Only one and a half human beings have been slain here by thee, O lord of men. . . . Unbelievers and men of evil life were the rest, not more to be esteemed than beasts. But as for thee, thou wilt bring glory to the doctrine of the Buddha in manifold ways; therefore cast away care from thy heart." "Thus exhorted by them the great king took comfort."[47]

The very inclusion of this passage in the chronicles of Ceylon, while ironic, is of immense import. While neither monarch nor Sangha in this guise could be a model, the tradition's refusal to gloss over murder and self-justification becomes instructive for history. As the conscience of the nation, the Sangha, sobered by unending warfare and intrigue, is recording its alarm. Though different stylistically from the Hebrew prophets, one detects a comparable judgment, upon themselves as upon those directly responsible. Again and again, the bhikkhu community through these chronicles records its own need for purification, alongside that of the nation. Part of the solemn charge given to the king is that of helping to maintain a strong and united Order. "It was his right to see that the religion was kept pure [*sodhesi sāsanam*] and in its pristine condition. Consecrated in the ceremonial of the *abhiṣeka* or "anointing" with rites at which in time the *sangha* assisted, the king was head of the state with power to purify the *sasana*, as he often did."[48] The monarch, in turn, was kept responsible by the Sangha, his meritorious works duly registered in the royal annals, his violations no less noted.[49] That there was friction between them one would expect, but that the *ideal* of reciprocity endured cannot be questioned. In essence, it was a symbiosis rooted in tradition and having consequences for what it meant to be a Buddhist community in the best sense of the word, a *sāvaka-saṇgha* or ideal social order.

As in every other way, the prototype for this relationship may be found in reports of the Buddha's life, here his associations with monarchs. The sovereignty of political power is subsumed under the sovereignty of the Dhamma in the *Dīpavaṃsa* account of King Bimbisāra's vision at the age of eight: "A Khattiya is in need of sovereignty; he, the Enlightened one, the bull among men, should arise in my kingdom; the Tathāgata should approach to show himself first to me, he should preach the everlasting norm, I should penetrate (into) the excellent (norm)."[50] Tradition cements the fealty of king to Dhamma in the appealing story of Asoka's attraction to and conversion by the young bhikkhu Nigrodha. Searching for "truth and untruth," "for the virtuous and skilful," Asoka tests person after person in vain and in discouragement asks: "When should I approach to have a sight of good men? Listening to this good saying I shall give my sovereignty along with the kingdom."[51] At one point he sees Nigrodha and addresses an aide: "Behold, quickly conduct that monk, the young man moving on the road like an elephant, graceful and peaceful by nature, fearless and possessed of the quality of tranquility."[52] Nigrodha is brought in and, "like the fearless king of gods, Sakka," mounts the imperial throne, to Asoka's amazement and delight. The king then utters the word which depicts the Sangha's vocation to monarch and people alike: "Teach me the Norm which you have learnt. You will be my teacher and I shall be taught by you. Oh great sage, I will act according to your word. Instruct me, I will listen to your instruction."[53] The monk speaks; the king listens; and the teachings of the Buddha come alive. Asoka then takes refuge in the Three Gems, bestowing upon the bhikkhu community his loyalty and his larder, saying, "as much as the monks desire I give them whatever they choose."[54] While a figment of later imagination, it takes root within the tradition.

What follows becomes the model of royal patronage to the Sangha in recognition of the Dhamma's true majesty. The monks' needs are met; vihāras without number are built; and in the Third Council the true Dhamma is compiled and preserved. One further test put to Asoka in answer to his question "Whose generosity toward the doctrine of the Blessed One was ever (so) great (as mine)?" shows even more the king's responsibility toward the Sangha and seals the eventual tie with Lanka. When told there was no one more generous than he, Asoka presses his luck and asks, "Is there a kinsman of Buddha's religion like unto me?" The reply of Moggaliputta Thera has implications not only for Asoka and succeeding monarchs, but for all people: "[Only] he who lets son or daughter enter the religious order is a kinsman of the religion and withal a giver of gifts."[55]

A great deal more could be said about the king's protection and support of the Sangha. The chronicles are replete with accounts of royal patronage to both Sangha and society; they are no less specific about lack of patronage as well.[56] Ideally, too, the ruler was expected to be the *fidei defensor*, protecting the Dhamma from heretical incursions, settling disputes among the bhikkhus, encouraging the teaching and spread of the doctrine. In actuality, kings were seen to support now one vihāra, now another, promoting "orthodoxy" at certain points in history, "heretical sects" at others. As with the misuse of power in general, the chronicles are candid about the infidelity of certain kings who fell into the clutches of wayward and lawless monks. One must always remember, however, that the story is being told from the Mahāvihāra point of view. In any case, our concern here is for the *image* of ideal reciprocity. On this score, the picture is unambiguous; it is a division of labor with both parties dedicated to the same goal. This is seen in the frequent offering of the kingdom to the Sāsana by the monarch, symbolizing his own recognition of the state's purpose. While always returned to him, it was a gesture of acknowledgement that his authority is both delegated and responsible.[57] The division of labor is seen also in the fact that, while it was the king's right and duty to insure that the doctrine be taught, it was in fact the Sangha's task to provide the instruction. The most poignant example of this may be noted in Duṭṭhagāmaṇī's attempt to propagate the faith himself. "He seated himself in the preacher's chair in the centre of the spacious hall and made ready to give the august assembly a discourse on some religious topic from the *Maṅgala-Sutta*. But, although he was quite familiar with the Sacred Scriptures, he could not proceed; he descended from the pulpit 'perspiring profusely'; he had realized how difficult was the task of the teachers, and his munificence towards them was made greater."[58]

It would be a serious mistake, on the other hand, to view the monarch's relationship to the Sangha independently of his relationship to society and the body politic as a whole. It would be more true to say that the ideal of symbiosis between *thera* and king was symbolic of the ideal reciprocity between all persons in the society. As the monarch can be portrayed as Cakkavatti at one end of the spectrum and Everyman at the other, so he can be in search of the Dhamma's meaning at the same time that he is its protector. It is this dual portrayal of each king which, as in the case of Asoka, commends him as an illustration of each person's striving toward "greater merit" in the short run and Nibbāna ultimately. The concept of reciprocity is paramount to the Buddhist notion of an ideal society. This is conceived in the *Sigālovāda Sutta*, sometimes regarded as the "Whole Duty" or *Vinaya* of the Buddhist layman. In it are depicted the ideal relationships between people in various roles or circumstances (e.g., husband-wife, parents-children, employers-servants, etc.). Though deceptively simple in presentation, it is a part of the Pāli Canon which has exercised immense influence because it catches the rhythm of authentic association. We shall explore this further in the final section. At this point let us examine the king's socio-political task in helping to make this reciprocity possible. It is in this regard that the idea of Dhamma has decidedly relevant social implications. This was put succinctly in the following statement:

> The early Buddhist philosophy of kingship is a compound of three distinct attitudes. Although the early Buddhists betray feelings of disquiet, bordering on fear, about the nature and functions of kingship as it existed in their times, they see no alternative to it and declare it to be absolutely essential to prevent humanity from lapsing into a state of anarchy. Finally, confronted with the fact of kingship and the absolute necessity for it for orderly human existence, they attempt to tame absolute political power by infusing into it a spirit of higher morality.[59]

Such a statement could have been affirmed either by Asoka or the Sinhalese chroniclers as the essence of the political task under Dhamma. The same ambivalence toward worldly power, the same acceptance of its inevitability, the same striving to make it responsible are as evident throughout Buddhist history as in its early days. The frequent assumption by Westerners that Theravada, especially, lacks a social ethnic cannot be maintained in the light of overwhelming evidence to the contrary. As with all social philosophy we are here talking about an ideal, but it must also be viewed as an ideal with policy repercussions. Again, the prime, but by no means only, example is that of Asoka. If Asoka provided the norm, it was one emulated in countless versions within Sinhalese, Burmese, and Thai history. In these and other cultural contexts can be seen a repeated clash of historic cruelty with the Asokan ideal. This should surprise no one; the chronicles themselves document this, reign after reign. Were this not so, the Dhamma would be fulfilled, not only preached. The carnage which supposedly brought Asoka's conscience into sensitivity was but a ripple in the world's history of slaughter, but the paradigm which his reported response provided continued to affect Buddhist communities. It was finally this which became the model and norm, not the political ideals of Kauṭilya.[60] In essence, this was to assert that the state is not an end in itself, but a means toward a higher end of which it is the servant. This is always the more difficult task than that of absolutism, for the higher end is always partially obscure and is never permanently reached within the political order.

It was this acceptance of the lesser but crucial task of creating a just order, which constitutes the crux of the Buddhist ideal of kingship. Acknowledgement of the limitations of its role makes the monarchy's reciprocity with the Sangha a viable one. The purpose of one was to create and maintain an ordered society within which men can pursue freely the greater goal beyond order. The purpose of the other was to discover this greater goal for themselves and to show all men the path to it. These two purposes were not at odds, only in tension. Order precedes liberation; liberation requires order. Besides, the type of order envisaged was one in which all men's basic needs were met; it was order at the heart of which was justice. It was the latter which reputedly prompted Asoka and later Buddhists to dig wells, provide rest houses, construct tanks, have mercy on animals, feed the poor and a host of other manifestations. But it was his reason for taking these and other steps which reveals the character of his concerns. "These are trifling comforts," he says. "For the people have received various facilities from previous kings as well as from me. But I have done what I have primarily in order that the people may follow the path of Dharma with faith and devotion."[61]

It was both the motive for his actions and the awareness that Nibbāna cannot be pursued when people's needs are ignored which made his political ethic a new entry into history. It created in the process a Buddhist ethos sometimes called *lokka-nibbāna* (or Nibbāna in this world), which is a confusing term when what it really connotes is the compatibility, even interdependence, between social concern on the one hand and the quest for tranquility (*upekkhā*) on the other. Far from being indifference to the world, it is only through upekkhā that genuine concern arises. Coupled with this was the pragmatic realization that the pursuit of Nibbāna necessitates leisured meditation and that this requires both economic sufficiency and a stable socio-political order.[62] The king's task, therefore, was to stabilize the natural and social order, not "change" society so much as "stabilize" it. The odyssey of the human spirit was viewed within a cosmological and historical pattern where there is no progress, only order and disorder, both relative, both filled with potential. Authentic progress comes only to the inner man; it is achieved by each man anew, moments building upon moments, each man, as the chronicles put it, going "according to his *kamma*" (*yathākammaṃ*). Over this no state, nor established religion, holds sway. It acts only as prelude, to facilitate or to obstruct. Like all worldly sovereignty, it is "sweet food mixed with poison."

IV. Society-Cosmos Relationship

The Aśokan concept of Dharma-vijaya (conquest through righteousness) pertained, in his thinking, not only to the present age but to the enduring future. If this eschatological note was not developed until later centuries, it was clearly struck in the emperor's hopes that his newly established pattern of conquest would become normative. One clue to this lies in his words that "whatever effort King Priyadarsī makes is for the sake of the life hereafter and in order that men may be saved from enslavement."[63] Like the chronicles of Ceylon the Edicts of Aśoka betray no illusion about the difficulty of the task, a task which "rich and poor alike will find . . . difficult to do . . . unless they make a great effort and renounce all other aims."[64] It remains for this final section to look at the *eschatological* dimensions of Dharma-vijaya, to see how it came increasingly over time to be united with certain cosmological assumptions about the nature of reality, certain emerging visions of the Ideal King, and certain growing expectations about the City of Righteousness.

While it is risky trying to date the emergence of these ideas, it is equally true that they were prominent in the time of the *Mahāvaṃsa* and that, in relatively undeveloped form, they can be found in the Pāli Canon. Tradition, indeed, ascribes them to the time of the Buddha himself, with the insistence by Mahayana that they represent the core of his teaching. Without stopping to argue these points, it is pertinent to this essay to observe their manifestation within the Sinhalese chronicles, especially within the *Mahāvaṃsa*, for upon these concepts depend the basic ingredients of an ideal social order as perceived by Theravada Buddhists. To reflect upon their meaning within this context affords a clearer understanding not only of what Buddhism construes by Dhamma but of the relationship between the three gems in which Buddhists take refuge.

1. The first of these concepts to be explored here stems from the sustained conviction within the Buddhist community about the essential oneness or interrelatedness of reality, a concept having both temporal and spatial dimensions.[65] The most seminal idea at this point is that of *paṭicca-samuppāda*, a notion central to all Buddhism which has been translated in various ways, though most frequently as "dependent origination." Basically, it suggests that, while there is no *original* causative agent or event, all reality is a network of causes and effects, producing various degrees of good and evil, order and disorder, and within it men can discover through discipline and eventually enlightenment the ability to cause or bring about their own liberation. In personal terms, it conveys the conviction that each man can come to realize the essential nonduality of "self" and "others," the fundamental union of all life, and the folly of clinging to the self-defeating notions of "me" and "mine." Fundamental to this realization is his awakening to the fact of impermanence (*anicca*) and his own capacity not simply to live tranquilly within it but to embody joy, harmony and compassion. In social terms, it conveys the sense in which the actions, words, and desires of each person fit into a framework of inter-relationship whereby what one does affects all. And, in cosmic terms, it conveys the more immense awareness that the entire universe is a fabric with parts dependent upon each other, a tissue of entities making up one whole.[66] It is intrinsic to Buddhist social concern that authentic community comes only through the unfolding consciousness of persons that their identity cannot be known apart from others. The most basic term for compassion, *karuṇā*, suggests a widening self-identification with all that lives.[67]

While this notion is common to all Buddhist testimony, its configurations in the Sinhalese chronicles are vivid and unique. One could do an entire study of the *Mahāvaṃsa* focussing on the personal, social and cosmic aspects of *paṭicca-samuppadā*, as they are manifold. Each chapter makes an assessment of the whys and wherefores of circumstances and events, interpreting them in the light of actions taken or ignored, tracing the destinies of kings, in particular, "according to their *kamma*." We shall focus here on the sense of cosmic consciousness which the chroniclers portray as they weave together the events of history with tradition's interpretation.

As might be expected, one finds the delineation of cosmic awareness peculiarly expressive in the accounts of royal consecrations, for at times like these relationships are made most explicit: those of monarch and Sangha and people to each other, those of time past to time present to time future, those of this place to all places. This is true with the kingly prototype, Asoka. "Straightway after his consecration his command spread so far as a yojana (upward) into the air and downward into the (depths of the) earth."[68] "The sense of this passage, not rightly understood up to the present time," Wilhelm Geiger quaintly suggests in a footnote, "is evidently this: not only men upon the earth but also the spirits of the air and the earth heard and obeyed Asoka's command."[69] Following this more general statement, the chronicle elaborates the organic harmony which comprised Asoka's rule:

> From the Himalaya did the devas bring for cleansing the teeth twigs of nāga-creeper. . . . The spirits of the air brought garments of five colours. . . . Out of the nāga-kingdom the nāgas (brought) stuff, coloured like the jasmine-blossom and without a seam . . .; parrots brought daily . . . waggon-loads of rice. Mice converted this rice, unbroken, into grains without husk or powder. . . . Perpetually did honey-bees prepare honey for him. . . . Karavīka-birds, graceful and sweet of voice, came and made delightful music for the king.[70]

Reference was made earlier to what happened at Devānaṁpiyatissa's consecration, as a result of his merit: "In the whole isle of Laṅkā treasures and jewels that had been buried deep rose to the surface of the earth."[71] The most tumultuous display of rhythmic harmony, uniting man and beast, is found in the depiction of the consecration festival of Parakkamabāhu, the Great, in 1154 A.D.[72] While more tailored to the local setting, it is no less cosmic in orientation.

All of these instances carry the conviction that the monarch's role in relationship to society and cosmos is to sustain the living harmony underlying all existence. Royal power is the instrument of cosmic power. As with the classic Chinese understanding of the emperor as the "Son of Heaven," the character of whose rule affected not only society but nature, so here one finds the assumed correspondence between an evil monarch and disasters in nature, or between goodness and harmony. The assumption throughout the *Mahāvaṃsa* is how much men of power can do, providing they have good understanding.[73] Sovereignty, when purged of poison, causes works which are sweet. Present in this view are both a "high" and a "low" estimate of royal power, estimates which are cautious, yet hopeful, at the same time. It is essentially a view of human nature which is realistic yet sensitive to man's potential. Above all, it stands awed before the power of the Dhamma. In commenting upon Eḷāra, the Tamil, who for forty-five years ruled justly over Lanka, the chronicler speculates, if a non-believer can be so good, how much more a believer![74]

It is again at this point that one sees the impact of the Sangha's relationship to the monarchy and why the latter remained pledged to the welfare of the Order. The ideal symbiosis between these institutions was the primal instance, the archetype, of what personal, social, and cosmic symbiosis involved. As an ideal, approximated in reality or not, it was the model of what all reciprocity entailed. When the Dhamma was protected, tradition counselled, the monarchy thrived, the Sangha became a blessing, and the people flourished. Any break in the continuum and disorder prevailed. The most symbolic presentation of this in the chronicles may be that chapter in the *Mahāvaṃsa* entitled "The Acceptance of the Mahāvihāra" in which Mahinda marks off locations in Anurādhapura, the sacred city, on which various buildings of the Great Vihāra will be constructed in future years. At each announcement there is a quaking of the earth. As with the account of the building of the Mahāthūpa later under Duṭṭhagāmaṇī, the tradition is making clear the connection between heaven and earth, between the present moment and all moments, between the sacrality of the Dhamma and all else. Ironically, the establishing of the boundaries (*sīmā*) is the removal of all boundaries. It is man's way of saying that in order to see continuity, to experience reciprocity, one must establish distinctions where in reality none exist. The planting of the Bodhi-tree and the bringing of the relics are ways of making visible, therefore present, what was never absent, though always invisible. At two points in the chronicles, both in relationship to the arrival or enshrining of relics, the same words are used: "Thus are the Buddhas incomprehensible, and incomprehensible is the nature of the Buddhas, and incomprehensible is the reward of those who have faith in the incomprehensible."[75]

It is in such a vein only that *samsāra* is *Nirvāṇa*,[76] for it is through the attaining of enlightenment that samsāra's full potential may be imagined, a potential which otherwise remains obscure because of the enslavement it more obviously reflects. It is faith in the very incomprehensibility of the transformation of ignorance into wisdom, of self-preoccupation into compassion for others, which is expressed devotionally within the chronicles. The profusion of festivals which color the pages of these documents and the seeming preoccupation with stūpa-building, image-making and celebration in general depict a community mindful of blessings received. To adorn is to be adoring, to bestow gifts is to acknowledge the worthiness of what has been received. In the words of the *Mahāvaṃsa*: "Commanded by the lord of men, they, filled with deep reverence for the Sage (Buddha), adorned the place in manifold ways."[77] It was a community having received a foretaste of what was possible for all men, of what society could become, and of what cosmic harmony would entail. The tension between the promise of a reconciled universe and the experience of a world in suffering made each more vivid. If the age of the Buddha (*Buddhavassa*) had begun, its consummation occurred only in the imagination. The Wheel of the Law had been turned, but Dharma-vijaya's fulfillment remained alive only in expectation.

2. Of one piece with this vision of unity and this continued experiencing of distress and enmity was the unfolding anticipation of an Ideal King, a monarch whose rule by righteousness would occasion and cement the reality of the universe's intrinsic oneness. At the heart of any apocalyptic vision is the awareness of a soteriological necessity. To the tradition's sensitivity to mankind's suffering was added the gradual acknowledgement of the king's role as *bodhisatta* (Sanskrit, *bodhisattva*) and of the appearance in new guise of the Cakkavatti figure. Unquestionably, this development reflects the influence of Mahayana sects upon Sinhalese consciousness, but it unfolded in ways which reinforced the orthodox insistence that man was the agent of his own release. This point has not yet been stressed enough in discussions of the interplay between the two major paths within Buddhist tradition. It is in part the intent of this section to highlight the compatibility of "taking refuge in oneself" with "taking refuge in Buddha, Dhamma and Sangha," both of which are essential to Buddhist soteriological understanding.

Many scholars have traced the appearance and increasing effect of the bodhisatta concept in India, Ceylon, and elsewhere. It is the task here to perceive its emergence within the Sinhalese chronicles, for the part it plays in Theravada generally stems from these developments, influenced by Indian concepts as they were. While one can read back into discussions of earlier reigns the same intent, the earliest explicit reference in the chronicles to the bodhisatta-like nature of any monarch is to Buddhadāsa who ruled in the mid fourth century A.D. The reference here, to be sure, is almost in passing, but it is unmistakable: "The Ruler lived openly before the people the life that bodhisattas lead and had pity for (all) beings as a father (has pity for) his children."[78] The significance of this comment can be minimized as a mere figure of speech and as one which may be found earlier in the Pāli Canon itself. It is, however, in the impression one gets of the nature and character of Buddhadāsa, who "shone like the Perfectly Enlightened One," and of his reign that one detects the beginning of a new phenomenon, a savior-king, one whose meritorious action heals the sick, woos men out of enmity, and creates happiness for all his subjects.[79] Even earlier, in the person of Sirisaṃghabodhi in the mid third century, we are put in the presence of one who, though not called a bodhisatta in the account, makes a self-oblation of his life that his realm may be freed from famine and drought.[80]

It is possible to discover at least four elements in the chronicler's judgment of what constituted a righteous monarch which contributed to, or were a part of, the emerging Cakkavatti image. The *first* relates to the qualities such a king should possess. While these may be found attributed to many rulers in various ways, the most succinct attributions are to Buddhadāsa and to his eldest son, Upatissa. "Endowed with the ten qualities of kings (*dasa rājadhammā*), while avoiding the four wrong paths, practising justice, [Buddhadāsa] won over his subjects by the four heart-winning qualities (*cattāri saṃghavatthūni*)."[81] Even more was ascribed to the son: "Shunning the ten sinful actions, he practised the ten meritorious works (*puññakiriyā*); the King fulfilled the ten royal duties and the ten *pāramitās*. By the four heart-winning qualities he won over the four regions of the world."[82] Geiger's footnotes detail these qualities, though, of course, these were familiar to all readers in ancient Lanka, indeed, to all bhikkhus and upāsakas, let alone to each monarch. The very cataloguing of the qualities was intended as a focus for meditation even more than as a description of certain kings. But there can be no questioning the lofty concept of kingship which these revealed.

The *second* element, present throughout portrayals of a righteous ruler, is one to which we have referred before, namely, his role as patron and supporter of the Sangha. This need not be elaborated except to say that one finds more explicit reference to social welfare measures appearing in the fourth and fifth centuries, and beyond, than earlier. The giving of alms, the concern for wages, the digging of wells, the planting of trees, and especially the construction of tanks and canals are of frequent mention. While all these obviously occurred before, the very increased mention says much about the king's function as not only an establisher of order but as a creator and maintainer of a just and thriving society, which was held to be an intrinsic part of the ideal. The most graphic figure of the monarch at this point is one assigned to Udaya II, who was "like to a wishing tree, a dispenser of blessings for all the needy," an image often used in Indian mythology to depict the bounty of heaven.[83] This corroborates Geiger's comment that "the greatest virtue of a king was considered to be charitableness" (*mahākaruṇā*), a quality stemming from identification with one's subjects, not simply from feelings of kindness.[84]

Thirdly, the ideal monarch is held to be a paragon of what it means to be a man, not just a patron of society or Sangha. As the king takes on the proportions of a Cakkavatti, with all the soteriological connotations, this depiction of him as a paragon for all men becomes increasingly important. There are a number of kings in the chronicles who are portrayed in this fashion, but two are especially intriguing, for different reasons: one (Sena II) seems almost the epitome of perfection and is therefore somewhat abstract, albeit no less a model of manhood; the other (Aggabodhi VIII) is portrayed in very concrete and human terms, albeit no less an image of perfection. To juxtapose comments about these persons helps create the impression of the tension, yet continuity, between the ideal as it was imagined and the reality which sometimes took flesh. "Showing conduct like that of the kings of the first age of the world, pious, wealthy, heroic, generous, impartial, succouring the needy . . . [Sena] represented in his spotless fame and his splendid ability, as it were, a union of the sun and the moon: richly gifted with unblemished qualities, practising every kind of virtue, devoid of all sin, weary of the cycle of births, his gaze fixed on the highest."[85] This statement is replete with connotations, religious and political, which might profitably be explored. Suffice it to say here that there could hardly be a more unstinted accolade of what Buddhist manhood should comprise than this. While beyond the reach of the ordinary layman, to be sure, it would at least constitute his understanding of the upāsaka vocation as well as engender in him a sense of the ideal king's paradigmatic nature.

Side by side with this may be put the portrayal of Aggabodhi VIII with whom identification may be more possible but who, nevertheless, embodies traits no less uncommon:

> The King found pleasure in the serving of his mother day and night. He went to wait on her already early in the morning, rubbed her head with oil, perfumed the parts moist with sweat, cleaned her nails and bathed her carefully. He clad her himself in a new garment, pleasant to the touch, and the castoff raiment he took and cleaned it himself. . . . After making obeisance before her three times, and walking, with right side facing, round her . . . he offered her delicious food with his own hand. . . . [Then] when he had put in order her chamber, fragrant with sweet odours, he carefully prepared there with his own hand her couch, washed her feet, rubbed her gently with fragrant oil, sat by her rubbing her limbs and sought to make her sleep. . . . Then happy at his action, and ever thinking of her, he went home. As long as she lived he served her in this way.[86]

The inclusion of this passage in the chronicles is hardly for reader interest alone. It bespeaks not only of true filial respect but of the essence of bodhisatta-like tenderness, the sort of reciprocity counselled in the *Sigālovāda Sutta*, of which we have spoken before. It is one, too, with the sense of fittingness which sees and responds to the needs of all creation. As was said about one king: "For the bhikkhu community, for the laity, for fishes, game and birds, for his kinsfolk and for the troops he did everything that was mete for them."[87] Lastly, it is one with the adoration and reverence shown toward the Buddha by pious followers, in token of blessings received. It is at the core of purity, which manifests itself in compassion, service, and self-oblation.

The *fourth* and crowning attribute of the ideal king is the catalytic effect his meritorious actions have upon other people. We are dealing here not simply with a paragon whose qualities are worthy of emulation but with a charisma and power which are said to call into existence traits dormant and unrealized in the lives of others. It is in this respect that the soteriological efficacy of the Cakkavatti takes on a dimension present but untapped in earlier tradition. As is true about the chronicler's judgment both of power and of human nature, the charisma of the ruler has demonic possibilities as well as beneficent, "for it is the rule with living creatures: what he who is master does, evil or good, the same is done by his subjects; let the wise man take heed of that."[88] The lesson of history, as recorded in these pages, makes clear the double-edged nature of the monarch's effect. But, in the same breath in which he cites this warning, he comments about the royal influence for good: "Thus he was in all his dealings one to whom the teaching of the Buddha was the highest (good), and vying with him all the people also fulfilled the (commands of that) doctrine."[89] About another king, he writes: "Everyone in his kingdom cultivated action which leads to Heaven, for as the monarch acts so do also his subjects."[90] Finally, about Duṭṭhagāmaṇī, whose own struggle with impurity and whose later meritorious actions are both seen as classic, the *Mahāvaṃsa* says: "Thus do the pious themselves perform pure deeds of merit, in order to obtain the most glorious of all blessings; and they, with a pure heart, make also others to perform them in order to win a following of eminent people of many kinds."[91]

In all these instances the basic assumption is made: like king, like subjects. It is possible to find plausible historic factors which influenced this development. Paul Mus has suggested that "the charismatic figure of the Wheel-wielding King (*cakravartin*) grew in size and was credited with increasing soteriological powers, as a compensation for and prospective help against too positive and immediate woes."[92] Walpola Rahula has pointed out its relationship to religio-nationalism, saying that "by about the tenth century, this belief had become so strong that the king of Ceylon had not only to be a Buddhist but also a Bodhisattva."[93] Undoubtedly, too, there were often quasi-magical elements present which trivialized and jeopardized the more profound implications. Without question, in the hands of some, the soteriological conception of the king was little more than a clever rationalization for state power. The validity of these and other explanations are pertinent, but they do not exhaust the internal meaning of the phenomenon and its relevance to the social order.

In essence, what one sees unfolding over many centuries, influenced both by the Sanskritic notion of kingship and by Mahayana ideas about the bodhisattva, was a merging of two distinct but overlapping notions of sovereignty: one, of the socio-political order; the other, of the cosmos at large. Paradoxically, the original choice of vocations which was put before the infant Siddhattha is now revealed as a false dichotomy, for as the Universal Ruler or Ideal King is also the Cakkavatti or Bodhisatta, so the Buddha is the supreme monarch, the master of heaven and earth. Whether viewed personally or cosmically, only one who rules himself is fit to rule others and he who teaches men Dharma-vijaya or conquest through righteousness is the ruler of all. In evidence is a kind of parabolic movement, which has obvious liturgical ramifications, from king to Bodhisatta King (Buddha) back to king again; an offering of self to one who taught release from self so that one may serve others with justice, compassion and tranquility. As Sarkisyanz points out in quoting from the *Kāka-Jātaka*, "a king laid his kingdom at the Bodhisattva's feet, but the Bodhisattva restored it to the king . . . beseeching him to shield all living creatures from harm."[94] One is struck by the identical symbolism here with that practiced by Sinhalese monarchs, as they offered their kingdom to the Sangha as vice-regent for the Buddha, or, in one case, to the newly arrived relics as the very presence of Gotama himself.

The explicit connection with the Buddha is, of course, central to the whole conception. Here too one can perceive a parabola-like movement, as, for instance, in the *Mahā-Sudassana Sutta* where the Buddha reveals himself to Ānanda as having been in another life the Great King of Glory. It is important to keep in mind that the only bodhisatta recognized by Theravada is the Buddha (or Bodhisatta) Metteyya, the Buddha-to-come. The expectations of his coming have played a major role in the social and political ethos of Theravada communities.[95] The aspirations of kings in both Ceylon and Burma were to become the Bodhisatta Metteyya in their next life. "Not only renovation but also fulfillment of Buddhism was expected from Mettaya (*sic*): universal compassion is to become through him a cosmic reality."[96] In this conviction we have a blending of the three ideas mentioned at the start of this section, namely, a conviction regarding the essential oneness of reality, a vision about the role of the Ideal King, and an expectation of the forthcoming City of Righteousness. In the various titles used for the Ideal King[97] it was manifest that in him was embodied a syzygy or genuine symbiosis by means of which, because the two wheels of the temporal and spiritual domains[98] were harmonized, there would emerge a harmonizing of heaven and earth, man and nature, king and people, society as a whole, and man with himself. The image of the Golden Age in the past was projected into the future as a time when all the ills of the present age would be cured and its antinomies reconciled. In the meantime, despite the strength of the expectation, there endured the awareness that we are living "between the times," in an age of decline between what once was and what in time will be. The vision of what will be is focused in the concept of a City of Righteousness.

3. Akin to the notion of an Ideal King, the City of Righteousness[99] may be seen by the mind's eye alone. As the presence of the Buddha within the relics, it is incomprehensible, accepted only by faith, made real only through enlightenment. It is the sāvaka-sangha, a spiritual community, invisible to all, whose members are known to none. It is a community of attainment where all striving has ceased. It is perceived in time but not limited by it; it occupies space but cannot be confined. It exists everywhere and in each place. It exists now and is eternal. No man is far from it, yet it remains unseen. To some, it seems fulfilled already, but this is blindness to suffering and to ignorance, especially their own. To others, it has no reality, for they place no hope in release from bondage, including their own. It is a city in which each learns from all and where none is lost. It is a community in which attainment has been reached, yet the horizons are unlimited. Here the glory of impermanence is understood, for each imagination has been opened to infinity. Here possession has no meaning, for no one is in need. Here fear is unknown, for love regards each person as himself.

The suttas, the commentaries, the chronicles, and a host of other testimonies bespeak of this City, yet no one who writes has more than glimpsed its possibility. The symbol of the Bodhi-tree, under which enlightenment first shone forth, is a primary image of the distance and of the closeness between wisdom and ignorance, between freedom and enslavement. In the epiphany symbolized by it we see the soil must be readied each time. The Buddha's visits to Lanka were to prepare yet another land for its transplant and growth. The vision told by the chronicler is of miracles taking place when preparation had occurred. "Hardly had he let it leave his hands but it rose up eighty cubits into the air, and floating thus it sent forth glorious rays of six colours."[100] "And while they all gazed, there grew, springing from it, eight shoots; and they stood there, young Bodhi-trees four cubits high."[101]

The glory of its springing forth and the tragedy that men remain ignorant is the essence of the chronicle's tale. The Wheel of the Law has been turned, yet men prefer to remain in Samsāra. Dharma-vijaya has been shown as the way, but conquest continues through force. The unity which exists as a present reality is spurned, as men still war against each other. The kings whose freedom could bring liberation now are everywhere, yet each lives in fear of its consequences. The city where righteousness could be known is at hand, though no one would be its first citizen. Men settle for the accumulation of merit and the promise of heaven, even while the peace of Nibbāna is more blissful still.

Yet it remains the genius of the Buddhist imagination that men must begin somewhere; therefore, no place of origin is despised. There will come a time when even relics will be extinguished (*dhātu-parinibbāna*), for the full presence will be known; in the meanwhile, these point the way. A time will unfold in which no monarchs are needed, for each will have achieved order by himself; though kings are needed yet. Finally, the ideal social order will have emerged, as each will have become righteous; though at present men still strain to perceive its configurations and to reject its demands.

Notes

1. *Dīpavaṃsa*, edited by B. C. Law (Maharagama, Ceylon: Saman Press, 1959), pp. 129-130.
2. The Venerable Walpola Rahula cites the main sources on which he based his *History of Buddhism in Ceylon*: namely, the Pāli Scriptures, the Asokan Edicts, the Ceylon Inscriptions, the Pāli Commentaries, Sinhalese Folk-tales, and miscellaneous works in Pāli and Sinhalese. Besides his work, most of the secondary sources used in this essay also deal extensively with this material. While considerable work remains to be done on the whole period in question, present scholarship is based upon a wealth of sources which corroborate and supplement the story told within the chronicles. Cf. Rahula, *History of Buddhism in Ceylon* (Colombo: M. D. Gunasena and Co., second edition, 1966), p. xix.
3. B. C. Law, *On the Chronicles of Ceylon* (Calcutta: *Journal of the Royal Asiatic Society of Bengal*, 1947), p. 43.
4. "For more than two thousand years the Sinhalese have been inspired by the ideal that they were a nation brought into being for the definite purpose of carrying the torch lit by the Buddha." D. G. Vijayavardhana, *Dharma-Vijaya (Triumph of Righteousness) or The Revolt in the Temple* (Colombo, Sinha Publications, 1953), p. 3.
5. Rahula, *op. cit.*, p. xxiv.
6. B. C. Law, Introduction to the *Dīpavaṃsa, op. cit.*, p. 5.
7. E. F. C. Ludowyk, *The Footprint of the Buddha* (London: George Allen and Unwin Ltd., 1958), p. 11.
8. The discontinuities are no less present, but by comparison during the classical period they seem subdued. One observes them in the breakdown of dynasties, in the resolute but

abortive resistance by orthodoxy to heretical doctrines, in the gradual decline of Sinhalese civilization itself beginning in the thirteenth century, to mention only three.

In an essay dealing in part with the influence of Indian thought upon Sinhalese it is inevitable that both Sanskrit and Pāli terms be used and that the same term be rendered first in one, then in the other (e.g., *Dharma, Dhamma*). The spelling used depends upon the context.

"Thus it was that a people who had very close cultural relations with each other were cast politically in the role of antagonists. By retaining their independence, the Sinhalese were enabled to develop their distinctive strand of civilization, though they owed much to Dravidian influences." Cf. S. Arasaratnam, *Ceylon* (Englewood Cliffs, New Jersey: Prentice-Hall, Inc., 1964), p. 60.

Wilhelm Geiger, *Culture of Ceylon in Medieval Times* (Wiesbaden: Otto Harrassowitz, 1960), p. 176.

The attainment of arahantship through beholding the miraculous, "with believing and joyous heart," need not be held inconsistent with the above, as this stage precedes that of final extinction. It should be noted, however, that the chronicles frequently record the mass attainment of arahantship in this manner. Cf. *Mahāvaṃsa*, Wilhelm Geiger, tr. (London: Luzac and Company, Ltd., 1964), p. 217, for one example.

Cakkavatti-Sīhanāda Suttanta, T. W. Rhys Davids, ed. (London: Luzac and Company, Ltd., 1965), pp. 74-75. The *locus classicus* of this is the *Mahāparinibbāna Sutta* of the *Dīgha Nikāya*, Vol. 2, pp. 108-109.

Mahāvaṃsa, p. 55. The responsibility is then delegated by Sakka to Viṣṇu.

Several studies have dealt with this subject in part, though no exhaustive treatment has yet appeared. Geiger's work mentioned above and an interesting article by B. G. Gokhale, entitled "Early Buddhist Kingship," are two among many. The latter will be discussed later.

Paul Mus, Preface to *Buddhist Backgrounds of the Burmese Revolution* by E. Sarkisyanz (The Hague: Martinus Nijhoff, 1965), p. vii.

Cūlavaṃsa, I, Wilhelm Geiger, tr. (Colombo: Ceylon Government Information Department, 1953), p. 30.

As we shall see later, through Mahayana influence he becomes both.

Mahāvaṃsa, p. 10.

Ludowyk, *op. cit.*, p. 88.

Ibid. E. W. Adikaram in his *Early History of Buddhism in Ceylon* shows how bhikkhus are encouraged in their efforts to lead a pure life by being reminded that they are "descended from the unbroken line of Mahāsammata," are grandsons of "the great king Suddhodana" and are younger brothers of Rāhulabhadda. See Adikaram (Colombo: M. D. Gunasena and Co., Ltd., 1946), p. 126.

Mahāvaṃsa, p. 49.

G. P. Malalasekera, *The Pāli Literature of Ceylon* (London: Royal Asiatic Society of Great Britain and Ireland, 1928), p. 54. He goes on to document the measures used to suppress this dissent. It is only fair to indicate that the attacks were reciprocal.

Mahāvamsa, p. 116.

377 B.C. - 1029 A.D.

Mahāvaṃsa, p. 216.

Ibid., pp. 78-79.

Ibid., p. 80.

Ibid. Rahula makes the point that it was Asoka who also conferred the honorific term *Devānaṁpiya* ("beloved of the gods") upon the Sinhalese King. While used in India even before Asoka, it was probably not used as a prefix in Ceylon prior to this time. It was a term used of Asoka himself and therefore reinforces the sense of continuity. Cf. Rahula, *op. cit.*, p. 27.

Rahula, *op. cit.*, pp. 59-60. Seven centuries later, the tide had reversed itself and various like Buddhaghosa in the fifth century A.D. made their way to Ceylon to translate the Sinhalese commentaries into Pāli and made their insight available beyond Lanka. With this event, symbolically, the wheel had turned full circle, so to speak.

31. Sarkisyanz, *op. cit.*, p. 33.
32. Ludowyk, *op. cit.*, p. 23. The reference in the first sentence is to the Buddha's footprint on Adam's Peak in south-central Ceylon.
33. *Ibid.*, p. 61.
34. *Mahāvaṃsa*, p. 42. As we shall see later when considering the concept of an Ideal King, the epithets for such a figure are myriad. *Dhammarājā* is one; *Priyadarśī rājā* is another. The latter means "one who sees to the good of others," i.e., the prototype of benevolence, and was apparently used only in reference to Aśoka. Cf. *The Edicts of Asoka*, ed. and tr. by N. A. Nikam and Richard McKeon (Chicago: University of Chicago Press, 1959), pp. 25-26.
35. Set into the poetic framework of the four cycles of history (the four *yūgas*) we find the beginnings of a new historiography which, while retaining much of the Brahmanic perspective, points forward to the expectation of the Buddha Metteyya and time's fulfillment, not unlike what occurred in later Hinduism as well, in the *bhakti-mārga* of Rāmānuja and others.
36. *Mahāvaṃsa*, p. 1.
37. Rahula, *op. cit.*, p. 162.
38. Ludowyk, *op. cit.*, pp. 107-108.
39. Mark 5:1-20.
40. *Mahāvaṃsa*, p. 4.
41. *Dīpavaṃsa*, p. 201.
42. *Ibid.*, p. 191. For a thorough discussion of the symbolism of the *yakkha* (Sanskrit, *yakṣa*) motif, primarily in its Indian setting, see Ananda K. Coomaraswamy, *Yakṣas* (New Delhi: Munshiram Manoharlal, 1971). The earlier edition was published in 1928.
43. According to Adikaram, the recitation of the *Parittas* (*Protection Suttas*) in Ceylon dates back at least to the late fourth century A.D., though they are part of the Pāli Canon itself. They are still used extensively. Originally, they had a public import and were chanted in times of famine, plague, or other ill. Cf. Adikaram, *op. cit.*, pp. 143-144.
44. *Mahāvaṃsa*, p. 266.
45. *Ibid.*, p. 177. "Sitting then on the terrace of the royal palace, adorned, lighted with fragrant lamps and filled with many a perfume, magnificent with nymphs in the guise of dancing-girls, while he rested on his soft and fair couch, covered with costly draperies, he, looking back upon his victory, great though it was, knew no joy, remembering that thereby was wrought the destruction of millions (of beings)."
46. *Ibid.*, p. 171.
47. *Ibid.*, p. 178. Regarding the one and a half: "The one had come unto the (three) refuges, the other had taken on himself the five precepts."
48. Ludowyk, *op. cit.*, p. 101.
49. Geiger, *op. cit.*, p. 204.
50. *Dīpavaṃsa*, p. 151. The "norm" referred to is the Dhamma.
51. *Ibid.*, pp. 172-173.
52. *Ibid.*, p. 174.
53. *Ibid.*, p. 175. The *Mahāvaṃsa* likewise describes this scene and adds an account of how the paths of these two had crossed in an earlier life, confirming the destined nature of their meeting and of Nigrodha's preeminence. Cf. *Mahāvaṃsa*, pp. 29-32. It is not clear why B. C. Law has capitalized "Norm" in this context and not, for instance, on page 151 (or vice versa). In any case, the meaning is the same.
54. *Dīpavaṃsa*, p. 178. The story of royal support for the economic needs of the Sangha has been told by many; Geiger's book referred to above is one example. Through the tax structure, through land grants, through sizeable endowments, among other measures, the Order received considerable fiscal assistance. Grants made to the bhikkhu community were known as *saṅgha-bhoga*. There also grew up the practice that whatever was produced in certain locales was for the *vihāra*, a practice known as *lābha-sīmā*, related as it was to the whole concept of *sīmā*, where boundaries of the Sangha are coextensive with the boundaries of the state. This kind of economic, social and political power granted to the Order made it in time influential in the making of policy. It was a secular force which no king could ignore, let alone a moral power of substance.

55. *Mahāvaṃsa*, pp. 42-43. The immediate son and daughter in question were, of course, Mahinda and Samghamitta who received the *pabbajjā* or ordination into the Order, but by extension the same criterion of kinsmanship applies to all parents.
56. Section four on the Ideal King will sketch further aspects of the monarch's role as patron.
57. Cf. Rahula, *op. cit.*, p. 75. The antiphonal nature of the oblation is caught in the *Mahāvaṃsa* description of Moggallāna's ascent to the throne: "He approached the community, greeted it respectfully and pleased with this community, he as a mark of distinction, presented it with his umbrella. The community returned it to him." (*Mhv.* 39.31). The white parasol or umbrella (*seta chatta*) was traditionally the prime symbol of royal authority.
58. Malalasekera, *op. cit.*, p. 38.
59. B. G. Gokhale, "Early Buddhist Kingship," *The Journal of Asian Studies*, Vol. XXVI (November 1966), No. 1, p. 15.
60. *Ibid.*, 21.
61. Nikam and McKeon, *op. cit.*, p. 64. Joseph M. Kitagawa has put it this way: "Asoka found in the Dharma a Universal principle, applicable both to religious and secular domains, as well as to all men, Buddhist and non-Buddhist alike." Cf. his article entitled "Buddhism and Asian Politics," *Asian Survey*, Vol. II, No. 5, p. 2.
62. Sarkisyanz, *op. cit.*, p. 56.
63. Nikam and McKeon, *op. cit.*, p. 48.
64. *Ibid.*
65. It goes without saying that these convictions are not developed "conceptually" either within the chronicles or within ancient Buddhist tradition. It is true, nonetheless, that the raw material for them may be found throughout the writings.
66. Cf. Edward Conze's essay "Dharma as a Spiritual, Social and Cosmic Force" in Paul Kuntz, ed., *The Concept of Order* (Seattle: University of Washington, 1967), pp. 239-252, in which he sees the same tripodic nature of the Buddhist orientation but develops it in a different direction.
67. Sarkisyanz, *op. cit.*, p. 41.
68. *Mahāvaṃsa*, p. 28.
69. *Ibid.*
70. *Ibid.*
71. *Ibid.*, pp. 77-78.
72. *Cūlavaṃsa*, I, pp. 347-348.
73. *Mahāvaṃsa*, p. 245.
74. *Ibid.*, p. 145.
75. *Ibid.*, pp. 120, 219.
76. Admittedly, a Mahayana claim, but made in other ways by Theravada.
77. *Ibid.*, p. 192. Cf. also, p. 242. This has a connotation similar to that of the Old English word "weorthscipe" (worthiness), from which "worship" (or paying reverence to that which is worthy) is derived.
78. *Cūlavaṃsa*, I, p. 10.
79. *Ibid.*, pp. 9-17.
80. *Mahāvaṃsa*, pp. 261-263.
81. *Cūlavaṃsa*, I, p. 10.
82. *Ibid.*, p. 17.
83. *Ibid.*, p. 159.
84. Geiger, *op. cit.*, p. 133.
85. *Cūlavaṃsa*, I, p. 147.
86. *Ibid.*, pp. 132-133.
87. *Ibid.*, p. 119.
88. *Ibid.*, p. 100.
89. *Ibid.*, p. 99.
90. *Ibid.*, p. 111. He continues: "Therefore should a wise king ever practice piety; in every place where men dwell he will become renowned and finally, surrounded by his compan-

ions, he enters Nirvana." In a footnote Geiger suggests the pragmatic advantages to a king to educate his people to piety, as it insures order in the realm. No doubt there were monarchs who practiced piety for just this reason, as well as those whose practice was otherwise motivated.

91. *Mahāvaṃsa*, p. 219.
92. Paul Mus, Preface to *Buddhist Backgrounds of the Burmese Revolution*, p. xviii.
93. Rahula, *op. cit.*, p. 62.
94. Sarkisyanz, *op. cit.*, p. 42.
95. *Ibid.* Sarkisyanz quotes Paul Mus as saying that it was largely through the Bodhisattva ethos that "Buddhism developed from an ethical sect into one of the *politically* most effective ethical systems in the world."
96. *Ibid.*, p. 44.
97. E.g., *Dhammarāja, Dhammiko Dhammarāja, Mahādhammarāja, Mahā-sudassana, Mahāsattva, Bodhisattva, Cakkavatti (Cakravartin), Bodhisattvāvatāra, Metteyya (Maitreya), Buddharāja,* et al.
98. Gokhale, *op. cit.*, p. 22.
99. For a discussion of this concept, which may be compared with that of the New Jerusalem, see *The Questions of King Milinda*, tr. by T. W. Rhys Davids (New York: Dover Publications, 1963), Part II, pp. 208-243.
100. *Mahāvaṃsa*, p. 132.
101. *Ibid.*, p. 133.

Kingship, The Sangha, and the Process of Legitimation in Anurādhapura Ceylon: An Interpretive Essay

Bardwell L. Smith

THE PROCESS OF legitimizing not simply power but authority in any society is a constantly evolving, complex and subtle phenomenon. While its configurations vary within all societies, the process reveals a number of interrelated features. This essay attempts to identify several of these features and to examine the process of legitimation within a particular society in its responses to opportunities and threats, both internal and external. The phenomena within this process are infinitely variable and the features selected, necessarily tentative. An interpretive essay of this sort seeks to highlight a few major ingredients of ancient Sinhalese history and test the usefulness of certain concepts in analyzing the legitimizing process itself.

The features examined are the following: *one*, the relationship between the precariousness of social and cosmic order as it is sensed by a tradition and the attempt to fashion forms of existence which appear less vulnerable to chaos or anarchy; *two*, the affirming of historical and even cosmic dimensions of legitimation, which provide the structures and values of a particular society with some transcending authority; *three*, the tensions existing between the claimants to legitimized power within any community, and the resultant balancing of power; *four*, the manner in which legitimation of authority is reinforced in symbolic, ritualistic and doctrinal modes; and, *five*, the validation of power through its ability to bolster a culture's "plausibility structure" in the face of crises threatening personal and communal existence and of pluralistic perceptions of reality. The interdependence of these features is clear, yet they hardly exhaust the theoretical possibilities. They serve simply as points of departure.[2]

I. The Precariousness of Order

Historical and comparative studies reveal how all societies struggle to cope with threats of disorder and to create forms of order which lend meaning, cohesiveness and durability to social and personal existence. The potential chaos which lurks both outside and within the perceived orders of every cultural ethos occasions alarm about whether any structure of meaning can be an enduring safeguard against disintegration and anomie. From social conflict and political crisis to psychic disorder and death the evanescent nature of life and the relativity of all forms of order are constantly experienced. In the face of human avarice and stupidity, of institutionalized injustice, and of the seeming irrationality of existence itself men vacillate between simple but shallow assurances on the one hand and terror on the other. History may be viewed as a series of scenarios in which the symbols of order and disorder clash for allegiance in the minds of men and in which societies embrace chaos-averting forces through the legitimizing process. History is in part a search for frameworks of meaning both to endure the threat of non-being and to discover dimensions of order, however fragile and incomplete. Human beings remain vulnerable to attacks upon their perceived definitions of reality and cannot escape the dilemma of having to legitimize authority and power (to counter the forces of disintegration) without silencing challenges to their legitimacy.

In Sinhalese history the interplay between the monarchy, the Sangha, and society at large portrays a continuing awareness of the precariousness of order in every sense of the word: cosmic, social and personal. There is repeated testimony about the contagious nature of disorder, especially when manifested within the Sangha or by kings. Disorder breeds disorder, just as order can be promoted by order. A kind of inevitability is expressed by the tradition, if only to dramatize that men in the grips of selfishness create forms of evil which then ensnare other men in the process. The Sinhalese experience of political realism arose from the broader Indian doctrine of *matsyanyāya* ("law of the fishes"), which cautioned rulers and their ministers that power left to its own devices issues in the law of the jungle, in the strong consuming the weak. This perception of political mores was used by astute rulers in various ways, from crass opportunism to the responsible but realistic exercising of power. Legitimation of power and authority receives its warrant from the fact that, unless the power of others is checked, threats to order keep recurring. In any case, the doctrine of *matsyanyāya* was not only part of the Sinhalese heritage from India in general, but specifically of the early Buddhist recognition within the Indian setting. In the *Dīgha-Nikāya* there is extensive discussion of the theory of the "Great Chosen One" (*Mahāsaṁmata*) to support the centralizing of power in kingly hands as a check to those who misappropriate power and in whose hands order becomes anarchy.[3]

The continuity between this theory and other teachings of the Buddha on the one hand and the manner in which power was said to be used by Aśoka is clear. The Buddhist doctrine of power and the Aśokan model were used repeatedly to alert later monarchs in Ceylon about the norms for legitimate authority. The *sine qua non* of all political legitimacy is protection from anarchy and its consequences.[4] From the *Manu-smṛti* and other Indian texts to the Chronicles of Ceylon this criterion is a constant. To the Sinhalese Buddhists this meant protection of the world (*loka*) from disorder, and of the *Sāsana* for the promotion of the *Dhamma*. Early in the *Mahāvaṃsa* the chronicler makes this clear as King Kālāsoka is first rebuked for being led astray by the Vesālī monks, prior to the Second Council, and then repents by promising to protect and further the doctrine.[5] Even more significant is the Buddha's last will and testament to Sakka (Śakra, Sanskrit), king of the gods: "In Laṅkā, O lord of gods, will my religion be established, therefore carefully protect him with his followers and Laṅkā."[6] Association is repeatedly made between the welfare of the *Buddhasāsana* and the well-being of society as a whole. The king who internalizes this kind of legitimacy becomes the *Dhammarāja*, the protector of men from worldly harm and privation and the active agent in founding social order upon the order of the cosmos. His kingship becomes one with the lord of gods (Sakka), with the Conqueror himself (Buddha Gotama).

On a larger scale, an ontological interdependence between several modes of order is perceived. This assumes mythic proportions in the symbolism of the Yakkhas and the Nāgas who represent at the very least threats to the human order. "At the time the plane of Laṅkā had big forests and great horrors; different kinds of *Yakkhas*, greatly terrible, cruel, feeding on blood, furious, and demons of various forms having different inclinations."[7] "All the snakes were endowed with miraculous power, all were terribly poisonous, all were faulty, fierce, haughty and dependent. The snakes were quick, greatly powerful, wicked, rough, harsh, irritable, extremely angry, and desirous of destruction."[8] On two of his legendary three trips to Lanka the Buddha encounters these forms of the demonic, reducing disorder to impotency, and ultimately enlists them in service to the Dhamma. Of one piece with this is the authority perceived by King Pasenadi of Kosala who marveled at how the Buddha "tames the untamed, calms the uncalmed," in reference to the dangerous robber Aṅgulimāla, "without stick or sword."[9] In artistic and doctrinal form these lingering evidences of the demonic, now rendered benign, remind men not only of the Buddha's power in earlier days but of the power of the Dhamma to exorcize latter-day Yakkhas, to contain all forms of destruction.[10]

These acts of the Buddha are given temporal perspective within the tradition by being placed within a continuum from the remote past where three previous Buddhas are said to have visited Lanka (freeing it successively from pestilence, drought, and "a hideous and life-destroying war") to the time identified by the chronicler when the doctrine was established by the bhikkhu Mahinda, traditionally said to be Asoka's son.[11] Each of these actions symbolically removes the consequences of disorder and bases the promise of order upon the implanting of the Dhamma in the minds and associations of men. The very establishing of the boundaries (*sīmā*) of the Mahāvihāra conterminous with those of the city, by Mahinda at the behest of Devānaṁpiyatissa, constitutes the conviction that earthly authority is grounded upon and gains legitimacy from a Dhamma having cosmic implications.[12] Centuries later, in the reigns of Buddhadāsa (337-365) and his son Upatissa I (365-406), the theme is repeated as both kings are shown to display the power of genuine authority in healing the sick and driving plague and famine from the land.[13] While the actions of virtuous men, the moral goes deeper than virtue; it points beyond the precariousness of order, beyond the readiness with which men revert to anomic existence, to the fundamental structure of reality which transcends yet makes possible the discovery of selfless freedom.

No less instructive, because equally part of the dialectic between order and chaos, is the insistence that the Dhamma's well-being depends upon the monarchy's residing in Buddhist hands. From the establishment of Sinhalese Buddhist kingship in the reign of Devānaṁpiyatissa to its final demise in the nineteenth century a continuing refrain attributes legitimacy only to monarchs who not only support the Sāsana but who perceive the Buddhadhamma as the essence of social order and harmony. "Just as religious legitimation interprets the order of society in terms of an all-embracing, sacred order of the universe, so it relates the disorder that is the antithesis of all socially constructed nomoi to that yawning abyss of chaos that is the oldest antagonist of all the sacred. To go against the order of society is always to risk plunging into anomy."[14] In this vein one can appreciate the relief expressed within the

Chronicles at the wresting of the monarchy from the Damiḷas by such kings as Duṭṭhagāmaṇī (161-137 B.C.), Vaṭṭagāmaṇī (89-77 B.C.), Dhātusena (455-473), and Vijayabāhu I (1055-1110), among others. The passages that "awaken serene joy (*pasāda*) and emotion (*saṃvega*)" in the minds of the faithful stress that the miseries of the world are healed only through the doctrine of the *Saṃbuddha*.[15]

II. The Ontological Status of Legitimated Authority

The safeguarding of authority rests not only with those who exercize power but with the institutions, laws and values of the society which sets criteria for legitimacy. While religious traditions are not unique in being engaged in the legitimation process, religion often invests social institutions with enduring significance, "bestowing upon them an ultimately valid cosmological status . . . by *locating* them within a sacred and cosmic frame of reference."[16] "The institutions are thus given a semblance of inevitability, firmness and durability . . . Their empirical tenuousness is transformed into an overpowering stability as they are understood as but manifestations of the underlying structure of the universe."[17]

If the transcendent sacred reality in which society is believed to be rooted provides meaning to historic existence, it also challenges every conventional basis on which men claim status, wisdom and dignity. The ontological reality by which men endorse their claims to legitimacy remains a double-edged sword haunting those by whom power is abused. One clear facet of legitimated authority is thus its provisional nature, its susceptibility to using power for its own sake, and its final accountability to that which it purports to serve. Grounding authority in the structure of the universe makes it more, not less, vulnerable to attack, yet it is essentially the incumbent who is liable, more than the values and traditions he represents. These are undergirded with a kind of finality, with immense implications for the process of legitimation.

The history of Sinhalese Buddhism during the Anurādhapura period provides repeated instances of authority being perceived in ontological terms. Often, it is difficult to discern the uniquely Sinhalese features of this process because of the broader Indian texture (both Buddhist and Hindu) from which the heritage of Ceylon derives. In other respects, Ceylonese culture is distinctive and original, especially in the manner by which Sinhalese Buddhism has appropriated and modified various elements of Indian models. Three of these will be examined here: the envisioning of a universe in sacramental terms, the enthroning of the Buddha on the sacred lotus-seat of Brahmā, and the attempted elevation of the monarchy itself to comparable heights. While these fall outside orthodox teaching, they are part of a mythology which orthodoxy seldom discouraged and which supported the sacred reality affirmed by that tradition.

1. Throughout the Chronicles there is a poetic envisioning of an organic harmony within the universe derived from the turning of the Wheel of Law. Despite the acknowledgement that most men ignore or violate the teachings of the Dhamma, the ontological structure of existence was seen to remain unfragmented. In *sacramental* terms, evidences are educed from a host of worlds to promote a vision of reality which portrays men drawn by the power of the

doctrine, enabled to participate in a universe of meaning beyond their separateness and outside the limits imposed by their fears. Early in the *Mahāvaṃsa* the stage is set for this vision as the chronicler, in reference to Asoka, writes: "Straightway after his consecration his command spread so far as a yojana (upward) into the air and downward into the (depths of the) earth."[18] Geiger's notes suggest that "not only men upon the earth but also the spirits of the air and the earth heard and obeyed Aśoka's command,"[19] the implication being that authority derived from faithfulness to the Dhamma elicits responses in kind from all corners of the universe. A similar notion emerges from the passage where Mahinda is depicted preaching to the devas, who, like his human congregations, are converted to the doctrine.[20] While these embellishments are partially to stress the Buddha's regnant status over gods as well as men, the coherent nature of reality is assumed and made vivid.

This last aspect is expanded in the many descriptions of wonders and miracles said to have occurred in the reigns of Devānaṁpiyatissa and Duṭṭhagāmaṇī. From the establishing of the Mahāvihāra to the coming of the Bodhi-tree, from the beginning of the Great Thūpa to the enshrining of the relics, the several events are depicted within a framework of cosmic majesty and as affirming the ontic unity within the universe. "Celestial instruments of music resounded, a celestial chorus pealed forth, the devatās let fall a rain of heavenly perfumes and so forth."[21] "All this was completed without hindrance by reason of the wondrous power of the king, the wondrous power of the devatās, and the wondrous power of the holy (theras)."[22] When one has seen the relics, in Mahinda's words, one has seen the Buddha. With their enshrinement in Lanka, the devotional transplanting of the Dhamma is complete. The transmission of the doctrine is not by words alone; what is really released is the empowerment to envision and make real dimensions of the sacred beyond the confines of our normal world. "There is, O *bhikkhus*, that which is not-born, not-become, not-made, and not-conditioned. If this not-born, not-become, not-made, and not-conditioned were not, then there would be no apparent release from that which is born, become, made and conditioned."[23] Whether in the logically clear, though cryptic language of the Buddha or in the allegorical flourishes of the chronicler, a continuity of perspective points to a universe which is sacramentally of one piece, beyond the divisions composing the history of mankind. The implications of this for the legitimation of power and authority are subtle, often unclear, and always indirect. The lesson is for each monarch, for the Sangha itself, and for all men to discover. But the assertion of the reality from which authority derives is a continuing theme in Buddhist doctrine and mythology.

2. If genuine authority is ontological by nature and if it embodies the truth of the Dhamma, then the Buddha himself is represented, whether in aniconic or image form, as *sovereign of the universe.* While the Chronicles speak from the vantage point of nearly 1000 years of Buddhist history (seven centuries within Ceylon alone), they strive to interpret the *meaning* of the relics, the Bodhi-tree, the stūpas, and the images for earlier generations as well as their own. Doubtlessly influenced by Mahayana symbolism and imposing later interpretations upon original forms, mid-Anurādhapura mythology was clearly in continuity with a progressively expanding ontological picture of the Buddha's nature. From very early days the stūpa was regarded not simply as a

repository for relics but as a symbol of the cosmos. "The relics enshrined within the *stūpa*, which at once symbolized the world and the Tathāgata, would convey the idea of the Tathāgata being immanent in the universe. The umbrella, the symbol of sovereignty, suggested to the faithful the idea of the Buddha being lord of the world."[24] It was therefore in relationship to sovereignty of this sort that the authority and power of kings could be legitimated.

One intriguing rendering of this theme argues that in the early centuries of Buddhist iconography, perhaps first in Gandhāra but shortly afterwards throughout India and in Ceylon as well, there emerged the common representation of the Buddha in symbolical form as ascendant to the throne of ultimate power. "The Buddha was, according to the canonical texts, a great Being (Mahāpurisa) far above any God or Brahmā (Devātideva, Brahmātibrahma). Thus when the Buddha was taken as the tangible object of worship he had to be represented in supreme qualities that behove of a great Being. The obvious result was the creation, through art, of a supreme Being, who had surpassed earthly limits."[25] This argument proceeds to analyze sculpture and architecture in early Ceylon, finally crystallizing in an artistic complex during the latter Anurādhapura period as well as at Polonnaruva which places the Buddha upon the sacred seat of Brahmā. While the chronology of this development is far from clear, a strong case is made for restructuring the Kailāsa myth whereby "the Buddha (Mahāpurisa) himself was enthroned thus making a suggestion that even the greatest Divine Being of the Hindu pantheon had succumbed before the Buddha by offering him his very lotus seat."[26] Though space does not permit elaborating on this interpretation here, the author depicts in detail several elements of this sculptural portrayal, providing further insight into the meaning not only of the principal figure but of the Nāga guardians (*dvārapāla*), the moonstones (*sandakaḍapahaṇa*), and the flight of steps leading to the cosmic mountain. In Mahayana imagery, especially in influencing Buddhist art among the Khmers, the Supreme Buddha takes on the abstract form of Vairocana. In Ceylon there is more a commingling of iconographic images (with primary stress upon the historic Buddha, albeit drastically reinterpreted) with the essential theme of his ontological priority over all beings, spiritual and worldly, divine and human. Through understanding this fundamental priority one can appreciate the willingness of Buddhists in Ceylon and elsewhere not simply to be tolerant of Hindu gods and local deities but to convert them into service of the Dhamma, a point to be discussed in the final section.

3. A third feature of the ontological grounding of legitimated authority proceeds from the above, namely, the association of kingship with the sovereignty of the Buddha. Beyond the direct historical ties of Gotama with pious kings such as Bimbisāra and beyond the transmission of Buddhist kingship from Aśoka to Devānaṁpiyatissa, there was the emerging conviction "that only a Buddhist had the legitimate right to be king of Ceylon," and by the tenth century that the king must be a Bodhisattva as well.[27] While the evolution of this is difficult to trace historically, there are nodal points along the way which suggest a definite elevation of kingship to divine status, or more precisely a direct ontological association between Buddhist kingship and the Lord Buddha. Canonical warrant for this is, of course, given in the *Cakkavatti* concept (*Dīgha-Nikāya*, II, 169f; and III, 62f) wherein the model of a World-

ruler is one who presides "over the four quarters of the earth, righteous in himself, ruling righteously, triumphant, enforcing law and order at home, possessed of the seven jewels."[28] But this remains abstract until specific kings claim for themselves or have ascribed to them direct association with this status.

Though partial ascriptions are made throughout the Chronicles of various monarchs, the most deliberate early assertion of ontological parity with the Buddha as Lord of the universe is that of Kassapa (473-491), the famed parricide king, who built his palace atop Sīgiriya. "As the *Cūlavaṃsa* categorically states, Sīgiri was built as a replica of Ālakamandā paradise on the top of Mount Kailāsa; and Kassapa resided there as the embodiment of Kuvera on earth."[29] While the chronicler's account of the whole Dhātusena-Kassapa-Moggallāna saga hits the salient didactic keys, it is basically restrained on this score. A translation with commentary by Dr. Paranavitana of a purported fifteenth century Sanskrit history of Sīgiri, on the other hand, unfolds the story of Siṁhagiri as an Alakā (paradise) on earth and of the attempts by both Dhātusena and Kassapa to be proclaimed *Parvatarāja*. "When it was questioned by Dhātusena what purpose there was in administering the kingdom from a place on the summit of a rock, the Maga Brāhmaṇa replied that *Parvata* was a synonym of *Megha*, i.e. the Cloud, that the Cloud was the source of all prosperity, that if the Cloud did not rain, the whole world would be destroyed and that it would be possible for anyone who had made the world to accept that he himself was the Cloud, [to] bring the whole world under his subjection."[30]

Cynicism prompts one to reject the whole account, or at least to view what it portrays as a bald power play, basing legitimation upon hoodwinking of the populace. However specious the supposed Brāhmaṇa's reasoning and however transparent his motives, the account nevertheless suggests the lengths to which the legitimizing process could proceed and the delicate line between genuine and spurious legitimation. As it is said in the *Manu-smṛti*, the king should "emulate the energetic action of Indra, of the Sun, of the Wind, of Yama, of Varuna, of the Moon, of the Fire, and of the Earth."[31] Likewise, the *Śukranīti* emphatically states that "the king is made out of the permanent elements of Indra, Vāyu, Yama, Sun, Fire, Varuna, Moon, and Kubera, and is the Lord of both the immovable and movable words."[32] With these legitimating mythologies underwriting political authority and with the even more potent ontological association with the Buddha seated upon the sacred throne of Brahmā, the power of kingship gave the appearance of durability. "To repeat, the historically crucial part of religion in the process of legitimation is explicable in terms of the unique capacity of religion to 'locate' human phenomena within a cosmic frame of reference. All legitimation serves to maintain reality – reality, that is, as defined in a particular human collectivity. Religious legitimation purports to relate the humanly defined reality to ultimate and sacred reality. The inherently precarious and transitory constructions of human activity are thus given the semblance of ultimate security and permanence. Put differently, the humanly constructed nomoi are given a cosmic status."[33]

III. The Extent and Limitation of Power

In traditional societies threatened by the continuous spectre of disorder, authority and power must be buttressed by more than appeals to ontological legitimacy, however acknowledged these may be. Men do not live by ideology alone; agreement on that level does not preclude serious discord about particular issues. Authority is therefore legitimated by the responsible exercise of power, not simply by where its ultimate grounding is perceived. In relatively stable social orders and within reasonably homogeneous communities, where traditions and values change gradually, concurrence about general goals comes more naturally. With the onset of social instability from whatever cause or with the absorption of heterogeneous sub-groups, basic agreements may dissolve and power is inevitably threatened. Appeals to legitimacy may then fall on deaf ears, or counterappeals may arise. At the very least, order again becomes a matter of highest importance and skill in political statecraft carries its own legitimation.

There is a political truism in the assertion that power seeks a vacuum. Maladministration, incompetence, or simply ignorance about the basic problems of a society finally undermine whatever ideological validation may exist. In a hierarchically structured body politic this means that leadership continues in name alone and that authority is retained only under duress. The fact that this authority is invested with ontological status may ironically become more of a liability than an asset, as blame is attached to those from whom benefits are supposed to flow. In a monarchy especially the kudos which attends kingship in times of plenty may suddenly collapse when conditions become critical, creating a crisis of confidence which places full responsibility upon the monarch in power. The jockeying for position which then emerges reveals the multiple loci of power comprising any society, however invisible these may be to the unsuspecting. In actuality, balancing of power occurs as much within a monarchy as in other forms of government. Attempts to secure absolute power are products of despair, resulting from the failure to extend legitimate authority throughout the system. Such efforts reveal that effective legitimation has been removed, that the mandate of authority is recalled, displayed as much by social disintegration as by inauspicious portents.

In this section the task is to examine the relationship between the concept of kingship and how kings actually exercised their legitimated power in ancient Ceylon. This does not mean ignoring the realms of ideology and rhetoric, since most of the source material is didactic by intention, but at least grains of realism become evident the more one explores the expansion, the use, and the curtailing of power. The areas to be viewed are the following: how the legitimation of authority is regularized and transmitted; how the actual power of kingship is expanded; how statecraft is envisioned and utilized; what bearing traditional expectations of kingship (stemming from legitimation) have for each monarch; and, what checks upon royal power effectually determine the shape and tenor of legitimacy.

1. In the entire history of Ceylon no event is accorded more importance for the establishment of legitimate political authority than the founding of Buddhist kingship upon the Aśokan model during the reign of Devānaṁpiyatissa (250-210 B.C.). This episode constitutes the classical designing both of what kingship means and of how it is to be regularized. This story is so well-known one needs only to mention the ingredients which became normative for the institution of the monarchy and how the Indian model of the ideal king, modi-

fied considerably by Aśoka, took root in Ceylon. If no direct lineage can be traced from the Mauryan dynasty to Ceylon, the fact that Aśoka's missionary, the bhikkhu Mahinda, is held responsible for Tissa's conversion to the Dhamma establishes a surrogate connection with the earliest of India's great empires. Lanka has, of course, related ambivalently throughout her history to this association with Indian prototypes, utilizing whatever served her own needs and becoming restive when threatened by political realities (especially from South India). In any case, the symbols of office, modes of consecration, and forms of administrative practice were largely Indian in origin.[34] It would be naive to imply these arrived full-blown with the advent of Mahinda, unfolding immediately with the *abhiṣeka* of Devānaṁpiyatissa, but over the centuries the regalia, the titles, the ceremonies, and much of the exercising of authority became more Indian in complexion, without losing their central legitimating feature, i.e., the claim of Dhamma.

2. More significant for our purposes than the acquiring and confirming of royal power are the means by which this power could be extended through a competent handling of the office. In line with the king's basic function of protection it is clear that military security and political stability were minimal conditions for the enhancement of the monarchy. As in the early days of any society, political leadership and military prowess were often merged. In India and Ceylon the caste basis of this solidified the connection even more. Among the greatest Sinhalese leaders were those whose strategic skills on the battlefield were noteworthy. The reverse is equally true, as many defeats by South Indian armies made clear. Without freedom from foreign attack or from civil strife legitimation was cast in doubt. The same was true with respect to economic welfare. Even with relative political stability the necessity of a productive agricultural base and a lucrative foreign trade regularly assumed major importance. The special climatic, terrain, and soil features of Ceylon led eventually, with population increases, to the extensive irrigation system which began to develop under Vasabha (67-111) and continued, though with many interruptions, until the final collapse of the Rājaraṭṭha civilization in the fourteenth and fifteenth centuries.[35] Safeguarding the economic base was therefore of no less consequence than political protection. In fact, the two were plainly intertwined, as was clear whenever foreign invaders took advantage of domestic unrest and weakness as the occasion to launch an attack.[36] While kings had certain rights over land usage and ownership, and possessed the privilege to levy various kinds of taxation, there was an unwritten law that these rights were in jeopardy unless basic economic and political conditions were met. The lesson for each king was clear – unless legitimation is rooted in effective response to the everyday needs of society, its claims to cosmic status are of small comfort. The converse is equally true, i.e., with the maintenance of these benefits royal authority is enhanced.

3. On the other hand, it is obvious that social conditions are rarely ideal and that consummate skills in governance can turn relative losses into relative success. As we shall see, though power is regularly held in balance by the presence of contending factions, shrewd leadership can defuse factious elements, even convert discord into harmony. While the process is a never-ending dialectic and while it can easily backfire, there were carefully developed principles

in the art of government (*daṇḍanīti*) which stood many a monarch in good stead. As Geiger indicates, the compiler of the first part of the *Cūlavaṃsa* (chapters 37-79) was well-versed in Indian *nīti* literature, especially in the *Arthaśāstra* of Kauṭilya, and attributed not only detailed knowledge of this to Gajabāhu II (1132-1153) but also showed how it was put into practice.[37] While earlier evidence of such statecraft is more fragmentary, one may find reference to it in the reigns of Kassapa V (914-923) and Dhātusena (455-473), whose bhikkhu uncle tutored him in these arts.[38]

Though few kings could meet Kauṭilya's high standards of intrigue and deviousness, rewarded by the successful manipulation of power, the evidence is considerable throughout the Chronicles that many Sinhalese monarchs were able practitioners of *realpolitik*. The standard education of any prince included study of the arts of warfare and of *nīti* in general. Political marriages regularly took place with princesses from South Indian dynasties from the outset of Sinhalese history. Bhikkhus, as well, engaged themselves at times in direct political involvement. In reference to Dāṭhāsiva, whose position at the court of Aggabodhi I (571-604) was similar to that of the *purohita*, Geiger notes this as "the beginning of political influence on the bhikkhus."[39] Long before this, however, in the late third century one can see in Saṁghamitta (during the reigns of Goṭhābhaya, Jeṭṭhatissa, and Mahāsena) a monk whose wiles and manipulation of power took second place to none, at least in the judgment of the Mahāvihāra.[40]

These examples should prove no surprise, for the climate of political practice in India and Ceylon made the knowledge of *daṇḍanīti* imperative. Even if Buddhist conscience did not normally approve of duplicity (*dvaidhībhāva*) or if circumstances did not always require spies (*guḍhapuruśas*), no leader could afford to be cavalier about the balancing of power (*āśana*), the prospect of anarchy (*matsyanyāya*), or the regularly practiced system of alliances (*maṇḍala*). While the influence of the Dhamma, as represented by the Sangha, doubtlessly exercised a moderating influence upon those who may have been tempted to excesses in statecraft, the Chronicles reveal that Sinhalese Buddhists in high places recognized that *daṇḍanīti* and tyranny did not need to be synonymous. Indeed, responsible statecraft and legitimation were more perceived to be hand and glove.[41]

4. In whatever ways a king's legitimacy is established and by whatever means he extends his authority, limits are set to his power both by the unpredictableness of circumstances and by other communities of power within his own society and beyond. As suggested earlier, the very inflation of status accompanying any ontological grounding of kingship produces a level of expectation and an automatic pinpointing of responsibility which ironically turn the monarchy into a precarious institution. When rainfall is sufficient and the crops flourish and the people prosper, the king may bask in the adulation of his citizens who, according to tradition, attribute all success to his righteousness, all bounty to his protection. When famine strikes, when plague decimates the populace, when a foe puts the king's troops to rout, blame is traditionally sought in the person of the monarch. "From Vedic times downwards the king has been regarded as the supporter and upholder of the law, the 'dharma.' It was believed that any unhappiness, misery and pestilence among the subjects were attributed to the failure of the king to conform to the duties (*rājadharma*) of

the king. It is said that even sugar and salt lose their flavour during the rule of an unjust king."[42] The very belief that kingly righteousness is the guarantee of heavenly blessing also attributes any nexus of afflictions to the absence of righteousness. "When kings become unrighteous, we are told in a canonical text (*Aṅguttara-Nikāya*, II, 74-76), the king's officers (*rājayutta*) also become unrighteous, this being so the Brāhmaṇas and the mass of ordinary freemen (*gahapati*), the townsfolk and the villagers in their turn become unrighteous, this being so the Sun and the Moon, the stars and the constellations go wrong in their courses; days and nights, months, seasons, and years are out of joint; the *devas* being annoyed do not bestow sufficient rain. This being so the crops ripen in the wrong season, and consequently men are short-lived, ill-flavoured, weak and sickly. Conversely, when kings become righteous all the reverse consequences follow."[43] A good king is therefore an incalculable blessing; a bad king, a disaster. What legitimation bestows, circumstances may remove, for authority is not inherent in the king. It is provisional, arising largely from an effective use of power for the benefit of others.

5. Finally, what factors served to check royal power from becoming tyrannous and contribute to a balancing of power whereby the legitimacy of kingship was actually enhanced?[44] *First*, on the level of theory, the fact that the king was supposed to rule according to the Dhamma created an image of sovereignty which had its effect upon incumbents, originally through their early education and later upon the throne. *Secondly*, there was always the threat of hostile public opinion, which could be capitalized upon by adversaries at home and abroad. *Third*, the lessons of history could provide sobering restraints as one reflected upon what happened when folly and injustice proceeded from the throne. *Fourth*, in the absence of instant communications and constant surveillance, local communities (the *gāma*, or basic unit of autonomy) and distant provinces (e.g., Rohaṇa) tended to promote a kind of functional independence within the general bounds of fealty. *Fifth*, the many centers of power within the court, the army, various corporations and guilds, all having their own diversity, were vehicles of support and potential threats to the king depending upon his ability to affect balances within and among these groups. *Sixth*, there was the factor of foreign mercenaries whose numbers grew in importance over the centuries and whose presence was ambiguous in relation to the various allies and foes among South Indian dynasties.

While all the above were important in limiting royal power, the most crucial factor was the bhikkhu Sangha. Because of the Sangha's closeness to the people and because of its role in lending cohesiveness to the realm, a unified monastic community was an invaluable asset to effective kingship. On the other hand, from the reign of Vaṭṭagāmaṇī (89-77 B.C.) on, the Sangha was not unified and was often seriously divided, a fact which regularly involved the king or his counsellors in disputes and which sometimes prompted them to take sides, creating further unrest. Kings were the primary patrons of the Sangha, but they could also become the target of abuse. The relationship between the monarchy and the monastic community deserves a great deal more attention than it has received thus far. The following summary at least begins to hint at the complexities at work and also suggests how royal power was both enhanced and limited in relationship to this community.

> Conflicts arose between the king and the Sangha when the king carried his patronage too far and interfered in the affairs of *uposathāgāra*. The Sangha also started

> taking more interest in politics as they became a landed aristocracy, and the existence of a division within the order aggravated the situation so that the monks tried to put their favourites on the throne in order to secure material benefits. As the orthodox church grew in power the king was forced to take sides with them, but disputes arose regarding the respective fields of power of these two institutions which led to the ultimate clash in the reign of Mahāsena. When the king realized that his power was no match for that of the orthodox church he made a sudden reversal of policy and instead of attempting to maintain the unity of the Sasana tried to bring about and maintain as many rival Viharas as possible, thereby to redress the balance.[45]

IV. The Nurturing of Legitimation

As in the political realm where power arrangements continuously shift, legitimation of authority and power is a process needing regularly to be renewed by means of symbolism, mythology and ritual. It is no more true in a monarchy than in representative government that once legitimated, always legitimate. Because most legitimation is "pretheoretical in character," as Peter Berger indicates, the legitimating formulas of any community need reaffirmation. Even where no threat or challenge exists, the process must become real to new members of the society and kept alive among those already accepting it in theory. "There is both an objective and a subjective aspect to legitimation. The legitimations exist as objectively valid and available definitions of reality. They are part of the objectivated 'knowledge' of society. If they are to be effective in supporting the social order, however, they will have to be internalized and serve to define subjective reality as well. In other words, effective legitimation implies the establishment of symmetry between objective and subjective definitions of reality."[46]

A second ingredient of this process is the need for reciprocity between key elements in the society to be experienced and confirmed. Legitimation is not simply of kingship but of the entire structure of which kingship is the most prominent feature. Authority and power are not granted to the throne for its own sake, but to offset the precariousness of order and to ensure the possibility of stability and reasonable prosperity. The very concept of reciprocity suggests that communal existence is a fabric whose integrity depends upon the strength of all its parts. Even in a society organized along hierarchical lines, where overt political power is lodged at the top and where no regular procedures exist for influencing policy or removing those in power, the recognition that order is essentially indivisible remains imperative. While reciprocity takes different forms, with different meanings at various levels of society, it is necessary to the legitimation process. "Without integration among the elite, integration between the elite and the masses is difficult to achieve; without integration between the elite and the masses, there cannot be an integrated political community."[47] The nurturing of legitimation remains, therefore, essential to any social organism.

Because most available source material from ancient Ceylon comes either from the bhikkhu community or from kings in the form of royal inscriptions, one would expect notions of reciprocity to dwell frequently on the relationship between the Sangha and the monarchy. While this is true, one may read between the lines for some picture of what was actually a more pluralistic reciprocity, with various groups within society and the populace in general being as central as the other two. Indeed, as recent anthropological studies of Ceylon, Burma and Thailand make evident, a rich heritage of ideology, symbolism, and ritual exists on the popular level throughout Theravada societies. While present forms of these cannot be projected upon previous centuries without considerable qualification, it is clear that a host of pretheoretical legitimating phenomena has existed from early Sinhalese experience. The following discussion identifies three aspects of the nurturing of legitimation, each involving the king, the Sangha, and the people in various ways: the notion of the Sangha as a merit field (*puññak-khutta*) whose purity was essential to society at large; the normative qualities of kingship, centering primarily on its responsibility to protect and further the Dhamma; and, the role of ritual and ceremony in keeping alive not just the memory of the Buddha but faith in the doctrine's power. These aspects of legitimation go far beyond underwriting royal authority; they attest to and buttress the entire universe of belief which makes up Sinhalese Buddhism.

1. The stress upon the Sangha's purity has been central from the tradition's beginning; the relating of this to an *ideology of merit* grew gradually over the centuries. Throughout Theravada Buddhism the injunction of the Buddha that "one of the six duties of a monk towards the laity is to show them 'the way to heaven' (*sagga*) . . . and not 'the way to emancipation' *(mokkhassa maggaṃ*)" has been taken seriously and helps to explain, with canonical support, the considerable encouragement given to pious practices of various sorts.[48] If the path to Nibbāna is too arduous for those not seeking it directly, the Sangha accepts the task of assisting laymen to build up merit for their next existence and of becoming through the quality of its own life a source of merit to others. The reasons for the Sangha's purity are therefore twofold: one, that this may enhance the chances of its own membership for attaining Nibbāna; and two, that the merit accrued by this quest may be transferred to pious followers.

The modern dynamics of this have been carefully discussed by S. J. Tambiah, who shows how the ascetic monk becomes "an appropriate intermediary who can reach up to mystical powers associated with the Buddha and the sacred texts, and who can in turn transfer these powers to the layman in a form that can positively sacralize this life and the next."[49] The doing of merit is thus accompanied by the receiving of merit, giving concrete form to the reciprocity which exists but needs actualizing to have meaning for the participants. As the king is ideally the mediator between the body politic and the cosmic realm, so the Sangha's mediatorial role helps to provide sacral meaning to mundane existence and the human odyssey. It is for this reason that the quality of bhikkhu life must ideally be *sans reproche.* Monks involved directly in political affairs, engaged in "monastic landlordism," or embroiled in strife among the nikāyas do not give the appearance of being merit fields for others. From the earliest days in India and Ceylon the king had an important role in prompting the Sangha to reform itself (*sodhana*) through a regulative act (*dhamma-kamma*) of the Vinaya. This did not place the king above the Sangha in ecclesiastical matters, but it reinforced the notion of reciprocity since the entire society had a stake in the Sangha's purity. Because the Sangha could be an effective check upon royal power that became tyrannous, a unified and healthy monastic community helped create political legitimacy. The ongoing process of purification was therefore a central ingredient in the nurturing of legitimation.

2. The role of the king as protector of the Dhamma was in direct correlation with his role as chief patron of the Sangha, though it went beyond this as well. Aside from the direct advantages of various land grants and other endowments which kings made available to monasteries, without which they could not have flourished, royal beneficence was also seen as a model for others, in spirit if not in kind. The importance attached by the compilers of the Chronicles to the generosity of kings was not simply out of appreciation for what the Sangha received materially. It was also recognition that monarchs well disposed toward the livelihood of the bhikkhus furthered the Dhamma in a number of ways, beyond the maintaining of order and justice within society.

As in other respects, Asoka was seen as a prime example. The *Dīpavaṃsa* records him as saying, "as much as the monks desire I give them whatever they choose."[50] It is also recorded that the monks had to restrain him in his liberality, though when he pressed the question to Moggaliputta as to whether there were "a kinsman of Buddha's religion like unto me," he received this response: "Even a lavish giver of gifts like to thee is not a kinsman of the religion; giver of wealth is he called, O ruler of man. But he who lets son or daughter enter the religious order is a kinsman of the religion and withal a giver of gifts."[51] It was only fitting then that Asoka's purported son, the bhikkhu Mahinda, should be the one to tell Devānaṁpiyatissa that not until someone native to Ceylon be ordained will the doctrine be planted in that country. Both examples suggest the nature of true giving, of self more than substance. And yet the very prodigality of royal patronage was stressed in order to inspire later generations. In response to the lavish gifts of Duṭṭhagāmaṇī, the chronicler writes: "Merit, that a man has thus heaped up with believing heart, careless of insupportable ills of the body, brings to pass hundreds of results which are a mine of happiness; therefore one must do works of merit with believing heart."[52] Such performance of "pure deeds of merit" prompts others to "give alms lavishly, with a mind freed from the fetters (of lust), mindful of the good of beings."[53] It was this sort of monarch who was said to walk among men even as a bodhisatta (e.g., Buddhadāsa in the fourth century) and to be endowed with the ten qualities of kings (*dasa rājadhamma*) and the four heart-winning qualities (*cattāri saṃgahavatthūni*).[54] The models of exemplary kingship are threaded throughout the Chronicles, in contrast to others whose lives of evil are due warning. Also, the stories of holy monks and nuns, collected in the *Ariyavaṃsa*, were ordered by Vohārika Tissa (209-231) to be read aloud for the edification of the people.[55] Protection of the Dhamma obviously, therefore, took a number of forms, involving support of the Sangha, construction of stūpas, and especially lives founded upon the teaching. In the process, not only was the Dhamma enhanced and nurtured; the whole process of legitimation was deepened through this internalization.

3. The most standard and conspicuous way by which society's roots in the sacred realm underwent reaffirmation was through ceremonies, festivals and other forms of ritual. While Aśoka's caution about the true nature of ceremony (*Dharmamaṅgala*) would rank proper respect for living creatures above the usual ceremonies people perform, he also placed "the gift of Dharma or the benefit of Dharma" above liberality.[56] The Chronicles make vividly clear,

however, that orthodoxy saw substantive benefits accruing to the Dhamma by the celebration of its power through ritual. Indeed, one of the more obvious emphases throughout the record of the *Mahāvaṃsa*, ending with the reign of Mahāsena (274-301), are its elaborate and unrestrained paeans in response to the rituals of stūpa-building, relic worship, reverencing of the Bodhi-tree, and other forms of paying homage to the Buddha. Unquestionably, the focus is upon the Buddha and the Dhamma, but it is upon their cosmic significance, not simply their historic features. Access to this realm comes preeminently perhaps through attitudes of reverence stimulated through symbolism, mythology and ritual. While many observers have suggested that these occasions were primarily for the populace, this argument is not convincing. The bhikkhu community was as much involved in the glorifying of the Buddha's relics and in celebrating the Wheel of the Law as any others. If the proper aspiration of each monk was the attainment of Nibbāna, paying homage to the Buddha formed an intrinsic avenue of approach even if the path finally required the extinction of all dependence.

It is true that the performance of ritual had its less elevated dimensions. Kings were often engaged in constructing dagabas and image houses, for instance, as much for their own merit as for the benefit these brought to the Dhamma. Political opportunism played its part as well, as a form of bread and circuses for the populace and building up credit with the Sangha. A touch of cynicism is appropriate in trying to assess motivations, though there was undoubtedly sincerity in the intentions of many monarchs, with a mixture of motivations being perhaps the norm among most kings and other members of the lay elite. At any rate, the value of renewing legitimation liturgically was not lost to the ingenuous and the scheming alike. Because men forget or disregard the ontic dimensions of their social existence, they need to be reminded regularly. "Religious ritual has been a crucial instrument of this process of 'reminding.' Again and again it 'makes present' to those who participate in it the fundamental reality-definitions and their appropriate legitimations. The further back one goes historically, the more does one find religious ideation (typically in mythological form) embedded in ritual activity. . . . The performances of the ritual are closely linked to the reiteration of the sacred formulas that 'make present' once more the names and deeds of the gods. . . . They restore ever again the continuity between the present moment and the societal tradition, placing the experiences of the individual and the various groups of the society in the context of a history (fictitious or not) that transcends them all."[57]

The single most important festival was that of the Tooth Relic, brought to Ceylon in the reign of Sirimeghavaṇṇa (301-328), which became an annual event continued down to the present and now accompanied by the Kandy Perahära. While associated with the Abhayagiri-vihāra and not even mentioned by the Pāli commentaries of the fifth century, the Tooth and the Alms-bowl (*pātra-dhātu*) of the Buddha came to be considered "essential for a prince who wished to be the recognized king of Ceylon."[58] Indeed, in an act of devotional symbolism Sirimeghavaṇṇa was said to have offered the whole kingdom to the Tooth Relic, whose annual festival scored the reliance of genuine sovereignty upon the sovereign rule of the Buddha in cosmic terms. Reinforced by the reverencing of the Hair Relic (*Kesadhātu*), begun in the reign of Silākāla (518-

531), "there were also public festivals in connection with the older objects of religious veneration, the Bodhi Tree and the *stūpas*, in which the king and the people took part. A festival regularly celebrated in honour of the Bodhi Tree was known as *sinānāpūjā*, the ceremony of bathing the holy tree, still conducted in the height of the drought as a means of causing rain to fall."[59] While it is not appropriate here to explore the vast subject of *pirit* (Pāli, *paritta*), it must at least be said that the importance of the Protection Suttas and their use in dealing with public and private calamity are central to the problem of evil which ensues when forms of anarchy threaten the cosmic order. While close to magic on one level, they may partake of spiritually more profound quests on another.[60]

In conclusion, it should be stressed that all forms of ceremony and ritualistic action on the public level in ancient Ceylon were party to the nurturing of legitimation, provided one interprets this as legitimation of society's definition of reality and not simply of royal authority and power. In this vein, for example, one may see the wider significance of stūpa-building, which has always been regarded in Theravada countries as the apogee of merit-making and which is also a form of ritual itself as well as the prime symbol of the Buddha's authority. The following comments by Edward Conze make this clear:

> It was because Buddhism assured this harmony with the cosmos on which all social welfare depends that the laity was so eager to support the Order, house its members, and erect fine monuments in honor of their teachings. The world would not have put up for long with a community of monks which would merely turn their backs on those who fed them if they had not given something priceless to the world which it could not get in any other way. The visible manifestations of this concern for cosmic harmony are the magnificent stupas which adorn all parts of the Buddhist world and are the tangible focus of the religion. It was the business of the laity to build those stupas, though only the relics of the Lord Buddha could give them life. The stupas are as fundamental to Buddhism as the four holy truths, and it has been shown beyond doubt that they have a cosmic significance, that they are representative of the universe. . . . This "cosmic architecture represents the world as a theatre for the working-out of the Dharma and for the awakening of all beings by its piercing rays." Each stupa is an "imitation" of the life, or rather lives, of the Tathagata . . ., they allowed a whole society to unite in one common celebration, and thus had not only great moral, but also political consequences.
>
> It was the French scholar Paul Mus who in his monumental work on Borobudur proved that the works of architecture, properly interpreted, show that the Buddhists felt responsible for the welfare of society as a whole, and that the Samgha . . . aimed at fostering and maintaining that cosmic harmony which is the source and basis of all social prosperity.[61]

V. The Collapse of Legitimation

It has been the thesis of this essay from the start that each human community requires for its social and psychic existence significant consensus about what Berger calls its "plausibility structure." This entails the definition of reality which that community uses to give ultimate meaning to its corporate life and to deal with the forces of disorder within and among people which make order itself seem precarious. The two most important ordering principles for human society are the political and the religious, both of which seek to relate the affairs of men, in different but complementary ways, to a perceived transcendent sacred reality. In this manner, genuine authority and power are identified and in various ways gain legitimacy, a legitimation more of the plausibility structure itself than of those comprising its leadership at any point in time. Furthermore, the structure by definition consists of whole cloth and cannot easily endure marked challenges to its authenticity without being radically affected. Lastly, the process of legitimation is a continuous one, needing reaffirmation regularly if its meaning is to persist.

A question which has become particularly acute in the second half of the twentieth century, as traditional forms of societies succumb to new means of ordering reality, is what happens to human communities in the face of immense pluralism when their plausibility structures are shattered or seriously threatened? The fact that we are more aware of this issue today does not mean the phenomenon is new. In the West, for instance, we have been dealing with this fact in a host of forms since the break-up of the Holy Roman Empire in the late Middle Ages. This does not suggest that new structures of meaning cannot emerge, for they obviously have. But they possess less scope and do not normally inspire the same confidence as those existing for centuries without successful challenge. On the other hand, history records successive efforts to weave new patterns from the ruins of the old, using many former threads but adding new ones besides. The process is thus no simple evolution from an originally affirmed plausibility structure, through its collapse, to the total absence of such a structure. More likely, the process is consensus, challenge, collapse, and attempts at new forms of consensus, ad infinitum. If consensus appears to be enduring, based indeed upon the perceived structure of reality, its collapse appears to preclude all possibility, at least until new visions become convincing.

The final section of a paper is no place to introduce new themes, but it is appropriate to suggest nuances of the original theme which could profit from further research and reflection. The history of the Anurādhapura period affords considerable evidence that the culture dominated by the ethos of Sinhalese Buddhism was in actuality remarkably diverse. This was somewhat true from the beginning, though it became more so through centuries of increased exposure to the political arenas of South India, the world trading community with which Ceylon was involved, and the changing patterns within Buddhism (in Theravada and Mahayana circles alike). The traditional documents for studying the Ceylon scene are well-known. While presenting an extraordinarily full picture, they would be enriched through comparative historical studies of other Theravada cultures especially, as well as further anthropological case studies of the sort done by Hans-Dieter Evers on the interplay between the vihāra, dēvāle and palace systems in the Kandy District.[62] This suggestion is made on the assumption that evidence for a fuller historic picture than we presently have of the diversity within the Sangha, the increasing influence of Purānic Brahmanism, and the impact of the national cults along with various forms of popular religion is obtainable.

The value of understanding this broader picture is obvious from a number of standpoints, but it is essential if one is to grasp more fully the factors leading to a radical challenge of the orthodox plausibility structure, beginning in the late Anurādhapura period. The final chapters of its collapse are not difficult to write, but to overstress the problems of this era when Ceylon fell victim to Cōḷa aggression would minimize the implications of expanding diversity over the centuries before. The main configurations of Mahayana history in Ceylon, from the reign of Vohārika Tissa (209-231) to the introduction of

Vajrayāna and Tantrayāna in the ninth and tenth centuries, are well known, but detailed studies of nikāya history (involving the problems of schism, sectarianism and Sangha unity) have not yet been broached. Likewise, knowledge about the general patterns of Brahmanic culture, especially in the North, is available, but further historical and case studies which seek to appraise in depth the influence of Indian popular religion, Sanskritized Tamil Brahmanism, and the highly important Bhāgavata cult upon forms of Sinhalese Buddhist life and practice remain to be attempted. Finally, while recent anthropological work of increasing sophistication has been done on the national cults of Ceylon and on various indigenous types of popular religion, it is crucial that these be studied on a comparative basis and that we learn further about their role historically in affecting more orthodox forms of mythology, symbolism, ritual, and piety.

While traditional forms of legitimation may retain their credibility long past their zenith, unless they absorb creatively new elements into the plausibility structure they are destined to become unconvincing. At that point they cease to exist and are irrecoverable. Until we know more about the history of relationships between the major vihāras and the nikāyas, not to mention their associations with political figures in Rājaraṭṭha and the provinces, we are forced to speculate about the tensions involved in the constant struggle over legitimacy. Glimpses of the picture are available. We know the side several kings took in disputes between monastic communities. Evidence affords some insight into the role of bhikkhu influence upon affairs of state. But only a skeletal perspective is thus far possible. The same holds for the manner in which diverse branches of the Sangha responded to the mounting Indian influence in the last two or three centuries before what the Chronicles calls the "pillage of Laṅkā" (by Māgha in 1215). A synoptic account exists, but we learn little about the dynamics of a culture wrestling desperately to retain its definition of reality in the face of competing alternative views. Were there, for instance, important attempts to fashion new syntheses which were nipped in the bud and never even reported? Does the Sangha's livelihood, in fact, depend upon patronage from the political arm? What creative resources emerge in such a community when it becomes clear that this dependence is no longer possible? Obviously, there were many stages in the history of Sinhalese Buddhism, long before the colonial and modern periods, when royal patronage and political stability were precarious or non-existent. How did the bhikkhu community deal with these crises? One may suspect that during these times the plausibility structure was at most in abeyance, not extinct, but we have inadequate insight into what this actually meant for the life of monks. Moreover, the picture of lay Buddhism during the vast scope of ancient times is inadequately known. While this was often true in the records of early societies, it is particularly so in this case. Again, here is where comparative historical and case studies from other Theravada societies might help speculation be more informed. To conclude, the process of legitimation involves the linking of mundane existence to a perceived sacred reality, indeed the perception of this reality *within* mundane existence. The more we discover about the dynamics of the process in detail, the more we see its fragile nature, its powers of renewal, its potential for accommodating new ingredients, the constant possibility of its collapsing, and the enduring importance of it for all communities.

Notes

This is a revised version of an essay originally published in *Buddhism in Ceylon and Studies on Religious Syncretism in Buddhist Countries: Report on a Symposium in Goettingen* (Goettingen: Akademie der Wissenschaften, 1978), a volume edited by Heinz Bechert and included in the series of the "Abhandlungen der Akademie der Wissenschaften in Goettingen." The conference took place in Goettingen in July, 1974. The author's participation was made possible by a travel grant from the American Council of Learned Societies. Reprinted with permission.

While the isolating of these particular features is my own, I am indebted to Peter Berger's discussion of the process of legitimation in his book *The Sacred Canopy: Elements of a Sociological Theory of Religion.* Cf. pp. 29-51, and *passim.* For an astute critique of broader aspects of Berger's thought, see Van A. Harvey, "Some Problematical Aspects of Berger's Theory of Religion," *Journal of the American Academy of Religion*, Vol. 41, No. 1 (March 1973), 75-93.

Dialogues of the Buddha, tr. by T. W. and C. A. F. Rhys Davids. London, 1921, III, 77-94. See also Vishwanath Prasad Varma, "Studies in Hindu Political Thought and Its Metaphysical Foundations," *Journal of the Bihar Research Society*, Vol. XXXVIII, Pts. 3-4, 454-466. As Varma says, "The 'law of the fishes' symbolizes the sheer prevalence of the cult of naked and unashamed force." (p. 466) Or, from the *Rāmāyaṇa*, tr. by Griffith, ii, lxvii: "In kingless lands no law is known,/And none may call his wealth his own;/Each preys on each from hour to hour,/As fish the weaker fish devour."

The Laws of Manu, tr. by Georg Bühler, p. 238. See also J. Gonda, *Ancient Indian Kingship from the Religious Point of View*, pp. 3-6, 17-19.

Mahāvaṃsa, IV. 1-44. The transliteration of Aśoka (Sanskrit) or Asoka (Pāli) will vary here according to the content referred to or the text cited. Also true of Dharma or Dhamma.

Ibid., VII. 1-5. The person referred to is Vijaya, who is said to have landed on Ceylon that same day, that of the Buddha's *parinibbāna*. Sakka (Indra) then handed over the guardianship to Vishnu (Upulvan). Indra is also seen as the god who makes possible the fecundity of nature, as he supplies both light and water. Kingship in association with Indra becomes, therefore, the bestower of blessings.

Dīpavaṃsa, p. 135. Also, *Mahāvaṃsa*, XV. 160-165.

Ibid., p. 139. These mythic beings are to be seen not literally as beasts, but as symbols of disorder, whose power is sought in the Dhamma's behalf.

Middle Length Sayings, II, p. 288.

Cf. Walpola Rahula, *History of Buddhism in Ceylon*, pp. 39-41, for other examples in India and Ceylon of conquering and controlling "yakṣas and nāgas." See also Edward Conze's essay "Dharma as a Spiritual, Social and Cosmic Force" in Paul G. Kuntz, ed., *The Concept of Order* (Seattle: University of Washington, 1968). On page 241 he writes: "Those parts of the world which have escaped the control of Dharma are marked by strife (*raṇa*) and turmoil (*ḍamara*). On a more or less poetical and allegorical level this is often shown in the scriptures by contrasting the serenity, peace and harmony of the world which is dominated by the Buddhas and Bodhisattvas (who are channels through which the transcendental Dharma reaches the world) with what is going on in the hells or among Mara's hosts."

Mahāvaṃsa, XV. 56-172.

Ibid., XV. 180-194.

Cūlavaṃsa, 37. 105-198.

Berger, *op. cit.*, p. 39.

Mahāvaṃsa, I. 3-4. See section III of this present essay for the way in which Sinhalese Buddhist ideology during this long period was strongly political in nature. See also the earlier chapter by the author entitled "The Ideal Social Order as Portrayed in the Chronicles of Ceylon."

Berger, *op. cit.*, p. 33.

Ibid., pp. 36-37.

Mahāvaṃsa, V. 23. The following verses (24-33) are a delightful depiction of this organic harmony within the natural world.

19. *Ibid.*, fn. 1.
20. *Ibid.*, XIV. 38-40. Besides the devatās, nāgas and their mortal foes (the supaṇṇas) also heard and were converted.
21. *Ibid.*, XXXI. 84.
22. *Ibid.*, XXX. 99.
23. *Udāna*, VIII. 3 (*Khuddaka-Nikāya*).
24. Senarat Parananvitana, *Sinhalayo* (Colombo: 1970, revised second edition), p. 20.
25. A. D. T. E. Perera, "Buddha on the Sacred Seat of Brahma," *World Buddhism Vesak Annual* (Colombo, 1973), p. 38.
26. *Ibid.*, p. 43. Kailāsa is the mountain paradise of Śiva, lying in Hindu cosmography to the east of Mount Meru. Cf. Himansu Bhusan Sarkar, "The Evolution of Śiva-Buddha Cult in Java," *Journal of Indian History*, Vol. 45 (1967), pp. 637-646, for the opposite process, i.e., the adoption of Buddha into the Hindu pantheon as one of the ten Avatāras of Vishnu. This happened by the eleventh century A.D., if not earlier. Cf. Senarat Parananvitana, *Ceylon and Malaysia* (Colombo, 1966), pp. 202-203, for an interesting statement on the development of the cosmic mountain theme in Southeast Asian Buddhist art.
27. Rahula, *op. cit.*, p. 62.
28. U. N. Ghoshal, "Principle of the King's Righteousness," *Indian Historical Quarterly*, Vol. 32 (1956), p. 309. One ruling over the four quarters was called *digvijayin.*
29. Paranavitana, *op. cit.*, p. 26. Kuvera (Kubera) is the god of wealth, whose paradise is Alakā.
30. Senarat Paranavitana, *The Story of Sigiri* (Colombo, 1972), p. 22. In general, both the Buddhists and the Jains rejected the divinity of kings, though the evidence is less clear than orthodoxy implies. Paranavitana's speculations on this topic have been subject to much criticism. See Sirima Kiribamune, "Some Reflections on Professor Paranavitana's Contribution to History," in *Ceylon Journal of the Humanities*, Vol. I, No. 1 (January, 1970).
31. *The Laws of Manu*, p. 396.
32. Balakrishna, "The Evolution of the State," *Indian Historical Quarterly,* Vol. 3 (1927), p. 325. The passage referred to is *Śukranīti,* i. 375.
33. Berger, *op. cit.*, pp. 35-36.
34. This is fully discussed in a number of studies. Cf. Tilak Hettiarchchy, *History of Kingship in Ceylon*, pp. 6-64; Wilhelm Geiger, *Culture of Ceylon in Mediaeval Times*, pp. 111-132; S. Paranavitana, ed., *The University of Ceylon History of Ceylon*, Vol. I, Part I, *passim*; H. Ellawala, *Social History of Early Ceylon*, pp. 11-27.
35. See K. Indrapala, ed., *The Collapse of the Rajarata Civilization* (Peradeniya, 1971).
36. As expressed in one famous maxim: "Watch for the weaknesses of others as a hawk watches its prey. And conceal your own weaknesses as a tortoise hides its soft body."
37. *Cūlavaṃsa*, 66. 126-158. Cf. also pp. vi and xiv.
38. Cf. *Cūlavaṃsa*, 52. 37-41, where it is said that Kassapa was "versed in statecraft" as well as being "a mine of virtues." Regarding Dhātusena, see *Cūlavaṃsa*, 38. 14-28, in which his uncle perceives that the boy Dhātusena "must be made a master in state-craft." The political aim of the chroniclers has been capably discussed by Heinz Bechert, who writes that "the basic idea of this ideology was that of the unity of nation and religion." See chapter 1 of the present volume.
39. *Ibid.*, p. 67, footnote 8.
40. *Mahāvaṃsa*, XXXVI. 110 - XXXVII. 31.
41. Extension of royal power came also through capable administration of justice, through the regular process of succession to the throne, through the power to make appointments to important positions and to make summary dismissals.
42. U. D. Jayasekera, *Early History of Education in Ceylon* (Colombo, 1969), p. 53.
43. U. N. Ghoshal, *op. cit.*, pp. 306-307. See also John W. Spellman, *Political Theory of Ancient India*, pp. 211-219. Also, the *Cakkavatti-Sīhanāda Sutta, Dialogues of the Buddha*, Vol. IV, pp. 59-76; and, *The Sutra of Golden Light*, pp. 57-62.
44. Cf. B. P. Sinha, "The King in the Kauṭilīyan State," *Journal of the Bihar Research Society*, Vol. 40, pp. 291-308; and, U. N. Ghoshal, "An Aspect of State Administration in

the Pre-Maurya Period–Influence of Public Opinion on Kingly Governments," *Journal of Indian History*, Vol. 40 (1962), 551-555.

Tilak Hettiarchchy, *History of Kingship in Ceylon up to the Fourth Century, A.D.*, p. 143. This is a very capable study of this subject. Especially excellent is his chapter on "The Relationship between the King and the Sangha," pp. 116-143, which is one of the more perceptive analyses of this topic that exists. It restricts itself, however, to the period before the fourth century A.D.

Berger, *op. cit.*, p. 32.

Ping-ti Ho and Tang Tsou, eds., *China in Crisis*, Vol. 1: *China's Heritage and the Communist Political System* (Chicago: University of Chicago Press), 1968, p. 279.

Rahula, *op. cit.*, pp. 251-2. The reference here is to the *Sigāla-sutta* of the *Dīgha-Nikāya*, III, p. 117. The Sigāla Homily is, of course, one of the most important suttas for expressing the nature of true reciprocity, though it focusses on what it means for the layman in the relationships of the "six quarters"–i.e., between parents and children, teachers and pupils, husband and wife, friend and friend, master and servant, laymen and religious "recluses and brahmins."

S. J. Tambiah, "The Ideology of Merit," in E. R. Leach, ed., *Dialectic in Practical Religion*, p. 116. For the growth of the concept of merit in post-canonical Theravada texts, see the article by Heinz Bechert entitled "Notes on the Formation of Buddhist Sects and the Origins of Mahāyāna," in *German Scholars on India: Contributions to Indian Studies*, Vol. I (Varanasi: Chowkhamba Sanskrit Series Office, 1973), pp. 16-17 especially.

Dīpavaṃsa, p. 178. The gift in that particular instance, apparently unsolicited from the monks, was said to be 84,000 monasteries, a figure merely symbolic of his munificence.

Mahāvaṃsa, p. 43.

Ibid., p. 190.

Ibid., pp. 219, 186.

Cūlavaṃsa, p. 10.

Mahāvaṃsa, p. 258. Cf. also Malalasekera, *op. cit.*, p. 51, who says that this custom existed before this time and also continues to be practiced today. As he was dying, Duṭṭhagāmiṇī expressed his fear of death to the bhikkhu Therasutābhaya, who comforted him and assured him of his great merit. The catalogue of his good deeds was then read to him out of the "Merit Book" (*Puññapotthaka*), which kings and other laymen often kept. As Geiger indicates in his Introduction to the *Cūlavaṃsa*, the source materials available to the compiler were mainly *Puññapotthakāni*, that is, "registers of meritorious works by which the prince had furthered the Church (*sāsana*) and the laity (*loka*)." See pp. iv-v.

N. A. Nikam and Richard McKeon, ed. and tr., *The Edicts of Asoka*, pp. 46-47.

Berger, *op. cit.*, pp. 40-41.

Rahula, *op. cit.*, p. 74.

S. Paranavitana, "Civilisation of the Period: Religion, Literature and Art," in *University of Ceylon History of Ceylon*, Vol. I, Part I, p. 384.

For an extremely suggestive interpretation of the protection ceremonies and the cosmic calendrical rites, which aim to ensure both public and public benefits, see Tambiah, *op. cit.*, pp. 118-120. In this section he writes: "Man, too, subjects himself to the moral order in these cosmic rites; his merit-making and selfless giving of gifts express this subjection; the Buddhist monk, through his form of ascetic subjection, appropriately chants and preaches about the Buddha's conquest of desire, pain and death. Perhaps at the back of these religious actions are the basic ethical ideas that man transcends his limitations by subjecting his animal nature, that it is by freely giving that he receives bountifully, that by refusing the grosser things in life he measures the value of life, and that by harnessing and releasing ethical energy, nature and agencies external to man can be brought into a single harmonious order. It is in this sense that Buddhist cosmic rites are not manipulative or instrumental in the manner of spirit cults or 'magical' rites. And this is why Buddhist values and action necessarily have a higher place in the hierarchy of values and acts that comprise the universe of religious action. . . . On the other hand, a coercive relationship of bargaining with spirits, their placation or domination, is again a statement of power relations which are an extension of and a contrast to the socially normal manipulative behaviour. . . . However ethically valued, both are stubbornly present in real life – for if either gains supremacy life will be heaven on earth or pure hell; both are improbable."

61. Conze, *op. cit.*, p. 250.
62. Hans-Dieter Evers, *Monks, Priests and Peasants: A Study of Buddhism and Social Structure in Central Ceylon* (Leiden: E. J. Brill), 1972.

References

I. Books

Adikaram, E. W., *Early History of Buddhism in Ceylon.* Colombo, 1946.

Arasaratnam, S., *Ceylon.* Englewood Cliffs, New Jersey, 1964.

Ariyapala, M. B., *Society in Mediaeval Ceylon.* Colombo, 1968.

Auboyer, Jeannine, *Daily Life in Ancient India.* London, 1965.

Berger, Peter L., *The Sacred Canopy: Elements of a Sociological Theory of Religion.* New York, 1969.

Bhandarkar, D. R., *Aśoka.* Calcutta, 1969.

Cakkavatti-Sīhanāda Suttanta, ed. by T. W. Rhys Davids, *Sacred Books of the Buddhists*, Vol. IV. London, 1965.

Choudhary, Radhakrishna, *Kautilya's Political Ideas and Institutions.* Varanasi, 1971.

Cūlavaṃsa (Parts I and II), tr. by Wilhelm Geiger and C. Mabel Rickmers. Colombo, 1953.

Devahuti, D., *Harsha: A Political Study.* Oxford, 1970.

Dīpavaṃsa, ed. by B. C. Law. Maharagama, Ceylon, 1959.

Drekmeier, Charles, *Kingship and Community in Early India.* Stanford, 1962.

Ellawala, H., *Social History of Early Ceylon.* Colombo, 1969.

Evers, Hans-Dieter, *Monks, Priests and Peasants: A Study of Buddhism and Social Structure in Central Ceylon.* Leiden, 1972.

Geiger, Wilhelm, *Culture of Ceylon in Mediaeval Times.* Wiesbaden, 1960.

Ghoshal, U. N., *A History of Indian Political Ideas.* London, 1966.

Gokhale, B. G., *Asoka Maurya.* New York, 1966.

Gokhale, B. G., *Samudra Gupta: Life and Times.* New York, 1962.

Gombrich, Richard F., *Precept and Practice: Traditional Buddhism in the Rural Highlands of Ceylon.* Oxford, 1971.

Gonda, J., *Ancient Indian Kingship from the Religious Point of View.* Leiden, 1969.

Hettiarchchy, Tilak, *History of Kingship in Ceylon up to the Fourth Century A.D.* Colombo, 1972.

Indrapala, K., ed., *The Collapse of the Rajarata Civilization in Ceylon and the Drift to the South-west.* Peradeniya, 1971.

Jayasekera, U. D., *Early History of Education in Ceylon.* Colombo, 1969.

Joshi, Lalmani, *Studies in the Buddhistic Culture of India (During the 7th and 8th Centuries A.D.).* Delhi, 1967.

Katikāvatas, ed. and tr. by Nandasena Ratnapala. München, 1971.

Kosambi, D. D., *The Culture and Civilisation of Ancient India in Historical Outline.* London, 1965.

The Laws of Manu, tr. by Georg Bühler. New York, 1969.

Leach, E. R., ed., *Dialectic in Practical Religion.* Cambridge, 1968.

Ling, Trevor, *The Buddha: Buddhist Civilization in India and Ceylon.* New York, 1973.

Liyanagamage, Amaradasa, *The Decline of Polonnaruwa and the Rise of Dambadeniya (circa 1180-1270 A.D.).* Colombo, 1968.

Ludowyk, E. F. C., *The Footprint of the Buddha.* London, 1958.

Mahāvaṃsa, tr. by Wilhelm Geiger. London, 1964.

Mahā-Sudassana Sutta, tr. by T. W. Rhys Davids, *Sacred Books of the East*, Vol. XI. Delhi, 1965.

Malalasekera, G. P., *The Pāli Literature of Ceylon.* Colombo, 1958.
The Middle Length Sayings (Majjhima-Nikāya), Vol. II, tr. by I. B. Horner. London, 1957.
Mookerji, Radha Kumud, *Ancient Indian Education (Brahmanical and Buddhist).* Delhi, 1969.
Mudiyanse, Nandasena, *Mahayana Monuments in Ceylon.* Colombo, 1967.
Nicholas, C. W. and S. Paranavitana, *A Concise History of Ceylon.* Colombo, 1961.
Nikam, N. A. and Richard McKeon, eds. and trs., *The Edicts of Asoka*, Chicago, 1959.
Nilakanta Sastri, K. A., *A History of South India.* London, 1966.
Paranavitana, Senarat, *Ceylon and Malaysia.* Colombo, 1966.
Paranavitana, Senarat, *Sinhalayo.* Colombo, 1970 (rev. 2nd edition).
Paranavitana, Senarat, *The Story of Sigiri.* Colombo, 1972.
Paranavitana, Senarat, ed., *The University of Ceylon History of Ceylon*, Volume I, Parts I, II. Colombo, 1959, 1960.
Pāṭimokkha, tr. by Ñāṇamoli Thera. Bangkok, 1966.
Raghavan, M. D., *India in Ceylonese History, Society and Culture.* New Delhi, 1969.
Rahula, Walpola, *History of Buddhism in Ceylon: The Anurādhapura Period (3rd Century B.C. - 10th Century A.D.).* Colombo, 1966.
Reynolds, C. H. B., ed., *An Anthology of Sinhalese Literature up to 1815.* London, 1970.
Saletore, Bhasker Anand, *Ancient Indian Political Thought and Institutions.* London, 1963.
Seligmann, C. G. and Brenda Z. Seligmann, *The Veddas.* Cambridge, 1969.
The Sutra of the Golden Light, tr. by R. E. Emmerick. London, 1970.
Shamasastry, R., tr., *Kauṭilya's Arthaśāstra.* Mysore, 1967.
Sharma, Ramashraya, *A Socio-Political Study of the Vālmīki Rāmāyaṇa.* Delhi, 1971.
Sharma, Ram Sharan, *Aspects of Political Ideas and Institutions in Ancient India.* Delhi, 1968.
Singh, Ram Charitra Prasad, *Kingship in Northern India (c. 600-1200 A.D.).* Delhi, 1968.
Sinha, H. N., *The Development of Indian Polity.* Bombay, 1963.
Smith, Bardwell L., ed., *The Two Wheels of Dhamma: Essays on the Theravada Tradition in India and Ceylon.* Chambersburg, Pennsylvania, 1972.
Spellman, John W., *Political Theory of Ancient India: A Study of Kingship from the Earliest Times to circa A.D. 300.* Oxford, 1964.
Spiro, Melford E., *Buddhism and Society: A Great Tradition and Its Burmese Vicissitudes.* New York, 1970.
Tambiah, S. J., *Buddhism and the Spirit Cults in North-east Thailand.* London, 1970.
Thapar, Romila, *Aśoka and the Decline of the Mauryas.* Oxford, 1961.
Warder, A. K., *Indian Buddhism.* Delhi, 1970.

Unpublished Monographs*

Adhya, G., *Studies in the Economic Life of Northern and Western India (200 B.C. - 300 A.D.).* Ph.D., 1962.
Gunawardana, R. A. L. H., *The History of the Buddhist 'Saṅgha' in Ceylon from the Reign of Sena I (833-853) to the Invasion of Māgha (1215).* Ph.D., 1965.
Indrapala, K., *Dravidian Settlements in Ceylon and the Beginnings of the Kingdom of Jaffna.* Ph.D., 1965.
Sinha, B. P., *Decline of the Kingdom of Magadha (c. 455-1000 A.D.).* Ph.D., 1948.
Siriweera, W. I., *Economic Conditions of Ceylon (c. 1070-1344 A.D.).* Ph.D., 1970.
Wijetunga, Mudalige Karunaratna, *The Rise and Decline of Coḷa Power in Ceylon.* Ph.D., 1962.

*The above monographs were Ph.D. dissertations done at the University of London.

The Kinsmen of the Buddha: Myth as Political Charter in the Ancient and Early Medieval Kingdoms of Sri Lanka

R. A. L. H. Gunawardana

"OF ALL THE chapters in religious anthropology," Claude Lévi-Strauss observed in his *Structural Anthropology*, "probably none has tarried to the same extent as studies in the field of mythology. From a theoretical point of view the situation has remained very much the same as it was fifty years ago, namely, chaotic. Myths are still widely interpreted in conflicting ways: as collective dreams, as the outcome of a kind of esthetic play, or as the basis of ritual."[1] Despite the noteworthy impact of his own theoretical work, it is not possible to say that the situation has become less chaotic during the score or so of years since Lévi-Strauss made this statement. The work of the foremost students of mythology like Malinowski, Boas, Kluckhohn and Lévi-Strauss himself has been concerned primarily with myth in "savage society." Malinowski was acutely aware of the need for the study of myth in ancient civilizations and believed that "the study of mythology as it functions and works in primitive societies should anticipate the conclusions drawn from material from higher civilizations."[2] In more recent times anthropologists and classical scholars have begun to pay close attention to the study of literate myths, particularly those of Mesopotamia and Greece. However, historians have been generally sceptical about the usefulness of the study of myth and hesitant about accepting it as a legitimate branch of their discipline. Thus, if the progress made in anthropology in the study of myth has not been impressive, in the field of historical research it is not possible even to assert that a serious beginning has yet been made. The present paper is explorative and experimental in character in attempting to draw on the theoretical work in anthropology for the study of a group of myths in Sri Lanka. It is hoped that this attempt, however tentative and limited, would contribute towards the development of conceptual tools for the historians of South Asia to enable them to approach the task of drawing on the considerable store of mythical material which has so far been largely ignored by them as irrelevant.

The two major chronicles of Sri Lanka, the *Dīpavaṃsa* and the *Mahāvaṃsa*, present detailed accounts of the three visits to the island that the Buddha is supposed to have made. These accounts are in Pāli verse. The *Dīpavaṃsa* presents the longer version which covers two chapters containing in all 150 verses. The *Mahāvaṃsa* devotes only one chapter with 84 verses to present a much more concise account of the visits. A third version, in prose, is to be found in the *Vaṃsatthappakāsinī*. Though this work is a commentary on the *Mahāvaṃsa*, the account presented therein differs in certain respects from the *Mahāvaṃsa* version.

The accounts of the three visits of the Buddha in these three sources are not corroborated by Indian material or even by the Pāli Canon preserved in

Sri Lanka. They contain descriptions of highly miraculous deeds. During all these three visits the Buddha is said to have had dealings with only non-human beings: *yakkhas, nāgas* and *devas.* Despite this, nineteenth-century writers like William Knighton, who published *The History of Ceylon* in 1845, found it possible to accept the historicity of these events.[3] For both Knighton and L. E. Blazé, the author of *A History of Ceylon for Schools* published in 1900, the *yakkhas* and *nāgas* represented the pre-Aryan inhabitants of the island.[4] The euhemeristic approach of these early European writers has been subjected to sharp criticism by later scholars nurtured in the traditions of empiricist historiography.[5] But there is little doubt that these stories were and are still believed to be true by the faithful among the Buddhists. The late Professor Senarat Paranavitana aroused a chorus of indignant protest by making a casual comment in a public speech delivered a few years before his death in 1972 that there was no justification for the belief that the Buddha did visit the island.

Though the stories concerning all three visits of the Buddha form a single group, there is reason to believe that even the chroniclers considered the first visit to be of special import. In the *Dīpavaṃsa*, for instance, the story of the first visit forms a separate chapter while both the second and the third visits are described in the second chapter. Further, the role of the Buddha in this story is quite inconsistent with the characterization presented in the Pāli Canon and the commentarial works. As would be seen in due course, in this story the Buddha is hardly the *mahākāruṇika*, the man of profound kindness, but a personality totally different from the type that one encounters in other Buddhist literary works. It becomes clear from an examination of the *Mahāvaṃsa* and the *Vaṃsatthappakāsinī* that there is also an inconsistency between the account of the first visit of the Buddha and the legend about Vijaya, "the first king of the island." The Buddha is said to have cleared the island of the *yakkhas* during his first visit, but, according to the Vijayan legend, Vijaya and his followers found within the island a kingdom of the *yakkhas.* Vijaya fought against these *yakkhas* and destroyed them with the aid of Kuveni before he founded the kingdom of Tambapanni. It would thus seem that these two sets of tales were of independent origin and had been deliberately strung together by the chroniclers.

According to the *Dīpavaṃsa*, the *yakkhas* were the original inhabitants of the island. At the time of the first visit of the Buddha they had all assembled at Mahiyaṅgaṇa. The Buddha appeared in the sky over this assembly and afflicted the *yakkhas* with rains and cold winds. Then he addressed them to ask for a place to sit in return for dispelling these calamities. The *yakkhas* readily consent to this and beseech him to provide heat to overcome the cold. The Buddha sits on his rug and makes it diffuse heat, unbearable in its intensity, compelling the *yakkhas* to flee. He then brings Giridīpa, another island, close to Lanka and, when the fleeing *yakkhas* clamber on to it, returns Giridīpa to its original place.[6]

In the variant version found in the *Mahāvaṃsa*, the *yakkhas* offer the Buddha the whole island if he would only relieve them of their distress. The Buddha sits on the ground, spreading his leather rug, and causes the rug to expand. Burning flames surround the rug. The *yakkhas* withdraw right up to the coastline and are transported away in the same manner as in the *Dīpavaṃsa* version.[7]

It is in the *Vaṃsatthappakāsinī* that this encounter is presented in the most dramatic manner.[8] The Buddha uses his supernatural powers to harass the *yakkhas* with eleven different types of afflictions. Torrential rains and hurricanes descend on them. They are pelted with showers of stones, weapons, burning embers, hot ashes and mud. Cold and humid winds, storms and darkness torment and terrify them. When the *yakkhas* appeal to the Buddha for succour, he demands a place to sit in return. They offer him the whole island. The Buddha expresses the doubt that this offer might be revoked later. The *yakkhas* then give a solemn promise (*sapatha*) that no one would ever hinder the right of the Buddha over the island. The Buddha seats himself on his leather rug and restores normalcy except for the fact that the cold continues to torment the *yakkhas*. The *yakkhas* appeal to the Buddha to release the heat rays of the sun. In response to this request, the Buddha causes his rug to emit heat. He also causes the rug to expand till, ultimately, it covers the whole island. The body of the Buddha, too, expands with the rug and it is said that, finally, the proportions of the island, the rug and the body of the Buddha were "the same." The *yakkhas* who retreat before the spreading rug reach the very shores and are convinced that "the island has been taken over by this great and powerful king of gods and lost to us."[9] The compassion of the Buddha is aroused by their plight and he brings Giridīpa in the manner described in the two chronicles to transport them away.

The Buddha's encounter with the *yakkhas* in the three different versions of the tale examined above contrasts sharply from descriptions of the "taming" (*damana*) of non-human beings in the Canon. In the story of the *yakkha* Ālavaka, for instance, it is the Buddha's kindness, tolerance and good temper unruffled by open hostility which win over Ālavaka.[10] Here, on the other hand, the Buddha is portrayed as one who harassed the *yakkhas* with devious afflictions. He asks the *yakkhas* for a place to sit, but finally drives them from their homeland. During the course of the story, he is often referred to as *jina* or "conqueror," a title which suits him here in its literal meaning. In this tale the Buddha is clearly the conqueror who has time for compassion only after a kingdom has been annexed. Indeed, he is cast in an unusual role.

Sri Lanka was one of the first countries where the Buddhist *saṅgha* developed a durable and close relationship with the state. It is possible to suggest that this growing rapprochement between the *saṅgha* and the state would have soon encountered serious problems. The early Buddhist ideal of kingship, as evident in the concept of the *cakkavatti* outlined in tales like the Mahāsudassana Sutta in the Pāli Canon, was one based on non-violence. The *cakkavatti* or the Universal Monarch tours the earth accompanied by his army and wins over the subservience of petty rulers through a mixture of eloquent expositions of the doctrine and pressure, without resort to violence.[11] Historical attempts to follow this ideal were few and, as would be expected, kings in actual life offered a distinct contrast to this ideal. Hence, though many kings associated closely with the Buddha and were his ardent patrons, politics (*khatta-vijjā*) is treated in the Brahmajāla Sutta as a "low science" (*tiracchāna vijjā, hīna-vijjā*).[12] According to the Mahābodhi Jātaka, politics represented the single-minded quest for power unhampered by codes of ethical conduct: Teachers of politics encouraged followers even to murder their own parents for the sake of self-advancement.[13] The attitude that the *saṅgha* should adopt towards the warrior-king, the manipulator of the foremost apparatus of organized violence in society, would have been a problem which rankled in the mind of many a monk in the formative phase of the relationship between the *saṅgha* and the state in Sri Lanka.

Placed in this context, it is possible to see in the myth of the first visit of the Buddha an attempt at mediating a contradiction. In the myth the Buddha is also a conqueror. His use of supernatural powers to harass the *yakkhas* is comparable with the king's resort to violence against foes. In explaining the need for the Buddha to take such extraordinary steps it is stated that the *yakkhas* were incapable of understanding the truth and were opposed to the *sāsana* and, therefore, had to be removed from the island.[14] Thus the myth presents an ethical principle distinct from those found in the Pāli Canon: violence is permissible in the interest of the *sāsana*, against those who do not understand the "true doctrine" and are opposed to it. This re-interpretation of the attitude towards violence facilitates the mediation of the contradiction between the ethical ideal and the practical behaviour of kings.

The story of Duṭṭhagāmaṇī in the *Mahāvaṃsa* is a clear instance of this new interpretation being invoked to justify the actions of a king. This king is credited with the construction of some of the principal Buddhist monuments at Anurādhapura. He was also a warrior whose campaigns for the unification of the island in the second century B.C. wrought great carnage. There was an obvious difficulty in presenting this successful warrior as a Buddhist hero. The mediation of this contradiction follows the same lines as in the myth. The campaigns of Duṭṭhagāmaṇī, the chronicle asserts, were not for personal glory but for the establishment of the *sāsana*, to make "the *sāsana* shine forth."[15] According to the chronicle, Duṭṭhagāmaṇī was overcome with remorse at the end of his campaigns when he recalled that a multitude of people had been killed. A group of *arahants* from Piyaṅgudīpa discerned his thoughts and came through the air to assure him that, though millions had fallen during his campaigns, he could be certain of being born in heaven. Only "one and a half" human beings could really be deemed to have been slain by him since of all those who had been slain only one had practiced the "five precepts" while another had uttered the *tisaraṇa* – the three statements professing the seeking of refuge in the Buddha, the *dhamma* and the *saṅgha.* All others were "unbelievers and men of evil life" and were not to be esteemed more than beasts. "But as for thee," the *arahants* exhort the king, "thou wilt bring glory to the doctrine of the Buddha in manifold ways; therefore cast away care from thy heart, O ruler of men."[16] The inconvenient question, whether from the Buddhist point of view the killing of men "who were like beasts" was not in itself an "evil action" is left unraised and, therefore, unanswered. It is significant that the chronicler closes the chapter by speaking of the "evil" arising from the murder of human beings through greed, thereby emphasizing the distinction between killing through greed and killing in the interest of the *sāsana.*[17] Later on, at the end of the chapter which describes the demise of Duṭṭhagāmaṇī, it is stated that he entered the Tusita heaven immediately after he left this world. The chronicler further predicts that he is destined to be the chief disciple of Metteyya, the future Buddha.[18] Thus the story of Duṭṭhagāmaṇī echoes the idea embodied in the myth of the first visit of the Buddha in implying that violence is not invariably associated with evil, and that a distinction has to be drawn between violence committed in the interest of the *sāsana* and that motivated by greed. The message is spelt out quite clearly: one who commits violence for the glory of the *sāsana* incurs no evil.

The myth of the first visit of the Buddha and the story of Duṭṭhagāmaṇī in the *Mahāvaṃsa* present a new principle which enabled a distinction to be drawn between permissible and non-permissible types of violence. This principle which is not found in the Pāli Canon was basic and vital for one of the most important ideas of kingship evolved in the island – the association of the king with the Bodhisattva. The term *mahāsatta*, an epithet of Bodhisattvas, is used in the *Mahāvaṃsa* to refer to Sirisaṅghabodhi who ruled in the third century A.D. This king was considered to be a paragon of virtue and a zealous patron of the faith.[19] The *Cūlavaṃsa* states that Buddhadāsa (A.D. 337-365) led the life of a Bodhisattva.[20] According to the same chronicle, Upatissa I (365-406) practiced the *dasapāramitā* – the ten principal virtues that a Bodhisattva should acquire.[21] Similarly, Aggabodhi I (571-604) and Sena I (833-853) are said to have aspired to Buddhahood.[22] By the reign of Mahinda IV (956-972), the ideas implicit in these statements seem to have reached full maturity. This king not only claims to have secured for himself "the way to *nirvāṇa*," but also speaks of the rulers of his dynasty as "the *kṣatriya* lords devoted to the Buddha, who of yore have received the assurance made by the Omniscient Lord of Sages, the pinnacle of the Sākya clan, that none but Bodhisattvas would become kings of prosperous Laṅkā."[23] It appears from this statement that by this time it was believed that indeed everyone who became king in Sri Lanka was a Bodhisattva. The elevation of the king to one of the highest positions that a layman could aspire to in the Buddhist social order represents an advanced stage in the development of the ideas of kingship in the island. It is noteworthy that the inscription bearing this statement was erected within the precincts of a monastery. In acquiescing in this idea, the *saṅgha* recognized the king as the leader of the laity in a political as well as a religious sense. Some of the kings who are described as Bodhisattvas are by no means saintly. The aspirations of Sena I to Buddhahood did not prevent him from sending his agents to India to assassinate Mahinda, a rival who was living there in exile.[24] Mahinda IV speaks with pride in his edicts about the victorious military campaigns prosecuted in his reign.[25] It was thus possible to recognize a future Buddha in a king who wielded the sword with vigour and eliminated his rivals through assassination, it is quite clear that by this time the contradiction between the warrior king and the Buddhist canonical ideal of kingship had in fact been mediated.

In analyzing the function of the myth of the first visit of the Buddha as a "political charter," it is possible to discern a second major theme. The myth clearly embodies the "message" that the island of Sri Lanka belonged to the Buddha. Not only was the island presented to him by the *yakkhas*, but also he acquired it by driving them away by the force of his supernatural powers. The interesting detail about the request of the Buddha for a place to spread his rug and sit and how the rug began to expand and finally covered the whole island is reminiscent of another myth, the foundation of Carthage which Virgil refers to in the terse, almost cryptic, verses in his *Aeneid*.[26] In the Roman myth, Dido, the devoted wife of Acerbas, flees from the kingdom of her brother who, being covetous of the wealth of Acerbas, had engineered his murder. On reaching the site of Carthage, she purchases land amounting to the area covered by an oxhide. But she cuts the oxhide into thin stripes and, by this clever strategem, becomes the owner of a large extent of territory on which the fortified city of Carthage is erected. The *Mahāvaṃsa* myth seems to suggest that the Buddha acquired the lordship over the island through similar means. Thus the island had been "given by the *yakkhas*," "acquired by strategem" and also "conquered": The Buddha had acquired a complete and unchallengeable right over the island.

The political significance of the "message" that the island belonged to the Buddha becomes clear when it is examined in association with another myth in the chronicles. According to the chroniclers, Vijaya was the first king of the island. But a new lineage begins when Paṇḍukābhaya, or Pakuṇḍa of the *Dīpavaṃsa*, ascends the throne. The *Dīpavaṃsa* devotes a short chapter to present his genealogy, while in the *Mahāvaṃsa* his life-story is given in great detail. The significance of the Paṇḍukābhaya legend has been the subject of considerable speculation by modern scholars. G. C. Mendis, for instance, has emphasized the artificial nature of the legend by pointing out the similarities between it and the stories about Krishna in the *Mahābhārata* as well as Buddhist canonical tales like the Ghata Jātaka.[27] According to the *Mahāvaṃsa*, the Sākya prince Paṇḍu, son of Amitodana, heard that both his homeland and his clan would be destroyed soon. He left his homeland and founded a new kingdom on the southern side of the river Ganges. Paṇḍu had seven sons and a daughter. Bhaddakaccānā, the daughter, was famed for her beauty and had many suitors. The king put her in a ship and set her adrift on the Ganges declaring: "Whosoever can, let him take my daughter." The suitors failed to halt the ship and it finally reached the shores of Sri Lanka where Bhaddakaccānā became the queen of Paṇḍuvāsudeva, the nephew of Vijaya. On hearing that their sister was living in Sri Lanka, six of her brothers came and settled in different parts of the island. Bhaddakaccānā had ten sons and a daughter. The daughter's name was Cittā, but she came to be known as Unmādacittā "since she drove men mad by the mere sight of her beauty." Soothsayers had predicted that her son would slay her brothers. So she was made to live in a chamber built on a single pillar to which access was only through the king's bed-chamber. Dīghāyu, one of the Sākya princes who had settled in the island, had a son called Gāmaṇī. This young man saw Unmādacittā and fell in love with her. He cleverly found a means of visiting her and the result of their union was Paṇḍukābhaya.[28]

This story and the tales about the boyhood of Paṇḍukābhaya which follow it bear a remarkable similarity not only with the Ghata Jātaka and the stories about Krishna in the *Mahābhārata*, as Mendis has noted, but also with the Greek myth of Perseus.[29] But what is most relevant to the present discussion is that the myth recounted above embodies a "message" contrapuntal to the one detected in the tale of the first visit of the Buddha. The story makes it quite clear that Paṇḍukābhaya was descended, through both his mother and fathers, from Amitodana. And Amitodana, according to the chronicle, was the youngest brother of Suddhodana. Though it is not specifically stated, it is not difficult for anyone who has listened to or read the story to deduce that Paṇḍukābhaya belonged to the Sākya clan and was a great grand-nephew of the Buddha. It thus becomes understandable why Paṇḍukābhaya is given so much prominence in the *Mahāvaṃsa*: The myth makes him the first Sākya prince on the throne of Sri Lanka. The chronicle alludes to the destruction of the Sākya kingdom and the annihilation of the Sākya clan by Vidūdabha[30] and thereby seems to suggest that Paṇḍu, the great grand-father of Paṇḍukābhaya, was the only member of the clan who survived. Thus the kings of the dynasty that Paṇḍukābhaya founded were not only Sākya princes but also descendants of the sole surviving member of the Sākya clan. Hence, if the Buddha had come to Sri Lanka as a conqueror and acquired the suzerainty over the island, the descendants of Paṇḍu would be the legitimate heirs. It would thus appear that the two myths, the tale of the first visit of the Buddha and the account of the genealogy of Paṇḍukābhaya, form the "point" and "counterpoint" as it were in conveying a politically significant message. They jointly serve the function of legitimizing the claims of the first dynasty of Anurādhapura to suzerainty over the whole island.

According to the chronicles, the first dynasty of Anurādhapura came to an end with the death of Yasalālaka Tissa (A.D. 52-59) and it seems reasonable to date the appearance of the group of myths under discussion to a period before this. Since the political unity of the island is implicit in these myths, it is tempting to consider the reign of Duṭṭhagāmaṇī (161-137 B.C.) whose campaigns led to the establishment of a unified kingdom as the *terminus a quo* of this period. However, till about the tenth century there is no actual instance of a king claiming membership of the Sākya clan. It does not seem to be a mere coincidence that during a period of intense political struggle like the tenth century when the Sinhalese kings were threatened by foreign invaders as well as regional factions and other local rivals their inscriptions refer insistently to the Sākya connection. It was the scholar-king Kassapa V (A.D. 914-923) who in his Mädirigiriya inscription first claimed descent from the legendary Sākya king Okkāka.[31] The chronicles state that it was Okkāka's son Okkāmukha who founded the Sākya dynasty of Kapilavastu and that the dynasty was known as Okkākaparamparā after Okkāka.[32] In the edicts of the successors of Kassapa V the claim to membership of the Sākya clan occurs in elaborate form. A prince called Lämäni Mihindu claims to be the "incomparable ornament" of the Sākya clan and a descendant of Paṇḍukābhaya in an inscription issued in the reign of Dappula IV (924-935).[33] A more detailed claim occurs in a fragmentary slab inscription found in the grounds of the Abhayagiri monastery and dated in the seventh year of a king identified as Mahinda IV (956-972). In this record, the king is described as "the pinnacle of the illustrious Sähä (Sākya) clan, who is descended from the lineage of Okāvas (Okkāka), who has come down in the succession of the great king Sudovun (Suddhodana) and who is descended from the lineage of the great king Paḍuvasdev Abhā."[34] The claims of the Sinhalese kings that through lineal descent they had the right to be the lords of "the maiden, the isle of Laṅkā" occurs in inscriptions from the time of Kassapa V.[35] If these edicts disregarded inconvenient matters of historical detail, like the fact that these kings of the tenth century belonged to a dynasty different from the one which Paṇḍukābhaya is said to have founded, they also did violence to the details in the myth which presented Amitodana, and not Suddhodana, as the Sākya prince from whom the kings of the first dynasty of Anurādhapura were descended. Yet, descent from Suddhodana is claimed in two more records – the Polonnaruva pillar inscription of Mahinda V (982-1029) and the Dimbulāgala inscription of Sundaramahādevī, the queen of Vikramabāhu I (1111-1132).[36] It is understandable that the Sinhalese kings preferred the father of the Buddha to his uncle as their ancestor. The modification of the myth brought them closer still to the Buddha himself. These inscriptions demonstrate how the myths were invoked in order to legitimize the rights of the Sinhalese kings to rule over Sri Lanka. It was but fit and proper that the island which had been acquired by the Buddha should be ruled by his kinsmen – the members of his own lineage.

The idea that the island belonged to the Buddha has another implication. Just as much as it buttressed the rights of the Sinhalese rulers over the island, it was also amenable to the interpretation that the kingdom belonged to the *sāsana* and that the *saṅgha* as the *buddhaputra* or the spiritual offspring of the Buddha were, collectively, heirs to the island. The idea that the island belonged to the *sāsana* is specifically stated only in the Polonnaruva North Gate inscription of Nissaṅka Malla.[37] An inscription found at Anurādhapura and attributed to the reign of Mahinda IV is useful in this connection. It describes both the king and the queen as belonging to the lineage of the Sākya king Okkāka and states that the kings of Sri Lanka were "wont to don the white scarf to serve the great community of monks on the very day they celebrate the coronation festival after attaining to the dignity of kingship, bestowed by the great community of monks for the purpose of defending their bowls and robes."[38] Two significant ideas are embodied in this statement. One is that the protection of the *saṅgha* and their possessions was the express duty of the king. A similar concept is found in the Polonnaruva inscription of the Veḷaikkāras. According to this record, Vijayabāhu I accepted the crown on the request of the *saṅgha* in order to defend the *sāsana*.[39] In his Hätadāge inscription Nissaṅka Malla states that the protection of the *sāsana* was a function of the kings of Sri Lanka.[40] The second idea embodied in the Anurādhapura inscription of Mahinda IV is that kingship was an office conferred by the *saṅgha.* The inscription refers, though not in very clear terms, to a ritual performed on the same day as the consecration, which emphasized this relationship between the *saṅgha* and the king. It would thus seem that the idea embodied in the myths that the island belonged to the Buddha was basic to the political ideas and the ritual pertaining to the investiture of the king reflected in the inscriptions. The myths, the political ideas and the ritual together reflect a political system in which the succession to power was based on lineal descent as well as on the concurrence of the *saṅgha* who enjoyed great prestige and wielded a profound influence in this society.

The emphasis on the function of myth as political charter in the preceding discussion does not imply that myth cannot be understood at more than one level. Myth could indeed be multi-functional, and this or that function could vary in importance according to situations and from time to time. Further, the analysis of a myth need not be limited to identifying its functions. For instance, the myths of the visits of the Buddha also underline the belief in the destiny of the island as the *dhammadīpa*, the home of the "true doctrine." The efflorescence of Buddhism in the island at a time when it was on the decline in its original home was conducive to the rise of such a belief. The *Dīpavaṃsa* and the *Vaṃsatthappakāsinī* state that soon after attaining Buddhahood, even before he rose from his seat after attaining Buddhahood, the Buddha foresaw the destiny of the island and the need for him to visit it.[41] It is also noteworthy that these tales are concerned with the sanctity of three main Buddhist shrines in different parts of the island: the *stūpa* at Mahiyaṅgana, the Rājāyatana-dhātu-vihāra in Nāgadīpa, and the *stūpa* at Kalyāni.[42] The *Dīpavaṃsa* states that during his third visit the Buddha also sanctified by his presence the sites of the Dīghavāpicetiya and the Bo-tree at the Mahāvihāra, while the *Mahāvaṃsa* adds four more places: the Sumanakūṭa and the sites of the Mahāthūpa, the Thūpārāma and the Silācetiya.[43] Another aspect of the myths is the characterization they present of three types of non-human beings: the *devas*, the *nāgas* and the *yakkhas*. Both the *devas* and the *nāgas* are presented as friends of the faith who accept the authority of the Buddha. On the other hand, the attitude towards the *yakkhas* is unmistakably hostile. The efficacy of the *paritta* incantations as a charm against the *yakkhas* is another of the "messages" that the myths convey. The *Dīpavaṃsa* states that soon after transferring the *yakkhas* to Giridīpa the Buddha recited the Metta-paritta, circumambulated the island and thus made it "protected for ever."[44] This detail is not found in the *Mahāvaṃsa*. But the *Vaṃsatthappakāsinī* takes up the theme again in stating that after transferring the *yakkhas* to Giridīpa the Buddha recited the *paritta* and thereby "established his authority." The authority of the Buddha "established on that day" is supposed to be as effective against the *yakkhas* as the flame-covered leather rug had been.[45]

While it is evident from the preceding discussion that the myths analyzed in this study could be understood and interpreted at more than one level, the justification of political dominance and of the claims of a specific dynasty to power became one of their principal functions. The myths also reveal the importance of the principle of "lineal descent" in legitimizing rights of overlordship. The analysis of myth in the present paper leans heavily, as its title suggests, on the theories of Malinowski, but it has also drawn on the theoretical work of other students of myth, in particular Lévi-Strauss. It demonstrates that some of the conceptual tools utilized in the study of myth in tribal society are useful even for the historians in the analysis of myths from more complex social formations. In literate societies witnessing a process of development leading to the emergence of the state or where the state has already come into being, myths would be to varying extents impregnated with political ideology. It would thus appear that in the study of the ancient history of South Asia historians will have to move away from their traditional methodology and pay greater attention to the study of myth as a noteworthy source of information on social and political ideology.

Notes

The author is indebted to Dr. Merlin Pieris for help with the passage quoted in footnote 26 and to Drs. H. L. Seneviratne, S. Kiribamune, and H. A. I. Goonetileke for useful suggestions. This paper was written for this volume but also appears in the *Sri Lanka Journal of the Humanities*, Vol. II, No. 1 (June 1976), 53-62.

1. Claude Lévi-Strauss, *Structural Anthropology* (London, 1969), p. 207. The relevant chapter was published as a separate paper in the *Journal of American Folklore*, Vol. 78, No. 270, 1955, pp. 428-444.
2. Bronislaw Malinowski, "Myth in Primitive Psychology," in *Magic, Science, and Other Essays* (New York, 1978), p. 145.
3. William Knighton, *The History of Ceylon* (London, 1845), pp. 8-11.
4. L. E. Blazé, *A History of Ceylon for Schools*, 10th edition, 1937, p. 8.

5. See, for instance, S. Paranavitana, *University of Ceylon History of Ceylon*, Vol. I, Pt. 1, 1961, p. 95.
6. *Dv.* Chapter 1.
7. *Mv.* 1.17-43.
8. *Vaṃsatthappakāsinī*, ed. G. P. Malalasekera (London, 1935), Vol. I, pp. 71-82.
9. *ayaṃ dīpo iminā mahesakkena devarājena pariggahito hutvā parahatthagato ahosi. Vap.*, Vol. I, p. 79.
0. *Saṃyutta Nikāya*, ed. Léon Feer (London, 1960), Vol. I, pp. 213-215; *Sāratthappakāsinī*, ed. F. L. Woodward (London, 1929), Vol. I, pp. 316-337.
1. *Dīgha Nikāya*, ed. T. W. Rhys Davids and J. E. Carpenter (London, 1947), Vol. II, pp. 169-199.
2. *Dīgha Nikāya*, Vol. I, p. 9.
3. *mātāpitaropi māretvā attameva attho kāmetabbo.* See *The Jātaka*, ed. V. Faüsboll (London, 1963), Vol. V, p. 228.
4. *te pana saccapativedhāya abhabbā sāsanassa avaruddhā. tato te mayā nīharitvā giridīpamhi vāsetabbā. Vap.*, Vol. I, p. 67.
5. *Mv.* 25.2-3, 17.
6. *Mv.* 25.101-111.
7. *Mv.* 25.116.
8. *Mv.* 32.75-83.
9. *Mv.* 36.73-97.
0. *Cv.* 37.109.
1. *Cv.* 37.180.
2. *aggabodhigatāsayo Cv.* 42.1; *buddhabhūmigatāsayo Cv.* 50.65.
3. *nobōsat-hu norajvanhayi sähäkula kot savaniya muniraj-hu. (viyāraṇ) lad . . . EZ,* Vol. I, p. 237 *ll.* B52-53 and p. 240.
4. *Cv.* 50.4.
5. See, for example, *EZ*, Vol. I, p. 33 *ll.* 5-6.
6. *The Aeneid of Virgil*, trsl. C. Day Lewis (London, 1954), p. 21. Justin gives a much more detailed account of the incident: *. . . itaque Elissa delata in Africae sinum incolas loci eius adventu peregrinorum mutuarumque rerum commercio gaudentes in amicitiam sollicitat, dein empto loco, quoad profisceretur, reficere posset, corium in tenuissimas partes secari iubet atque ita maius loci spatium quam petierat occupat, unde postea ei loco Byrsae nomen fuit . . . Historicae Philippicae,* 1802, n.p., p. 198.
7. G. C. Mendis, "The Mahābhārata Legends in the Mahāvaṃsa," *Journal of the Ceylon Branch of the Royal Asiatic Society*, New Series, Vol. V, 1956, pp. 81-84.
8. *Mv.* 8.18-19.27.
9. Apollodorus II.2.1,4 and Pausanias II.16.2,25.6. See William Smith, *Dictionary of Greek and Roman Biography and Mythology* (London, 1867), Vol. I, p. 14 and Vol. III, p. 205.
0. G. P. Malalasekera, *Dictionary of Pāli Proper Names*, Vol. II, pp. 171, 857.
1. *EZ*, Vol. II, p. 30 *ll.* 6-8.
2. *Mv.* Chapter 2.
3. *paḍu abhā naranind-hu parapuren ā . . . sähä kulaṭ ektalā ṭikvä siṭi . . . EZ*, Vol. III, pp. 222-223 *ll.*A17-B1, B15-17.
4. *siribar sähä kulaṭ kot okāvas [parapuren] n baṭ sudovun maharaj-hu anva [ye] n ā paḍuvasdev abhā maharaj-hu parapuren bat . . . EZ*, Vol. III, p. 227 *ll.* 1-4 and p. 228. I have changed "Sähä clan."
5. See *EZ*, Vol. I, p. 25 *ll.* 4-5; p. 46 *ll.* 2-3; p. 117 *l.* 2; p. 130 *l.* 2; p. 246 *ll.* 2-3.
6. *EZ*, Vol. II, p. 95 *l.* 1; Vol. IV, p. 64 *ll.* A12-14.
7. *budu sasunata himi lakdivata . . . EZ*, Vol. II, p. 161 *ll.* B8-9.
8. *tumā pay sivur rak (nubas) mahasaṅg-hu piḷiväyū rajsiri pämiṇä säṇä bisev vindna (da) vas saṅg-haṭ meheyaṭ uvasarvas (sevel) bandna . . . EZ*, Vol. I, p. 237 *ll.* 53-55. D. M. de Z. Wickremasinghe translated *tumā pay sivur* as "the bowl and robe of the Buddha." *EZ*, Vol. I, p. 240. This is inaccurate.

39. *buddhaśāsanaṃ rakṣikka vēṇḍi saṃgha-niyogattāl tirumuḍi-śudi* . . . *EI*, Vol. XVIII, p. 336 *ll.* 8-9.
40. *EZ*, Vol. II, p. 97 *ll.* 3-4.
41. *Dv.* 1.17-27; *Vap.*, Vol. I, pp. 66-69.
42. In its account of the second visit of the Buddha, the *Dv.* does not specify that the incident took place in Nāgadīpa. But it is clear from its description of the visit that it is referring to the same shrine mentioned in the *Mv. Dv.* 1.52-53, 2.52; *Mv.* 1.21-24, 47, 67-68, 75.
43. *Dv.* 2.60-61; *Mv.* 1.77-83.
44. *Dv.* 1.80.
45. *parittaṃ katvā āṇam bandhitva* . . . *taṭā pana baddha-āṇaṃ tesaṃ nisīdacammaṃ iva ahosi. Vap.* Vol. I, p. 81.

Buddhism and Royal Prerogative in Medieval Sri Lanka

Sirima Kiribamune

IT IS NOT infrequently that the question of eligibility for kingship comes up in ancient and medieval Sri Lanka. This is inherent in the case of an institution which had evolved over a period of time. The ideals of ancient and medieval Sri Lankan polity have to be gleaned from actual practices noticed in historical sources and casual references in them, for we do not have a single treatise on the political or legal institutions of this period. From the oft-repeated palace coups and wars of succession mentioned in the early chronicles of Sri Lanka, it is evident that at various times there were differences of opinion regarding eligibility for kingship. It would even seem that there were occasions when rules were adjusted to suit certain situations and persons. However, these same sources make it abundantly clear that by the twelfth century A.D. at least, if not earlier, a certain stability had been reached regarding the institution of kingship. By this time there seems to have been a definite rock-bed of accepted opinion regarding the legal status of a monarch and the pre-requisite conditions for such status. If these requirements were not fulfilled, a ruler could be denied the *abhiṣeka* or royal consecration and consequently the status of a legal monarch. In fact, these concepts have been brought into sharp focus by two clear instances of rulers who administered the country without the royal consecration, without the right to use their regnal years for purposes of official dating and without the right to issue a fresh coinage. They were Vikramabāhu I (1111-1132) and his son Gajabāhu II (1132-1153). Why had this to be so? In the answer would lie the key factors in the legitimation of royal power in medieval Sri Lanka.

Before embarking on our main quest it might be useful to place Vikramabāhu I and Gajabāhu II in their proper historical perspective, with a view to understanding the particular circumstances which led to their assumption of office. Consequent to the expulsion of the Coḷas, Vijayabāhu I (1055-1110) effected the political unification of the island. His brother Jayabāhu was the recognized heir to the throne and Vikramabāhu, the son of Vijayabāhu I, was given the title of *ādipāda* and entrusted with the administration of the province of Rohaṇa.[1] The basic assumption in this scheme was that Jayabāhu would succeed Vijayabāhu I and that Vikramabāhu would be next in the line of succession. However, this scheme was set aside by Jayabāhu's sister Mittā and her three sons, Mānābharaṇa, Kīrtiśrīmegha and Śrī Vallabha. On the death of Vijayabāhu I they placed Jayabāhu on the throne (no departure from the original scheme so far), but Mānābharaṇa and not Vikramabāhu was recognized as next in line of succession. Vikramabāhu, who naturally took objection to this, fought against Jayabāhu and the sons of Mittā and conquered Polonnaruva. In the process he lost both Rohaṇa and the province of Dakkhiṇadesa to Mānābharaṇa and his brothers, who ruled them independently of Polonnaruva. It is to this depleted kingdom of Polonnaruva that Gajabāhu later succeeded.

The above sequence of events is narrated in the *Cūlavaṃsa*, the main chronicle dealing with the history of this period. The opinion of the chronicler himself is that the recognition of Mānābharaṇa as the heir to the throne after Jayabāhu was against former custom.[2] There is no doubt that the customary law of succession was along the paternal line, but Mānābharaṇa was the sister's son of Jayabāhu. Inheritance through one's mother's brother is an essential characteristic of a matriarchal society, and such tendencies were not totally absent in Sri Lanka during this period. However, it would not have been possible to push this line of argument for the succession to the throne without precedent. Also, if mother-right was the argument in favor of Mānābharana, his claims should have been advanced over those of Jayabāhu as well. What then were the arguments in favor of Mānābharaṇa? Perhaps the more pertinent question is what were the arguments against Vikramabāhu, in spite of his natural claims to the throne? These no doubt were the same arguments used later to deny Vikramabāhu and his son Gajabāhu the status of consecrated monarchs, despite their gaining authority over Polonnaruva.

That Vikramabāhu was not consecrated is specifically stated in the *Cūlavaṃsa.*[3] Mānābharaṇa of Dakkhiṇadesa and his brothers ruling Rohaṇa are made to express the view that Vikramabāhu's position at Polonnaruva was illegal as he was not a consecrated monarch.[4] The chronicle, however, is silent on the question of Gajabāhu's consecration. He is said to have taken possession of the kingdom (*hatthagataṁ katvā*)[5] after the death of Vikramabāhu I. This does not convey the conviction that Gajabāhu's was an acceptable succession. It is perhaps worth noting that neither the *Pūjāvaliya*[6] nor the *Rājāvaliya*[7] mentions Gajabāhu II in their king-lists.

The epigraphical records of Vikramabāhu I and Gajabāhu II provide the best proof that they did not enjoy complete status as sovereign rulers. Inscriptions belonging to their reigns are invariably dated in the regnal years of Jayabāhu I, whenever it was considered necessary to do so. The regnal period of Jayabāhu can be worked out with evidence from a Tamil inscription found at Polonnaruva. According to this, the fifteenth year of Gajabāhu corresponded to the thirty-eighth year of Jayabāhu. This would leave twenty-three years for both Jayabāhu and Vikramabāhu, the intervening ruler. According to the *Cūlavaṃsa* Vikramabāhu ruled for 21 years. Thus Jayabāhu reigned for only two years. But there are inscriptions dated in the eighth,[8] twenty-third,[9] twenty-fourth,[10] twenty-seventh,[11] thirty-fifth,[12] thirty-eighth,[13] fortieth[14] and forty-third[15] years of Jayabāhu's reign. It cannot be argued that the practice may have been continued because Jayabāhu was still alive. His death is announced in the reign of Vikramabāhu,[16] but his regnal years continue to appear in inscriptions almost throughout the reign of Gajabāhu, the forty-third year of Jayabāhu corresponding to the twentieth year of Gajabāhu. Among these dates there is only one instance when the regnal year of Gajabāhu is mentioned, but that it was of doubtful validity is clear from the fact that it is preceded by a date in Jayabāhu's regnal years.[17] All this clearly indicates that both rulers lacked legal status. Vikramabāhu was denied the royal consecration according to the *Cūlavaṃsa* and there is little doubt that Gajabāhu suffered the same privation.

The kings of this period are known to have used alternately two consecratory titles, *Siri Saṅgabodhi* and *Abhā Salamevan* (Pāli – *Salāmeghavaṇṇa*; Tamil – *Calāmega*). Neither Vikramabāhu nor Gajabāhu are specifically referred to by these titles, which of course is not particularly surprising. However, the reference to a *Vikkirama Calāmega Īśvara* of *Vikkirama Calāmegapura* in an inscription[18] dated in the eighth year of Jayabāhu (this would correspond to the sixth year of Vikramabāhu) poses a problem. The practice of naming cities and temples after rulers is not uncommon in Sri Lanka and the only contemporary king with the Vikrama name was Vikramabāhu I. This would necessarily mean that Vikramabāhu was entitled to the *Salamevan* title. Vijayabāhu I has the title of *Siri Saṅgabodhi*[19] and Jayabāhu I, as was customary, used the alternate title, *Salamevan* (*Calāmega*).[20] In the normal course of events, Vikramabāhu should have had the *Siri Saṅgabodhi* title, but it would seem that he continued to use the title adopted by Jayabāhu. The only possible explanation is that an unconsecrated ruler could use the consecratory title which was last recognized, for the alternative title could only be conferred on consecration. Perhaps the title was in some way linked with the official chronological scheme and regnal periods were considered in terms of the Salamevan year or Siri Saṅgabodhi year. Thus kings whose legal status was not recognized were not only expected to use the year which was current at the time of their accession but could also use the consecratory title linked with it. This assumption must, however, remain tentative until we have direct evidence that Vikramabāhu in fact used an official title. The present evidence is of a somewhat indirect nature where a king's titles are conferred on a city and a deity, and the evidence which suggests that the king in question is Vikramabāhu I is purely circumstantial.

That Vikramabāhu and Gajabāhu did not enjoy valid legal status is further confirmed by the fact that there are no extant coin issues by either of them. Numerous coins issued by the monarchs of Polonnaruva have come to light and it cannot be assumed that the coins of these two monarchs were singled out for destruction or have escaped detection.

As far as the *de facto* position of the two rulers was concerned, it must be pointed out that the above disabilities did not seriously undermine their authority to rule. They are known to make land grants[21] which were obviously valid, their commands in this connection being referred to by the legal term *vyavasthā*. In the Kapuruväḍu Oya inscription,[22] Gajabāhu is seen enjoying all the trappings of executive authority. He sits in the *Citrakūṭamaṇḍapa* or Assembly Hall, surrounded by his ministers, performing the functions of royal office and making royal proclamations for whatever was deemed necessary. In the light of these facts the *de jure* position of Vikramabāhu and Gajabāhu becomes even more bewildering.

The qualifications for kingship are at times set out explicitly in our sources, but more often they are implicit in certain situations. The cases of Vikramabāhu and Gajabāhu could be tested against these criteria and by a process of elimination it would perhaps be possible to discover the reasons behind their predicament.

Neither Vikramabāhu nor Gajabāhu ruled over the whole island. The statement in the *Cūlavaṃsa* which compares Vikramabāhu and his contemporaries who ruled the provinces of Dakkhiṇadesa and Rohaṇa to village chiefs (*gāmabhojaka*), who did not desire the royal consecration,[23] could be taken to imply that dominion over the entire country was a necessary pre-requisite for the *abhiṣeka*. Many examples can be quoted to the contrary, but the case of Jayabāhu I alone would suffice. His legal position is in no doubt and he did not control the province of Rohaṇa. Therefore, it cannot be said that authority over a united Sri Lanka was a *sine qua non* for the royal consecration.

That a monarch, to be acceptable, should be born of royal parents of equal birth is implied in many situations noticed in the chronicles.[24] In this respect neither Vikramabāhu nor Gajabāhu could be found wanting.[25] Also they both had consorts of equal status,[26] yet another requirement for royal consecration.[27] The reasons behind the plight of these two rulers still seem elusive.

The custody of the Tooth and Alms-bowl Relics of the Buddha were fast becoming an attribute of kingship during this period, and neither Vikramabāhu nor Gajabāhu had possession of these Relics. An inscription, which can definitely be dated to the period after Vijayabāhu I and more approximately to the period of political confusion on the eve of the accession of Vikramabāhu I, states that the Tooth Relic was entrusted to a group of mercenaries known as the *Veḷaikkāras* for its protection. Those responsible for this act were the ministers of state and the monk Mugalan of the Uttaramūla.[28] According to the *Cūlavaṃsa*, the Tooth and Alms-bowl Relics of the Buddha were removed to Rohaṇa by the Buddhist monks because of the anti-Buddhist activities of Vikramabāhu.[29] It would seem that the Relics were in Polonnaruva at the time Vikramabāhu captured the throne. Whether he attempted to take custody of them and failed is a problem which cannot be settled in the present state of our knowledge. The Relics remained in the custody of the Rohaṇa rulers until they were secured by Parākramabāhu I. During the intervening period Mānābharaṇa of Rohaṇa tried to establish himself at Polonnaruva and brought the Relics with him, perhaps with the idea of buttressing his claims.[30] Later on, Parākramabāhu I waged a protracted war in Rohaṇa, a major consideration in it being the securing of the Relics. There is no doubt that during this period the custody of the Tooth and Bowl Relics of the Buddha gave added prestige and power to a ruler, but it cannot be maintained that without them the consecration of a ruler was not possible. Parākramabāhu, according to the *Cūlavaṃsa* was consecrated twice, the first time when he took over the kingdom of Polonnaruva consequent to the death of Gajabāhu[31] and the second time after he had defeated Mānābharaṇa who had challenged his position and taken temporary control of Polonnaruva.[32] It was only after both these events that he was able to secure the Relics.[33] This makes it amply clear that the absence of the Tooth and the Bowl Relics of the Buddha would not have stood in the way of the consecration of either Vikramabāhu or Gajabāhu.

In two of his inscriptions, Nissaṁkamalla (1187-1196) addresses his mind to the problem of eligibility for kingship. He, of course, is dealing with a peculiar political situation where he and his dynasty faced opposition from various factions both local and foreign, and, therefore, the rules laid down by him were no doubt tailored to meet his own situation. Nevertheless, they might shed some light on the accepted principles relating to kingship during this time. The inscribed records of Nissaṁkamalla make it quite clear that he was looking out for popularity for himself and his dynasty and therefore he might not be expected to promulgate rules and regulations which were contrary to customary practice.

The Galpota inscription of Nissaṁkamalla[34] lays down that after the death of a king, his children who held the titles of *āpa* and *mahapā* should be considered for the throne. The position is slightly different in his inscription at the north gate of Polonnaruva.[35] This opens the door to all royal princes, failing the heir to the throne (*yuvarāja*). Vikramabāhu and Gajabāhu do not stand disqualified on this score. Both inscriptions agree that in the absence of royal princes, the choice should fall on the queens. Two other points on which these two epigraphs agree are: (1) members of the Govikula should not be considered for kingship and (2) non-Buddhist rulers such as Coḷas and Pāṇḍyas (Coḷas and Keraḷas in the inscription at the north gate) should not be placed on the throne. The inscription at the north gate adds that this should be so as the country belongs to Buddhism.

There is no question that Vikramabāhu and Gajabāhu belonged to the royal family which claimed to be of the Kshatriya caste, and so the strictures placed on the Govikula should not apply to them. As for the second objection, these two rulers were neither Pāṇḍyas, Coḷas nor Keraḷas. Here one should not, however, miss the point that these people were disqualified not because they were foreign, for Nissaṁkamalla himself was a foreign prince; but because they were not Buddhists, and Sri Lanka, asserts one record, belongs to Buddhism. Could this be of any relevance to the problem at hand? Was Nissaṁkamalla only appealing to popular emotion in order to deal with a situation peculiar to his time? Or, were there time-honored strictures against non-Buddhists who attempted to gain the throne of Sri Lanka?

That kingship was closely tied up with Buddhism is a point that cannot be easily missed even by one who takes a cursory look at the sources relating to the early history of Sri Lanka. This association seems to have been of significance even for the consecration ceremony. The Jetavanārāma slab inscription of Mahinda IV[36] states that it was decreed by the Buddha that those who were not Bodhisattvas[37] will not be kings of Sri Lanka. It goes on to say that kingship was bestowed on a person by the community of bhikkhus for the purpose of defending the religion of the Buddha and that at the time of consecration the king ties a white scarf, signifying the attention he would pay to the community of monks. There is also the instance of Vijayabāhu I whose consecration took place in the hall which housed the Tooth Relic of the Buddha and he is said to have placed the throne on his head at the request of the Sangha.[38] From this evidence it would seem that Buddhist monks played a prominent part in the inauguration of a ruler. We often find the chronicles laboring the point that the king's main duty was to protect the people and Buddhism[39] and they do not tire of listing the services rendered to Buddhism by individual rulers. Similar sentiments are often expressed in the inscriptions also.[40] A statement in the *Dāṭhāvaṃsa* might also be relevant in this connection. Parakkama, the general who helped Līlāvatī to ascend the throne for the third time (1210-1211) is said to have trained (with a view to kingship) a Pāṇḍyan prince named Madhurinda in the arts and made him conversant with the doctrines of Buddhism.[41] It is very likely that this prince was not born a Buddhist and Parakkama, who was aware of the strictures imposed on non-Buddhist aspirants to the throne of Sri Lanka, tried to remedy the situation in his own way. The underlying assumption in all these statements is that the king was expected to be a Buddhist by religion. Thus Nissaṁkamalla was only emphasizing the point – no doubt in the interest of his dynasty – when he raised the cry that Pāṇḍyas, Coḷas and Keraḷas should not be considered for the throne because they were non-Buddhists.

From this arises two questions (1) were Vikramabāhu and Gajabāhu not Buddhists? (2) If so, could they have been denied consecration on this count?

Vikramabāhu was the son of Tilokasundarī, a foreign princess, chief queen of Vijayabāhu I.[42] Although there is no direct reference to her religious leanings, there are certain indications that she was perhaps not a Buddhist. The *Cūlavaṃsa* states that she broke the rule which made Buddhist monasteries places of refuge and for this offence she was deprived of all her revenues and was led out of the city by her neck. In this way the king is said to have appeased the community of monks.[43] For the chief queen to have been so disgraced in order that the monks be placated, it is very likely that she was not only a non-Buddhist but also that her actions were directed against Buddhism. Furthermore, the *Cūlavaṃsa*, while summing up the reign of Vijayabāhu I, lists the Buddhist works of the ruler and adds to it certain Buddhist monuments put up by the *yuvarāja* and by one of his daughters, Yasodharā. There is no mention of anything undertaken by his queens or his other children. In the circumstances there was every chance for Vikramabāhu to have come under the influence of his mother. If her disgrace had made any impression on his mind, he could not have harbored very kindly thoughts towards the community of Buddhist monks.

Direct evidence which confirms the above deductions is not lacking. The *Cūlavaṃsa* has a somewhat lengthy account of the privations suffered by the Buddhist monks and their monasteries at the hands of Vikramabāhu. It is said that temple lands were given over to those who were in his service and monasteries in the capital city were made the dwelling places of foreign soldiers. The wealth that had been offered to the Tooth and Bowl Relics, the king is supposed to have used as he pleased, and because of all this the monks are said to have removed the Relics to Rohaṇa.[44] Obviously they did not expect Vikramabāhu to grant due honor to the Relics. All this smacks of a non-Buddhist ruler, but for some unknown reason the *Cūlavaṃsa* is reluctant to make this admission. The furthest it goes is to say that Vikramabāhu and his associates were behaving like heretics (*titthiya tulyānaṁ*) when they harmed the Buddhist religion.

The inscriptional evidence supports the position taken up in the preceding discussion that Vikramabāhu was not a Buddhist. To cite the negative evidence first, there is no contemporary record of any Buddhist monument or even a grant to a Buddhist institution which can be credited to Vikramabāhu. On the other hand, the second inscription at Budumuttāva shows that a Śaiva temple was named after him.[45] This alone is no proof that Vikramabāhu was a Hindu, for even good Buddhists like Vijayabāhu I lent their names to Śaiva monuments.[46] Evidence of a more direct nature is found in the Kahambiliyāva slab inscription of Vikramabāhu.[47] The king's virtues and prowess are described in a number of epithets. Among them are two epithets of a religious significance – *Pārvatī-pati-dattāsir-vīra-mahā-vṛṣa*, "the heroic great bull who has been given the blessings of the husband of Pārvatī (Śiva), and *Rāja Nārāyana*, a king like Viṣṇu." Both have very clear Hindu associations. It is also significant that none of the epithets applied to Vikramabāhu in this record have the slightest connection with Buddhism. It is fairly clear from the evidence cited so far that Vikramabāhu I was not a Buddhist.

Gajabāhu I seems to have been somewhat of an eclectic person. Practising the traditional policy of toleration usually followed by the rulers of Sri Lanka, he gave his patronage to both Buddhism and Hinduism and the many records of his reign show that both these religions were freely patronized by private individuals as well. Foremost among the Buddhist devotees of his time was his mother Sundaramahādevī, the chief queen of Vikramabāhu I.[48] The king's own patronage of Buddhism is attested by contemporary records. A grant made to a Buddhist temple at Polonnaruva is the subject of a Tamil inscription.[49] Although the position is not very clear, this was possibly a royal grant, for the inscription is wound up with the statement that whoever acted contrary to its provisions would be disobeying the orders of the king. The Ruvanvälisāya also shared in the munificence of the king, being in receipt of a land grant.[50] Gajabāhu held the Buddhist Sangha in high esteem, so much so that his political rivals enlisted its support when they wished to come to terms with him. Mānābharaṇa of Rohaṇa came to Gajabāhu in the company of Buddhist monks when he wished to enter into an alliance with him.[51] Gajabāhu himself sought the help of the Sangha when he was driven to dire straits by the armies of Parākramabāhu, in order to reach a settlement with the latter.[52] The agreement itself was said to have been inscribed on a stone at Maṇḍalagiri vihāra,[53] a copy of which has been found at the Sangamu vihāra.[54]

Patronage of Buddhist temples and good relations with the Sangha do not necessarily mean that the king was a Buddhist. The only possible arguments in favor of such an assumption arise from the Sangamu vihāra inscription and the Nelubāva Pillar inscription.[55] The former, which is a political agreement between Gajabāhu and Parākramabāhu I, ends with the statement, "anyone who acts contrary to this would be going against the authority of the Triple Gem." It could be argued that the Triple Gem was invoked by the Buddhist monks, through whose active intervention this agreement was brought about. Also one of the parties to the agreement was Parākramabāhu I, an acknowledged Buddhist. The Nelubāva Pillar inscription which records a grant to the Ruvanvälisāya ends with a request to future kings to protect this grant, acquiring the merit accruing from it, as if they themselves had made the donation. These might be interpreted as sentiments peculiar to a Buddhist, but in view of the religious eclecticism of the time a Hindu ruler could very well have been conscious of the merit accruing from a donation to a Buddhist temple.

Apart from private grants to Brāhmaṇas and places of Hindu worship which can be dated in the reign of Gajabāhu II, two inscriptions bear witness to the king's own patronage of Hinduism. One of them records the setting up of a pillar as a boundary mark for the Brahmadeya village of Kantalay[56] and the other is a grant made by Gajabāhu to a certain Dāperä Rangidāge Hinābi, who made an image of Skanda and other gods for a *lakṣapūjā*.[57] The propitiation of Skanda and other attendant deities is a clear indication of the king's Śaivite leanings. The king is also credited with the patronage of Brāhmaṇas attached to the Konesvaram temple at Trincomalee in the *Takṣiṇa Kailāca Purānam*.[58]

Although the *Cūlavaṃsa* does not refer directly to Gajabāhu's religious leanings, certain statements in it seem to imply that under him Buddhism could not expect the patronage usually accorded to it by a Buddhist ruler. The chronicle does not attribute any Buddhist monuments to him. He is accused of bringing over nobles of heretical faith from abroad.[59] The rationale for the war between

Parākramabāhu I and Gajabāhu is made out to be the welfare of the people and Buddhism.[60] Even when the Buddhist monks intercede with Parākramabāhu I on behalf of Gajabāhu, they argue that Gajabāhu was old and close to death and he had no sons or brothers, and Parākramabāhu would soon have the opportunity to work for the welfare of the people and Buddhism. As this particular section of the *Cūlavaṃsa* is specially bent on eulogizing Parākramabāhu I, one cannot ignore the subjective bias of the author. The position taken up by the *Cūlavaṃsa*, however, seems to rest on something more tangible than the fertile imagination of the author. The most significant piece of evidence which supports this view is contained in the Devanagala inscription of Parākramabāhu I.[61] Here it is claimed that he waged war with Gajabāhu and Mānābharaṇa in order to restore Buddhism which had been ruined for a period of forty-two years since the death of Vijayabāhu. This is not a vague generalization of a royal bard which can be brushed aside as pure eulogy. It is a specific statement which involves a precise period, and that includes the reign of Gajabāhu II, hence its significance. Moreover, the record is dated in the twelfth year of Parākramabāhu I, which is roughly about twelve years after the death of Gajabāhu, when memories were still fresh and it is very unlikely that Parākramabāhu would have made a public statement such as this without any basis.

One other clue which suggests Gajabāhu's leanings towards Hinduism is his retirement to Gaṅgātaṭāka (Kantalay) after he had come to terms with Parākramabāhu I and settled the succession to the throne in the latter's favor.[62] After a period of long and bitter fighting, Gajabāhu had come to the end of the road as it were and whatever hopes and aspirations he had entertained earlier had to be abandoned with the recognition of Parākramabāhu as his heir. The choice of Gaṅgātaṭāka at this stage of his career might have been prompted by religious considerations. The Pālmoṭṭai Tamil inscription, which can be dated in the forty-second year of either Vijayabāhu I or Jayabāhu I, shows that Kantalay was clearly a Hindu center. According to this inscription Kantalay was called *Vijayarāja Caturvedimaṅgalam* and the Śiva temple found here was known as *Ten Kailāsam* (Southern Kailāsam).[63] *Caturvedimaṅgalam* is the term usually applied to a village granted to a corporation of learned Brahmins. That Gajabāhu had associated himself with this Brahmin settlement is known from his Kantalay inscription referred to already.[64] That this area continued with its Hindu associations much longer is proved by the Kantalay Stone Seat inscription of Nissaṁkamalla which refers to the region as Caturvedi Brahmapura.[65] An alms hall built by this ruler was named after Pārvatī, the consort of Śiva. Archaeological evidence also supports the assumption that this was a center of Śaiva worship.[66] Thus it would seem that Gajabāhu II, bereft of all hope, chose to spend his last days in a Hindu atmosphere, where he could devote his time to religious activities.

If religion was the determining factor as regards the status of Vikramabāhu I and Gajabāhu II, it should be possible to test this against other non-Buddhist rulers of Sri Lanka. However, such testing need not cover the entire dynastic history of the country, for, as pointed out at the beginning of this paper, rules and practices were liable to change from time to time. The period from Vijayabāhu I (1055-1110) to the end of the reign of Māgha (1236 A.D.) is the most relevant period for such an investigation, but unfortunately for us there is only one ruler who was definitely known to have been a non-Buddhist – this being

Māgha. There is no ambiguity about the religion of Māgha in the *Cūlavaṃsa*, which refers to him as one who held false beliefs.[67] On the basis of the arguments advanced so far, Māgha would not be entitled to the royal consecration. However, the information in the *Cūlavaṃsa* is that he was consecrated.[68] In the face of this, the entire argument falls. However, a closer examination of the *Cūlavaṃsa* shows, that this consecration of Māgha was not recognized. The consecration itself was said to have been performed by his chief warriors,[69] who had accompanied him from Kaliṅga.[70] Such a consecration would not have been very meaningful in the local context, and that it was not acceptable is patently clear from the statements of the chronicle itself where the regnal period of Māgha is referred to as a *rājantara* or interregnum.[71] The *Pūjāvaliya* speaks of Māgha's reign as the *Demaḷa arājitaya*,[72] conveying similar sentiments. Thus Māgha's reign does not seem to have been officially recognized and it would follow that the so-called *abhiṣeka* of this ruler was not legally valid. No coins of Māgha have been found and there are no inscriptions so far found which can be attributed to him. Therefore the case of Māgha seems to support the contention that kings of Sri Lanka had to be Buddhists in order to gain official recognition. These same sentiments are reiterated in the *Cūlavaṃsa* while commenting on the religious activities of Parākramabāhu II. It says that Lanka does not remain (for long) in the hands of heretical kings but it flourishes under kings of the true faith.[73] The author of the *Pūjāvaliya* comes out even more strongly in the same context when he says that it was not proper for heretical kings to rule Lanka which befits only those of the true faith. This he says is an established truth (*ekānta dharmayeka*).[74]

This then was probably the "established" law and it was perhaps this law that operated against Vikramabāhu I and Gajabāhu II. Sri Lanka was the Island of Buddhism – *Dhammadīpa* and its rulers were expected to be Buddhists. Those who were not were tolerated but grudgingly.

Notes

This is a slightly revised version of an article entitled "The Royal Consecration in Medieval Sri Lanka: The Problem of Vikramabāhu I and Gajabāhu II" sent to the *Sri Lanka Journal of South Asian Studies*, Vol. I, No. I (1976), edited by K. Indrapala and published by the Faculty of Humanities, University of Sri Lanka, Jaffna Campus, Jaffna, Sri Lanka.

Cūlavamsa (Cv.), ed. W. Geiger, Pali Text Society, London 1925, Chs. LVIII and LIX.

Ibid., Ch. LXI, v. 4.

Ibid., Ch. LXI, v. 47.

Ibid., Ch. LXI, v. 30.

Ibid., Ch. LXIII, v. 19.

Ed. A. V. Suraweera, Colombo 1961 – a thirteenth century work which has a chapter on the dynastic history of Sri Lanka.

A Sinhalese chronicle which can be dated in the eighteenth century.

S. Paranavitana, "Two Tamil Inscriptions from Budumuttāva," *Epigraphia Zeylanica (EZ)*, Vol. III, No. 33.

S. Paranavitana, "Kahambiliyāva (Kaudulu-väva) Slab Inscription of Vikramabāhu I," *ibid.*, Vol. V, No. 39. [Professor Paranavitana is mistaken in his assumption that the 23rd year mentioned in this inscription is a date in the regnal year of Vikramabāhu I. The Polonnaruva inscription cited earlier would give 23 years to both Jayabāhu and Vikramabāhu. Thus on Paranavitana's reckoning Vikramabāhu should have captured the throne in the very first year of Jayabāhu's reign. This seems highly improbable.

The *Cūlavaṃsa* assigns a 21-year regnal period to Vikramabāhu. Therefore the 23rd year should be taken as a date in the regnal years of Jayabāhu I, this being the official scheme of dating in current use.]

10. K. Indrapala, "A Pillar Inscription from Mahakirindegama," *Epigraphia Tamilica, (ET)*, Vol. I, Pt. I, No. 2.
11. D. M. de Z. Wickremasinghe, "Dimbulāgala: Māravidiye Rock Inscription," *EZ*, II, No. 34.
12. W. S. Karunaratne, "Kaṭagamuva Slab-Inscription of Mānābharaṇa," *EZ*, V, No. 11.
13. H. C. P. Bell, *Archaeological Survey of Ceylon, Annual Report (ASCAR)*, 1909, p. 27.
14. K. Indrapala, "An Agampaḍi Inscription from Hingurakdamana," *ET*, I, Pt. I, No. 4.
15. K. Kanapathi Pillai, "Mānkanai Inscription of Gajabāhu II," *University of Ceylon Review*, XX, No. I, pp. 12 ff.
16. *Cv.*, Ch. LXIII, v. 1.
17. *ASCAR*, 1909, p. 27.
18. *EZ*, Vol. III, No. 33.
19. D. M. de Z. Wickremasinghe, "Ambagamuva Rock Inscription of Vijayabāhu I," *EZ*, II, No. 35.
20. K. Kanapathi Pillai, *op. cit.*
21. *EZ*, Vol. V, Nos. 38 and 39.
22. *Ibid.*, No. 38.
23. *Cv.*, Ch. LXIV, vv. 33-35.
24. *Ibid.*, CH. XXXVIII, vv. 1-2 and v. 80 ff.
25. *Ibid.*, Ch. LIX, vv. 29-32; *EZ*, Vol. II, No. 34.
26. *EZ*, Vol. II, No. 34; *Cv.*, Ch. LXVI, vv. 146-9.
27. *Mahāvaṁsa*, ed. W. Geiger, Pali Text Society, London, 1934, Ch. VII, v. 47; Ch. VIII, vv. 17-27.
28. D. M. de Z. Wickremasinghe, "Polonnaruva: Slab Inscription of the Velaikkāras," *EZ*, II, No. 40.
29. *Cv.*, Ch. LXI, vv. 54-61.
30. *Ibid.*, Ch. LXX, v. 310.
31. *Ibid.*, Ch. LXXI, vv. 19-32.
32. *Ibid.*, Ch. LXXII, vv. 311-329.
33. *Ibid.*, Ch. LXXIV, v. 126.
34. D. M. de Z. Wickremasinghe, "Polonnaruva: Galpota Slab Inscription," *EZ*, Vol. II, No. 17.
35. D. M. de Z. Wickremasinghe, "Polonnaruva: Slab Inscription at the North Gate of the Citadel," *EZ*, II, No. 28.
36. D. M. de Z. Wickremasinghe, "Jetavanārāma Slab Inscription of Mahinda IV," *EZ*, I, No. 20.
37. Persons destined to be Buddhas.
38. D. M. de Z. Wickremasinghe, *EZ*, II, No. 40.
39. *Cv.*, Ch. LXXX, vv. 9-14.
40. D. M. de Z. Wickremasinghe, "Polonnaruva: Slab Inscription of Sāhasamalla," *EZ*, II, No. 36.
41. Ed. Uduwe Narada, Colombo 1946, Canto I, vv. 4-8.
42. *Cv.*, Ch. LIX, vv. 29-32.
43. *Ibid.*, Ch. LX, vv. 54-55.
44. *Ibid.*, Ch. LXI, vv. 54-61.
45. *EZ*. Vol. III, No. 33.
46. S. Paranavitana, "A Tamil Slab Inscription from Palamoṭṭai," *EZ*, IV, p. 194.
47. *EZ*, Vol. V, No. 39.

Ibid., Vol. II, No. 34.

ASCAR, 1909, p. 27.

W. S. Karunaratna, "The Nelubāva Pillar Inscription," *EZ*, VI, Pt. I, No. 23.

Cv., Ch. LXX, vv. 179-82.

Ibid., vv. 327-330.

Ibid., Vol. VI, No. 23.

S. Paranavitana, "Sangamu Vihāra Rock Inscription," *EZ*, IV, No. 1. .

EZ, VI, Pt. I, No. 23.

K. D. Swaminathan, "An Inscription of Gajabāhu II," *Ceylon Historical Journal*, Vol. X, Nos. 1-4, 1960-61.

EZ, Vol. V, No. 38. The *laksapūjā* is the same as *laksa-arcanā*. Offerings are made to the accompaniment of the recital of a lakh of names of the god. This figure is made up by the repetition of the *sahasranāma* a hundred times. "A Study of Śaivism of the Epic and Puranic Periods." Unpublished Ph.D. thesis, K. Kailasanatha Kurukkal, Poona, 1960, p. 635.

Ed. P. P. Vaittiyalinka Tecikar, 1916, vv. 95-97.

Cv., Ch. LXX, vv. 53-55.

Ibid., vv. 210 and 248.

EZ, Vol. III, No. 34.

Cv., Ch. LXXI, v. 1.

EZ, Vol. II, No. 42.

See footnote 56.

D. M. de Z. Wickremasinghe, "Kantalai Gal-āsana Inscription of Kīrti Nissaṁkamalla," *EZ*, II, No. 42.

EZ, Vol. IV, pp. 191-192.

Cv., Ch. LXXX, v. 56.

Ibid., v. 73.

Ibid.

Ibid., vv. 59-60.

Cv., Ch. LXXXI, vv. 1 and 31; LXXXIV, v. 7; LXXXVII, v. 46.

Ch. 34, p. 785.

Cv., Ch. LXXXII, v. 9.

Ch. 35, p. 787.

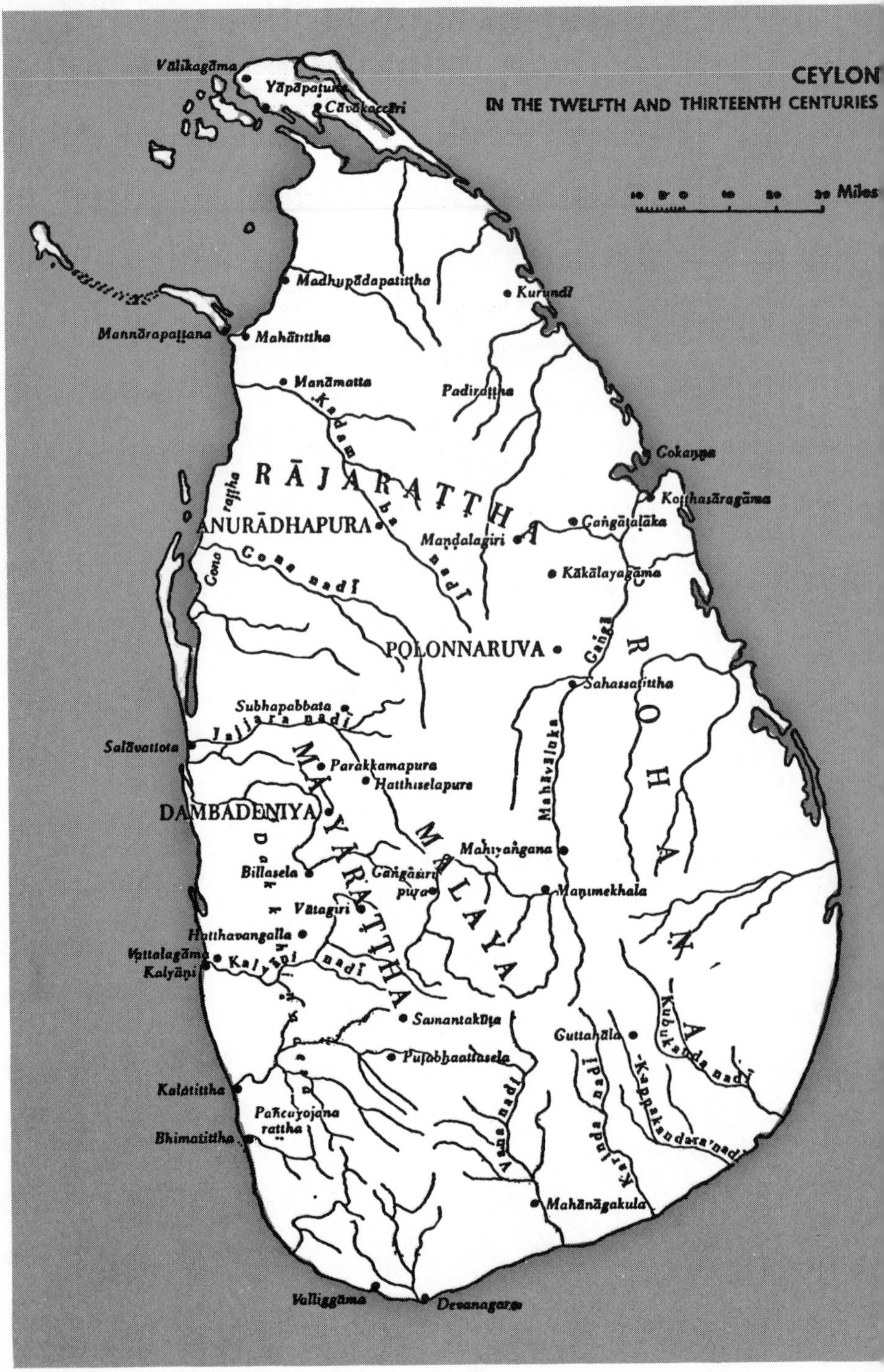
CEYLON
IN THE TWELFTH AND THIRTEENTH CENTURIES
Miles
Vālikagāma
Yāpāpaṭuna
Cāvākaccāri
Madhupādapatittha
Kurundī
Mannārapaṭṭana
Mahātittha
Manāmatta
Padiraṭṭha
Kadamba nadī
Gokaṇṇa
RĀJARAṬṬHA
Koṭṭhasāragāma
ANURĀDHAPURA
Maṇḍalagiri
Gaṅgātaḷāka
Kākālayagāma
Gona raṭṭha
Gona nadī
POLONNARUVA
Gaṅgā
Sahassatittha
ROHAṆA
Subhapabbata
Jajjara nadī
Salāvattota
MAYĀRAṬṬHA
Parakkamapura
Hatthiselapura
DAMBADENIYA
MALAYA
Mahāvāluka
Mahiyaṅgana
Billasela
Gaṅgāsiripura
Maṇimekhala
Vātagiri
Hatthavangalla
Vattalagāma
Kalyāṇi
Kalyāṇi nadī
Samantakūṭa
Guttahāla
Kubukanda nadī
Puṇṇabhaattasela
Kalatittha
Pañcayojana raṭṭha
Bhimatittha
Valave nadī
Karinda nadī
Kappakandara nadī
Mahānāgakula
Valligāma
Devanagara

The Polonnaruva Period (ca. 993-1293 A.D.): A Thematic Bibliographical Essay

Bardwell L. Smith

WHILE SRI LANKA (Ceylon) experienced invasions from South India several times in its long history (foreign rule lasting 66 years in the second century B.C.), Sinhalese political history turned a corner in the reign of Kassapa V (914-923), beginning its involvement more deeply than ever in struggles abroad. Siding with a former enemy, the Pāṇḍyas, with whom they had been at war twice in the previous century, Kassapa launched on a policy of resistance to the emerging Cōḷa kingdom, setting into motion an era whose polity and economic changes were irreversible. While no single step in this development was responsible, the politics of Ceylon and South India had become so increasingly intertwined throughout the preceding hundred years that by the early tenth century internal conflicts within Ceylon were all but inseparable from what was happening on the continent. Whether cause or effect, dynastic entanglements abroad entailed larger numbers of often recalcitrant mercenaries (most were foreign themselves), repeated internecine struggles among Sinhalese nobility complicated by relations with Pāṇḍyans and Kaliṅgas (with frequent involvement by bhikkhus, notably that of the Paṃsukūlin sect of the Abhayagirivihāra), and, above all, threats to fundamental unity by continuing tensions between the court and factions based within Rohaṇa to the south.

Though the long Anurādhapura period (third century B.C. to tenth century A.D.) had its own share of problems, the complexity of developments leading to the decline of Anurādhapura, the conquest and occupation by the Cōḷas in 993, and the establishment of their capital at Polonnaruva (Pulatthinagara) issued in a phase of Sinhalese history whose configurations lasted over five centuries. While seemingly under the shadow of Anurādhapura, the latter being the capital for more than a millenium before, Polonnaruva became in all respects the political and ceremonial center of the nation when the original capital was vacated. In a variety of ways it embodied a cultural and political complex, even when occupied by enemy forces; it became a stage of history which was both in significant continuity with the past and finally, through the infusion of new elements and the structural transformation of society, was markedly discontinuous with old ways of life. Polonnaruva and the culture at large underwent a change from being essentially orthogenetic in character to a

---

*While the principal focus of this essay is the Polonnaruva period, many references dealing with other periods of Ceylonese history are provided which help one to understand the tenth through the thirteenth centuries. Also, as will be stressed later, this includes a number of recent anthropological studies, which unquestionably illuminate factors in the basic process of religious assimilation, a process which may be observed throughout Ceylon's history but which was especially interesting in the Polonnaruva period.

stage of being not yet heterogenetic but a precarious combination of diverse elements, some of which were incorporated into a new synthesis, others which ultimately were rejected. At stake throughout this transformation was the nature of Sinhalese identity. The encounter with changing religious, intellectual, political and economic forces from within and abroad was both intense and relatively rapid. Responses ranged from confusion and indecisiveness to ones which were bold and powerful. The interpretation of these forces and of responses to them is far from simple. Even the dating of the period can be argued. As early as the late seventh century kings made Polonnaruva their base from time to time, though Anurādhapura remained the capital, in fact and/or symbolically, until its final collapse with the Cōḷa occupation. At the other end of the period one may date Polonnaruva's demise with the emergence of successful resistance out of Māyāraṭṭha to another invader, the Kaliṅga ruler Māgha (1215-1236), and the beginning of the Daṁbadeṇiya, Yāpahuva and Kuruṇāgala period (1232-1341). And, yet, it is clear that Polonnaruva retained its symbolic hold upon the Sinhalese imagination through Parākramabāhu III's reign (1287-1293), when it succumbed to a host of forces moving the base of operations and the critical mass of Sinhalese population to the southwest.

The present essay points to one among many ways to understand the main forces at work in the Polonnaruva period. It was written as a bibliographic counterpart to another essay published elsewhere, entitled "Polonnaruva as a Ceremonial Complex: Sinhalese Cultural Identity and the Dilemmas of Pluralism," in which the same four approaches to this theme of identity and pluralism in tension are explored more fully.[1] Both essays were intended to be suggestive, to raise more questions than they settle. The *first* of the approaches inquires into the political and socio-economic developments which were fundamental to this three-hundred-year period and to see what implications these had for Polonnaruva as well as other regions of the country. The *second* approach is to examine the bases for legitimizing authority within this era. What alternative concepts of kingship emerged out of this changed political context and were these in continuity with notions about legitimacy which had characterized the Anurādhapura period? *Thirdly*, as part of the response toward cultural and social pluralism, it is important to examine how the Buddhist Sāsana in Ceylon dealt with forms of Mahayana and Mantrayana which were especially strong in the early Polonnaruva period and in the century or two before. And, throughout the period, with the vital bhakti movements within Hinduism, not to mention the continuing elements of folk religious belief and practice. *Finally*, both in relation to new forms of religious expression and to the whole phenomenon of a ceremonial complex, it is pertinent to examine developments in rite, symbol and cosmology. Again, to what degree are these essentially continuous with traditional formulations of reality, as expressed in the Dhammadīpa mode, and to what degree are they new departures? These four sections will be preceded by one which deals with the basic source material that is available for a study of this period.

I. Historiographical Problems and Sources

For specialists on various periods in Sinhalese history source materials in Sanskrit, Pāli, Sinhalese, and various South Indian languages (not to mention earlier inscriptional materials in Brāhmī script) remain central for serious research. For the non-specialist studying this important period of Sinhalese history, yet untrained in these languages, as well as for the specialist there is a wealth of material written in English and an increasing number of translations from Pāli and Sinhalese. While dozens of bibliographies include entries on Polonnaruva life and institutional history, none supplies the reader with a carefully selected, annotated, and at the same time reasonably comprehensive sample. Without question, the most helpful systematic guide to the entire scope of materials published on Ceylon in Western languages from the sixteenth century to the present is the three-volume work of H. A. I. Goonetileke entitled *A Bibliography of Ceylon* (Zug, Switzerland: Inter Documentation Company, 1970 and 1976). This is a basic resource guide to published and unpublished materials on all aspects of culture in every period of Ceylonese history. Goonetileke has also prepared a number of annotated bibliographies on special topics. While all of them deal with the various periods of history, three may be mentioned here: (1) "A Bibliography of Ceylon Coins and Currency: Ancient, Mediaeval and Modern," *Ceylon Journal of Historical and Social Sciences*, Vol. 6, No. 2 (July-December 1963), 187-239; (2) "Writings on Ceylon Epigraphy: A Bibliographical Guide," *Ceylon Historical Journal*, Vol. 10, Nos. 1-4 (July 1960-April 1961), 171-207; and (3) *The Art and Architecture of Ceylon: A Bibliographical Guide to Literature in the Western Languages* (1958, unpublished), xxv, 252 leaves. In Volume I of his work, *A Bibliography of Ceylon*, see also his select list of bibliographical sources and periodicals on pages xxxi-lxiv and his annotations of reference works (including manuscripts and printed books in South Asian and Western languages, indexes to periodicals, and other bibliographies) on pages 10-53. One further bibliographical guide is pertinent, namely, an essay by Sirima Wickramasinghe (afterwards Sirima Kiribamune) entitled "The Sources for a Study of the Reign of King Parākramabāhu I," *Ceylon Historical Journal*, Vol. IV, Nos. 1-4 (July and October 1954 and January and April 1955), 169-182.[2] In this she deals with literary (historical and non-historical); archeological (epigraphic, monumental, and numismatic); and secondary sources. It is the best single introductory guide to the study of this reign.

As implied before, in order to understand what was taking place within the Polonnaruva period it is necessary to see that era in relationship to the long classical period of Ceylonese history during which Anurādhapura was the capital. Without question, the most valuable survey from pre-history to the coming of the Portuguese in 1505 is the two-volume *University of Ceylon History of Ceylon* (Colombo: Ceylon University Press, 1959 and 1960) under the general editorship of H. C. Ray.[3] This important work, now out of print, deals with political and cultural history and provides a synoptic view of this long period of nearly two millenia. As a necessary supplement to this material one should also consult several works by K. A. Nilakanta Sastri: (1) *The Pāṇḍyan Kingdom from the Earliest Times to the Sixteenth Century* (London, 1929); (2) *The Cōḷas*, Volumes I and II (Madras: University of Madras Press, 2nd edition, 1955); and (3) *A History of South India from Prehistoric Times to the Fall of Vijayanagar*, 3rd edition (London: Oxford University Press, 1966).

Before mentioning the sizeable number of specialized histories, both published volumes and doctoral dissertations, the primary source material must be stressed. A large body of extant literature exists in chronicle and commentarial form, not to mention the Buddhist Pāli canon itself and Buddhist Sanskrit texts which influenced the Sāsana in Ceylon. Though these chronicles and commentaries are didactic in nature, they represent an immense store of information about the life and culture of this society. This material has been systematically studied and much of it is now translated into English. While not the place to discuss this literature, mention must at least be made of the following: (1) *The Dīpavaṃsa, an Ancient Buddhist Historical Record*, edited and translated by Hermann Oldenberg (London: Williams and Norgate, 1879), which remains the only reliable translation and is to be preferred over the *Dīpavaṃsa*, translated, edited, and with an introduction by B. C. Law, published in the *Ceylon Historical Journal*, Vol. VII, Nos. 1-4 (July and October 1957 and January and April 1958); (2) the *Mahāvaṃsa*, translated and an introduction by Wilhelm Geiger (London: Luzac & Company, Ltd., reprinted in 1964); and (3) the *Cūlavaṃsa*, Parts I and II, translation and introduction by Wilhelm Geiger (Colombo: Ceylon Government Information Department, 1953). These Pāli chronicles may be studied endlessly for insight into the nature of religious and secular history in Lanka, but those portions which are particularly pertinent to understanding the Polonnaruva period are from Chapter 50 in Part I of the *Cūlavaṃsa* through Chapter 90 in Part II. The former picks up the story in the reign of Sena I (833-853), who suffered a severe but not lasting defeat by the Pāṇḍyans, and the latter contains the denouement of Polonnaruva with the demise of Parākramabāhu III in 1293. These four hundred pages are an invaluable record for the social and cultural historian even though more than half deal with the saga of Parākramabāhu I and thereby slights long periods of time. Though not yet translated into English, the *Vaṃsatthappakāsinī* or *Mahāvaṃsa Tika* should be mentioned. It is a commentary on the *Mahāvaṃsa*, variously attributed to a period ranging from the seventh to the twelfth century A.D., and has been edited by G. P. Malalasekera for the Pali Text Society.

Among scholarly works on this material the following are noteworthy: (1) G. P. Malalasekera, *The Pāli Literature of Ceylon* (Colombo: M. D. Gunasena & Co., Ltd., 1958), examines the full sweep of this literature from the writing down of the canon in the reign of Vaṭṭagāmaṇī (89-77 B.C.) up to the modern period; (2) E. W. Adikaram, *Early History of Buddhism in Ceylon* (Colombo: M. D. Gunasena & Co., Ltd., 1953), focuses on the state of Buddhism as portrayed in the Pāli commentaries, or aṭṭhakathās, of the fifth century A.D.; (3) Wilhelm Geiger, *Pāli Literature and Language* (Delhi: Motilal Banarsidass, 1968), a reprint of the 1943 authorized English translation by B. Ghosh (University of Calcutta Press) of *Pāli, Literatur und Sprache* (Strassburg: K. J. Trübner, 1916), whose first section is still a very useful survey of information on Pāli literature including works from Ceylon; (4) Bimala Churn Law, "Pāli Chronicles," *Annals of the Bhandarkar Oriental Research Institute*, Vol. 13 (1931), 250-299, surveys the major works of this kind from the *Dīpavaṃsa* of the fourth century to the Burmese *Sāsanavaṃsa* of the nineteenth; (5) Bimala Churn Law, *A History of Pāli Literature*, 2 volumes (London: Kegan Paul, Trench, Trübner and Co., Ltd., 1933), reprints the article on the chronicles and also discusses Pāli literary pieces in Vol. II, 517-596, 611-629; (6) Bimala Churn Law, *On the Chronicles of Ceylon* (Calcutta: Royal Asiatic Society of

Bengal, 1947); and (7) G. C. Mendis, "The Pāli Chronicles of Ceylon," *University of Ceylon Review*, Vol. 4 (October 1946), 1-24, examines scholarly opinion about them since 1879 and judges the approach of Geiger to be the most reliable. A recent publication of considerable importance is the volume of collected essays of Wilhelm Geiger, *Kleine Schriften zur Indologie und Buddhismuskunde*, edited by Heinz Bechert (Wiesbaden: Franz Steiner Verlag, 1973), which contains a complete bibliography of Geiger's writings, indices, as well as articles published in older journals which are sometimes difficult to obtain. This collection includes Geiger's article, "The Trustworthiness of the Mahāvaṃsa," originally published in the *Indian Historical Quarterly*, Vol. VI, No. 2 (June 1930), 205-228. As for the historiographical material, the best and most detailed study is still that by Wilhelm Geiger, *The Dīpavaṃsa and Mahāvaṃsa and their historical development in Ceylon* (Colombo, 1908), the original German version of which is W. Geiger, *Dīpavaṃsa and Mahāvaṃsa und die geschichtliche Überlieferung in Ceylon* (Leipzig, 1905), which is a study of the Pāli chronicles followed by a survey of the Sinhalese sources and is in no way replaced by other studies available thus far.

Three recent essays are more directly pertinent to the theme of this bibliography in trying to assess the sort of historiographic tradition created in the *Mahāvaṃsa*, as well as in its continuation, the *Cūlavaṃsa*, a tradition which "is not a dead relic of the past but continues more than ever to inspire a people, determine their attitudes and ideals, and to some extent fashion their conception of history." With these words L. S. Perera begins an important analysis of "The Pāli Chronicles of Ceylon," in C. H. Philips, ed., *Historians of India, Pakistan and Ceylon* (London: Oxford University Press, 1961), 29-43. A second essay, by Heinz Bechert, "The Beginnings of Buddhist Historiography: *Mahāvaṃsa* and Political Thinking," seeks to examine the motivation of the earliest historiographers and to raise important questions about the implicit cultural and political ideology.[4] Another essay along similar lines looks at the origins of this ideology and at the earliest Sinhalese prototype; see Alice Greenwald, "The Relic on the Spear: Historiography and the Saga of Duṭṭhagāmaṇī."[5] Also of importance, though not yet published, is the doctoral dissertation by Frank Perera, "The Early Buddhist Historiography of Ceylon" (accepted by the Phil. Fak., University of Göttingen, 1974, 221 pp.), which discusses at length the problems of Buddhist historiography in Ceylon, with an extensive survey of the history of studies in this field.

While several other chronicles exist, three in English translation are particularly germane to this study. In the period of intensified contact between Ceylon and South India just prior to and throughout the Polonnaruva period the influence of Sanskritic literature came into serious vogue.[6] Three Pāli texts, translated into English, exist as important supplements to the main *Mahāvaṃsa/Cūlavaṃsa* account of this age. The first is the *Dāṭhāvaṃsa*, edited and translated by Bimala Charan Law (Lahore: Moti Lal Banarsi Das, 1925), which is an account of the Tooth Relic of the Buddha from its Indian origins to its arrival in Ceylon during the reign of Kitti Sirimeghavaṇṇa (301-328). An earlier English translation of this text was done by Mutu Coomāra Swāmy. See *The Daṭhāvansa; or, The History of the Tooth-Relic of Gotama Buddha* (London: Trübner and Co., 1874). Traditionally ascribed to the year 310 A.D., it was written in Sinhalese by an unknown author and then translated about

1200 into Pāli by Mahāthera Dhammakitti, a disciple of the renown Sāriputta. Though not dealing with events beyond the fourth century, the chronicle's reappearance in its late twelfth or early thirteenth century Pāli version underscores the continuing and even growing influence of the relic both politically and devotionally. This fact will be explored subsequently in the essay. Mention should be made of *A Manual of Buddhist Historical Traditions (Saddhamma-Saṁgaha)*, a non-canonical Pāli work, whose compilation was ascribed to Dhammakitti and which was translated into English by Bimala Churn Law (Calcutta: University of Calcutta, 1941). This account is essentially about the compiling and writing of the Pāli canon and of its commentarial literature from the Buddha's Parinibbāna to the twelfth century in Ceylon. Pages 83-89 especially deal with the time of Parākramabāhu I.

One generation or more later there appeared a Pāli text, the *Thūpavaṃsa*, attributed to Vācissaratthera, who may be placed some time between 1236 and 1270. This figure had at his disposal an earlier Pāli version of this chronicle as well as a more ancient *Siṃhala Thūpavaṃsaya*. The theme is the history of the Mahāthūpa in Anurādhapura, whose construction was begun by Duṭṭhagāmaṇī toward the end of his life, though again the tale begins with the vow the Bodhisatta (later Gotama Buddha) made under the Buddha Dīpaṅkara, linking this to early Buddhism in India and the enshrinement of relics, as a foreshadowing of the Buddha's association with Ceylon, i.e., the Dhamma's living reliquary. In his introduction to the English translation of this text, N. A. Jayawickrama, ed., *The Chronicle of the Thūpa and the Thūpavaṃsa* (London: Luzac and Company, Ltd., 1971), writes: "The comparative silence of Dpv. on Duṭṭhagāmaṇī is an outcome of popular tradition not meeting with the approval of the monastic chroniclers responsible for that work. The Thūpavaṃsa, on the other hand, which upholds the so-called 'priestly tradition' makes full use of the elements of the heroic epic, even to a far greater extent than Mhv., for purposes of religious edification. It is thus patently clear that in spite of all the efforts of the author to conceal the fact, the central figure in Thūp. is Duṭṭhagāmaṇī. He is the ideal hero and the ideal lay disciple." This is an important statement by Jayawickrama and he properly places this story into the *jātaka* and *apadāna* tradition, the understanding of which is crucial to an appreciation of epic figures such as Aśoka, Duṭṭhagāmaṇī, Parākramabāhu I, and others. In fact, one could go further and speculate that it was no accident that the *Thūpavaṃsa* was translated again in the mid-thirteenth century, so soon after the passing of Parākramabāhu I, whose exploits (both military and religious) could easily be compared with those of Duṭṭhagāmaṇī. As such, the Polonnaruva era was being woven not only into the fabric of classical Sinhalese history but into the wider cloth of the Dhamma.

The third chronicle of this same period is the *Hatthavanagallavihāravaṃsa*, written some time between 1247 and 1266 in the reign of Parākramabāhu II (1236-1270). This very popular text was translated twice into Sinhalese, in the fourteenth and fifteenth centuries, and represents an astute associating of the saintly king Sirisaṁghabodhi (247-249), the account of whose short reign comprises two-thirds of the text, with Parākramabāhu II, the high point of whose pious career is the miracle of the Tooth Relic described in the final chapter of this chronicle (as well as in Chapter 82 of the *Cūlavaṃsa*). The English translation of this text, rendered with copious notes and an extensive introduction, is by James d'Alwis, *The Attanagalu-vansa or The History of the Temple of Attanagalla* (Colombo, 1866). Besides these three chronicles, two others should be mentioned because of the perspective they give to the Sinhalese accounts. One is *The Sheaf of Garlands of the Epochs of the Conqueror*, which is a translation into English of the Thai Pāli text, the *Jinakālamālīpakaraṇaṁ*, by N. A. Jayawickrama (London: Luzac & Company, Ltd., 1968). This text gives considerable coverage to the Sāsana's history in Ceylon up to the coming of the Tooth Relic, as well as the bringing of a famous Sinhalese Buddha image to Siam in the fourteenth century and the pilgrimage of Thai and Burmese monks to Ceylon in 1423/4.[7] Finally, there is the nineteenth century *Sāsanavaṃsa (The History of the Buddha's Religion)*, translated by Bimala Churn Law (London: Luzac & Co., Ltd., 1952), which deals primarily with Burmese Buddhism after an initial chapter on the spread of the Sāsana from India and a second one on its development in Ceylon up to and including the time of Buddhaghosa (with scattered references beyond). Important especially as a chronicle of the king-Sangha relationship in Burma, it is not vital for an understanding of Sinhalese Buddhism.

As for more specific items of the tradition concerning the views of the earlier history of Ceylon held during the Polonnaruva period, one should also mention Herbert Günther, "Einige überlieferungsgeschichtliche Bemerkungen zum Duṭṭhagāmaṇī-Epos," *Wiener Zeitschrift für die Kunde des Morgenlandes*, vol. 49, pp. 115-125. Günther (who is none other than Herbert V. Guenther now known as a specialist in the field of Tibetan studies) discusses the peculiar way in which the story of Duṭṭhagāmaṇi was rewritten in Vedeha's *Rasavāhinī* and other contemporary sources. The *Rasavāhinī*, which was composed by Vedeha Thera in the thirteenth century, is by far the most important source on the more popular aspects of Sinhalese Buddhism of the later Polonnaruva period and should be referred to, though there is no complete translation of it in a Western language yet. However, Friedrich von Spiegel did translate the first four stories in his *Anecdota Pālica* (Leipzig 1845); some other stories from the first section were translated by Sten Konow in *Zeitschrift der Deutschen Morgenländischen Gesellschaft*, vol. 43 (1889), pp. 297 ff., by P. E. Pavolini in *Giornale della Società Asiatica Italiana*, vol. 8 (1895), pp. 179 ff., and *ibid.*, vol. 10 (1897), pp. 175 ff. The whole of Vagga II was translated by Magdalene and Wilhelm Geiger: *Die zweite Dekade der Rasavāhinī* (München: Königlich Bayerische Akademie der Wissenschaften, 1918), along with an edition of the Pāli text of this Vagga. Selected stories from the *Rasavāhinī* were translated into Danish by Dines Andersen: *Rasavāhinī, Buddhistiske Legender* (Copenhagen, 1891). In this context, the short monograph by Sten Konow, *Vedehathera* (Videnskabsselskabets Skrifter, II. Kl. 1895, No. 4, Copenhagen, 1895) on Vedeha and his times may still serve as a useful piece of information.

The other body of literary source materials is that in Sinhalese (Siṃhala). As we know, it was largely in translating Sinhalese commentaries on the Pāli canon into Māghadibhāṣā and in rendering his own masterful commentaries on the canon that occupied Buddhaghosa in the early fifth century. While those ancient Sinhalese materials no longer exist and while the earliest extant work in this language dates from the tenth century, the literature (both religious and secular) since the thirteenth century especially is extensive. The best survey to date of this material is that by C. E. Godakumbara entitled *Sinhalese*

Literature (Colombo: The Colombo Apothecaries' Co., Ltd., 1955), which traces the development mainly in prose and poetry, but also treats popular literature, scientific literature, and some modern works.[8] More recently, a useful selective translation has appeared, edited by Christopher Reynolds, *An Anthology of Sinhalese Literature up to 1815* (London: George Allen & Unwin, Ltd., 1970). Since few translations of Sinhalese religious literature exist, this publication is a welcome one. Over half of the material in this anthology deals with thirteenth century literature and thus represents great value for the student of the Polonnaruva period in its final decades. The most important texts for this purpose are the *Amāvatura*, the *Pūjāvaliya*, and the *Saddharmaratnāvaliya*. In this connection one can mention M. B. Ariyapala's *Society in Mediaeval Ceylon* (Colombo: Department of Cultural Affairs, 1956), which is a thorough description of Ceylonese society as depicted in the *Saddharmaratnāvaliya* and other thirteenth century literature. (Various sections of this book will be referred to later.)

Beyond these, two works exist, translated from Sinhalese into English, which are significant source materials. The first is *The Katikāvatas: Laws of the Buddhist Order of Ceylon from the 12th Century to the 18th Century* (München: R. Kitzinger, 1971), critically edited, translated and annotated by Nandasena Ratnapala. Katikāvatas, or codes of regulations agreed upon by the community of Buddhist monks, are first noted in the latter half of the Anurādhapura period and may be of two types: Vihāra Katikāvatas, which differ from one Vihāra to another and whose jurisdiction "did not extend beyond the boundaries of that Vihāra where they were promulgated"; and Sāsana Katikāvatas, which apply to the entire Order and whose form includes a long historical introduction linking "events from the birth of the Buddha up to the establishment of the Katikāvatas by different monarchs."[9] Of the five Sāsana Katikāvatas translated in this edition two are relevant for this bibliography, namely, the Mahā Parākramabāhu Katikāvata promulgated by Parākramabāhu I in 1165 and the Daṁbadeṇi Katikāvata established by Parākramabāhu II in 1266/7. While the monarch's role in assisting the Sangha to purify itself of corruption and disunity harks back to Aśoka and was not uncommon in Ceylon, these particular regulations, especially the first, afford major insight not only into the condition of the Order at these times but also into changes which were beginning to emerge in the king-Sangha relationship. These changes, which accented the need for unity within the community of bhikkhus and which prefigured later developments of organizational centralization, stemmed directly from political and social events of the twelfth and thirteenth centuries. The calling for order and unity within the Sangha was clearly a response to the uncertain and confused nature of the times. The other document in Siṃhala to be noted is the *Nikāya Saṇgrahawa: Being a History of Buddhism in India and Ceylon* (Colombo: H. C. Cottle, 1908), translated by C. M. Fernando, revised and edited (with introduction, analytical survey, and notes) by W. F. Gunawardhana. Written by Dhammakitti, who was Saṅgharāja in the reign of Bhuvanekabāhu V (1372-1408), this is a concise history of the Sāsana from its beginnings in India through the middle of this monarch's reign. It is especially interesting because of the focus upon heretical movements within the Sāsana and again attests to concerns about unity.

For descriptions of important literary works of the Polonnaruva and the

Daṁbadeṇi periods, see Heinz Bechert's articles on the Sinhalese works *Amāvatura, Paricchedapota, Pūjāvaliya,* and *Saddharmaratnāvaliya* and on the Pāli works *Rasavāhinī* and *Upāsakajanālaṅkāra* which are published in *Kindlers Literatur Lexikon* (Zürich: Kindler Verlag, 1965 ff.), partly in the supplement volume. In addition, see his articles on the later works *Nikāyasaṅgrahaya*, on the *Saddharmālaṅkaraya* (which is based on the *Rasavāhinī*), on the *Saddharmaratnākaraya* (fourteenth/fifteenth cent., which contains a historical chapter largely based on the *Nikāyasaṅgrahaya*), on the *Attanagaluvaṃsaya* (which is the Sinhalese version of the *Hatthavanagallavihāravaṃsa*), as well as on the *Rājāvaliya* contributed to the *Kindlers Literatur Lexikon*. All serve a useful purpose because of their detailed bibliographical references. As for the *Rājāvaliya*, this chronicle of the Sinhalese kings deserves a place in enumerating the Sinhalese historiographical works, though the available versions date from the fifteenth to the eighteenth century only (cf. C. E. Godakumbura, "Historical Writing in Sinhalese," *Historians of India, Pakistan and Ceylon*, ed. C. H. Philips, London 1961, pp. 75-81). The standard version of the *Rājāvaliya* was translated as *The Rājāvaliya: or, A Historical Narrative of Sinhalese Kings from Vijaya to Vimala Dharma Surya II*, by B. Gunasekera (Colombo, 1900).

To conclude this section on basic source materials, two other categories of works bear referring to, i.e., published works on specialized topics or periods of time and unpublished doctoral dissertations. In almost all cases these are based upon extensive research into primary materials and therefore represent important guides to the theme under discussion. In the first category five books may be singled out as especially valuable. One of the best known of these is Walpola Rahula's *History of Buddhism in Ceylon: The Anurādhapura Period, 3rd Century B.C.–10th Century A.D.* (Colombo: M. D. Gunasena & Co., Ltd., second edition, 1966). Though not extending into the period under question, it provides a fundamental survey of pre-Buddhist Ceylon, the establishment and development of Buddhism, as well as the nature of monastic and lay life up to the Polonnaruva period. A second short, but very helpful book is Tilak Hettiarachchy's *History of Kingship in Ceylon* (Colombo: Lake House Investments, Ltd., 1972), which, while stopping with the reign of Mahāsena (274-301), is the best monograph on this subject and is particularly suggestive regarding the traditional relationship between king and Sangha, providing a background against which one may see the changes of the Polonnaruva period and beyond. A work of major import is Wilhelm Geiger's *Culture of Ceylon in Mediaeval Times*, edited by Heinz Bechert (Wiesbaden: Otto Harrassowitz, 1960). Identifying the ancient period as prior to 362 A.D., Geiger deals with the post-Mahāsena period (whose dates he gives as 334-361/2), limiting his focus primarily to materials post-dating the *Mahāvaṃsa*. As such, it is complementary to Hettiarachchy's volume, though it explores a broader range of subject matter and is among the more valuable treatments of Buddhism, Hinduism and popular religion during this long period.[10] The fourth work has already been cited, namely, Ariyapala's *Society in Mediaeval Ceylon*, which examines intensively the thirteenth century in its political, religious and social aspects. It is the only thorough treatment of this subject, but it may be read in combination with Amaradasa Liyanagamage's *The Decline of Polonnaruwa and the Rise of Dambadeniya* (Colombo: Department of Cultural Affairs, 1968). These two monographs are exceedingly valuable studies of Polonnaruva

Ceylon. The latter is particularly important for an understanding of the time between 1180 and 1270, a period during which the society was undergoing changes that were fundamental for later developments.

The final category of source materials consists of doctoral dissertations, most of which were done at the School of Oriental and African Studies, University of London, between 1958 and 1970.[11] Since these works are less easily available and since I am currently working on a project that will utilize them more extensively, reference will only be made to them in passing here. They represent, nevertheless, research of immense value to the serious student of this period. The order in which they are listed is essentially chronological in terms of the subject matter covered: (1) R. A. L. H. Gunawardana, *The History of the Buddhist "Saṅgha" in Ceylon from the Reign of Sena I (833-853) to the Invasion of Māgha (1215)*, Ph.D., 1965; (2) Mudalige Karunaratna Wijetunga, *The Rise and Decline of Cōḷa Power in Ceylon*, Ph.D., 1962; (3) Gallege Sirimal Ranawella, *A Political History of Rohaṇa from c. 991-1255 A.D.*, Ph.D., 1966; (4) Wathuge Indrakirti Siriweera, *Economic Conditions of Ceylon (c. 1070-1344)*, Ph.D., 1970; (5) Sirima Wickramasinghe, *The Age of Parākramabāhu I*, Ph.D., 1958; (6) Yatadolawatte Dhammavisuddhi, *The Buddhist Saṅgha in Ceylon (ca. 1200-1400 A.D.)*, Ph.D., 1970; (7) Karthigesu Indrapala, *Dravidian Settlements in Ceylon and the Beginnings of the Kingdom of Jaffna*, Ph.D., 1965; (8) Sivasubramaniam Parthmanathan, *The Kingdom of Jaffna (c. A.D. 1250-1450)*, Ph.D., 1969; (9) W. M. Sirisena, *Ceylon and Southeast Asia: Political, Religious and Cultural Relations, A.D. 1000-1500*, Ph.D., Australian National University, 1970; and (10) K. L. Hazra, *Religious Intercourse among Theravada Countries, 11th to the 16th Centuries A.D.*, Ph.D., University of Ceylon, 1968. This list doubtlessly needs to be updated and augmented by the mention of comparable work done elsewhere. This is part of the project referred to above.

II. Political and Economic Trends – Late Anurādhapura and Polonnaruva

"The civil war of the seventh century which lasted nearly three fourths of a century had far reaching repercussions on the political history of the island. Trends that had their origin in this period of civil strife lasted throughout the late Anuradhapura and Polonnaruwa periods and only ceased to exist after the abandonment of the Raja rata. This civil war, it is true, was a dynastic struggle fought by the rival claimants to the throne with mainly mercenary troops in a limited area around the capital, but the indirect results of this period of prolonged struggle on the political conditions of the country was disastrous." This statement by B. J. Perera, in an article entitled "Some Political Trends in the Late Anuradhapura and Polonnaruwa Period," *Ceylon Historical Journal*, Vol. X, Nos. 1-4 (July 1960 to April 1961), 60-76, begins a shrewd analysis of the many complex factors leading to the decline of the ancient capital, the establishment of a new one, and the gestation of forces which altered Sinhalese society and culture markedly.

In order to assess the impact of pluralistic influences upon Sinhalese cultural identity in this period of time it is necessary to examine the social, political and economic landscape. Beyond the primary materials of a literary and inscriptional nature and beyond the secondary sources discussed earlier (see especially the *University of Ceylon History of Ceylon* and the works of Geiger, Liyanagamage and Ariyapala), there are many relevant articles, though no definitive history has yet been written. A helpful starting place is the Perera article mentioned above. His identifying of the key trends from the seventh to the tenth centuries sets the stage for perceiving later developments: namely, (i) dynastic struggles which contributed to regional factionalism, with Rājaraṭṭha, Rohaṇa and Dakkiṇadesa frequently pitted against each other; (ii) Tamil mercenaries implicated in these struggles and then neither sent back to South India nor absorbed within the local population; (iii) rising independence of the Sinhalese nobility in relationship to the court at Anurādhapura, with Kaliṅgan elements introduced by certain monarchs to offset Sinhalese aristocratic power; (iv) economic insecurity arising out of political confusion and producing its own dynamics, which included peasant revolts and increasingly feudal structures "in which the topmost strata possessed extensive lands"; and (v) invasion and occupation by the Cōḷas, beginning in 993, which was largely enabled by the centrifugal tendencies preceding it and which occasioned in the end a momentum toward centralization anticipated in the reign of Vijayabāhu I (1055-1110) and confirmed under Parākramabāhu I (1153-1186).

Among recent articles on the early Polonnaruva period is one by George W. Spencer entitled "The Politics of Plunder: The Cholas in Eleventh-Century Ceylon," *Journal of Asian Studies*, Vol. XXXV, No. 3 (May 1976), 405-419, which utilizes both South Indian and Ceylonese sources in an effort to understand the basic rationale for Cōḷa incorporation of Ceylon into its political and economic orbit. His main premise is that "Chola kings utilized long-range plundering raids as the principal tactic in a dual strategy of (1) sustaining and enlarging the supply of 'free-flowing' resources to the royal court, and (2) providing an occasion for royal coordination and direction of a common enterprise among the diverse elements of a markedly decentralized socio-political system, i.e., as an integrative activity."[12] In this essay he provides a different interpretation to that discussed by W. M. K. Wijetunga, "Some Aspects of Cola Administration of Ceylon in the Eleventh Century," *University of Ceylon Review*, Vol. XXIII, Nos. 1-2 (April-October 1965), 67-81, who accents the administrative structure of the Cōḷa presence in Rājaraṭṭha and its stabilization of political and economic forces in comparison to the relatively anarchic period of the century before. The Spencer article discusses the interplay between Cōḷa forces in Ceylon and the foreign mercenaries there on the one hand and the foreign and domestic mercantile groups on the other. This piece may be supplemented by K. Indrapala's "South Indian Mercantile Communities in Ceylon, circa 950-1250," *Ceylon Journal of Historical and Social Studies*, N.S., Vol. 1, No. 2 (July-December 1971), 101-113. Another article that is instructive about the first century of the Polonnaruva period is K. A. Nilakanta Sastri,, "Vijayabāhu I, the Liberator of Laṅkā," *Journal of the Royal Asiatic Society (Ceylon Branch)*, N.S., Vol. V (1954), 45-71, which not only chronicles the events of his career in mobilizing support that eventually ended the Cōḷa occupation and in establishing an important but passing period of stability, but also sheds light on the import of the Vēḷaikkāras who, as foreign mercenaries in Ceylon, exercised considerable influence throughout this century and beyond. While the above articles are helpful, we still have but a fragmentary picture of the eleventh century. Further evidence may simply not be available, but those attempts which bear on the economic aspects may in the long run prove more discerning. It is here that one can perceive more fundamentally what developments were in process in the tension between centrifugal and centripetal elements which emerged in clearer fashion in the twelfth century, an age of immense pluralism. One suspects that these elements were no less present in the era of Vijayabāhu I, but that they had not yet coalesced.

The generation following the death of Vijayabāhu in 1110 is not known in its details, but it was obviously one of political anarchy in which local princes settled for their own fiefdoms and the people suffered. A famous sentence in the *Cūlavaṃsa* captures the mood: "In their insatiability and money lust they squeezed out the whole people as sugar cane in a sugar mill, by levying excessive taxes." (Chapter 61:53) The remaining verses of this chapter afford a vivid picture of the chaos which characterized the period and set the stage for the emergence of the great hero-king and unifier, Parākramabāhu I. Beyond the extensive treatment of this figure in the chronicle (Chapters 62-79) and the thorough discussion of his reign in the doctoral dissertation by Sirima Wickramasinghe, one may consult Chapters IV, V, VII and VIII of the *History of Ceylon*, Vol. I, Part II. Also, the special issue referred to earlier, of the *Ceylon Historical Journal*, Vol. IV, Nos. 1-4 (July & October 1954 and January & April 1955), 7-182, on the Polonnaruva period contains a useful selection of essays on various aspects of twelfth century political, economic and cultural history. While some will be mentioned in a later section, others are pertinent here: (1) A. L. Basham, "The Background to the Rise of Parākkamabāhu I," 10-22, traces the changing faces of Ceylon's adversaries from the Pallavas to the Pāṇḍyans to the Cōḷas and correlates the Sinhalese scene with changes occurring on the continent; (2) K. A. Nilakanta Sastri, "Parākramabāhu and South India," 33-51, focuses mainly on the long military campaign waged, unsuccessfully in the end, by Sinhalese forces against the Cōḷas on South Indian soil (cf. the same author's history of *The Cōḷas*, Vol. II, 97-107, 120-130); (3) Wilhelm Geiger, "Army and War in Mediaeval Ceylon," 153-168 (reprinted from the *Indian Historical Quarterly*, Vol. XIV (1938), 511-531), recreates the military picture from the chronicle's account, providing in the process at least an indirect confirmation of *Arthaśāstra*-like tactics used by Sinhalese forces, especially those of Parākramabāhu, during this period, though Geiger replaced this treatment of the subject in his *Culture of Ceylon in Medieval Times*, pp. 149-163; (4) C. W. Nicholas, "Sinhalese Naval Power," *University of Ceylon Review*, Vol. 16, Nos. 3 and 4 (July-October, 1958), 78-92, is a survey of this topic with special reference to the Polonnaruva period; and (5) H. W. Codrington, "Notes on Ceylon Topography in the Twelfth Century," 130-152 (reprinted from the *Journal of the Royal Asiatic Society, Ceylon Branch*, Vol. XXIX, No. 75 and Vol. XXX, No. 78), provides a map through the jungles of names confronting one in the accounts of campaigns and skirmishes. C. W. Nicholas, "Historical Topography of Ancient and Medieval Ceylon," *Journal of the Royal Asiatic Society (Ceylon Branch)*, N.S., VI, Special Number (1959), 1-223, exhaustively details this subject and is a crucial reference.

By far the most suggestive recent essay on the internal developments in Ceylonese society during this time is one by Keith Taylor, "The Devolution of Kingship in Twelfth Century Ceylon," in Kenneth R. Hall and John K. Whitmore, eds., *Explorations in Early Southeast Asian History: The Origins of Southeast Asian Statecraft* (Ann Arbor: Center for South and Southeast Asian Studies, University of Michigan, 1976), 257-302. The thirteenth century is viewed as "profoundly different from anything previously seen in Ceylon, in terms of its geography, economic base, and political organization" and the author analyzes aspects of the previous four centuries (with special attention to the reigns of Vijayabāhu I and Parākramabāhu I) to identify the causes. He begins by offering three conclusions of his analysis. "First, the transition can be broadly identified as one which sees the end of the traditional organization of Ceylonese society and politics and the emergence of new, more fragmented, social and political patterns of which the imperial rule of Parakkamabāhu I is only the first and most successful example. Parakkamabāhu I's empire, though not an example of political fragmentation, was only possible by the destruction of the traditional order and the welding together of the resulting fragments through sheer physical force. Second, since the nature of Parakkamabāhu I's rule shows more continuity with what follows than with what went before, the breaking-point of the transition must be placed prior to his accession. Finally, the central theme of the transition was the struggle of the Ceylonese monarchy to survive in the age of Cōḷa power. Yet, while the continental pressures cannot be denied, they cannot be used as an excuse for the demise of the Ceylonese monarchy. This paper will emphasize the decline of the monarchy as a result of primarily internal difficulties." This exceptionally rich essay is difficult to summarize in a few lines, but the concept of "transition" provides the clue to his overall thesis. The era of dynastic warfare from the death of Vijayabāhu I to the accession of Parākramabāhu I in 1153 is the breaking-point of the transition. After this, "non-traditional patterns are the rule": (i) the collapse of old feudal patterns with strongholds particularly in Rājaraṭṭha and Rohaṇa and the shift to a pattern of personal loyalty on either the chieftain (*vannī*) or imperial level; (ii) the shift from a predominantly peasant-based agriculture to one that was more diversified and included a rising merchant and artisan class; (iii) the move toward isolating the Sangha from political involvement, coupled with either more imperial supervision of Sāsana affairs or, later, the creation of more organizational structures to guarantee self-regulation; and (iv) the final crushing of Rohaṇa-stimulated movements of political resistance, which while this facilitated momentary national unity under the aegis of Parākramabāhu I also undermined traditional centers of power and led to a more severe regionalizing of Sinhalese authority in the Southwest.

The post-Parākramabāhu I era, through the reign of Parākramabāhu II (1236-1270), has been explored most fully by Amaradasa Liyanagamage in the volume referred to before. Separate chapters are on the following topics: the disintegration of the Polonnaruva kingdom; the foundation of the Daṁbadeṇiya kingdom and the reign of Vijayabāhu III (1232-36); the beginnings of Parākramabāhu II and the policies of Māgha (1215-1236); the Jāvaka and the Pāṇḍya invasions; and the importance of the reign of Parākramabāhu II. No other treatment of comparable importance exists on this relatively neglected period in Ceylonese history. One may also consult two chapters in the *History of Ceylon*, Vol. I, Part II, namely, Sirima Wickramasinghe, "Successors of Parakramabahu I: Downfall of the Polonnaru Kingdom," 507-528, and S. Paranavitana, "The Dambadeni Dynasty," 613-635; see also B. J. Perera, "An Examination of the

Political Troubles that Followed the Death of King Parākramabāhu I," *Journal of the Royal Asiatic Society (Ceylon Branch)*, N.S., Vol. V (1957), 173-182.

Mention should also be made of the notorious Kaliṅga theory of Professor Paranavitana, in which he identifies the Kaliṅga of Māgha of the thirteenth century not with India but with Malayasia. The following materials should be consulted, though a more complete listing may be found in Goonetileke's three volume bibliography: (1) S. Paranavitana, "Ceylon and Malayasia in Mediaeval Times," *Journal of the Royal Asiatic Society of Great Britain and Ireland (Ceylon Branch)*, New Series, Vol. VII (1959), 1-42; (2) K. A. Nilakanta Sastri, "Ceylon and Sri Vijaya," *Journal of the Royal Asiatic Society (Ceylon Branch)*, New Series, Vol. VIII (1962), 125-140; (3) S. Paranavitana, "Ceylon and Malayasia: A Rejoinder to Nilakanta Sastri," *Journal of the Royal Asiatic Society (Ceylon Branch)*, New Series, Vol. VIII, Part 2 (1963), 330-377; (4) S. Paranavitana, *Ceylon and Malaysia* (Colombo: Lake House Investments Limited, 1966), which is his most extensive treatment of the subject and deals not only with contacts between these two areas in the Polonnaruva period but also before and afterwards; (5) K. Indrapala, critical review of *Ceylon and Malaysia* in the *Journal of the Royal Asiatic Society (Ceylon Branch)*, New Series, Vol. IX (1967), 101-106; (6) R. A. L. H. Gunawardana, "Ceylon and Malaysia: A Study of Professor S. Paranavitana's Research on the Relations Between the Two Regions," *University of Ceylon Review*, Vol. XXV, Nos. 1 and 2 (April-October, 1967), 1-64; (7) Sirima Kiribamune, "Some Reflections on Professor Paranavitana's Contribution to History," *Ceylon Journal of the Humanities*, Vol. 1, No. 1 (January, 1970), 76-92; and (8) W. M. Sirisena, "The Kaliṅga Dynasty of Ceylon and the Theory of its South-east Asian Origin," *Ceylon Journal of Historical and Social Studies*, New Series, Vol. 1, No. 1 (January-June, 1971), 11-47. Present scholarly judgment is unable to accept Paranavitana's theory and is also critical of a number of his other theories (see Kiribamune's article especially), albeit indebted to him for his important research on Ceylonese history.

Among the frequently debated topics about the Polonnaruva period is why it ended in the permanent shift of population away from the area and toward the so-called wet zone. A number of papers have been collected in a volume, edited by K. Indrapala, entitled *The Collapse of the Rajarata Civilization in Ceylon and the Drift to the South-west* (Peradeniya: Ceylon Studies Seminar, University of Ceylon, 1971). Among several essays in this collection, the following help to suggest the complexity of the issues: (1) H. W. Codrington, "The Decline of the Medieval Sinhalese Kingdom," 6-20 (reprinted from the *Journal of the Royal Asiatic Society, Ceylon Branch*, N.S., Vol. VII, 1959, 93-103), accents, as causative factors, reliance upon mercenaries, the steady influx of Tamil immigrants, the fact that trade was largely in foreign hands, decay of the revenue system, and breakdown of the old irrigation system; (2) Rhoads Murphey, "The Ruin of Ancient Ceylon," 21-48 (reprinted from the *Journal of Asian Studies*, Vol. 16, No. 2, February 1957, 181-200), rules out as adequate explanations foreign invasion, climatic changes, soil deterioration, or siltation of tanks and channels, but instead stresses the breakdown of the bureaucratic and administrative system which had previously maintained the dry-zone irrigation, followed eventually by widespread malaria which discouraged reoccupation of the area; (3) S. Paranavitana, "The Withdrawal of the Sinhalese from the Ancient Capitals," 49-59 (reprinted from *History of Ceylon*, Vol. I, Pt. II, 713-720), underscores, among other factors, the breakdown of the local infrastructure (epitomized by the *kulīnas* or local chiefs) caused by the trend toward centralization under Parākramabāhu I especially; (4) Amaradasa Liyanagamage, "The Disintegration of Polonnaruva," 60-72 (reprinted from his book, *The Decline of Polonnaruwa and the Rise of Dambadeniya*, 67-75), agrees with Murphey and Paranavitana in seeing as a major factor the weakening of local administration and the resultant deterioration of the irrigation system, hence the entire economy, all an inadvertent consequence of centripetal trends in the twelfth century and their aftermath; (5) K. Indrapala, "Invasions from South India and the Abandonment of Polonnaruva," from his doctoral dissertation, *Dravidian Settlements in Ceylon and the Beginnings of the Kingdom of Jaffna*, University of London, 1966, stresses the importance of foreign invasions, especially that of Māgha in 1215, which led to the dislocation of the administrative machinery, hence the breakdown of the reservoir system, hence economic decline, hence the resettlement of large numbers of people and the creation of two kingdoms (in Jaffna and the Southwest); and (6) W. I. Siriweera, "The Decay of the Dry Zone Reservoir System of Ancient Ceylon," 89-98, from his doctoral dissertation, *Economic Conditions in Ceylon, c. 1070-1344*, University of London, 1970, 160-65 (revised), concurs with Murphey's basic thesis but believes that the collapse of the dry zone reservoir system was a long process and cannot be attributed to recent forms of centralization.

The debate will continue, but at least the core of it relates to the main theme of this bibliographical essay, namely, the tension between forces of centralization and provincial or localized autonomy. In order to understand this more thoroughly a number of articles on the irrigation system and on land tenure are instructive. (1) C. W. Nicholas, "A Short Account of the History of Irrigation Works up to the 11th Century," *Journal of the Royal Asiatic Society (Ceylon Branch)*, N.S., Vol. VII (1959), 43-69, shows that while considerable advances were made, beginning in the first century A.D., in tank size and technical achievement the village tank system continued alongside the great reservoirs and canals. (2) C. W. Nicholas, "The Irrigation Works of Parākramabāhu I," *Ceylon Historical Journal*, Vol. IV, Nos. 1-4 (Special Issue, 1954-55), 52-68, shows how the construction and maintenance of major new irrigation ventures were intrinsic to that monarch's efforts at political and economic cohesion. (3) S. Paranavitana, "Some Regulations concerning Village Irrigation Works in Ancient Ceylon," *Ceylon Journal of Historical and Social Studies*, Vol. I (1958), 1-7, deals mainly with the situation in fifth century Ceylon and before, as revealed in Buddhaghosa's *Samantapāsādikā*, and looks at regulations applying to reservoirs or tanks which were privately or corporately owned, confirming the importance of local networks as well as the state built and run system. (4) R. A. L. H. Gunawardana, "Irrigation and Hydraulic Society in Medieval Ceylon," *Past and Present*, No. 53 (November 1971), 3-27, is an excellent analysis of the dynamism which existed in a society where the government was not alone in irrigation activity. The economic power of the monastic estates is stressed (monastic officials often taking the place of royal officials), as is that of the increasingly independent gentry class in various parts of the country which thrived until Māgha (1215-36) was ruthless both with it and the monasteries. Gunawardana's thesis is that "a multi-centered society with power devolving on the gentry and the monastic institutions in particular appears to be more true of the social structure of Ceylon than the concept of a centralized bureaucratic system of despotic rule." (5) E. R. Leach, "Hydraulic Society in Ceylon," *Past and Present: A Journal of Scientific History*, No. 15 (April 1959), 2-26, tests Wittfogel's famed thesis about hydraulic societies and oriental despotism with respect to Ceylon, and concludes that the hydraulic societies of India and Ceylon are cellular, not centralized in structure.

Finally, there are a few articles which discuss the nature of land tenure and of revenue in pre-colonial Ceylon, shedding light on this very important topic. (1) Lakshman S. Perera, "Proprietary and Tenurial Rights in Ancient Ceylon," *Ceylon Journal of Historical and Social Studies*, Vol. 2, No. 1 (January 1959), 1-36, deals only up to the eighth century but does so in a detailed fashion and also compares literary and inscriptional evidence in Ceylon with Indian perspectives found in the Code of *Manu* and in the *Arthaśāstra*. (2) W. A. de Silva, "A Contribution to the Study of Economic and Social Organization in Ceylon in Early Times," *Journal of the Royal Asiatic Society (Ceylon Branch)*, Vol. XXXI, No. 81 (1928), 62-76, uses a fourteenth century Sinhalese work, the *Saddharmālankāraya*, to gain insight into the period circa 200 B.C. to 200 A.D. (3) W. I. Siriweera, "The Theory of the King's Ownership of Land in Ancient Ceylon: An Essay in Historical Revision," *Ceylon Journal of Historical and Social Studies*, N.S., Vol. I, No. 1 (January-June 1971), 48-61, should be read in conjunction with his other article, "Land Tenure and Revenue in Mediaeval Ceylon (A.D. 1000-1500)," *Ceylon Journal of Historical and Social Studies*, N.S., Vol. II, No. 1 (January-June 1972), 1-49. The second of these articles is especially important in showing that, while the king did not have sole ownership over land, he did have certain rights regarding the land: e.g., taxation on grain; the right to unoccupied wasteland, to abandoned land, to land with no heirs; and various categories of royal land. Siriweera spells out the nature of service tenure (*rājakāriya*) to the king; the granting of immunities by the king to individuals, or monasteries, or other groups; the nature and extent of temple lands; the types and amount of taxation on or revenue from paddy land, trade and irrigation water, as well as other sorts of royal revenue.[13] (4) R. A. L. H. Gunawardhana, "Some Economic Aspects of Monastic Life in the Later Anurādhapura Period: Two New Inscriptions from Mädirigiriya," *Ceylon Journal of Historical and Social Studies*, N.S., Vol. II, No. 1 (January-June 1972), 60-74, shows how a Buddhist monastery of the late ninth or early tenth century could become a corporate land-owning institution with tenurial rights which excluded the authority of royal officials from them. This was apparently the beginning of what was later to be known as "monastic landlordism."

III. Dhamma and Daṇḍa: The Dual Basis of Legitimacy

The grounds for legitimating power in Ceylonese history is a subject on which considerable source material exists, yet curiously there is little analytical reflection. More to the point, there have been few attempts at perceiving the historic tension between the religious basis for kingship and the tradition of secular statecraft (clearly present within the Polonnaruva period, but also before). Part of the explanation for this relative dearth, perhaps, is that the dynamics of the tension are difficult to assess; one is often forced to speculate about motivations. While this difficulty will inevitably remain, it is useful to note the principal configurations of the *dhamma-daṇḍa* tension (perceivable in the *Cūlavaṃsa* particularly) as another approach to the theme of Sinhalese cultural identity and the dilemmas of pluralism.

Among the possible configurations at least five exist which, in combination, help to refine analysis about the problem. The *first* concerns the very basis on which legitimate power is acquired, maintained and transferred; its preoccupation is not simply accession to the throne but accession undergirded by an ontological mandate. The *second* involves utilizing power either to maintain or re-establish basic order and stability; the monarch's role as protector of the realm is a sine qua non of legitimacy itself. The *third* is inseparable from the requirement of order and casts the king (indeed, the entire bureaucratic system) in the role of provider as well as protector, economic welfare being one with political and military security. The *fourth* combines the previous two and directs the focus upon the vocation of royal power (and all other power by derivation) to promote the well-being of the Buddha Sāsana. While patronage of other religious communities often accompanies patronage of the Dhamma, it cannot be at the latter's expense. And, *fifth*, there are symbolic, cosmological and ritualistic aspects to the definition and enactment of legitimated power which are double-edged; they are as much a challenge to power as they are its reinforcement. When minimal stability and security are absent, legitimacy collapses. These five will be discussed in three categories below.

1. As with each of these configurations, succession to the throne combines elements of statecraft (realpolitik) with legitimation through association with the Sāsana. At stake in the former obviously is the basis of dynastic legitimacy, compounded as it was in the Polonnaruva period by regular struggles between dynasties involving Pāṇḍya and Kaliṅga factions. While a very complex subject, royal succession is profitably discussed in the following: (1) Thomas R. Trautmann, "Consanguineous Marriage in Pali Literature," *Journal of the American Oriental Society*, Vol. 93, No. 2 (1973), 158-180, which compares Indian and Ceylonese marriage patterns, including the use of marriage as a branch of diplomacy in Ceylon; (2) M. B. Ariyapala, "Succession to the Throne in Ancient Ceylon," *University of Ceylon Review*, Vol. XII, No. 4 (October 1954), 195-216, who argues that succession was normally from father to son, except where not possible, in contrast to those who maintain it was from brother to brother and then to the eldest son of the eldest brother; (3) Heinz Bechert supports Geiger's original thesis, in contrast to Ariyapala's primogeniture argument, in "Mother Right and Succession to the Throne in Malabar and Ceylon," *The Ceylon Journal of Historical and Social Studies*, Vol. 6 (1963), 25-40, originally in German: "Mutterrecht und Thronfolge in Malabar und Ceylon," *Paideuma*, Vol. 7 (1960), 179-192; (4) S. Paranavitana, "Matrilineal Descent in the Sinhalese Royal Family," *Ceylon Journal of Science (G.)*, Vol. II, Pt. 3 (October 17, 1933), 235-240, cites some aspects of this topic during the Polonnaruva period; (5) Sirima Kiribamune, "The Royal Consecration in Medieval Sri Lanka: The Problem of Vikramabāhu I and Gajabāhu II," *Sri Lanka Journal of South Asian Studies*, Vol. I, No. 1 (January 1976), 12-32, examines in detail the qualifications for kingship and concludes that these two monarchs ruled without royal consecration because, at least by the twelfth

century, non-Buddhists were not given the Sangha's imprimatur; and (6) S. Paranavitana, "The Kāliṅga Dynasty of Ceylon," *Journal of the Greater India Society*, Vol. III, No. 1 (January 1936), 57-64, which, unlike his later speculations about the identity of Kaliṅga as Malaysia, outlines the traditional view of Ceylon's long relationship with this part of India, focusing especially on the twelfth and thirteenth centuries and on the dynastic connections between the two regions.

Even more prominent within the chronicle account is the weight given to auspicious signs and marks as these foretell greatness and embody legitimacy itself. While the *kāvya* and *praśasti* traditions in South Asia generally are clearly panegyric after-the-fact, the instances in which these are used attest to the meaning of genuine legitimacy. Those whom the chroniclers so honor fit the pattern of epic heroes and are not only legitimated in the usual sense but are exemplars of kingship in the Sinhalese Buddhist mode. Regarding the young Prince Kitti (later Vijayabāhu I and easily one of Ceylon's great figures) an astrologer noted his marks of power, insight and courage, saying: "Even in Jambudīpa he would, I believe, be capable of uniting the whole realm under one umbrella, how much more so in the Island of Laṅkā!" (*Cv.* 57.50) More dramatic, though in obvious continuity, was the scene in which Vijayabāhu sees on his daughter Ratanāvalī signs auguring true greatness: "This thy body shall be the place for the birth of a son, who will surpass all former and future monarchs in glorious qualities, generosity, wisdom and heroism, who will be able to keep Laṅkā ever in safety and united under one umbrella, who will be in perfect wise a patron of the Order, and who will display an abundant and fine activity." (*Cv.* 59.37-9) The son in question was the future Parākramabāhu I, who ranks with Duṭṭhagāmaṇī as Ceylon's epic king par excellence and who was born with marks on his hands and feet which led the *purohita* and other *brāhmaṇas* to exclaim: "Apart from the island of Laṅkā he is able to unite under one umbrella and to rule even the whole of Jambudīpa." (*Cv.* 62.49) The obvious extension of his potential domain and the resemblance of his birth story to that of Siddhattha Gotama link Parākramabāhu not only with the "pure dynasty of the Moon" but with the lineage of *cakkavatti* kings. Among many articles, these three discuss wider implications of such encomia: (1) R. S. Copleston, "The Epic of Parakrama," *Journal of the Royal Asiatic Society (Ceylon Branch)*, Vol. XIII, No. 44 (1893), 60-77; (2) B. C. Law, "The Life of King Parākkamabāhu I," *Ceylon Historical Journal*, Vol. IV, Nos. 1-4 (1954-55), 23-32; (3) L. S. Perera, "The Pali Chronicle of Ceylon," in Philips, ed., *Historians of India, Pakistan and Ceylon* (London: Oxford University Press, 1961), 29-43. See also a novel about Parākramabāhu I entitled *Self-Portrait of a King* (Colombo: Print/Design, 1971).

2. Beginning with the reign of Sena I (831-851) we can see the handwriting on the wall both with respect to Indian *maṇḍala* politics and Rohaṇa-Rājaraṭṭha rivalry. After the seizure of Anurādhapura by the Pāṇḍyas, who left "the splendid town in a state as if it had been plundered by yakkhas," and then through involvement in the internal politics of Rohaṇa, Sena became the first king to establish a substantial base at Pulatthinagara (Polonnaruva) as a strategic post further from Indian attack and closer to the source of potential turbulence in the south. From this point in the mid-ninth century to the end of the Polonnaruva period the chronicle is filled with discussion about the balancing of power.

Involved both with what transpires in South Indian politics and with the growing threat represented by Rohaṇa and Dakkhiṇadesa, the monarchs of Rājaraṭṭha stand or fall on their ability to play the game of power (*daṇḍa*) and invest increasing resources in military expenditure. Predictable cycles unfold – with the growth of dynastic and regional factionalism comes the greater likelihood of foreign invasion and conquest, and with the tyranny and ignominy of conquest comes the invitation to strong-armed leadership to rid Lanka of the "blood-sucking yakkhas" and possess it.

The theme of unity becomes the overriding one both on the sub-continent as the Cōḷas under Rājarāja (985-1016) break up the confederacy of Pāṇḍya, Cera and Ceylon, and on Lanka as Vijayabāhu I (1055-1110) begins and Parākramabāhu I (1153-1186) completes the process of centralization. The concern to bring all Ceylon under one umbrella is epitomized in the soliloquy of Parākramabāhu I in Chapter 64 of the *Cūlavaṃsa*, as he weds statecraft with normative tradition in his determination to take possession of all Lanka and in associating himself with the heroism of old. From his lips fall names from the Jātakas, the *Rāmāyaṇa*, the *Mahābhārata*, from Itihāsa tales and the wisdom of Cāṇakka (Kauṭilya). Here in one canticle is *nīti* ethics solemnized and legitimated by association with the entirety of tradition. The king as protector, as the establisher of order, is being elevated by the Sāsana tradition. The Mahāsaṃmata of old appears in new form and legitimates his power by protecting the powerless, by dispelling the forces of *adhamma*, whether yakkhas from abroad or rebels in Rohaṇa. The influence of the *Arthaśāstra* is unmistakably present not just in this monarch's words but in his whole campaign to capture power, centralize the forces of government, establish a broad economic base, flex his military muscles abroad, unify the Sangha and disengage it from political involvement, and in his expansive artistic and cultural endowments. The clear blending of Indian and Sinhalese elements is nowhere more present in Ceylon's history than in this reign. The chronicle is replete with evidence. For one moment the tension between Sinhalese cultural identity and the forces of pluralism is exceedingly rich. The two wheels of dhamma (*dhammacakka* and *āṇācakka*, the wheel of righteousness and the wheel of power) seem to coordinate. But the moment passes and the yakkhas return. The story of this blending and of its continually precarious nature has not yet been adequately portrayed, but the most interesting backdrop for its portrayal has been depicted in the essay, mentioned before, by Keith Taylor entitled "The Devolution of Kingship in Twelfth Century Ceylon."

3. The king as provider and as patron of the Sāsana may be viewed together for purposes of this context. Aside from the primary material and the various historical works discussed earlier, there are a number of articles which provide perspective on this topic. These fall into three general categories: Indian and Southeast Asian concepts of state and kingship; Sinhalese Buddhist Dhammadīpa ideology; and the monarch as provider. Since several of the essays in the first category are well known, they may be mentioned in passing. (1) Louis Dumont, "The Conception of Kingship in Ancient India," *Contributions to Indian Sociology*, Vol. 6 (December 1962), 48-77 [reprinted in his book *Religion, Politics and History in India: Collected Papers in Indian Sociology* (Paris: Mouton, 1970), ch. 4] has proven to be a stimulating and frequently debated essay. Since Buddhism arose within a Brahmanic setting, one can scarcely

avoid dealing with various Indian positions on authority and power, as well as the uniquely Ceylonese ones.[14] This article and other of Dumont's writings explore the hierarchical relationship between *dharma* and *artha*, as seen in the Brahman/Kshatriya relationship, which is suggestive for the normative Sangha/king pattern within the chronicles of Ceylon. A symposium on Dumont's work has recently been published; two articles are of especial interest here: (2) Pauline Kolenda, "Seven Kinds of Hierarchy in *Homo Hierarchicus*," 581-596; and (3) J. Duncan M. Derrett, "Rājadharma," 597-609, in the *Journal of Asian Studies*, Vol. XXXV, No. 4 (August 1976). In different ways these provide critical perspective on Dumont's important work. Three essays by Balkrishna Govind Gokhale are also helpful in understanding the formative years of Buddhism's relationship to the state in India: (4) "Dhamma as a Political Concept in Early Buddhism," *Journal of Indian History*, Vol. 46 (April 1968), 249-261; (5) "The Early Buddhist View of the State," *Journal of the American Oriental Society*, Vol. 89, No. 4 (October-December 1969), 731-738; and (6) "Early Buddhist Kingship," *Journal of Asian Studies*, Vol. XXVI, No. 1 (November 1966), 15-22. (7) An essay by Frank Reynolds examines early Buddhism's combining of soteriological goals (both other-worldly and more immediately within this world) with a concern for establishing and maintaining proper order in the world: "The Two Wheels of Dhamma: A Study of Early Buddhism," in Bardwell L. Smith, ed., *The Two Wheels of Dhamma: Essays on the Theravada Tradition in India and Ceylon* (Chambersburg, Pa.: American Academy of Religion, Studies in Religion, No. 3, 1972), 6-30. (8) Reynolds looks at Buddhism as a bearer of tradition and as a conveyor of new meaning in "Dhammadipa: A Study of Indianization and Buddhism in Śri Lanka," *Ohio Journal of Religion*, Vol. II, No. 1 (April 1974), 63-78. (9) The relationship of Buddhism to the state is beyond the scope of this essay, but mention can at least be made of an important article by Robert Heine-Geldern, "Conceptions of State and Kingship in Southeast Asia," *Far Eastern Quarterly*, Vol. 2 (November 1942), 15-30, reprinted as Data Paper No. 18, Southeast Asia Program, Cornell University, April 1956, 1-14. While some of his analysis applies only to the Southeast Asian context, much of it is helpful for understanding the Polonnaruva complex with its considerable influence from Hindu and Mahayana elements. (10) Finally, the monarch served the Order partially by helping it to be renewed when necessary through the Sangha in Burma and Thailand, and by enabling it when strong and vital to have contact with various lands in Southeast Asia. See the following articles: Sirima Wickremasinghe, "Ceylon's Relations with South-East Asia, with Special Reference to Burma," *Ceylon Journal of Historical and Social Studies*, Vol. 3, No. 1 (1960), 38-58; G. H. Luce, "Some Old References to the South of Burma and Ceylon," in *Felicitation Volumes of Southeast-Asian Studies. Presented to Prince Dhaninivat*. Vol. II (Bangkok: The Siam Society, 1965), 269-282; C. E. Godakumbara, "Relations between Burma and Ceylon," *Journal of the Burma Research Society*, Vol. 49 (December 1966), 145-162; and S. Paranavitana, "Religious Intercourse between Ceylon and Siam in the 13th-15th Centuries," *Journal of the Royal Asiatic Society (Ceylon Branch)*, Vol. 32, No. 85 (1932), 190-213.

The second category of articles on this topic deals specifically with traditional Sinhalese Buddhist ways of perceiving the Sāsana and political order relationship. In this category one finds history interpreted by ideology, as much Sinhalese as Buddhist, but this makes it all the more important to understand.

(1) Heinz Bechert, "The Beginnings of Buddhist Historiography: *Mahāvaṃsa* and Political Thinking," in Bardwell L. Smith, ed., *Religion and Legitimation of Power in Sri Lanka* (Chambersburg, Pa.: Anima Books, 1978) goes beyond previous essays in making explicit the political ideology which underlies the chronicle tradition in Ceylon. (2) Regina T. Clifford, "The *Dhammadīpa* Tradition of Sri Lanka: Three Models within the Sinhalese Chronicles," in Bardwell L. Smith, ed., *op. cit.*, examines this tradition by looking at Devānaṁpiyatissa, Duṭṭhagāmaṇī and Parākramabāhu I and shows the dynamic nature of this interpreted past. (3) Bardwell L. Smith, "The Ideal Social Order as Portrayed in the Chronicles of Ceylon," in Bardwell L. Smith, ed., *op. cit.* (originally published in *The Two Wheels of Dhamma*, see above), provides a picture of this normative order as seen through the chronicles within the Anurādhapura period. (4) Bardwell L. Smith, "Kingship, the Sangha, and the Process of Legitimation in Ancient Ceylon (Anurādhapura Period)," in Bardwell L. Smith, *op. cit.* (originally published in Heinz Bechert, ed., *Buddhism in Ceylon, and Studies on Religious Syncretism in Buddhist Countries: Report on a Symposium in Goettingen* (Goettingen: Abhandlungen der Akademie der Wissenschaften, 1978), explores the political, religious and symbolic aspects of legitimation. The above essays, while not focussing primarily on the Polonnaruva period, shed light on traditional Sinhalese patterns of thought about power and protection of the Sāsana. (These essays are in a collection with eight others which also look at various aspects of this relationship.) (5) Heinz Bechert, "Theravāda Buddhist Sangha: Some General Observations on Historical and Political Factors in Its Development," *Journal of Asian Studies*, Vol. XXIX, No. 4 (August 1970), 761-778, concentrates mainly on Sāsana reform, the state-Sangha relationship, and the organizational structure of the Order in different periods of Ceylonese history; see also his "Sangha, State, Society, 'Nation': Persistence of Traditions in 'Port-traditional' Buddhist Societies," *Daedalus, Journal of the American Academy of Arts and Sciences*, Winter 1973, 85-95, which adds some new viewpoints to his 1970 *JAS* article.

The final category stresses the king's role as provider, a role intrinsic to both Brahmanic and Buddhist tradition. It is so prevalent in discussions about kingship and its obligations that it becomes de rigueur, treated almost as a ritualistic act and presented as such frequently within the chronicles. There is a deeper meaning to it, however. On the one hand, it is part of a reciprocal relationship with the Sangha, indeed, part of a more profound reciprocity between the social order and the cosmic order, between form and formlessness, to be alluded to in Section Five. On the other hand, it is a serious political commitment, which is breached at the monarch's peril. As in most traditional societies, there is a perceived correspondence between legitimate sovereignty and economic well-being. When drought and famine strike, evil in high places is often thought to be at stake.[15] By whomever the mandate is given, it may be removed for perceived cause. It should be no wonder then that Sinhalese monarchs, along with kings elsewhere, should draw attention to the bounty brought by their reign. The most famous vow in this regard is that of Parākramabāhu the Great: "Truly in such a country not even a little water that comes from the rain must flow into the ocean without being made useful to man." (*Cv.* 68.11) It is clear that the greatness of monarchs in Ceylon is frequently measured by the extent of their irrigation projects, which is in many respects a correlate of economic and social prosperity. While provision comes in many forms, often indirectly, there is a continuing suspicion that the elements and the social order are bound together.

Though illustrations of this are repeated within the chronicles, there has been little discussion of it in the secondary literature. And those that have appeared have often been maligned, in part because they seemed far-fetched and in part because such matters blur the line between "precept" and "practice" in Buddhist contexts. In any case, there is value in pointing to what is a constant refrain, while being cautious about what conclusions may be drawn. Perhaps the most notorious example in modern scholarship is Paranavitana's interpretation of Sīgiriya, the rock-fortress of Kassapa (473-491 A.D.), as an intended relic on earth of Ālakamandā, the dwelling place of Kuvera, the god of wealth and lord of the yakshas.[16] His article "Sīgiri, the Abode of a God-king," *Journal of the Royal Asiatic Society (Ceylon Branch)*, N.S., Vol. 1 (1950), 129-183, is an imaginative interpretation, albeit speculative, of Kassapa's intention to be associated in the popular mind with Kuvera, the provider par excellence. Kassapa the parricide, alienated from the Sangha and living in constant fear of his half-brother's return from India, seeks to ingratiate himself with the populace and gain legitimacy through association with the divine bestower of wealth. In a later and even more speculative interpretation, unaccepted by most thus far, Paranavitana published a book entitled *The Story of Sigiri* (Colombo: Lake House Investments Ltd., 1972). Two more articles by Paranavitana may be mentioned, which, while also speculative in interpretation, are suggestive. This is particularly true of "The Sculpture of Man and Horse near Tisāväva at Anurādhapura, Ceylon," *Artibus Asiae*, Vol. 16 (1953), 167-190, which looks symbolically at kings as the bringer of clouds, water and thus prosperity, seeing this interpretation within "the canonical as well as in the exegetical literature of the Theravāda Buddhists," and as part of a general strain found not just in the Vedic tradition but in pre-Buddhist popular practices as well. Finally, "The Statue near Potgul-vehera at Poḷonnaruva, Ceylon," *Artibus Asiae*, Vol. 15 (1952), 209-217, argues that the king is here portrayed bearing the burdens of state, evenly as if on a scale, providing yet another image of how kingship was perceived in a normative fashion. All of these instances combine *dhamma* and *daṇḍa* in one mode or another.

IV. The Buddha Sāsana and Religious Pluralism

While the impact of Mahayana Buddhism in Ceylon has generally been underplayed, sufficient evidence exists (of a doctrinal, iconographic and cultic sort) to show that Sinhalese Buddhism has accommodated itself to a variety of religious influences, including those of Mahayana, over the centuries. If one took literally the thrust of the chronicles, one would have a picture of so-called orthodox Buddhism (i.e., that of the Mahāvihāra in alliance with key monarchs) as "defensor fidei," staving off influences of a Mahayanist and Brahmanic nature, not to mention folk religious beliefs and practices. In actuality, the picture is otherwise. Buddhism in Ceylon was itself more diverse than has often been assumed and Sinhalese Buddhism became exceedingly skilled in adjusting to other religious traditions. This was nowhere more evident than during the period under consideration. In fact, it was during the Polonnaruva period that Ceylon began to relate to and influence strongly various Buddhist communities in Southeast Asia. It is ironic that the form of

Theravada which emerged after periods of intense exposure to Mahayana and Mantrayana elements, with their rich and complex ingredients, was the form that was taken as the standard of orthodoxy in these other countries. The actual process of assimilating certain new forms while rejecting others reveals the tensions which arise in the encounters between a specific tradition and plural elements within and outside itself, and is thus analogous to the political problems of balancing centripetal and centrifugal forces. This section points to material which illuminates these phenomena and this process. Though much of it falls outside the Polonnaruva period, it is basically germane to understanding that era as well as others.

1. The first category of material depicts folk beliefs and practices of an indigenous or semi-indigenous variety. While difficult to separate from popular forms of Buddhism and/or Hinduism, folk religion has been the subject of several studies. In a summary article entitled "Pre-Buddhist Religious Beliefs in Ceylon," *Journal of the Royal Asiatic Society (Ceylon Branch)*, Vol. 31, No. 82 (1929), 302-327, S. Paranavitana examines briefly *yakṣa* cults, tree worship, patron deities of various trades, astrological cults, phallic worship, alongside early forms of Brahmanism, Jainism, and certain communities of wandering ascetics. Other general treatments may be found in the following books: Wilhelm Geiger, *Culture of Ceylon in Mediaeval Times* (Wiesbaden: Otto Harrassowitz, 1960); M. D. Raghavan, *India in Ceylonese History, Society and Culture* (Bombay: Asia Publishing House, 2nd revised edition 1969); James Cartman, *Hinduism in Ceylon* (Colombo: M. D. Gunasena & Co. Ltd., 1957); L. A. de Silva, *Buddhism: Beliefs and Practices in Sri Lanka* (Colombo, 1974). The most thorough study of the earliest known community in Ceylon is *The Veddas* (Cambridge: Cambridge University Press, 1911) by C. G. Seligmann and Brenda Z. Seligmann; see especially its chapters on religion, magic, ceremonial dances and invocations. See also O. Pertold's three-part article "The Ceremonial Dances of the Sinhalese: An Inquiry into the Sinhalese Folk-Religion," *Archiv Orientalni*, Vol. 2, Nos. 1-3 (1930), 108-138, 201-254, 385-426, which includes a helpful bibliography. (For more extensive references one should consult the three volume *Bibliography of Ceylon* by H. A. I. Goonetileke, mentioned earlier.) Two shorter articles by Pertold are of interest: "Foreign Demons: A Study in the Sinhalese Demon-Worship," *Archiv Orientalni*, Vol. 1, No. 1 (1929), 50-64; and "The Conception of the Soul in the Sinhalese Demon-Worship," *Archiv Orientalni*, Vol. 1, No. 3 (1929), 316-322. Other articles and books which examine folk religion within Hindu or Buddhist contexts will be mentioned below. See also Dandris de Silva Gooneratne, "On Demonology and Witchcraft in Ceylon," *Journal of the Royal Asiatic Society (Ceylon Branch)*, Vol. IV, No. 13 (1865-6), 1-117; Edward Upham, *The History and Doctrine of Buddhism, popularly illustrated with notices of The Kappooism or Demon Worship and of the Bali or Planetary Incantations of Ceylon* (London, 1829); and E. R. Sarachchandra, *The Folk Drama of Ceylon* (Colombo: Government Press of Ceylon, second edition, 1966). The latter explicitly discusses the relation between folk religion and Buddhism, especially as this relationship manifests itself in ritual, ceremony and drama.

2. The influences of Mahayana and of Hinduism upon Sinhalese Buddhism may be seen in a wealth of artistic, literary and ritualistic evidence. One place

to start is the influential article by S. Paranavitana entitled "Mahāyānism in Ceylon," *Ceylon Journal of Science (Section G. Anthropology)*, Vol. 2, Pt. 1 (1928), 35-71, which provides an historical sketch from the second century to the eighth century A.D. using literary materials, then summarizes epigraphical and sculptural evidence from the eighth and ninth centuries, and discusses at length the various Bodhisattva cults of Avalokiteśvara (Nātha), Samantabhadra (Saman or Sumana), and Upulvan (Uppalavaṇṇa, later associated with Vishnu) which combined Buddhist, Hindu and folk-religion features. (The books mentioned in the preceding paragraph by Geiger, Raghavan, Cartman and de Silva also deal with certain aspects of similar material, as do the primary sources discussed earlier and the *University of Ceylon History of Ceylon.*) Discussions of the various divisions within the Sangha, many of which stemmed from the Mahayana presence, may be found in the following: Vincent Panditha, "Buddhism during the Polonnaruva Period," *Ceylon Historical Journal*, Vol. IV, Nos. 1-4 (1954-55), 113-129; D. J. Kalupahana, "Schools of Buddhism in Early Ceylon," *Ceylon Journal of the Humanities*, Vol. 1 (July 1970), 159-190; R. A. L. H. Gunawardana, "Buddhist Nikāyas in Mediaeval Ceylon," *Ceylon Journal of Historical and Social Studies*, Vol. 9(January-June 1966), 55-66; Heinz Bechert, "Notes on the Formation of Buddhist Sects and the Origins of Mahāyāna," *German Scholars on India: Contributions to Indian Studies*, Vol. 1 (1973), 6-18. Another part of this picture was the spreading influence of Sanskrit during the Polonnaruva period, which contributed to the rise of Mahayana and Hinduism. See O. H. deA. Wijesekera, "Sanskrit Civilization among the Ancient Sinhalese," *Ceylon Historical Journal*, Vol. 1, No. 1 (1951), 23-29; O. H. deA. Wijesekera, "Pali and Sanskrit in the Polonnaruva Period," *Ceylon Historical Journal*, Vol. IV, Nos. 1-4 (1954-55), 91-97; Sukumari Bhattacharji, "The Indian Pantheon in the Early Buddhist Sanskrit Literature," *Anvīkṣā* (Jadavpur Journal of the Department of Sanskrit), Vol. 3, Pt. 2 (March 1971), 35-53, which though not dealing with Ceylon shows how Buddhism in India assimilated selectively both the high gods of Brahmanism and various tutelary divinities; and Sumana Saparamadu, "The Sinhalese Language and Literature of the Polonnaruva Period," *Ceylon Historical Journal*, Vol. IV, Nos. 1-4 (1954-55), 98-112.

For the beginnings of Mahayana in Ceylon, see Bechert, "Buddha-Feld und Verdienstübertragung: Mahāyāna-Ideen im Theravāda-Buddhismus Ceylons," *Bulletin de la Classe des Lettres et des Sciences Morales et Politiques, Académie Royale de Belgique*, 5e série, Vol. 62 (1976), 27-51 (in German with summary in French). Here, the relation of the early sects of Ceylon with Mahayana is discussed and a work composed by Ceylonese "Mahāyāna-Sthaviras" (i.e., by Theravadins professing Mahayana) is traced in the canon itself. Bechert challenges Kalupahana and Gunawardana, who do not agree with each other, in their identifications of sects (see above) and also discusses the origins and development of the notions of *patti* and *anumodanā* which are so characteristic of mediaeval Ceylonese Buddhism, and the Mahayana influence thereupon. Some of the information discussed in this paper is repeated (with additional information on Mahayana works) in Bechert's "Mahāyāna Literature in Sri Lanka: The Early Phase," which is to appear in *The Prajñāpāramitā and Related Systems: Studies in Honor of Edward Conze* (Berkeley Buddhist Studies Series, Vol. 1). An English version of the discussion on Gunawardana's and Kalupahana's opinions on the sects will be found in "Sanskrit Literature in Sri

Lanka as a Paradigm of Regional Sanskrit Literature," scheduled to appear in: *Malalasekera Commemoration Volume* (Colombo) in 1977.

Perhaps the clearest indication of both Mahayana and Hindu impact upon Sinhalese Buddhism in this era exists in the artistic remains. To perceive what occurred in the capital city of Polonnaruva one must examine the large Anurādhapura complex and its developing features over several centuries. The best single treatment of this is the recently published study by Senake Bandaranayake, *Sinhalese Monastic Architecture: The Vihāras of Anurādhapura* (Leiden: E. J. Brill, 1974), which is a thorough analysis of the monastic plan, the building types, and the architectural form of structures erected at that site from Devānaṁpiyatissa (250-210 B.C.) to the Cōḷa conquest in 993 A.D. It is indispensable for any student of this subject. Another valuable study is S. Paranavitana, *The Stūpa in Ceylon, Memoirs of the Archeological Survey of Ceylon*, Vol. V (Colombo: Ceylon Government Press, 1946), which deals with Polonnaruva as well as Anurādhapura and relates Ceylonese styles to those in India from early Sāñchī to later forms. Among the most informative studies of Buddhist art in Ceylon is Nandadeva Wijesekera, *Early Sinhalese Sculpture* (Colombo: M. D. Gunasena & Co. Ltd., 1962), which covers material from the earliest period up to 1200 A.D., with an especially helpful chapter on the "Evolution of Sinhalese Sculpture" regarding the various layers of influence upon this long development. The same author's *Early Sinhalese Painting* (Maharagama: Saman Press, 1959) is of some help as well. Of more pertinence is Nandasena Mudiyanse, *Mahayana Monuments in Ceylon* (Colombo: M. D. Gunasena & Co. Ltd., 1967), which describes in detail both stone and metal images, as well as inscriptions, showing how the third, sixth and ninth centuries were times of strong Mahayana activity and how the Mahāvihāra had accepted many Mahayana doctrines by the end of the Anurādhapura period, including belief in Bodhisattvas and emphasis upon devotion (*bhakti*). For sources on mediaeval art, Hans Ruelius, "Mañjuśrībhāṣita-Citrakarmaśāstra: A Mahayanistic Śilpaśāstra from Sri Lanka," *Buddhism in Ceylon, and Studies on Religious Syncretism* (see above) is important, because the śilpaśāstra described by Ruelius in all probability dates from the Polonnaruva period and is the only work of its kind. The work *Śāriputra*, a Ceylonese Sanskrit text on the proportions of the images of the Buddha, seems to belong to roughly the same period. It was edited and translated by Hans Ruelius, *Śāriputra und Ālekhyalakṣaṇa, Zwei Texte zur Proportionslehre in der indischen und ceylonesischen Kunst*, Goettingen, 1974 (printed doctoral dissertation, University of Goettingen).

Among a large number of articles on the subject of Mahayana and Hindu artistic impact, the following are of special interest: (1) L. Prematilleke and R. Silva, "A Buddhist Monastery Type of Ancient Ceylon Showing Mahāyānist Influence," *Artibus Asiae*, Vol. 30 (1969), 61-84; (2) S. Paranavitana, "The Art and Architecture of the Polonnaruva Period," *Ceylon Historical Journal*, Vol. IV, Nos. 1-4 (1954-55), 69-90, plus 39 plates; (3) P. E. E. Fernando, "Tantric Influence on the Sculptures at Gal Vihara, Polonnaruva," *University of Ceylon Review*, Vol. 18 (1960), 50-66, alongside an appendix entitled "Tantric Influence at Gal-Vihara, Polonnaruva" in Mudiyanse, *op. cit.*, 107-119; (4) P. Sarvesvara Iyer, "Puranic Saivism in Ceylon during the Polonnaruwa Period," *Proceedings of the First International Conference Seminar of Tamil Studies* (Kuala Lumpur: University of Malaya, 1968), 462-474; (5) P. Arunachalam, "Polonnaruwa Bronzes and Siva Worship and Symbolism," *Journal of the Royal Asiatic Society (Ceylon Branch)*, Vol. XXIV, No. 68 (1915-16), 189-222, plus 11 plates; (6) C. E. Godakumbara, "Bronzes from Polonnaruva," *Journal of the Royal Asiatic Society (Ceylon Branch)*, N.S., Vol. VII, Pt. 2 (1961), 239-253; (7) S. Paranavitana, "Śaṁkha and Padma," *Artibus Asiae*, Vol. 18 (1955), 121-127, which shows how the palace of Vijayabāhu I (1055-1110) at Anurādhapura was symbolically guarded by these two retáiners of Kuvera, i.e., how Sinhalese kings were regularly protected by Hindu gods or mythical semi-human beings, a theme also evident in D. T. Devendra, "The Symbol of the Sinhalese Guardstone," *Artibus Asiae*, Vol. 21 (1958), 259-268; (8) Nandasena Mudiyanse, "Architectural Monuments of the Mahayanists of Ceylon," in *The Indo-Asian Culture*, Vol. XIX, No. 3 (July, 1970), 13-30; and (9) Nandasena Mudiyanse, *The Art and Architecture of the Gampola Period (1341-1415 A.D.)* (Colombo: M. D. Gunasena & Co. Ltd., 1963), which, while beyond the period under consideration, shows how some of the same themes continued after the shift of the capital away from Polonnaruva, with Dravidian influences being especially strong.

3. Along with textual material, as well as evidence of an archeological or inscriptional nature, one of the more instructive ways to understand the dynamics of religious pluralism is through carefully done anthropological studies. Clearly, studies which reflect present circumstances must be used with caution if one is trying to assess what was involved in past periods of history, but the more perceptive anthropologists use historical documents along with field studies and present significant diachronic portrayals of Buddhism in response to changing and continuing patterns of a religious and social nature. Two of the more important book length investigations along these lines are by Hans-Dieter Evers and Richard Gombrich. Evers' book, entitled *Monks, Priests and Peasants: A Study of Buddhism and Social Structure in Central Ceylon* (Leiden: E. J. Brill, 1972), analyzes the social, religious and economic organization of the great Lankātilaka Vihāraya, founded in 1344 A.D., and the interrelationship between the vihāra, dēvāle and palace systems which characterized this important complex from the fourteenth to the nineteenth centuries and, in altered but still significant ways, up to the present. While one way to understand the religious and socio-economic dynamics of the Kandyan period and region, it affords insight into the same factors not only today but to some extent into developments occurring from at least the eleventh century onward and in more fragmentary forms from the beginning of Ceylonese history. One should consult, however, a critical and extensive review of this book by Heinz Bechert, shortly to appear in *Orientalistische Literaturzeitung*, in which he questions particularly Evers' view that strong religious influences from Southeast Asia can be traced in the religion of the Sinhalese. The study by Richard F. Gombrich, a philologist using anthropological methods as well, entitled *Precept and Practice: Traditional Buddhism in the Rural Highlands of Ceylon* (Oxford: Clarendon Press, 1971) is a valuable attempt to assess "the tensions between the cognitive and the affective belief system and value system" in Sinhalese Buddhism. Of especial interest here are two long chapters on "The Buddha," pages 80-143, and "A Sketch of the Universe as Seen from Migala," pages 144-213, in which he depicts the enormously rich composite of traditional Buddhist practices and beliefs alongside the coexistence of folk religion, Hindu ingredients, and diverse forms of Buddhist ritual and belief which con-

stitute the Sinhalese tradition. Though the combinations of these elements vary with circumstances of time and place, their presence in one form or another throughout the culture's long history makes Gombrich's study valuable in attempting to speculate about the nature of their existence in the Polonnaruva period as well. Two other studies, both by S. Paranavitana, are similarly suggestive in terms of the interrelationship between Buddhist, Hindu and other religious traditions: (1) *The Shrine of Upulvan at Devundara, Memoirs of the Archeological Survey of Ceylon*, Vol. VI (Colombo: Ceylon Government Press, 1953) shows how the god Upulvan (P. Uppala-vaṇṇa) was early associated with Varuṇa (Protector of the Waters), was delegated by Sakka, King of the Gods, to protect Lanka upon the Buddha's bidding, becoming the Sinhalese national god (with a pilgrimage place in the extreme south), and was finally by the sixteenth century associated with Vishnu through Hindu influence; and (2) *The God of Adam's Peak* (Ascona: Artibus Asiae, 1958), links the importance of pilgrimage to this holy site with several religious communities, including the Sinhalese belief in the Buddha's visit there in earliest times and the assimilating of the god Saman (Sumana, Yama) to his cause. This site becomes increasingly important to Buddhists with the Polonnaruva period as several monarchs, notably Vijayabāhu I and Parākramabāhu II, went to considerable ends to facilitate pilgrims' visitation to Samantakūṭa, now known as Adam's Peak, to see and revere the Buddha's footprint (Śrī Pāda).

A number of influential anthropological essays have appeared since 1960 in an attempt to analyze the structure of the Sinhalese pantheon and the relationship in belief and practice between the various levels within it, from the Buddha at the apex, followed by the various Indian guardian deities as protectors of the Sāsana in certain areas as well as more localized gods, with demons and ghosts at the bottom whose potentially malevolent inclinations must be propitiated or transformed. Again, while no deductions may automatically be made about how these dynamics operated in other periods of Ceylonese history, these studies assist one to read between the lines and speculate with some intelligence about similar, albeit constantly changing phenomena in earlier times. Among the more important essays are the following: (1) Gananath Obeyesekere, "The Great Tradition and the Little in the Perspective of Sinhalese Buddhism," *Journal of Asian Studies*, Vol. XXII, No. 2 (February 1963), 139-153; (2) Gananath Obeyesekere, "The Buddhist Pantheon in Ceylon and Its Extensions," in Manning Nash et al., *Anthropological Studies in Theravada Buddhism* (New Haven: Yale University, Southeast Asia Studies, 1966), 1-26; (3) Gananath Obeyesekere, "Social Change and the Deities: The Rise and Fall in the Sinhalese Buddhist Pantheon," unpublished manuscript, read at a symposium on Religion and Social Change in Southeast Asia held at Swarthmore College in April, 1972, 1-47; (4) Michael M. Ames, "Ritual Prestations and the Structure of the Sinhalese Pantheon," in Manning Nash et al., *op. cit.*, 27-50; (5) Nur Yalman, "On Some Binary Categories in Sinhalese Religious Thought," *Transactions of the New York Academy of Sciences*, Vol. 24, series II, 29 pages; and (6) Nur Yalman, "Dual Organization in Central Ceylon? or The Goddess on the Tree-top," *Journal of Asian Studies*, Vol. XXIV, No. 3 (May 1965), 441-457 (reprinted with minor revisions in Manning Nash et al., *op. cit.*, 197-223).

4. Part of the process of analyzing the interrelationship between Buddhism and other religious beliefs and practices, whether at the folk level or in contexts

where the intermingling gains what is tantamount to official blessing, is the whole phenomenon mistakenly called "syncretism."[17] Because the meaning of this term is easily misunderstood, I would prefer to identify the process as one in which a tradition (in this case Sinhalese Buddhism) assimilates, subordinates, transforms, and is itself modified by elements of belief and practice from other religious traditions or communities. The process is subtle, complex, frequently reciprocal, dynamic, and found in the areas of ritual, symbol, cosmology and institutional structure. A careful reading of the chronicles of Ceylon provides repeated raw material for study, but it is especially in cultic practices as these may be observed in the present that one can understand more deeply the process of assimilation and synthesis which occurs in varied ways and at different rates throughout history. Because the Polonnaruva period was exceptionally rich from the standpoint of religious pluralism, it is important to examine the dynamics of this phenomenon, as another method of assessing what was occurring from the tenth to the thirteenth century. The literature on this subject is considerable; the following essays are selective but representative: (1) Paul Wirz, *Kataragama: The Holiest Place in Ceylon* (Colombo: Lake House Investments Ltd., second edition, 1972), examines briefly what has become the most popular pilgrimage place for Buddhists, Hindus and Muslims in Ceylon, resulting in a fusing of pietistic beliefs and practices on the folk level (alongside deliberate attempts at retaining distinctions) centered around the God Kataragama (Kārttikeya, Subrahmanya, Skanda, Murukan); (2) Ponnambalam Arunachalam, "The Worship of Muruka or Skanda (the Kataragam God)," *Journal of the Royal Asiatic Society (Ceylon Branch)*, Vol. XXIX, No. 77 (1924), 234-261; (3) Manmatha Mukhopadhyay, "Some Notes on Skanda-Kārttikeya," *Indian Historical Quarterly*, Vol. 8 (1931), 309-318; (4) K. Kailasanatha Kurukkal, "A Study of the Karttikeya-cult as reflected in the Epics and the Puranas," *University of Ceylon Review*, Vol. XIX, No. 2 (October 1961), 131-137; (5) Heinz Bechert, "Eine alte Gottheit in Ceylon und Süd-indien," *Beiträge zur Geistesgeschichte Indiens, Festschrift für Erich Frauwallner, Wiener Zeitschrift für die Kunde Süd- und Ostasiens*, Vols. 12/13 (1968-69), 33-42, examines with great care the evolving identification of the North Indian god Skandakumāra with South Indian and Ceylonese gods of a similar nature from the fourteenth century on; (6) Edmund R. Leach, "Pulleyar and the Lord Buddha: An Aspect of Religious Syncretism in Ceylon," *Psychoanalysis and the Psychoanalytical Review*, Vol. 49 (1962), 80-102, shows how the Hindu god Ganesha (son of Śiva and brother of Skanda) becomes Pulleyar, a feudal dependent of the Lord Buddha among Buddhists in North Ceylon; (7) H. L. Seneviratne, "The Äsala Perahära in Kandy," *Ceylon Journal of Historical and Social Studies*, Vol. 6, No. 2 (July-December 1963), 169-180, and also his doctoral dissertation entitled *The Natural History of a Buddhist Liturgy (Being a Study in the Nature and Transformation of Kandyan Sinhalese Metropolitan Ritual)*, Ph.D., University of Rochester, 1972 (forthcoming as *Rituals of the Kandyan State*, Cambridge University Press, 1977), both of which depict the subsuming of Hindu gods and the provincial chiefs to the centralizing process at work in Kandyan Buddhism and Kandyan political administration; (8) Gananath Obeyesekere, "The Structure of a Sinhalese Ritual," *Ceylon Journal of Historical and Social Studies*, Vol. 1 (1958), 192-202, reveals the interdependence yet differentiation of caste groups and relates an annual ritual to the whole question of national and ethnic identity in the midst of religious and cultural pluralism; (9) M. D. Raghavan, "The Pattini Cult as a Socio-Religious Institution," *Spolia Zeylanica*, Vol. 26 (1951), 251-261; (10) Richard Gombrich, "Food for Seven Grandmothers: Stages in the Universalisation of a Sinhalese Ritual," *Man*, N.S., Vol. 6, No. 1 (March 1971), 5-17; and (11) Gananath Obeyesekere, "Gajabāhu and the Gajabāhu Synchronism: An Inquiry into the Relationship between Myth and History," in Bardwell Smith, ed., *Religion and Legitimation of Power in Sri Lanka* (Chambersburg, Pa.: Anima Books, 1978), which is an extremely important essay in the area of religious assimilation. The last three essays deal with the Pattini cult, which is a locus classicus of the process whereby Buddhist belief and practice overlap with and absorb features of other religious communities.

Finally, a few articles exist which more explicitly discuss the topic of assimilation and syncretism. One is an essay by Kitsiri Malalgoda, "Sinhalese Buddhism: Orthodox and Syncretistic, Traditional and Modern," *Ceylon Journal of Historical and Social Studies*, N.S., Vol. 2, No. 2 (January-June 1972), 156-169, which is a review article of Gombrich's book, *Precept and Practice.* Malalgoda faults Gombrich for not having taken into account the Sinhalese works written over the past thousand years. This raises the important question of the changes that occur within the organizational structure and belief system of a tradition over long periods of time. One theoretical essay of significant value in this respect is Thomas F. O'Dea's "Five Dilemmas in the Institutionalization of Religion," *Journal for the Scientific Study of Religion*, Vol. 1, No. 1 (October 1961), 30-41, which analyzes the tension between a tradition's need to respond to new historic circumstances afresh and its need to interpret and pass on these responses to others. For a more important review essay of Gombrich's study, see that of Heinz Bechert in a forthcoming issue of the *Indo-Iranian Journal.* Another essay by Malalgoda, "Millennialism in Relation to Buddhism," *Comparative Studies in Society and History*, Vol. 12, No. 4 (October 1970), 424-441, examines in an interesting fashion the way in which millennial expectations emerge with the rise of frustrations when a community's image of its identity clashes with the actual reality it faces in periods of self-confusion and rapidly increasing pluralism. The relationship of this phenomenon to Sinhalese Buddhism's long-term stress upon its Guardian Deities is of great importance. The essay by Obeyesekere on the Gajabāhu synchronism, mentioned above, is very much to the point here. Both these articles show how subtle and extensive is the manner in which Buddhism has accommodated itself to changing needs and new circumstances. Another essay, by Frank E. Reynolds, "Dhammadipa: A Study of Indianization and Buddhism in Śri Lanka," *Ohio Journal of Religion*, Vol. II, No. 1 (April 1974), 63-78, makes a careful case for how the Mahāvihāra community in Ceylon reacted over centuries to the stimulus of Mahayana and Mantrayana forms of Buddhism on the one hand and to varieties of Hinduism on the other hand, not by a "grudging acceptance of the newer views and practices" but by a "persistence and resilience" which enabled Sinhalese Buddhism to sustain a balance between significant continuity with its historic tradition and significant change in the face of major threats and challenges. The result was a perceptively altered form of Buddhism which became the model for the forms the Sāsana took in Burma, Thailand and Cambodia.

An important recent publication in a related area is the one mentioned above, edited by Heinz Bechert, *Buddhism in Ceylon, and Studies on Religious*

Syncretism in Buddhist Countries (Goettingen, 1978). Here, the relevant contributions are: H. Bechert, "On the Popular Religion of the Sinhalese"; R. F. Gombrich, "Kosala-bimba-vaṇṇanā"; H. Ruelius, "Netrapratiṣṭhāpana, eine singhalesische Zeremonie zur Weihe von Kultbildern"; as well as R. F. Gombrich, "The Buddha's Eye, the Evil Eye, and Dr. Ruelius" which aims at a refutation of the methodology used by Dr. Ruelius in his contribution. The particular importance of the volume is that the problem of relations of Buddhism and "folk religion" in Sri Lanka was discussed here, for the first time, in the context of a comparative survey of syncretism in Buddhist countries (with contributions by S. Lienhard on Nepal, by J. Ensink on Java and Bali, by R. Heinemann on Japan, and by G. Roth and H. Bechert on Bengal). For future work in this particular field, a comprehensive survey of the facts has been provided by Heinz Bechert in his contribution to the mythological dictionary, which contains also a complete bibliography of writings on Sinhalese popular religion up to 1974: H. Bechert, *Mythologie der singhalesischen Volksreligion*, which forms Lieferung (fascicle) 15, pp. 509-656, of the "Wörterbuch der Mythologie," ed. by H. W. Haussig (Stuttgart: Klett-Verlag 1976). Under 207 catch-words, the material is arranged with bibliographic references, so that, e.g., all significant bibliographic information on folk religion given by Pertold and Goonetileke is found there, as well as material not found in either of these two.

Two other essays are of interest in a comparative sense: (1) Lowell W. Bloss, "The Buddha and the Nāga: A Study in Buddhist Folk Religiosity," *History of Religions*, Vol. 13, No. 1 (August 1973), 36-53, shows how Buddhism relates to other religious phenomena not simply by a process of accretion or assimilation but often by a kind of dialectic or tension whereby it accepts and at the same time rejects elements of popular belief and practice, in different ways at different times; (2) Lawrence Palmer Briggs, "The Syncretism of Religions in Southeast Asia, especially in the Khmer Empire," *Journal of the American Oriental Society*, Vol. 61, No. 4 (October-December 1951), 230-249, examines in detail the syncretism of Śaivism and Vishnuism and the syncretism of Hinduism and Buddhism, especially that of the Śivaic Maheśvara and the Mahayanist Lokeśvara between the sixth and twelfth centuries in the Khmer kingdom.

V. Ritual, Cosmology, and Cultural Identity

The final section overlaps to some extent the previous one by including both anthropological and artistic materials, also by going beyond the Polonnaruva period itself in order to understand that period, but the section differs in singling out areas of concern which are more symbolically basic to personal and cultural identity, namely, those appearing in ritual, ceremony and cosmology. There is, of course, no substitute for reading the various primary materials to which attention has been given earlier. The various writings in Pāli and Sinhalese give sufficient account of developments in the areas of both rite and cosmology during the Polonnaruva period to indicate this was an era of immense change in this respect. As one observer perceptively put it: "For Parākramabāhu I, in the historical mythology of Lankā, is regarded as the Sinhalese ecumenicist *par excellence* whose greatest kingly act was the reconciliation of Ceylon's Buddhist sectaries and the restoration to ecclesiastical supremacy of the followers of the Theravāda. Still, the Mahāyānist character of the Wata-dā-ge at Polonnaruva, and of its model, does not reflect a cultural abnormality. The role of the Mahāyāna in the cultural development of Ceylon has been grossly underrated, both in the traditional histories and in modern commentary. (It may be said also that the special character of ecclesiastical reform in ancient Ceylon has not been understood.) The archaeological remains alone suggest a widespread Mahāyāna cult flourishing from the seventh century until the devastation of Anurādhapura in the tenth. And there is considerable evidence for the survival of Mahāyāna institutions well into the fifteenth century."[18]

The same case could be made for Brahmanic influence during this period and the centuries prior to the coming of the Portuguese. The point here is not to elaborate on these and more indigenous influences but to indicate what sorts of developments were in progress and what areas of future research might prove rewarding. Underlying this section, as well as the entire essay, is the assertion that the Polonnaruva period presents a rich scholarly field which has as yet not been explored in terms of its overall implications. While it has been the subject of many excellent monographs and articles, its more fundamental themes lie essentially untapped. The following bibliographical references are but a start.

In three very different sorts of essays, all of which deal with the relationship between ritual, mythology and identity, Gananath Obeyesekere provides considerable perspective on the problems of pluralism, religious and social assimilation, and the "sense of belonging to a moral community": (1) "Sinhalese Buddhist Identity in Ceylon," in *Ethnic Identity: Cultural Continuities and Change*, edited by George de Vos and Lola Ross (Palo Alto: Mayfield Publishing Company, 1975), deals in part with the concept of an "obligatory pilgrimage," helping one to understand what was becoming of major importance during the entire Polonnaruva period as pilgrimage to holy sites such as Adam's Peak was being encouraged by Vijayabāhu I, Parākramabāhu II and Parākramabāhu III, and as celebration of the Tooth Relic was being more actively enjoined by various monarchs and the Sangha; (2) "Gajabāhu and the Gajabāhu Synchronism: An Inquiry into the Relationship between Myth and History," in Bardwell L. Smith, *op. cit.*, shows the evolution of the Gajabāhu story from a matter of fact account within the chronicles to an elaborate myth in the *Pūjāvaliya* in the reign of Parākramabāhu II (1236-70) and especially in the *Rājāvaliya* four centuries later, an evolution providing major evidence of a dynamic ritualistic process at work in which South Indian and Sinhalese elements on the one hand and diverse religious and mythic ingredients on the other were gradually amalgamated; (3) "The Pataha Ritual: Genesis and Function," *Spolia Zeylanica*, Vol. 30, Part II (1965), 279-296, spells out the nature of a ceremony of first fruits after the harvest or "in times of crisis like pestilence, famine and drought" (with the goddess Pattini presiding) in which a major theme is the tension between kingship as traditionally legitimated and kingship gone astray, a theme fitting into the *daṇḍa-dhamma* tension discussed above but also showing how ritual often inverts the meaning of myth, exposes its nonconformance with reality, and acts as an assimilating agency of new ingredients over time.

Another cluster of essays deals with Buddhism's accommodation with a variety of age-old ways to resolve or at least cope with problems arising within a world characterized by *dukkha*. Theoretically, Buddhism's efforts are towards the cessation of *dukkha*, but in fact most forms of Buddhism have encouraged religious beliefs and practices which serve to assist mankind in avoiding or lessening pain. This modus vivendi has been true from the beginnings of Buddhist history, as within every religious tradition. Regarding the Sinhalese tradition the book by Richard Gombrich, *Precept and Practice*, mentioned above is an important study. Others of value would include the following: (1) Michael M. Ames, "Magical-animism and Buddhism: A Structural Analysis of the Sinhalese Religious System," *Journal of Asian Studies*, Vol. XXIII (June 1964), 21-52, which was published as a special issue, edited by Edward B. Harper, entitled *Aspects of Religion in South Asia*; (2) Michael M. Ames, "Buddha and the Dancing Goblins: A Theory of Magic and Religion," *American Anthropologist*, Vol. 66 (1964), 75-82; (3) Nur Yalman, "The Structure of Sinhalese Healing Rituals," *Journal of Asian Studies*, Vol. XXIII (June 1964), 115-150, also in Harper, *op. cit.*, looks in detail at various rites and their practitioners from *pirit* (Pāli, *paritta*) rituals performed by bhikkhus to *dēvayā, yakkuva* and *grahayo* rituals performed by *kapurālas* (Hindu priests), astrologers, and "general practitioners" in turn; (4) Richard Gombrich, "The Consecration of a Buddhist Image," *Journal of Asian Studies*, Vol. XXVI, No. 1 (November 1966), 23-36, describes the *nētra pinkama* ceremony (festival of setting the eyes in a newly consecrated image of the Buddha), which, like the *pirit* ritual, is an example of an evil-avoiding ceremony and which, Gombrich indicates, was referred to first by Buddhaghosa in the fifth century A.D., was practiced by Parākramabāhu I (*Cv.* LXXIII, 78), and was apparently an annual festival with some Buddha images in the Polonnaruva period and beyond; (5) J. F. Dickson, "Notes Illustrative of Buddhism as the Daily Religion of Ceylon and Some Account of Their Ceremonies before and after Death," *Journal of the Royal Asiatic Society (Ceylon Branch)*, Vol. VIII, No. 29 (1884), 203-236, depicts the ten modes of *pinkama* or meritorious acts which a layman can perform (as outlined in the Pāli canon and as practiced by laymen) with the Sangha's blessing and assistance; (6) Gananath Obeyesekere, "Theodicy, Sin and Salvation in a Sociology of Buddhism," in E. R. Leach, ed., *Dialectic of Practical Religion* (Cambridge: Cambridge University Press, 1968), 7-40, analyzes among other things the important concept of "merit transfer" through the special qualities of the *vanavāsīn* (hermit monk) in Theravada and its implications for lay soteriology; (7) O. Pertold, "A Protective Ritual of the Southern Buddhists," *Journal of the Anthropological Society of Bombay*, Vol. XII, No. 6 (1923), 744-789, examines the Pāli and Sinhalese texts of a *paritta* (*pirit*) nature historically and describes their use in Ceylon fifty years ago; (8) Ernst Waldschmidt, "Das Paritta, Eine magische Zeremonie der buddhistischen Priester auf Ceylon," in Ernst Waldschmidt, *Von Ceylon bis Turfan* (Göttingen, 1967), 465-478, for an excellent description of paritta; and (9) Peter Schalk, *Der Paritta-Dienst in Ceylon* (Lund: Bröderna Ekstrands Tryckeri AB, 1972), which is the most thorough study of *paritta* texts and ceremonies in any language and is a major resource for the study of this extremely important subject. Finally, see the articles by Bechert, Gombrich and Ruelius in the above-mentioned *Buddhism in Ceylon, and Studies on Religious Syncretism in Buddhist Countries* (Göttingen, 1978).

Along similar lines but exploring the subject at greater depths are several essays which depict the ritualistic or symbolic crossing of various boundaries.

Almost by definition these involve pluralistic elements and suggest both the extreme difficulty with which a culture or a person may encounter threats to identity and the manner in which practices of a very specialized nature may have implications for society more broadly. One example is the still common practice of exorcism in Ceylon. The best known study of this is Paul Wirz, *Exorcism and the Art of Healing in Ceylon* (Leiden: E. J. Brill, 1954), which remains crucial for this topic. The original German edition of this book, *Exorzismus und Heilkunde auf Ceylon* (Bern, 1941), unlike the translation, has an Index, which is essential to an intelligent grasp of the material presented by Wirz. Also of importance is Gananath Obeyesekere, "The Ritual Drama of the *Sanni* Demons: Collective Representations of Disease in Ceylon," *Comparative Studies in Society and History*, Vol. 2 (1969), 174-216, and the response to this article by Jerrold E. Levy, "Some Comments upon the Ritual of the *Sanni* Demons," 217-226. A third perceptive treatment is by John Halverson, "Dynamics of Exorcism: The Sinhalese Sanniyakuma," *History of Religions*, Vol. 10, No. 4 (May 1971), 334-359, which describes at length how the demonic (specifically here the *sanniyaku* or demons of ill health) is assimilated in ritualistic fashion and is thereby domesticated. The process is one which combines the need both for integration (a centripetalizing activity) and individuation (an expressive or centrifugal mode); a process having psychic, communal and cosmic dimensions. One is reminded of Giuseppe Tucci's classic development of the symbolism and liturgy of the *maṇḍala* as a means towards reintegration in *The Theory and Practice of the Maṇḍala* (New York: Samuel Weiser, 1971), which elaborates on both Hindu and Buddhist uses of this practice. Another essay, more specifically within Sinhalese monastic practice (namely, the *Upasampadā* or rite of ordination), discussing the manner in which the boundary (*sīmā*) between "this world" and another form of existence is symbolically crossed is H. L. Seneviratne, "The Sacred and the Profane in a Buddhist Rite," Ceylon Studies Seminar 1969-70, Series, No. 7 (University of Ceylon, 1970). See also his doctoral dissertation, *The Natural History of a Buddhist Liturgy, being a Study in the Nature and Transformation of Kandyan Sinhalese Metropolitan Ritual*, Ph.D., University of Rochester, 1972.[19]

Finally, an article by S. Paranavitana, "The Significance of Sinhalese 'Moonstones'," *Artibus Asiae*, Vol. 17 (1954), 197-231, serves to focus attention on how a specific Buddhist symbolic complex both assimilates and transforms Brahmanic and folk elements for its own purposes and how this symbolic gestalt may then be used in ritualistic fashion. Moonstones first appeared around the fourth century A.D. in Anurādhapura, with Indian counterparts earlier, and continued to be made through the Polonnaruva period. The significance of Paranavitana's imaginative interpretation is his portrayal of the relationship between the moonstone, which represents the plane of suffering (*bhava-cakra* or *saṁsāra*), and the image shrine or mount upon which the Buddha sits (*pabbata*). The pilgrimage symbolically is from the *saṁkhāra-loka*, or world of psychic suffering, to the *Brahmā-loka*, or the Abode of Pure Beings, where *taṇhā* has been extinguished. At considerable length Paranavitana discusses the iconographic and floral detail, relating this to Brahmanic and Buddhist mythology and elaborating upon its spiritual implications. The import of his discussion deals with the basic process of symbolization, i.e., the attempt to make what is essentially unknowable intelligible through the use of symbols or ritual or cosmology, all of which interpret the unknown by analogy with what is really, or supposedly, known.[20] Thus, by recognizing the pluralistic nature of all symbolic interpretations and the resultant sense of inadequacy of all symbolizations, one is led to the non-symbolic, whether in the aniconic representations of the Buddha or in the doctrine of the *Trikāya* which is ultimately the non-symbolic beyond infinite symbolization. Without question, the most comprehensive and perceptive study of this entire topic is Paul Mus, *Barabuḍur: Esquisse d'une histoire du Bouddhisme fondée sur la critique archéologique des textes*, 2 volumes (Hanoi: Imprimerie d'Extrême-Orient, 1935). Mus' final paragraph is an appropriate conclusion to this essay which has sought to suggest part of what constituted the intellectual and religious currents in a very complex period in the history of Sri Lanka:

> Laissons le dernier mot à la *Sumaṅgalavilāsinī.* Voici comment se termine son commentaire du *Tevijja sutta: Atha kho rūpārūpāvacarakammaṃ eva kāmāvacaram mah' ogho viya parittaṃ udakaṃ pharitvā pariyadiyitvā attano okāsam gahetvā tiṭṭhati* . . . "Mais au contraire le *karman* des mondes de la Forme Pure et au delà de la Forme agit envers le Monde du Désir comme le débordement d'un grand fleuve qui recouvre un petit ruisseau, le supprime, prend sa place et s'y épand (*tiṭṭhati*)."

Notes

1. See Bardwell L. Smith, "Polonnaruva as a Ceremonial Complex: Sinhalese Cultural Identity and the Dilemmas of Pluralism," in A. K. Narain, ed., *Essays in the History of Buddhism*, forthcoming. In his article "The Capital of Ceylon during the Ninth and Tenth Centuries," *Ceylon Journal of Science (Section G. Anthropology)*, Vol. 2 (1930), 141-147, S. Paranavitana makes a reasonable case for Anurādhapura's remaining the capital, however precarious its hold, during this time.
2. This was a special issue commemorating the 800th anniversary of Parākramabāhu's accession to the throne in 1153. Besides her essay there are ten others, to be noted later.
3. These two volumes are known as Volume I, Parts 1 and 2. (The dating used in this essay has followed that of these volumes.) There is also *A Concise History of Ceylon* (Colombo: Ceylon University Press, 1961), edited by C. W. Nicholas and S. Paranavitana, which is not recommended for the serious student. Part 1 of the two volume study has a helpful bibliographical chapter by L. S. Perera on the sources of Ceylon history, pages 46-73; and Part 2 has a comprehensive bibliography of materials in all pertinent languages, pages 795-841. A good summary chapter on Sinhalese history may be found in S. Arasaratnam, *Ceylon* (Englewood Cliffs, N.J.: Prentice-Hall, Inc., 1964), 41-97.
4. See Chapter One in the present volume. This is a revised version of a paper originally given at the Ceylon Studies Seminar, 1974 Series, No. 2. This subject was first discussed in Bechert's "Zum Ursprung der Geschichtsschreibung im indischen Kulturbereich," in *Nachrichten der Akademie der Wissenschaften in Göttingen, Philologisch-historische Klasse*, 1969, No. 2, pp. 35-68, which covers additional subject matter not found in the English version.
5. *Ibid.* For an interesting structural analysis of "quasi-historical" and "mythical" sources, as a supplement to the "historical" accounts, see the article on Duṭṭhagāmaṇī, who reigned from 161 to 137 B.C., by Marguerite S. Robinson, "'The House of the Mighty Hero' or 'The House of Enough Paddy'?: Some Implications of a Sinhalese Myth," in E. R. Leach, ed., *Dialectic in Practical Religion* (Cambridge University Press, 1968), 122-152.
6. See Malalasekera, *op. cit.*, pp. 147-237. For a thorough discussion of source materials for this period, see pages 1-33 of Amaradasa Liyanagamage's *The Decline of Polonnaruwa and the Rise of Dambadenia (circa 1180-1270 A.D.)* (Colombo: Department of Cultural Affairs, Government Press, 1968).
7. Chinese accounts of Buddhism in Ceylon are also important. See *A Record of Buddhistic Kingdoms: Being an Account by the Chinese Monk Fa-Hien of His Travels in India and Ceylon (A.D. 399-414) in Search of the Buddhist Books of Discipline*, translated by James Legge (New York: Dover Publications, Inc., 1965), 101-110; and "Chino-Sinhalese Relations in the Early and Middle Ages," *Journal of the Royal Asiatic Society (Ceylon Branch)*, Vol. XXIV, No. 68 (1915-16), 74-123, which is a translation with notes by John M. Sena-

veratne of the article by M. Sylvain Lévi on Chinese references to Ceylon, published in the *Journal Asiatique* (1900).

8. See also his essay entitled "Historical Writing in Sinhalese," in Philips, *op. cit.*, 72-86.

9. See pages 6-8 of Ratnapala's introduction. Also, on page 221 he lists nine prior instances of Sāsana purification effected by kings from the third to the tenth century. Ratnapala's study was a doctoral dissertation at the University of Goettingen and was stimulated by the research of Heinz Bechert on the question of Sāsana reform. See Bechert, "Zur Geschichte der buddhistischen Sekten in Indien und Ceylon," *La Nouvelle Clio* (Bruxelles), Vols. 7-9 (1955-57), 311-360, in which the history of sects in Ceylon is discussed in detail in the context of examining the nature of Buddhist nikāyas or sects from India to Southeast Asia. Also, see Bechert, "Ways of Sāsana Reform in Theravāda Buddhism," *Rhys Davids Memorial Volume* (Colombo, 1965), 145-157.

0. Of lesser value to this bibliography but worth mentioning are: (1) H. Ellawalla, *Social History of Early Ceylon* (Colombo: Department of Cultural Affairs, 1969), which deals with this subject up to the fourth century A.D. and includes a chapter on the effect of Buddhism upon society, dealing with Brahmanism and popular cults as well; (2) U. D. Jayasekera, *Early History of Education in Ceylon* (Colombo: Department of Cultural Affairs, 1969), which also stops with the fourth century A.D.; (3) E. F. C. Ludowyk, *The Footprint of the Buddha* (London: George Allen & Unwin, Ltd., 1958), which, while intended for broad readership, is a capable portrayal especially of the establishment of Anurādhapura as a sacred city and, more briefly, of the royal palace of Sigiriya and the royal capital of Polonnaruva; (4) Reginald Stephen Copleston, *Buddhism Primitive and Present in Magadha and Ceylon* (London: Longmans, Green, and Co., second edition, 1908), which reveals at least how modest Western scholarship on Sinhalese history has been until recently. The work by Tilak Hettiarchchy on kingship in Ceylon has been brought forward to cover the period up to the tenth century A.D. by Sujatha Gunasena in a doctoral dissertation, which I have not seen, from London University (1974).

1. The published volumes, discussed above, by Ariyapala, Ellawalla, Hettiarachchy and Liyanagamage were also originally doctoral dissertations done at SOAS since 1949. The first eight of the ten listed here were done at the University of London. Of these ten, those by Gunawardana and Sirisena are scheduled to be published.

2. See also two other articles by him which spell out further the interrelationships between the king, the various religious networks, and agrarian institutions and groups in the Chola sphere of influence on the continent: (1) "Temple Money-Lending and Livestock Redistribution in Early Tanjore," *Journal of the Indian Economic and Social History Review*, Vol. V, No. 3 (September 1968), 277-293; and (2) "Religious Networks and Royal Influence in Eleventh Century South India," *Journal of the Economic and Social History of the Orient*, Vol. XII, Part I (1969), 42-56.

3. For further discussions of this subject, see H. W. Codrington, *Ancient Land Tenure and Revenue in Ceylon* (Colombo, 1938); review of this book by Julius de Lanerolle, with exchanges between him and Codrington, in the *Journal of the Royal Asiatic Society (Ceylon Branch)*, Vol. XXXIV, No. 91 (1938), 199-230. Also, see relevant sections in Ariyapala, *op. cit.*; Geiger, *Culture of Ceylon in Mediaeval Times*; Ralph Pieris, *Sinhalese Social Organization: The Kandyan Period* (Colombo: Ceylon University Press, 1956), 39-139, 233-261; H. W. Tambiah, *Sinhala Laws and Customs* (Colombo: Lake House Investments Ltd., 1968), 157-212; and the *Bibliography on Land Tenure and Related Problems in Ceylon* (Colombo: Department of Information, n.d.).

4. Among the vast literature on Indian political theory the following are important examples: J. Gonda, *Ancient Indian Kingship from the Religious Point of View* (Leiden: E. J. Brill, 1969); Charles Drekmeier, *Kingship and Community in Early India* (Stanford: Stanford University Press, 1962); John W. Spellman, *Political Theory of Ancient India* (Oxford: Clarendon Press, 1964); R. Shamasastry, tr., *Kauṭilya's Arthaśāstra* (Mysore: Mysore Printing and Publishing House, 1967, 8th edition); Thomas R. Trautmann, *Kauṭilya and the Arthaśāstra* (Leiden: E. J. Brill, 1971); U. N. Ghoshal, *A History of Indian Political Ideas* (London: Oxford University Press, 1966); R. P. Kangle, *The Kauṭilīya Arthaśāstra* (Bombay, 1965). As for the influence of Kauṭilya in Ceylon, it was Wilhelm Geiger who discovered and first discussed it: Wilhelm Geiger, "Kenntnis der indischen Nītiliteratur in Ceylon," *Beiträge zur Literaturwissenschaft und Geistesgeschichte Indiens, Festgabe für Hermann Jacobi* (Bonn, 1926), 418-421 (reprinted in: Geiger, *Kleine Schriften*, pp. 422-425). Earlier authors had misread the relevant passages of the *Cūlavaṃsa*

(*kocallādisu nītisu* instead of *koṭallādisu nītisu* as conjectured by Geiger). The mediaeval Sinhalese used the alternative form of Kauṭilya's name, viz. Kauṭalya, as seen from the Pāli Koṭalla.

15. John W. Spellman discusses the connection between water, *dharma*, and the king in "The Symbolic Significance of the Number Twelve in Ancient India," *Journal of Asian Studies*, Vol. XXII, No. 1 (November 1962), 79-88. He also shows the relationship between the god Varuṇa and the king in this respect. This fact had considerable importance in Ceylon as well.
16. According to the Bhāgavata Purāṇa, Kuvera first dwelt in Lanka (then situated on Mount Meru and a city of unrivalled splendor), only to be driven from it by Rāvana. Ironically, however, Vāyu the wind god broke Lanka off from Mount Meru, hurling it in the sea, and it became Ceylon, then to be possessed by Rāvana. Kuvera, meanwhile, fell heir to Ālakā, the wealthiest of celestial cities, located on Mount Mandara, a spur of Meru.
17. In the essay mentioned in footnote 1 above I examine this matter at some length.
18. Diran K. Dohanian, "The Wata-dā-gē in Ceylon: The Circular-Relic-House of Polonnaruva and Its Antecedents," *Archives of Asian Art*, Vol. 23 (1969-70), p. 37. For an extensive treatment of this subject, see his unpublished doctoral dissertation at Harvard, 1964, entitled *The Mahāyāna Buddhist Sculpture of Ceylon*.
19. For further study of this subject historically one should consult A. M. Hocart, *The Temple of the Tooth in Kandy, Memoirs of the Archeological Survey of Ceylon*, Vol. IV (Colombo: Ceylon Government Press, 1931); and the review article of this work by Victor Goloubew, "Le Temple de la Dent à Kandy," *Bulletin de l'École Française d'Extrême-Orient*, Vol. 32 (1932), 441-474.
20. Eric Voegelin, *Order and History* (Baton Rouge: Louisiana State University Press, 1956), p. 5.

Gajabāhu and the Gajabāhu Synchronism: An inquiry into the relationship between Myth and History

Gananath Obeyesekere

IT IS A well-known fact that ancient literary works and chronicles are full of material of a patently mythological character. Sometimes it is easy to distinguish the mythical from the historical, but at other times this becomes extremely difficult, particularly if the events mentioned have some kind of historical core or base. Matters become even more complicated when the mythic events or personages mentioned in ancient literature (and sometimes the literature itself) are closely involved with regional or national patriotism so that scholars are tempted to reify myth as history in order to prove a point of national honour, or enhance the glory of the past. In Sri Lanka, fortunately for us, in addition to the traditions recorded in the chronicles, there exists a rich tradition of myth and ritual sung or performed in well-known religious ceremonies. It is therefore possible to control the data found in the literary works with that of myth, so as to throw some light regarding the historicity or the mythical nature of the events or personages mentioned in these sources. In this paper we will be mostly concerned with one such personage – Gajabāhu – an important Sinhala King appearing in historical chronicles and literary works as well as in the contemporary Sinhala ritual tradition.

My interest in Gajabāhu emerged from my research on the Pattini Cult. The rituals associated with the goddess Pattini are performed in the Sinhala low country in a large scale ceremony known as the *gammaḍuva* ("village hall"). There are also *dēvāles* for this goddess in almost every part of the country, and during annual *dēvāle* celebrations, myths of the goddess are sung, and rituals are performed in her honour. One such ritual is the famous "water-cutting ritual," which, according to myth, commemorates the cleaving of the ocean by Gajabāhu. This episode is recounted in the *Gajabā Katāva* ("the story of Gajabāhu"), one of the ritual texts sung in the Pattini rituals of the *gammaḍuva*.

In the course of my research, I realized that an analysis of Gajabāhu, from a non-historical and anthropological point of view, may help us to clear some of the ambiguities and contradictions that center on this figure, both regarding his role in Sinhala culture and history, and also in relation to the Tamil Saṅgam

This paper was originally presented at the University of Sri Lanka, Sri Lanka Studies Seminar, on December 13, 1968. The paper was revised in the light of criticisms and comments made by several colleagues, especially Dr. G. C. Mendis, Dr. R. A. L. H. Gunawardena, Dr. K. Indrapala and Mr. Thananjayarajasingham. I am very grateful to Dr. B. P. J. Hewawasam of the Department of Sinhala, University of Sri Lanka (Colombo) for loaning me his copies of the Karikāla texts in Sinhala. The present essay is a slightly revised version of the one appearing under the same title in the *Ceylon Journal of the Humanities*, Vol. I, No. 1, January, 1970, 25-56. Reprinted with permission.

Epic, the *Śilappadikāram.* The problem as far as the *Śilappadikāram* is concerned pertains to what is known as the "Gajabāhu synchronism," i.e., the attempt to date the *Śilappadikāram* on the basis of references to Gajabāhu (Kayavāgu) of Sri Lanka found in that work. The Gajabāhu synchronism relates to the reference in the *Śilappadikāram* that Gajabāhu (Kayavāgu) was present at the consecration ceremony of the Pattini temple inaugurated under the patronage of Śeṅguṭṭuvaṉ. Since Gajabāhu lived in the late second century, according to the *Mahāvaṃsa*, the "Gajabāhu synchronism" has been of crucial importance for South Indian historical and literary chronology. Most scholars, of every persuasion, with a few exceptions, are inclined to accept the Gajabāhu synchronism. Scholars of the more patriotic persuasion (for example, Dikshitar), admit it in toto, i.e., they are convinced that King Gajabāju of Sri Lanka was not only present at Śeṅguṭṭuvaṉ's capital for the ceremony, but also, that he introduced the Pattini Cult to Sri Lanka as the commentator's addendum in the *Śilappadikāram* states. Several scholars of the tough-minded sort accept it with reservations. They are impressed by the fact that the*Śilappadikāram* refers to both Gajabāhu and Śeṅguṭṭuvaṉ as contemporaries. Though the *Śilappadikāram* was written much later, they believe that the reference to the two kings was based on a valid historical tradition.

The importance of the Gajabāhu synchronism for South Indian chronology could be illustrated by a few representative quotations from leading scholars.

(a) "This allusion to the King of Ceylon enables us to fix the date of Imaya Varman. . ."[1]

(b) "The synchronism of Senguttuvan with Gajabahu I of Ceylon is the sheet anchor of the chronology of early Tamil literature."[2]

(c) Dikshitar, after reviewing the "evidence," confidently affirms: "Thus the Gajabahu synchronism is explained and the date of the composition of the *Silappadikāram* settled once and for all."[3]

(d) Kamil Zvelebil, the fmous Czech scholar of Tamil, says that "the majority of historians agree with the so-called Gajabahu synchronism, that is, the conception according to which the Ceylonese King Gajabahu I (171-193 A.D.) was a contemporary of the Cera monarch, Senguttuvan."[4] Though in his more recent work on Tamil Literature Zvelebil denies the exaggerated claims for the antiquity of the *Śilappadikāram.*

(e) Nilakanta Sastri says that "it is not unlikely that the legend preserved the memory of a historically correct synchronism."[5] Paranavitana also gives assent to this view.[6]

In the following pages we shall demonstrate that the Gajabāhu synchronism is worthless for purposes of historical chronology, since the Gajabāhu of the *Śilappadikāram* is a mythical, not a historical personage. This consideration will also take us to an analysis of the Gajabāhu myth.

The Gajabāhu Synchronism

In the *Śilappadikāram* proper the reference to Gajabāhu of Sri Lanka is as follows:

> The monarch of the world circumambulated the shrine thrice and stood offering his respects. In front of him the Arya Kings released from prison, kings removed from the central jail, the Kongu ruler of Kudagu, the King of Malva and Kayavāgu (Gajabāhu), the King of sea-girt Ceylon, prayed reverentially to the deity thus: "Please grace our countries just as you have done this auspicious day, a fete-day at Imayavaramban's sacrifice." Then a voice from the welkin issued forth: "I have granted the boon."[7]

Scholars like Vaiyapuri Pillai have noted that this account merely mentions that

Gajabāhu was present at the ceremony. The reference to his having introduced the Pattini Cult to Sri Lanka occurs in *Uraiperukatturai*, which was added to the *padikam* by an early editor.[8] This account actually seems to contradict the former. It states that famine devastated the Pāṇḍyan Kingdom after Pattini destroyed Madura so that the successor to the late King "propitiated the Lady of Chastity by sacrificing a thousand goldsmiths, and celebrated a festival when there was a downpour causing fertility to the land .... On hearing this Gajabāhu of Sri Lanka encircled by sea, built a shrine for the Lady of Chastity where daily sacrifices were performed. Thinking that she would remove this distress (of his land), he also instituted annual festivals commencing with the month of Adi; then the rains came to stay and increased the fertility of the land so as to produce unfailing crops. . . ."[9]

Thus, this part of the story merely states that Gajabāhu introduced and instituted the Pattini Cult in Sri Lanka. These contradictions, in combination with other reasons, have led Vaiyapuri Pillai to deny the validity of the Gajabāhu synchronism, as well as the account of his presence in the court of Śeṅguṭṭuvaṉ. He considers these later interpolations.[10] While agreeing with Vaiyapuri Pillai, let us submit the Gajabāhu episode to a further scrutiny employing an anthropological analysis of the episode.

The arguments advanced by the more dogmatic scholars are briefly as follows: Gajabāhu of Sri Lanka is mentioned in the *Śilappadikāram*; there were two Gajabāhus mentioned in Sri Lankan chronicles, one in the second and the other in the twelfth century; the twelfth century is palpably too late a date; ergo, Gajabāhu of the *Śilappadikāram* is Gajabāhu I who reigned in the second century. That things are much more complicated is apparent from a critical examination of the Sri Lankan chronicles. The earliest reference to Gajabāhu I appears in the *Dīpavaṃsa* compiled by Sri Lankan monks about the middle of the fourth century. There is a brief, succinct account which states that Gajabāhu was the son of Vaṅkanāsikatissa. "Tissa's son Gajabāhukagāmiṇī caused a great *thūpa* to be built in the delightful Abhayārama. This royal chief constructed a pond called Gāmiṇī, according to the wish of the mother; this lord ordered the *ārāma* called *Rammaka* to be built. He ruled twenty-two years over the Island."[11] The *Mahāvaṃsa*, compiled in the fifth century is only slightly more detailed. Several references to pious deeds omitted in the earlier account are included here.[12] There are no references here to the Pattini Cult, or to Gajabāhu's visit to South India. These references are found in *Rājaratnākara*, a sixteenth century work, and the *Rājāvaliya*, written probably in the seventeenth century. Both these are written in Sinhala as against the Pāli of the early chronicles. The latter text mentions that Gajabāhu did go to South India and brought back Buddha relics and the anklets of the Goddess Pattini. Before we consider these latter accounts, let us examine the implications of the *Dīpavaṃsa* and *Mahāvaṃsa* accounts of Gajabāhu.

The *Dīpavaṃsa* and *Mahāvaṃsa*, composed as they are in the fourth and fifth centuries, are close to the events of Gajabāhu I's reign. Moreover, the compilers of the two chronicles used pre-existent accounts kept by monks in Buddhist temples. It is therefore surprising that Gajabāhu's visit to India finds no reference here. Some writers (Dikshitar, Gulasekeram) argue that the lack of reference to this incident is due to Buddhist compilers who did not wish to be associated with a non-Buddhist cult like that of Pattini. This argument seems to me highly improbable, for both chronicles are replete with references to so-called "non-Buddhist" practices and beliefs. Actually, according to popular Sinhala tradition, Pattini is not a Hindu but a Buddhist deity and an aspirant to future Buddhahood. Moreover, according to Sinhala tradition, as embodied in the later accounts, Gajabāhu also brought back with him Buddha relics. It is even more surprising, therefore, that no reference was made to Gajabāhu's visit in the early accounts. Hence we shall draw certain *tentative* generalizations, which will be spelled out in detail later.

(a) The *Mahāvaṃsa* and *Dīpavaṃsa* make no reference to Gajabāhu's visit to South India because Gajabāhu I of the chronicles made no such visit.

(b) The likelihood is that the Pattini Cult was not prevalent in Sri Lanka at the time of the composition of these chronicles. Nowhere in them is there a reference to the Goddess Pattini. Since the later Sinhala chronicles do mention Pattini, one could tentatively conclude that the cult was introduced to Sri Lanka some time after the fifth century but before the sixteenth.

These conclusions will be spelled out in more detail in the analysis of the later Sinhala accounts.

Let us now consider the sixteenth and seventeenth century Sinhala accounts of the Gajabāhu episode. The Sinhala accounts in the two chronicles are basically the same, but since the *Rājāvaliya* is the more detailed one let us consider it.

> Gajaba, son of king Bapa Vannassi, succeeded to the throne. One night, when walking in the city, he heard a widow weeping because the king of Soli had carried away her children. He said within himself, "Some wrong has been done in this city" and having marked the door of her house with chalk, returned to his palace. In the morning he called his ministers and inquired of them what (they knew of any) acts of justice or injustice in the city. Thereupon they replied, "O great king, it is like a wedding house." The king, being wroth with his ministers, sent for the woman, the door of whose house he had marked with chalk, and asked her (why she wept). The poor woman replied, "I wept because among the 12,000 persons taken captive by the Soli king were my two sons." On hearing these words the king expressed anger against his royal father, and saying "I will go tomorrow to the Soli country," assembled an army and went to Yapapatuna, thinking "I will (myself) bring back the people forcibly carried off by the king of Soli," and having declared it openly, he dismissed the army. Taking the giant Nila with him he went and struck the sea with an iron mace, divided the waters in twain, and going quietly on arrival at the Soli capital, struck terror into the king of Soli, and seated himself on the throne like king Sak; whilst the giant Nila seized the elephants in the city and killed them by striking one against another.
>
> The ministers informed the king of Soli of the devastation of the city thus being made. Thereupon he inquired of Gajaba, "Is the Sinhalese host come to destroy this city?" Gajaba replied, "I have a little boy who accompanied me; there is no army," and caused the giant Nila to be brought and made to stand by his side. Thereupon the king of Soli asked "Why has your Majesty come alone without an army?" Gajaba replied, "I have come in order to take back the 12,000 persons whom your royal father brought here as prisoners in the time of my father." To this the king of Soli saying, "A king of our family it was who, in time past, went to the city of the gods and gained victory in the war with the Asuras," refused to send for and deliver the men. Then Gajaba grew wroth and said, "Forthwith restore my 12,000 people, giving 12,000 besides them; else will I destroy this city and reduce it to ashes." Having said this, he squeezed out water from sand and showed it; squeezed water from his iron mace and showed that. Having in this way intimidated the king of Soli he received the original number supplemented by an equal number of men, as interest, making 24,000 persons in all. He also took away the jewelled anklets of goddess Pattini and the insignia of the gods of the four devalas, and also the bowl-relic which had been carried off in the time of king Valagamba; and admonishing the king not to act thus in future, departed.
>
> On his arrival he landed the captives; sent each captive who owned ancestral property to his inherited estate, and caused the supernumerary captives to be dis-

tributed over and to settle in these countries, viz., Alutkuruwa, Sarasiya pattuwa, Yatinuwara, Udunuwara, Tumpane, Hewaheta, Pansiya pattuwa, Egoda Tiha, and Megoda Tiha. This king reigned 24 years, and went to the world of the gods."[13]

On reading this version, the reader will note that it agrees with the *Śilappadikāram* only in one respect – that Gajabāhu visited South India and was associated with the Pattini Cult. It contradicts or omits details in the *Śilappadikāram*. In the *Rājāvaliya* the reference is to Gajabāhu having visited Coḷa (Soli), not Cera where Śeṅguṭṭuvaṉ reigned. It is unlikely that he ever went to Cera (assuming for argument's sake that this account has some historicity), for he brought back the anklets of the Goddess Pattini *from Coḷa.* If this is correct, the Pattini Cult must have been already fully institutionalized in Coḷa in the second century. Thus the *Śilappadikāram* account which says that it was *started* in Cera by Śeṅguṭṭuvaṉ is, according to the Sinhala accounts, wrong. Gajabāhu is presented in a role subservient to Śeṅguṭṭuvaṉ in the *Śilappadikāram*. In the *Rājaratnākara* and the *Rājāvaliya* he is presented as a grandiose hero. He brings back the insignia of the Gods of the four *dēvāles*, the bowl relic of the Buddha, and 12,000 Tamil prisoners. There is no reference to his having introduced the Pattini Cult to Sri Lanka. On the contrary, the assumption in these two accounts is that the Pattini Cult was already in existence in Sri Lanka, hence the importance of bringing back with him the anklets of that deity. Moreover, as we shall show presently, Sinhala sources state clearly elsewhere that Gajabāhu did *not* introduce the cult. We will therefore have to dismiss the preposterous claims of some scholars who, like Natesan, say that "the introduction of the Pattini Cult to Ceylon by Gajabāhu I is confirmed by the *Rājāvaliya*, the Ceylon chronicle."[14]

Even a cursory glance at the Gajabāhu story suggests that the account has no historical veracity. The highly improbable ignorance of the King regarding the fact that 12,000 prisoners were taken captive in his father's reign till reminded of this by an old widow, the cleaning of the ocean in two and other miraculous events show that this is hardly historical, though it may be based on some historical event whose nature we are in no position to infer. The account, however, is almost in point-by-point agreement with the Gajabāhu myth sung in watercutting rituals. The inference is irresistible: the Gajabāhu story is not a historical episode at all, but a mythical one associated with watercutting (and probably other customs) and incorporated into the two Sinhala chronicles. Thus the reason why the earlier *Mahāvaṃsa* account does not mention the episode is that it simply did not take place historically. This is not only true of the Gajabāhu episode but of others as well. Another famous origin myth – that of the *pūna yāgaya* (ritual of the *pūna* pot) as well as the Kandyan *kohombā kankāriya* – deals with the illness of King Paṇḍuvāsudeva, Vijaya's nephew. The *Mahāvaṃsa* is singularly silent about this episode, whereas the *Rājāvaliya* restates almost *in toto* the mythic version of the episode. Once again, the conclusion is that the myth evolved after the fifth century but before the sixteenth and is based on ritual data. But for some scholars these seem incontrovertible historical facts. K. K. Pillay, Professor of History of the University of Madras writing on South Indian colonization in Sri Lanka asserts: "One of the early references to such settlements is heard of in connection with the reign of Paṇḍuvāsudeva. It is said that for the purpose of curing the illness of the King, certain Brahmins were brought from South India and they were settled in the capital."[15]

To sum up what we have said so far: The Gajabāhu episode in the *Rājāvaliya* and *Rājaratnākara* is probably derived from the origin myth of the water-cutting ceremony, or from similar myths, and has nothing to do with the historical Gajabāhu of the *Mahāvaṃsa* who lived in the second century. The myth, which associates Gajabāhu with the Pattini Cult in a manner opposed to the *Śilappadikāram* account, evolved after the fifth century A.D. The *ritual* of water-cutting is probably older than the *myth* of origin. For example, even in Sri Lanka water-cutting is also associated with festivities involving Skanda (Kataragama), Ganesh and Śiva; here different myths of origin are involved. The probability is that the Gajabāhu episode was used to explain the origin of water-cutting after the Pattini Cult became the dominant fertility cult in Sinhala Sri Lanka. The Gajabāhu story itself may have been current before then, i.e., before the Pattini Cult became dominant. Indeed, Gajabāhu is a typical Sinhala culture hero figure who like Vijaya, Paṇḍuvāsudeva, and Malala Rajjuruvo of the Sinhala ritual tradition was the "originator" of various ritual and religious customs and institutions of the Sinhalas. If there was any historicity in these figures, they have been completely transformed in the myth-making process. Further analysis of the Gajabāhu episode as depicted in the two Sinhala chronicles and in our myths will make this process of mythicization clearer.

An important difference exists between the *Rājāvaliya* account and the myth of Gajabāhu of the water-cutting ritual. The *Rājāvaliya* states that the 12,000 captives brought to Sri Lanka by Gajabāhu were settled in the following regions: Alutkuruva, Sārasiya Pattuva, Yaṭinuvara, Uḍunuvara, Tumpanē, Hēvāhäṭa, Pansiya Pattuva, Egoda Tiha, Megoda Tiha. The water-cutting ritual ignores this detail. A historical literalism in the analysis of the episode would mean that Gajabāhu I, who lived in the second century, waged a war in the Coḷa country – brought back many prisoners, and settled most of them in certain parts of the Sinhala hill country. By contrast, the Coḷa King who lived in Gajabāhu's father's reign put his Sinhala captives to work in damming the Kāverī, a useful irrigation enterprise. It was singularly foolish of Gajabāhu not to have used this human labor for similar construction purposes, for the hill country and the coastal regions where his captives were settled were, in the second century, a remote, inaccessible and inhospitable region, "a home of rebels and lost causes."[16] An anthropological analysis, treating this episode as a myth, yields a different set of conclusions. This version of the Gajabāhu story is what I call a "colonization myth," functionally similar to the Moses myth of the Bible. As an origin myth, it explains the existence of South Indian settlers in parts of Kandyan provinces and coastal regions. These settlers may have come for various reasons – through waves of conquest, peaceful immigration, or "introduced" by the Sinhala kings themselves. The myth, like other myths of this genre, is an explanation of the existence of these groups probably justifying their "anomalous status," to use Malinowski's words, in the Sinhala social structure. Even now there are communities of low subcastes of the *goyigama* (farmer) caste in the Kandyan areas (e.g., near Ampiṭiya I have come across one such village) who claim their origin from this source. Their position is slightly inferior to the majority of the *goyigama* castes: their inferiority, as well as their origin, is explained in terms of the identical myth. The myth served as a useful mechanism for incorporating immigrant populations into the Sinhala social structure till recent times. In the Sinhala low country there are castes of *karāva, salāgama* and *demala gattara* (lit. Tamil *gotra*) who claim to have descended from those captives thus providing a mythical charter, in Malinowski's sense, for these groups.[17]

The earliest reference to Gajabāhu's colonization is in the sixteenth century *Rājaratnākara*, which only states that the captives were settled in Alut Kuruva, near Negombo. A *Kaḍaimpota* (an account of geographical boundaries), quoted by Bell, has another account of Gajabāju's colonization of Alut Kuruva.

> In olden times, after the Rawana War, from Kuru Rata there came to this Island a queen, a royal prince, a rich nobleman, and a learned prime minister, with their retinue, and by order of King Rama dwelt in a place called on that account Kuru Rata. In the year of our great Lord Gautama Buddha, Gajabahu who came from Kuru Rata, settled people in the (second Kuru Rata), calling it Parana-Kuru-Rata. In another place he sent 1,000 persons, and gave it to them calling it Alut Kuruwa.[18]

Alut Kuruwa is today populated by the *karāva* or Fisher caste, who in their myths trace their ancestry to the Kauravas (Kuru) of the *Mahābhārata* war. The major waves of *karāva* immigration to Sri Lanka occurred in the fifteenth century and after.[19] The Gajabāhu myth, in its *Rājaratnākara* version, probably explains and justifies the existence of these and similar South Indian groups. The *Kaḍaimpota* version has actually converted Gajabāhu to a *karāva* hero, whose home was not Sri Lanka but India. Furthermore, he is a contemporary of the Buddha. No further evidence is required to illustrate the mythic character of Gajabāhu.

The viability of the Gajabāhu myth as a mythical charter for incorporating immigrant groups into the Sinhala social structure continued till recent times. The *demala gattara* caste of the Sinhala low country who were recent immigrants to Sri Lanka also trace their ancestry to Gajabāhu's captives. The *salāgama* (*Hāli, Caliya* originally weavers, later cinnamon peelers) who were earlier immigrants also have similar myths. The Portuguese historian of Sri Lanka, Father de Queyroz, writing in the seventeenth century about the exploits of the Sinhala says: ". . . and once they captured 12,000 foreigners with whom they peopled the country of Dolosdaz-Corla and from these, they say, are descended the Chaleaz who are obliged to get the cinnamon."[20] Doḷosdās-Kōrale is in the Matara District where once again there are groups of the *salāgama* caste.

Thus, the Gajabāhu myth has been a continually viable one, justifying and explaining the existence of South Indian settlers in Sri Lanka. But at what period did this version of the myth arise? Two references in the Sinhala chronicles give us important clues. Firstly, the areas where the captives were settled were in the Kandyan region and the coastal areas. These regions came into prominence in the fourteenth century and after, particularly with the founding of the Gampoḷa Kingdom. The movement to the Kandyan areas was consequent to disastrous invasions by the Coḷas (tenth century) and later of Māgha (thirteenth century), which ruined the magnificent civilizations of Anurādhapura and Polonnaruva. It is most likely that *this version* of the colonization myth evolved after the fourteenth century. Moreover, these place names were hardly known in the second century. Secondly, the *Rājāvaliya* version mentions that Gajabāhu brought back with him the insignia of the gods of the Four Dēvāles. The "Four Dēvāles" refer to the temples for the four deities – Skanda (Kataragama), Pattini, Nāta, Vishṇu in Kandy. The "Four Dēvāles" came into prominence in the reign of Kīrti Śrī Rajasiṃha in 1775 A.D., though it existed at the time the *Rājāvaliya* was composed, i.e., the seventeenth century.[21] The *Mahāvaṃsa* and *Cūlavaṃsa* make no mention of the Four Dēvāles. The probability is strong that the concept of the Four Dēvāles also evolved after the fourteenth century in Kandyan times. We can therefore roughly place this version of the Gajabāhu myth between the fourteenth and seventeenth centuries.

There is some further evidence which is of some importance. The *Rājaratnākara* written in the sixteenth century makes no mention of Gajabāhu bringing back with him the anklets of Pattini or the insignia of the Four Gods. The rest of the episode, however, is recounted. The *Pūjāvaliya*, a thirteenth century Sinhala text, has even less to say about Gajabāhu:

> Waknaha Tissa's son Gajabahu "learning that during the reign of his royal father, people were sent from Lanka to work at Kaveri, sent for his ministers, and having made inquiries was highly displeased and took in his hand the iron mace made for him by his royal father. Accompanied by his warriors, with the iron mace in his right hand, to lift which fifty persons were required, circumambulating the sea from right to left, he struck it (with the mace); divided the waters in two by virtue of his meritorious deeds; went to the sea-coast of Soli without wetting his feet; displayed his power; took away twice as many persons as went to work at Kaveri; made a law that henceforth the inhabitants of Lanka shall not go to work at Kaveri; placed guards round the coast; issued a proclamation in Lanka by beat of tom-tom; celebrated his triumph; performed many meritorious deeds; reigned for twenty-two years; and went to the divine world.[22]

The *Pūjāvaliya* account makes no mention of his association with the Pattini Cult, with the Four Dēvāles or with settling down captives in specific places, or the number of captives involved. Moreover, nowhere in the *Pūjāvaliya* or in any of the other literature of the thirteenth century, as far as I could gather, is there any reference to the Pattini Cult. The evolution of the myth, as it is found in the chronicles, could be presented in the following table.

	Cleaves Ocean	Brings Captives	Settles Them	Brings Buddha Relics	Brings Insignia of Four Dēvāles	Brings Anklets of Pattini	Builds Specific Tanks and Temples
Dīpavaṃsa – 4th century							+
Mahāvaṃsa – 5th century							+
Pūjāvaliya – 13th century	+	+					
Rājaratnākara – 16th century	+	+	+	+			
Rājāvaliya – 17th or 18th century	+	+	+	+	+	+	

Does this mean that the cult was not dominant enough to be recorded in the *Mahāvaṃsa* and *Dīpavaṃsa*? There are probably many important incidents that have occurred in Sri Lanka's history which find no mention in the *Mahāvaṃsa* or *Dīpavaṃsa*; thus the absence of reference in the *Mahāvaṃsa* to a certain historical event is no real proof of its non-occurrence. But note that these two early chronicles actually mention Gajabāhu; the "miraculous" exploits of Gajabāhu are, however, not mentioned, though these chronicles are full of "miracle" particularly when it comes to religious matters. It is therefore reasonable to assume that these works which contain enough "miracle" would not hesitate to record grandiose events regarding heroic figures if these events were current information at periods in which they were written. There is then a remarkable evolution of the Gajabāhu story from the matter-of-fact historic accounts in the *Dīpavaṃsa* and *Mahāvaṃsa* to the elaborate myth of the *Rājāvaliya.* The mythic elements are present in the thirteenth century *Pūjāvaliya*, and absent in the fifth century. In the latter three accounts factual references to the construction of buildings and tanks are omitted. During this period the Gajabāhu of history has been transformed into the Gajabāhu of myth. The *Pūjāvaliya* version commences the myth-making process by reference to the cleaving of the ocean and the bringing back of captives.

We noted that the contemporary water-cutting ritual celebrated the cleaving of the ocean by Gajabāhu and that this origin myth or a similar one was incorporated into the *Rājāvaliya*, in all likelihood. It is now obvious that this myth is also included in the earlier *Pūjāvaliya, but without any association with Pattini.* The conclusions we can derive are the following:

(a) The water-cutting ritual is even today not only associated with Pattini but also with other deities.

(b) In all probability it is a rite antecedent to the Pattini Cult.

(c) In the Pattini Cult in Sri Lanka water-cutting is associated with Gajabāhu, but the only substantive connection between the two myths in terms of their content is that Gajabāhu brought back with him the anklets of the deity.

(d) The *Pūjāvaliya* account makes no reference to these anklets or to Pattini.

(e) It therefore looks as if the Gajabāhu myth was the origin myth of water-cutting even before the Pattini cult was dominant in Sri Lanka, or that it was a myth independent of the Pattini Cult.

As a matter of fact there is some internal evidence in the *Pūjāvaliya* account to suggest that even this reference has to do with a ritual. Note that in this account Gajabāhu circumambulated from right to left before he split the ocean with his mace. Such circumambulation rites are performed as a prelude to any propitious ritual even today and it is conceivable that this episode also refers to a ritual. Incidentally, clockwise circumambulation (right to left movement) is viewed as propitious; anti-clockwise circumambulation (left to right movement) is unpropitious, or inferior. Unhappily, there is some controversy regarding the problem of Gajabāhu's circumambulation of the ocean in Sinhala editions of *Pūjāvaliya*. The word for circumambulation is *pradakṣiṇā*; whereas all recent editions of the *Pūjāvaliya* give the word as *dakṣinākoṭa. Dakṣinā* could best be translated as gift or offering, and *dakṣinākoṭa* could read as "having made a gift or offering." However, Gunasekara, who translated this section of the *Pūjāvaliya* in 1895, also published the Sinhala edition in 1893.[23] His version, which is the result of the collation of several palm-leaf manuscripts, has *pradakṣinā-koṭa* "having circumambulated." Scholars whom I consulted agreed with "*dakṣinākoṭa*" as the correct word; the reason they gave was that it was an impossible feat for Gajabāhu to have circumambulated the ocean! My own view is that *pradakṣinā-koṭa* ("circumambulated") is the correct interpretation, and *dakṣinā-koṭa* is simply a result of a literal interpretation of this episode by editors. The final solution to this problem must await the collation of old palm leaf manuscripts of the *Pūjāvaliya.*

Thus we state on the basis of the preceding argument that the Gajabāhu myth originated about the thirteenth century, and that this myth was not associated with the Pattini Cult. It is probable that this lack of association between the "Gajabāhu Cult" and the Pattini Cult continued through to the fifteenth century, for the *Rājaratnākara* also has no reference to Pattini. However, according to this account, Gajabāhu brought back with him the Buddha's almsbowl taken to South India in the time of Valagambā (29-17 B.C.). What is the mythic significance of this inclusion? According to the *Mahāvaṃsa* Tamil chiefs from South India captured the revered bowl relic and took it to India.[24] The *Cūlavaṃsa*, which continues the *Mahāvaṃsa* narration, states that in King Upatissa's reign (365-406 A.D.) the stone bowl was used by the king himself for a rainmaking ritual.[25] No reference to the bowl having been brought back is however given in the *Mahāvaṃsa.* A strange *lacuna*, and not a very comforting one for mass religiosity.

Yet, what about the *stone* bowl in Upatissa's reign? The *Mahāvaṃsa* in the early references does not mention that the bowl was of stone, and it is unlikely that the Buddha used a bowl made out of this particular mineral. The conclusion is again irresistible. The bowl relic was, next to the tooth relic, the major object of mass adoration and also associated with sovereignty. It was taken to South India and lost in Valagambā's reign. Yet mass religiosity cannot brook this loss, and a stone bowl was substituted. (This course of events, incidentally, is identical with that of the history of the tooth relic which suffered similar vicissitudes but always managed to get back to Sri Lanka.) But there is a serious lacuna here for, if the bowl relic was lost in the second century B.C. and yet existed in the fifth century A.D. and thereafter, who recovered it and how? Gajabāhu, of course. Thus, by the sixteenth century when the *Rājaratnākara* was written Gajabāhu the culture hero was credited with this great achievement. Thus this version of the Gajabāhu myth accounts for the presence of the stone bowl in Sri Lanka.

In the *Rājāvaliya* account of the seventeenth or eighteenth century two more elements are added to the Gajabāhu myth: Gajabāhu brings back the insignia of the gods of the Four Dēvāles and the anklets of the Goddess Pattini. What are the Four Dēvāles, and who are its Gods? The Four Dēvāles are the temples of the Four Gods (*hatara deiyo*) - Nāta, Vishnu, Pattini and Kataragama located near the Temple of the Tooth in Kandy. One of the four gods is Pattini; thus Gajabāhu brings the insignia of Pattini (one of the Four Gods) and her anklets, *which are her insignia*! These contradictions which arise from a literalist interpretation of the episode are resolved if we approach it once again as a myth.

The Four Dēvāles are typically associated with Kandyan Kingship, for victory in war and for success in secular undertakings. Though the Four Dēvāles may have existed earlier, they came into prominence in the time of Kīrti Śrī Rājasiṃha (1747-1782 A.D.). Kīrti Śrī Rājasiṃha also inaugurated the procession or *perahära* of the Temple of the Tooth with the four *dēvāles* participating in it.[26] One origin myth of the *perahära* (there are others) states that it was inaugurated to celebrate the victory of Gajabāhu in Coḷa. Thus the significance of the insignia of the Four Gods is obvious: it is linked to the inauguration of the *perahära* by Gajabāhu. What about the separate reference to Pattini's anklets? The likelihood is that by the time the *Rājāvaliya* was composed the Pattini Cult had come into prominence and the water-cutting ritual was associated with other rites performed during annual Pattini rituals, as it is done even today in the *gammaḍuva* rituals for Pattini. If so, the Gajabāhu myth of water-cutting had to be linked with Pattini. This was done through that final version of the myth, which stated that Gajabāhu brought back with him the anklets of the deity.

We are not yet done with the Gajabāhu myth. Gajabāhu, we noted, is the culture hero to whom are attributed several deeds of cultural significance for the Sinhala people. The earliest extant form of the myth is the thirteenth century. It was clearly absent in the fifth. The question is at what period between the fifth and thirteenth centuries could the myth have evolved? A psychological interpretation of the content of the myth may give us a clue. Gajabāhu is the hero leading his people from captivity in the Tamil Kingdom. He is like Moses of the Bible; he cleaves the river with a rod and parts the seas. Gajabāhu is accompanied by Nīlamaha Yōdaya, who appears as a demon Kaḷu Kumāraya in other Sinhala myths.[27] He brings back 12,000 Coḷas in addition to the 12,000 Sinhalas. The number is explained by Spellman in his essay on the ritual significance of the number twelve in Indian culture. Spellman also quotes a Jain myth, strikingly similar to the Gajabāhu one, where an ascetic predicting a twelve-year famine led 12,000 of his people to a more fruitful land.[28] Gajabāhu is the great hero, performing miraculous deeds, vanquishing the detested Tamils. The tone and contents of the myth are highly "nativistic," though not millenarian. It seems a wish-fulfilment more than a reality, a boost for the self-esteem of a group subject to serious vicissitudes of fortune. The mythic fantasy is, we suggest, the opposite of reality. The question that arises then is, what period between the fifth and thirteenth centuries was conducive to the formation of this myth? The intervening historical events provide the answer.

The low point in Sinhala fortunes commenced in the late tenth century with systematic South Indian invasions, unlike the more sporadic incursions of the earlier periods. Sri Lanka was a principality of Coḷa till 1070 when the Sinhala chieftain Kīrti raised the standard of revolt successfully and assumed the Crown as Vijayabāhu I (1055-1110 A.D.). After Vijayabāhu there was a temporary resurgence of Sinhala civilization culminating in the reign of Parākrama Bāhu the Great. The old capital of Anurādhapura had to be moved to Polonnaruva as a result of the Coḷa invasions, and under Parākrama Bāhu I Sinhala civilization reached new heights. But the respite was temporary. In 1215 Māgha of Kaliṅga landed in Sri Lanka with a large army and wrought utter destruction. The *Cūlavaṃsa* gives a detailed account of the destruction caused by Māgha. The *Pūjāvaliya*, written soon after Māgha's invasion, also mentions the tragedy of the Sinhalas. Both accounts mention the number of Keraḷa troops as 24,000, a figure which we pointed out cannot be taken literally. The *Rājāvaliya* gives the number as 20,000 in its brief account of the conquest which is quoted below:

> As moral duties were not practised by the inhabitants of Laṅkā, and the guardian deities of Laṅkā regarded them not, their sins were visited upon them and unjust deeds became prevalent. The king of Kaliṅga landed on the island of Laṅkā with an army of 20,000 ablebodied men, fortified himself, took the city of Polonnaruwa, seized King Parākrama Pāṇḍi, plucked out his eyes, destroyed the religion and the people, and broke into Ruwanväli and the other dagabas. He caused the Tamils to take and destroy the shrines which resembled the embodied fame of many faithful kings, the pinnacles which were like their crowns, and the precious stones which were as their hearts, and the relics which were like their lives. He wrought confusion in castes by reducing to servitude people of high birth in Laṅkā, raising people of low birth and holding them in high esteem. He reduced to poverty people of rank; caused the people of Laṅkā to embrace a false faith; seized those who were observant of morals, and mutilated them,

> cutting off hands, feet, etc., in order to ascertain where they had concealed their wealth; turned Laṅkā into a house on fire; settled Tamils in every village; and reigned 19 years in the commission of deeds of violence.[29]

While Māgha was holding sway over the old capitals of Anurādhapura and Polonnaruva, Vijayabāhu III established a Sinhala Kingdom in Daṁbadeṇi (the Daṁbadeṇiya dynasty) to the south of the Old Kingdom. He was succeeded by Parākrama Bāhu II, his son (1236-1270). His period was one of intense literary and cultural activity, though he also could not reunite the whole of Sri Lanka under his dominion. The *Pūjāvaliya*, which gives the first written account of the Gajabāhu episode, was written during this period.

The socio-historical ethos of the time was conducive to the development of a nativistic myth. The late tenth and eleventh centuries saw a serious decline in Sinhala fortunes with the Coḷa conquest; there was a rapid rise to new heights of glory in the twelfth century; and then in the early thirteenth it sank to the lowest yet in the history of the Island. If we are right that the fantasy in the myth is the opposite of the reality, the period of the depredations of Māgha was probably the time when the myth evolved. We noted that while Māgha was ruling in the old kingdom, Vijayabāhu III established the Daṁbadeṇiya dynasty – the myth may have evolved in this region. If so, the *Pūjāvaliya* written soon after merely committed to writing an existent myth.

When we compare the Gajabāhu myth and the Māgha account, we realize again that the former is a myth which is the opposite of the later "reality": Māgha invades Sri Lanka with 24,000 (or 20,000) Keraḷa troops; Gajabāhu brings back 24,000. Māgha plunders and terrorizes the Sinhalas killing their king; Gajabāhu terrorizes the Coḷas. Māgha populates Sinhala villages with Tamil *conquerors*; Gajabāhu does it with Tamil *captives*. Even more important than these polarities are the social psychological functions of the myth which are to boost the self-esteem of the peoples whose "morale" had sunk low in an era of troubles. We note that these heroic exploits are foisted on Gajabāhu who, as a result, was transformed from a historical into a mythological figure. Unlike millenarian myths the heroic exploits mentioned are projected into a glorious past, rather than a paradisal future. Both types of myths, however, express a "fantasy" which is contrasted with the current reality. If so, the danger in a literalist interpretation of the myth is obvious. As a typical example of such a literalist interpretation we shall quote from one eminent scholar.

> In the reign of the next king a small army of Coḷians invaded Ceylon and carried off much booty and a considerable number of prisoners. This insult was avenged by his son and successor, Gajabāhu (the Elephant-armed), who invaded Tanjore with a large army. The king of Tanjore, intimidated by the sudden attack, acceded to all demands without a single act of hostility. It was the first expedition of the Sinhalese outside their island home, and their success brought about several important and interesting results. Twelve thousand Coḷian prisoners accompanied Gajabāhu on his return home, and they were settled in various parts of the country, where they quite soon became part of the permanent population. Their descendants are scattered in many districts even at the present time, and their language has influenced Sinhalese speech in no small measure. A large number of Coḷian words found their way even into the literary dialect of the Sinhalese. The king of Coḷa also presented Gajabāhu with the jewelled anklets of the Hindu goddess Pattini and the insignia of four Hindu deities, Viṣṇu, Kārtikeya, Nātha and Pattini. The cult of these gods and goddesses was thus introduced into the island; an extensive literature and folklore grew up around these names; special families dedicated themselves to their service, and observances and ceremonies connected with these deities continue to this day. A large number of books dealing with the cult of Pattini are still available.[30]

What light does the preceding analysis of the Gajabāhu myth throw on the *Śilappadikāram* and the chronology of the early South Indian history? One thing is clear: in so far as the Gajabāhu of the Pattini Cult is not the historic Gajabāhu who lived in the second century, the "Gajabāhu synchronism" has to be abandoned once and for all. Secondly, since the Gajabāhu myth probably evolved in the period of the tenth to thirteenth century, a late date for the *Śilappadikāram* is more in consonance with the Sinhala evidence. However, there are several problems yet unsolved, for even the most cautious Indian scholars place the *Śilappadikāram* not later than the ninth century.

If so, the Gajabāhu reference, like Iḷangō Aḍigal's kinship with Śeṅguṭṭuvaṉ, must be later interpolations, a characteristic feature of early literature. Some writers have used the independent references to Gajabāhu in the *Śilappadikāram* and the Sinhala chronicles as proof of the historical authenticity of the protagonist (e.g., Gulasekeram). For the anthropologist this should prove no problem, for myths have circulated in the Indo-European orbit from the earliest times. The Gajabāhu myth evolved in Sri Lanka and probably diffused to South India, since channels of intercommunication between the two countries existed. When myths get diffused, they may be adapted to the socio-historical context of the recipient nation. Hence we see the difference in attitude to Gajabāhu in the two countries. In Sri Lanka, Gajabāhu is the grandiose hero who saved his people from servitude: we noted that the nativism of the myth was conducive to the ethos of the tenth to thirteenth centuries, for this was a period where South Indian invasions were intensest. What about the ethos in South India (especially Coḷa and Keraḷa, i.e., Cera) from where the invasions sprang? The reverse of the Sri Lanka situation must surely be true. This factor is given expression in the Indian adaptation of Gajabāhu, for in the *Śilappadikāram* Gajabāhu is not the hero of Sinhala myth. He is subservient to Śeṅguṭṭuvaṉ who is the grandiose hero in the Tamil epic, also performing improbable adventures. Thus the two different adaptations of Gajabāhu are a fascinating example of a mythic figure adapted to suit divergent socio-historic conditions in two neighboring countries.

It also explains the different roles of Gajabāhu in relation to the Pattini Cult. In the Indian version he introduces the cult to Sri Lanka under the patronage of the Cera king; in the Sinhala version he terrorizes the Coḷa king and brings back the anklets of the deity, a religious object of great veneration. Looking at the Sinhala versions *in toto* Gajabāhu's action here is strictly analogous to his action in respect of the prisoners. The Coḷa king captures 12,000 Sinhala prisoners. Gajabāhu brings them back and in addition 12,000 more South Indian prisoners. A Tamil captures the bowl relic in Valagamba's reign; Gajabāhu brings this back *and in addition* brings back the anklets of Pattini and the insignia of the Four Dēvāles. There is method in the organization of the myth, but this cannot be elucidated by a literal examination of the myth.

The *Śilappadikāram*, we noted, states that Gajabāhu introduced the Pattini Cult to Ceylon under the patronage of the king of Cera, Śeṅguṭṭuvaṉ. The Sinhala Gajabāhu myth does not agree with this. What do the Sinhala *ritual* sources say about the Pattini Cult in Sri Lanka? The text of the *maḍu upata*, sung in Pattini rituals, gives us the answer: the Pattini Cult was introduced by Sēraman ("Ceraman") appears in the Śaṅgam literature as a prefix for several South Indian rulers.[31] A literalist may now argue on the basis of this that the Pattini

Cult was introduced by a king of Cera, probably Śeṅguṭṭuvaṉ. But this is as far-fetched as the Gajabāhu hypothesis as far as we are concerned. Sēraman Raju, like the kings of Pāṇḍi and Soli, in other Sinhala rituals, is also a mythical figure. Consider his case as described in the myths. He had a headache as a result of a frog (who carried an enmity towards the king from a previous birth) having entered his nose. He came to Sri Lanka (for some inexplicable reason) and had a ritual performed. Divinities like Viśvakarma, the divine architect, and Sakra, King of the Gods, came to his aid. This event occurring in mythical times is a prototype of the present *gammaḍuva* ritual. Thus no historicity can be attributed to this myth. However, while it is true to say that the action of the episode is set in mythic times, the myth like any other was composed in historical times.[32] One plausible historical inference we may make from this myth is that the Pattini Cult was introduced by Cera (Keraḷa) colonists from Malaladesa (Malabar?). In Sinhala ritual the words like Malaladesa, Pāṇḍi and Soli refer to South Indian people generally, rather than a specific geographic region in South India. Hence the only cautious inference one can make is that the cult of Pattini was introduced to Sri Lanka by South Indian colonists in all likelihood after the tenth century.

Gajabāhu and Karikāla

One of the fascinating problems that emerge in the study of the Gajabāhu myth is the reference in the *Pūjāvaliya* and *Rājāvaliya* to Sinhala people taken captive by the Coḷa king in the reign of Gajabāhu's father to work at the river Kāverī. It was these people that Gajabāhu (like Moses) went to rescue. The name of the Coḷa king is not mentioned, but the reference is clearly to the great Coḷa king, Karikāla, who according to Nilakanta Sastri reigned around the second century A.D., about the time of the historical Gajabāhu's father. Post eighth century Telegu and Tamil literary and epigraphic accounts state that one of the achievements of Karikāla was the enlargement of the river. What are we to make of this synchronism? Does it enhance the historicity of these events, or does it reflect an interrelated corpus of myth common to South India and Sri Lanka? An examination of Karikāla, both as a historical and a mythical figure, will help elucidate this problem.

We are fortunate that Nilakanta Sastri in his scholarly work on Coḷa history and administration has sifted the literary and epigraphical evidence to disentangle the historical facts about Karikāla from the mythical accretions which developed much later. In fact, the development of the Karikāla story follows almost the same pattern as that of Gajabāhu – from the factual accounts of contemporary or near contemporary sources to the improbable and grandiose accounts of later works.[33] Nilakanta Sastri sums up some of the facts of Karikāla's reign from the early literature as follows:

> He inherited the throne of Cola as a boy; illegitimate attempts were made by his relatives, for a time successfully, to keep him out of his birthright; by his own ingenuity and strength, and with the assistance of friends and partisans from outside, among whom may have been the maternal uncle Irumbidarthalai, Karikala after some years of confinement in a prison, effected his escape from it and succeeded in making himself king. An early accident from fire which maimed him in the leg for life seems to be rather well attested and to furnish the true explanation for his name.[34]

Even much of this seems legendary, strongly suggestive of the prototypical myth of the birth of the hero. The first part is reminiscent of the Krishna-type myth, while the latter reference to the maimed foot is tantalizingly reminiscent of Oedipus. From the eighth century the Karikāla of history gradually becomes converted into the Karikāla of myth in Telegu and Tamil accounts. He is credited with several achievements, two of which are relevant for our purposes here, viz. his construction of the flood banks of the Kāverī, and his conflict with the three-eyed king variously known as Trinetra Pallava or Trilocana Pallava ("Three-eyed Pallava"). The seventh or eighth century *Mālēpādu* plates of *Punyakumāra* (Telegu) mention that Karikāla was the worker of many wonders, "like that of controlling the daughter of Kāverī, overflowing her banks."[35] The tenth and eleventh century records known as the *Tiruvālangādu* plates of Rājendra I, and the Leyden grant, repeat this story, while the *Kanyākumārī* stone inscription adds a very important detail in its reference to kings who worked as slaves for Karikāla. "(Karikāla) who was as bright as the sun and who curbed the pride of the insubordinate, controlled the Kāverī – which, by its excessive floods, caused the earth to be deprived of its produce – by means of a bund formed of earth thrown in baskets carried in hand by (enemy) kings."[36]

In the *Kalingattupparani* further exploits of Karikāla are narrated and a probable reference to his having wiped out the third eye of an enemy; this reference is clearly made in the Ulās of *Oṭṭakkūttan* of the twelfth century: "The Cola Karikala who took the eye of him who did not come to raise the Kaveri banks which took the earth carried on the heads (of subordinate kings)."[37] The same poet in his poem on Kulōttuṅga II makes it clear it was a third eye of one Mukhari that was lost, in all probability by sorcery based on imitative magic: ". . . we know of the wiping out of one eye traced on the picture so that the inimical Mukhari lost one of his three eyes."[38] The fourteenth century work, the *Navacōlacarita*, a Telegu rendering of a Kannaḍa work, expands this and introduces two further elements – the construction of a tank and a war waged against insubordinate kings. Karikāla decides

> that he should raise the banks on either side of the river and dig a tank and earn for himself the religious merit thereof. So he sent his *sāmantas* (subordinate chiefs) from the various parts of the realm and all of them came up, with the exception of Bhāskara-Cōla and Mukkanti Cōla and others who held themselves back on account of their noble birth and other like reasons. The king undertook a *daṇḍayātrā* (expedition) against them, conquered them, and took them captives and compelled them to work on the construction of the banks of the Kaveri until the task was completed.[39]

Though this work does not mention the three-eyed king, Telegu epigraphy of the fourteenth century states that the person who lost the third eye was a Pallava king.

The reader should bear in mind the following features in the development of the Karikāla myth.

(1) Karikāla raises the banks of the Kāverī.

(2) Subordinate kings work like common laborers in the project. One account mentions the loads they carried on their heads.

(3) A three-eyed king – known as Mukari, or Trinetra Pallava, or Trilocana Pallava, defied Karikāla who, probably through magic, wiped out the third eye of the former.

(4) The *Navacōlacarita* does not mention the three-eyed king; instead, it refers to several subordinate kings who defied Karikāla, and against whom Karikāla waged successful war.

(5) The account also mentions the construction of a tank by Karikāla, though it is by no means clear what relationship this has with the bunding of the Kāverī.

Let us now examine how these elements of the myth are related to the Gajabāhu and other related myths of Sri Lanka.

The connection between the Gajabāhu myth and that of Karikāla is the reference in the *Pūjāvaliya* and the *Rājavaliya* that Sinhala people were taken captive by the Coḷa king and put to work in the river Kāverī. The reference is clearly to the Karikāla myth, though that myth in its South Indian forms makes no mention of Sinhala captives.

The *Gajabā Katāva*, the Sinhala ritual text mentioned earlier, explicitly states how the Sinhala captives were forced to work in the Kāverī. The first part of the *Gajabā Katāva*, sometimes known as the *Ankoṭa Haṭana* ("the conflict of the short-horn"), states that in the time of Gajabāhu's father there lived a poor Sinhala villager who owned a buffalo with a pair of short horns. This buffalo was forcibly used by other villagers for their ploughing. The owner complained to the king, but the king only heeded the counter-complaints of the other villagers and offered no redress to the owner of the short-horn buffalo. The latter therefore decided to go to Soli-rata (the country of Coḷa). The king of Soli is described thus in the following verse:

> The great King of Pandi possessing three eyes
> He (Soli) destroyed; he broke Pandi's might;
> he dammed the waters.
> "I have no other recourse but to seek his help,"
> Thus he prepared to leave for the country of Soli.

Our Sinhala exile ingratiated himself into Soli's confidence and persuaded the king to dam the waters of the Kāverī. The king of Soli sent messages to the rulers of the eighteen realms; they all came to work in the Kāverī. But try as they might the waters of the Kāverī river washed out the mud used for the construction. The exile now told the king that he would find the men to build the dam. With a large fleet and many soldiers he sailed for Sri Lanka and landed at Māgama. He ordered the soldiers to capture Sinhala villagers; they captured 12,000 Sinhalas all in one night and returned to Coḷa where they were employed as laborers in the Kāverī.

One could, I think, reasonably conjecture the manner in which the Gajabāhu myth was linked up with Karikāla. The Gajabāhu myth in the form in which it is expressed in the *Pūjāvaliya* and *Rājāvaliya* is, we noted, a "colonization myth," providing a charter for the existence of South Indian peoples in Sri Lanka. According to the myth, Gajabāhu, like Moses, brings his people from captivity. How did the captivity theme appear in the myth? I think the answer is a simple one. Alien South Indian groups who were settled in Sri Lanka had in some ways to justify or legitimize their existence here. Thus a charter had to be provided for explaining the obvious fact that they were alien, and yet, at the same time, show that they were *not* alien and really belonged to the country in which they were naturalized. This is a problem for any immigrant group in a larger society. The theme of captivity provides a resolution to the problem of how immigrant groups could be alien and not alien at the same time, for the myth states that in fact they were originally Sinhalas settled in South India (Coḷa) after being dispossessed from their original home in Sri Lanka. Thus the myth provides a charter of legitimation for the immigrant group. The dominant Sinhalas among whom they were planted could however keep them as a group apart by activating the same myth, and stating that they were in fact aliens, Coḷa slaves captured by their great King Gajabāhu. For, it should be noted that Gajabāhu brought back with him two categories of people – the original Sinhalas captured by the Coḷa king in his father's reign, and an equal number of Coḷas as captives. The further question of how these original Sinhala people were made captives is neatly resolved by linking the Gajabāhu myth with the Karikāla myth; for Karikāla was preeminently the Gajabāhu-type culture hero for South Indian peoples, performing improbable deeds, putting "captives" to work in the Kāverī. What Gajabāhu is to Sri Lanka, Karikāla is to South India. Indeed, Karikāla like Gajabāhu, is a kind of colonizer, for according to several versions of that myth he was responsible for rebuilding the city of Kāñchī and settling it with immigrants. It is therefore highly apposite that the Gajabāhu and Karikāla myths should be interlinked in this manner.

Karikāla Lore in Sinhala Ritual

The relation between the Gajabāhu myth and that of Karikāla does not exhaust the study of the Karikāla traditions of Sri Lanka. There are two other Sinhala mythical traditions, somewhat contradictory to the one described earlier, drawing upon the mythical lore contained in the South Indian Karikāla traditions. These several accounts unmistakably suggest that the South Indian Karikāla traditions were widespread even in Sri Lanka, and were adapted to the socio-economic conditions of the country into which they were diffused. We will deal firstly with Sinhala myth and ritual which indirectly draw upon the Karikāla lore of South India described by Nilakanta Sastri. The Sinhala text that we will use is known as the *Pataha* ("tank") and is enacted dramatically in the *gammaḍuva* ceremony. Since I have analysed this ritual elsewhere, I will only present those aspects of the ritual which show their relationship to the Karikāla myths.[40]

The *Pataha* ritual is a dramatic enactment of the following myth. The king of Pāṇḍi is an evil, arrogant king, possessing three eyes, one of which is located in the middle of his forehead. He had a most wonderful city built by the divine architect Viśvakarma himself, resembling the city of the gods. The king, ruler of the eighteen realms was also a cruel tyrant. The songs state that –

> No kind thought ever ripened in his mind,
> His power however ripened from day to day.
> His mind like a fearful demon's "ripened,"
> Like Warrior Ravana ripened his strength.

The king of Pāṇḍi feels that he should build a "tank," so that his city will resemble that of the god Sakra, who also had a large pond. He therefore ordered his ministers to build a tank for him. The king, however, in his arrogance ignored traditional custom – he started work on an inauspicious day and hour.

The work on the tank got started and people worked there like slaves. The king himself supervised the work:

> Wearing robes worth a thousand gold pieces,
> Brandishing his sword studded with a thousand gems
> Like Ravana entering the field of battle
> Comes the great Pandi king to the tank.
> He grabs hold of idlers and beats out their brains.
> He cuts their bodies and slaughters the lads . . . .

A wave of fear and discontent runs around the camp, and people complain thus:

O foolish king, in spite of his broad forehead
To please him we carry large baskets on our heads.
We suffer a thousand sorrows and misfortunes
Our heads are bald by carrying these baskets!

Now the king ordered the rulers of the eighteen realms to come and work in his tank. All came, except the king of Soli (Coḷa), and they were made to work like common laborers.

Even the kings who lived in the shade of goodness
Didn't have a thing to eat the live-long day
They draw loads of earth and heap them on both sides
They suffer terribly like rounded-up cattle.

The king of Soli not only refused to come but insulted the king of Pāṇḍi's emissary by lopping off his nose and ear and feeding him with excrement. Yet in the ritual, Soli is presented as a just king, contrasted with the evil Pāṇḍi. Various stereotyped acts of justice attributed to many South Indian kings (including Eḷāra of Sri Lanka) are also attributed to Soli. Soli's insult to Pāṇḍi aroused the latter's wrath. Pāṇḍi decided to wage war against Soli, and marched into the country of Soli with his army. Soli undeterred, blew his conch and his friend, the God Sakra who heard this, created a huge downpour that engulfed and destroyed Pāṇḍi's army. Pāṇḍi himself managed to escape back to Madura, where he cursed Soli. As a result of his curse the land of Soli was devastated by a drought, which brought in its wake pestilence and famine. Another myth, also enacted in the form of a ritual drama known as the *amba vidamana* ("shooting of the mango"), describes how Sakra came down to earth and wiped out the third eye of Pāṇḍi, and ended the drought in the country of Soli.

It is obvious that the *Pataha* ritual practised by the Sinhalas draws on the same body of mythological lore from which the Karikāla myths derive. The similarities are striking. There are references to the building of a tank (as in the *Navacōlacarita*), the employment of crowned kings and their suffering, and above all to the three-eyed king. Though some historians have tried to prove the historicity of these events, the Sinhala data add greater cogency to Nilakanta Sastri's view that they are myths. Indeed, it is also probable that these myths were originally enacted as ritual dramas, even in their South Indian home. The wiping out of the third eye of Mukhari (or Trinetra Pallava) strongly suggest a ritualistic act, analogous to the wiping out of the third eye of Pāṇḍi in Sinhala ritual drama.

In the *Gajabā Katāva* the king of Coḷa constructs a dam; he destroys an enemy, the three-eyed king of Pāṇḍi (always presented as the embodiment of evil in Sinhala myth). In the *Pataha* these two persons coalesce; the evil three-eyed king of Pāṇḍi (Trinetra Pallava of South Indian texts) builds a tank and he has a conflict with Soli, one of the rulers of the eighteen realms. All these myths derive from a common source. In the *Pataha* ritual they are adapted to serve different social ends, as I have demonstrated elsewhere.[41]

Sinhala Myths of Karikāla

In the preceding ritual Soli and Pāṇḍi are not historical figures but mythical beings acting out a grand conflict between good and evil. However, there is another set of myths, related to the preceding one, in which the king of Soli is explicitly identified with Karikāla. These myths are the following: *Kāverī Ganga Diya Helīma* ("the dropping of the waters of the Kāverī river"), *Karikāla Upata* ("the birth of Karikāla"), *Ganga Bändīma* ("damming of the river"), *Diyakeli Katāva* ("story of the water sports"). All these, like the preceding myths we had described, are part of the cycle of myths associated with the Pattini Cult.

This set of Karikāla myths takes off from the description of the drought in the kingdom of Soli described in the *Pataha* ritual. *Kāverī Ganga Diya Helīma* describes how the gods had assembled in heaven to review the affairs of the world, and saw with concern the drought that ravaged the kingdom of Soli. One god, Mā Muni ("the great sage," i.e., Agastya), decided to help Soli and went to the *anōtatta vila*, the pond sacred to Sakra. However, this pond was protected by a snake named Kāli. When the sage asked permission from Kāli for some water from this pond, the snake refused. Then the sage took the guise of a *gurulu* bird (the enemy of snakes), chased the cobra away, and collected some water from the pond, into a pot. The angry cobra complained to the gods, who decided to help the cobra. One of the gods took the form of a crow, and flew down to where the sage was bathing with the pot of water lying near him. The crow tried to open the lid of the pot and the sage who saw this clapped his hands to scare the crow away. The crow, frightened, spilled the water from the pot; this flowed out into the country of Soli and became the river Kāverī.

Karikāla Upata describes the birth of Karikāla. A king of Soli went out hunting with his followers. They saw a pond in which there were fish. The king ordered the pond to be filled with mud (in order to kill the fish). This was done and all the fish died. As a result of this heinous sin, there occurred a continuous shower of mud, which killed (?) the king and his followers and destroyed much of the realm. The queen, who was pregnant, however, managed to escape and sought shelter with a Brahmin couple. The text describes the various stages of the pregnancy and the arrival of the time of delivery. The actual delivery had to be delayed because the time was astrologically dangerous. In order to delay the birth the legs of the queen were tied with a silk cloth and, at the astrologically propitious time, this cloth was untied. The text then goes to describe the growing up of the boy and an incident that led to his becoming king. The state elephant of Soli got intoxicated with alcohol and went on a rampage. The young prince brought the elephant under control and the elephant went down on its knees before him. The people who soon assembled there brought a seat which was placed on the back of the elephant and the prince sat on it. The mother of the prince then rubbed charcoal on his feet and he was led triumphantly into the city and was accepted as the king of Soli. Since he was smeared with charcoal, he was named Karikāla.

Ganga Bändīma describes the construction of the dam across the Kāverī by Karikāla with the help of feudatory monarchs. Several attempts failed, but at last they succeeded when they used *kumbal mäti* ("potter's clay") and *tala tel* (sesame seed oil) for constructing the dam. *Diyakeli Katāva* describes the water sports held in order to celebrate the completion of the dam.

Several conclusions can be drawn from the evidence given above. Firstly, the Karikāla myths of South India were also common to Sri Lanka and were associated with the corpus of the Pattini Cult. However, the content of some of these myths seems to contradict the content of others. For example, according to the *Ankoṭa Haṭana*, Sinhala captives were made to work on the Kāverī, whereas according to the *Ganga Bändīma* this was done by the feudatory monarchs of Karikāla. Such contradictions are expectable when attempts are made to link up one body of mythology with another body of related myths. Secondly, the lore mentioned in South Indian Karikāla myths (such as the blinding of the three-eyed king, and the king's use of feudatory monarchs to construct a tank) is found in a totally different context in Sinhala myths, such as the *Pataha*. This suggests that the lore contained in the Karikāla tradition was part of a larger mythological corpus common to both South India and Sri Lanka. Thirdly, the Sinhala myths of Karikāla draw much of their content from a body of lore in South India stretching from about the period of the *Śilappadikāram* to the seventeenth century. For example, the statement in the Sinhala text that Karikāla's birth was delayed by tying the legs of his mother with a silk cloth has its earliest echo in a fourteenth century annotation to the third century text *Pattupāṭṭu* which states that "Karikāla's birth was delayed by unnatural means and that he was retained in his mother's womb until the auspicious moment came for him to be delivered."[42] The Sinhala text *Diyakeli Katāva* seems to be derived from canto VI, II of the *Śilappadikāram*. The earliest reference in South Indian literature to the elephant incident mentioned in the *Karikāla Upata* is found in a commentary to the sixth century text, *Paḻamoḻi*, and repeated in more detail in the *Śevvandippurāṇam*, a seventeenth century work.[43] This work also mentions the destruction of Uṟaiyūr in a sandstorm, which is probably the "rain of mud" described in the *Karikāla Upata*. The Sinhala evidence clearly indicates that the Karikāla myths recorded in the later period of South Indian history did not constitute a disconnected series, but represented a viable continuing tradition.

The Gajabāhu Myth in Social Action

In the preceding pages I have dealt with the following problems: the evolution of Gajabāhu from a historical to a mythic figure; the lack of validity of the Gajabāhu synchronism; the relationship between the two culture heroes, Gajabāhu and Karikāla; and finally the link between Karikāla myths and the Sinhala text, the *Pataha*. In the course of the analysis I have discussed the functions of one version of the Gajabāhu story as a colonization myth used to justify the existence of South Indian settlers, legitimize their presence and anomalous status and incorporate them into the larger Sinhala society. Let me develop this theme further and illustrate how this myth is actually used by some contemporary social groups.

My first illustration is from the *karāva* fishermen of Negombo. There exist today bilingual fishermen in the area between Chilaw and Negombo, speaking both Sinhala and Tamil. They are therefore groups who are "anomalous" in respect of the exclusively Sinhala speaking fisherfolk, south of Negombo, and the exclusively Tamil-speaking groups north of Chilaw. They are thus marginal groups sandwiched between two exclusive linguistic areas. South of them are predominantly Sinhala-speaking fishermen belonging to three castes – the *karāva, durāve* and *goyigama.* From the point of view of the latter groups they have a problem in relation to the former – how is it that while these bilingual fishermen are like themselves in some respects, they are also so different? The Gajabāhu myth is again used to justify the anomalous status of the bilingual groups living in close proximity to the Sinhalas: they are Coḷa (Soli) captives of Gajabāhu settled by him in this region. When recent immigrants from South India become better assimilated into the Sinhala social structure – when they become exclusively Sinhala-speaking – the myth has to be refashioned so as to give a higher status to the better assimilated immigrant group. This point could be neatly illustrated in respect of the *karāva* community of Alut Kuruva, south of Negombo. The sixteenth century *Rājaratnākara* states that Gajabāhu settled his captives in Alut Kuruva. Thus, this form of the myth is the same as the one used to refer to present day bilingual fishermen. It is very likely that at the time the *Rājaratnākara* was written the Alut Kuruva fishermen were also recent immigrants, and hence they were treated as the Coḷa captives of Gajabāhu, rather than the original Sinhalas rescued by him. Today, however, Alut Kuruva is Sinhala-speaking and its people have a clear Sinhala identity. The Sinhala *karāva* groups also believe that they are descended from the prestigious *Kauravas* mentioned in the *Mahābhārata.* The Kaḍaimpota version of the colonization of Alut Kuruva quoted by Bell is probably a later version of the myth to suit the changed status of the fishermen of Alut Kuruva. In this account Gajabāhu is a contemporary of the Buddha who brought with him settlers from Kururata where the prestigious Kauravas lived.

The Gajabāhu myth then is not a static one but expresses a dialectic between various social groups. Our second example from the North Central Province will illustrate this status dialectic carried to an extreme. From the point of view of the higher castes of the region the blacksmiths of Roṭāveva are inferior. Their inferiority is explained by saying that they are captives of Gajabāhu settled in this region. However, the Veddahs of the North Central Province give a different twist to this myth. As far as the Veddahs are concerned, they (the Veddahs) are the original settlers of Sri Lanka; the blacksmiths of Roṭāveva, as well as the *goyigama* folk (*raṭē minussu*), are all later immigrants and aliens in territory that is rightfully theirs. Thus Veddahs state that all groups in the North Central Province, excluding the Veddahs, are descendants of Gajabāhu's captives. They are no doubt correct, for it is very likely that most, if not all, Sinhala groups in this island were at some period or other immigrants from South India. The Gajabāhu myth is a symbolic way of expressing this sociological fact.

Notes

1. V. Kanakasabhai, *The Tamils Eighteen Hundred Years Ago*, second edition (Tirunelveli, 1954).
2. S. Natesan, "The Sangam Age in Tamilnad," *History of Ceylon*, Vol. I, H. C. Ray, Editor-in-Chief. (Colombo: University of Ceylon Press, 1959), 206-207.
3. V. R. R. Dikshitar, *Silappadikāram*, (Oxford, 1939).
4. Kamil Zvelebil, "Tamil Poetry Two Thousand Years Ago," *Tamil Culture* (1963), X, 19-30.
5. K. A. Nilakanta Sastri, *History of South India*, second edition (Oxford, 1958), 112.
6. S. Paranavitana, "Lambakaṇṇa Dynasty: Vasabha to Mahāsena," *History of Ceylon*, Vol. I, 179-191.
7. Dikshitar, *Silappadikāram*, 342-343.
8. *Ibid.*, p. 6.
9. *Ibid.*
10. S. Vaiyapuri Pillai, *History of Tamil Language and Literature* (Madras: New Century Book House, 1956), 144.

11. B. C. Law (ed.), *Dīpavaṃsa*, in *The Ceylon Historical Journal* (Colombo, 1958), Vol. 7.
12. Wilhelm Geiger (trans.), *Mahāvaṃsa* (Colombo: Government Printer, 1911), 254-255.
13. B. Gunasekara (trans.), *The Rājāvaliya* (Colombo: Government Printer, 1911), 47-48.
14. Natesan, "The Sangam Age in Tamilnad," *History of Ceylon*, Vol. I, 212.
15. K. K. Pillay, *South India and Ceylon* (Madras: University of Madras Press, 1963), 136.
16. G. C. Mendis. The quotation is from Dr. Mendis (personal communication).
17. B. Malinowski, *Magic, Science and Religion* (New York: Doubleday, 1955), 101.
18. H. C. P. Bell, *Report on the Kegalle District* (Colombo: Government Printer, 1904), 2.
19. M. D. Raghavan, *The Karava of Ceylon* (Colombo: K. V. G. de Silva, 1961)
20. Father Fernando de Queyroz, *The Temporal and Spiritual Conquest of Ceylon* (Colombo: Government Printer, 1930), Book 1.15.
21. R. H. Aluwihare, *The Kandy Perahara*, second edition (Colombo: Gunasena, 1964).
22. B. Gunasekara (trans.), *A Contribution to the History of Ceylon, Translated from "Pujavaliya"* (Colombo: Government Printer: 1895), 21-22.
23. B. Gunasekara (ed.), *Pūjāvaliyen upuṭāgannālada laṅkākatāva* (Colombo: Government Printer, 1893), 21.
24. Wilhelm Geiger (trans.), *Mahāvaṃsa* (Colombo: Government Press, 1934), 232-233.
25. Wilhelm Geiger (trans.), *Cūlavaṃsa* (Colombo: Government Printer, 1953), 19.
26. Aluwihare, 2-3.
27. Paul Wirz, *Exorcism and the Art of Healing in Ceylon* (Leiden: Brill, 1954), 34-39.
28. John W. Spellman, "The Symbolic Significance of the Number Twelve in Ancient India," *Journal of Asian Studies*, Vol. XXII, No. 1, (1962), 79-88.
29. B. Gunasekara (trans. and ed.), *Rājāvaliya* (Colombo: Government Printer, 1900), 61-62.
30. G. P. Malalasekera, *The Pāli Literature of Ceylon* (Colombo: Gunasena, 1958), 50.
31. Vaiyapuri Pillai, *op. cit.* 95-99, 110-159.
32. Some traditions of the *gammaḍuva* refer to Gajabāhu having built a temple for Pattini, but I have encountered this only in two ritual traditions. All ritual traditions, however, mention the Sēraman myth. The former references are, I suspect, attempts to link Sinhala ritual with the *Śilappadikāram* tradition.
33. K. A. Nilakanta Sastri, *Studies in Cola History and Administration* (Madras, 1932).
34. *Ibid.*, 44.
35. *Ibid.*, 27.
36. *Ibid.*, 28.
37. *Ibid.*, 30-31.
38. *Ibid.*, 44.
39. *Ibid.*, 35-36.
40. G. Obeyesekere, "The Pataha Ritual: Genesis and Function," *Spolia Zeylanica* (Colombo: Government Press, 1965), Vol. 30, Part II, 3-20.
41. Though it is not possible to date with accuracy when these myths diffused to Sri Lanka, it is nevertheless important that we can trace its origins in South India from the eighth to fourteenth centuries. It is likely that they also reached Sri Lanka during the systematic South Indian conquests of the tenth to thirteenth centuries. Since working on the Gajabāhu myth I have revised some of my views on the *Pataha* ritual, specially regarding its antiquity. However, my general analysis of the *Pataha* ritual is unchanged. I believe that it is a ritual of protest by ordinary villagers against the utilization of forced services by Sinhala kings to build public works like tanks. It is also likely that the Karikāla myths of India served similar social functions.
42. K. A. Nilakanta Sastri, *op. cit.*, 20-21.
43. *Ibid.*, 24, 36-37.

Religion and Legitimacy of Power in the Kandyan Kingdom

H. L. Seneviratne

EVER SINCE ITS introduction to the island, certain organized aspects of the Buddhist religion have been inextricably bound with the concentration of political authority. The regnancy of Buddhism over the land and the people is well expressed in a consistently arranged order of symbols found in the *Mahāvaṃsa* and ingrained in the memory of society – the legendary vision of the Buddha himself that the doctrine (*Dhamma*) would shine in Ceylon; the footprint of the Buddha on a majestic peak believed to be visible from all parts of the island; the dedication of the island to the religion by Devānaṁpiya Tissa (250-210 B.C.), the implantation of the Bodhi Tree to take firm root in the land; and more. According to the Jetavana slab inscription of Mahinda IV (956-972), kingship is a status bestowed upon the ruler for defending the Bowl and the Robe (EZ, 234, 237, 240). Wars have often been proclaimed as mere attempts to defend and propagate the religion. The author of the *Mahāvaṃsa* describes Duṭṭhagāmaṇī as marching against the Tamils having "a relic put into his spear" (*Mv.*, 170) and attributes the following to this hero, about to take to the battlefield: "give us, that we may treat them with honor, bhikkhus who shall go on with us, since the sight of bhikkhus is blessing and protection for us" (*loc. cit.*).[1]

It cannot, however, be maintained that this repetitive pattern of royal munificence toward the religion was merely an attempt at the legitimation of political power, "domestication of the masses," as Weber stated. A look at the ideological basis of the Buddhist polity reveals a different facet of the close association between ruler and religion. This ideology is scattered throughout the Buddhist corpus, the most direct statements to be found in the *Nikāya* literature such as *Dīgha, Saṁyutta* and *Aṅguttara*. Excellent secondary accounts are found in Gokhale (1953, 1966). However, for the present purposes I can do no better than refer to the imaginative work of Tambiah,[2] a work enriched also by his extensive knowledge of Thailand, the only Buddhist kingdom not colonized by a Western imperial power, where there is "a persistence of certain patterns that other Southeast Asian polities have irrevocably lost" (*op. cit.*: 2). In Tambiah's exposition, Buddhist polity consists of three entities: the religion characterized by the three jewels, Buddha, Dhamma and Sangha; kingship idealized in terms of a universal righteous emperor who is also an embryo Buddha; and a people whose historical destiny is the preservation of religion and kingship. Tambiah states that "the strain to identify the Buddhist religion with the polity, and the Buddhist polity in turn with the society were deep structure tendencies in the Buddhist kingdoms of Southeast Asia . . . ." (*op. cit.*: 3).

It is sometimes argued that the heightened involvement of the state with Buddhism during the era of the Nāyakkar kings of Kandy (1739-1815) is the result of a conscious attempt on the part of these kings who were "aliens in race, language, religion and culture" (Dewaraja, 1972:20) to legitimize their power. I have tried to suggest elsewhere[3] that these kings were really not so alien as they are often portrayed to be by historians. At least, it is legitimate to ask the question, "alien to whom?" They were certainly not any more distant, idealized or alien to the vast majority of the people than the Sinhalese kings themselves were. Besides, the alleged "religious revival under the Nāyakkars," upon close examination, appears to have started long before their advent. Heightened religious activity, I would like to suggest, was a cyclical phenomenon in Ceylonese history. Close association between state and religion was a constant and is in keeping with the notions of Buddhist polity referred to above. It is not my intention to deny that the Nāyakkar kings, particularly the first to succeed to the throne of Kandy, were blind to the copious use to which religion might be put in consolidating their government. The point worth noting here is that palace intrigue was by no means unknown in the long history of the island and there would have been many *Sinhalese* kings – not "aliens" – who were much more uneasy on the throne than the Nāyakkars. In view of these facts it does not stand to reason that their being Nāyakkar was the sole or even the determining factor that made these kings involve themselves in religious activity. Under Sēnarat (1604-1635), Vimaladharmasūrya II (1687-1707), and Narēndrasiṃha (1707-1739), the "cultural revival" had already started to swell and the Nāyakkars who immediately followed these three kings only rode its crest.

Bearing in mind that the association between state and religion was a continuing factor in Ceylonese history, let us examine how specifically the Nāyakkars translated this association into practice. It should not surprise us to find the translation to be one which suited their political interests. Two broad mundane goals emerge as the rationale of the religious policy of the Nāyakkar kings, in particular the first two, Śrī Vijaya Rājasiṃha (1739-1747) and Kīrti Śrī Rājasiṃha (1747-1782): (1) political integration of the kingdom and the enhancement of centripetality, and (2) idealization of the king by resort to identification with religion and culture and hero-kings of the past. The second goal embraces many of the activities involving the building and repair of religious monuments, and the organization of religious festivals. Let me hasten to add that one or both these goals could also be considered the rationale for religious activity for most kings of the past. We will try to illustrate the pursuit of these goals by reference to concrete acts as recorded in the major source book for the period, the *Cūlavaṃsa*. It must be added that many of these acts overlap in their effect in the achievement of the above goals. It is rather obvious that these acts have, of necessity, to be combinations of the spiritual and the temporal.

II

Let us first look at some acts that illustrate the goal of political integration and centripetality. The temples the Nāyakkars built or restored were scattered all over the island. Royal visits to these sites, which the inauguration and other festivals of these temples occasioned, had the sociological function of strengthening the king's hold over the provinces. From the *Cūlavaṃsa* descriptions we can infer that these visits were quasi-military: they had the character of a temporary movement of the capital to the particular provincial site. These "festivals" themselves were smaller scale repetitions of the military displays that were periodically made in Kandy in the guise of religious festivals. The visits of the Siamese envoys to the sacred places performed a similar sociological function. The envoys would have wished, undoubtedly out of piety, to visit places of religious interest as the author of the *Cūlavaṃsa* states (284). The opportunity, however, was seized by the king both to display to the provinces the bearers of the doctrine and to send along with them a "retinue," a term which the *Cūlavaṃsa* and other traditional works often mention. These "retinues" cannot but be construed as displays of military ceremonial. The Wheel of Righteousness was rolled into the provinces – but by the king's military men.

The vessel carrying the Siamese monks arrived in Trincomalee and in conducting the monks to Kandy the king again displayed his association with religion on the one hand and power on the other. The King's commander-in-chief (*mahāsenāpati*) was sent to fetch the distinguished guests. Rest houses were built on the route between Trincomalee and Kandy and as the monks were conducted in pomp and ceremony the king exemplified the moral and physical forces by marching to meet the delegation at the entrance to the city "with the army in piety" (*Cv.*, 259, n.2). We see here again the pattern, characteristic of Nāyakkar rule, of diluting the coercive with the spiritually desirable.[4]

Always a fine instrument of political power, the annual Äsala festival and pageant in Kandy was reorganized by Kīrti Śrī in revivalist directions which were simultaneously directions of enhancement of his control over the provinces. Each year in the month of Äsala after a week or so of preliminary ritual the insignia of the four principal gods of Kandy (Nātha, Vishnu, Kataragama and Pattini) were taken in solemn procession in the streets of the capital. Ostensibly a religious pageant, the *Äsala perahära*, as it was called, also microcosmically represented the civil and military departments of the state, both central and provincial. Religious imperatives compelled the annual participation of the provincial chiefs in the pageant thereby bringing them annually to the king's presence for a period of about a month, a period in which "the refractory were punished, the loyal rewarded, and new regulations were promulgated that they might be carried to the more distant districts of the land" (Pridham, 1849:331). Kīrti Śrī's innovation in the Äsala pageant was the introduction of a section that carried the Tooth Relic enshrined in a golden casket. He placed this section at the head of the pageant, thereby giving it primacy over the sections that carried the insignia of the gods. Such an arrangement was a dramatic representation of the place the king accorded Buddhism in relation to the worship of the gods who were associated with the Hindu religion. The king did not fail to make himself conspicuous by riding in the pageant "in royal splendor" (*Cv.*, 260-61). The centralization of the ordination ceremony by confining it to a consecrated spot (*sīmā*) in Kandy also contributed to political centralization, as pointed out by Malalgoda (1976). Monks who annually visited the capital from all over the island were undoubtedly reinforced in their evaluation of the king and central authority. The visit of the provincial chiefs and monks to Kandy for the Perahära and ordination, respectively, expressed in reverse the same principle of contact with the provinces embodied in such religious acts as the king's pilgrimages to the sacred sites situated away from Kandy, and visits to the provinces by central officials.

Kīrti Śrī ascended the throne in 1747, only eight years after the elevation of the first Nāyakkar king Śrī Vijaya Rājasiṃha (1739-1747). Although Śrī Vijaya had intensified the "religious revival" and had engaged in many endeavors designed to receive political support among the people, eight years is hardly a long enough period to achieve stable control over the kingdom. It is quite understandable then that Kīrti Śrī Rājasiṃha, then a youth of sixteen, would have been rather uncomfortable on the throne. He could not have asserted himself by appeal to physical force, nor could he have felt secure without the exercise of it. The circumstance was one that called for an exhibition of muted power, the desired medium between all force and all piety:

> . . . moving along with royal magnificence, the Great King whose merit was now having its effect, marched round the town, his right side turned towards it, thus making it known that the realm of Laṅkā, bereft of its king had again a king . . . ." (*Cv.*, 255-256).[5]

Marching in this manner is reminiscent of the type of worship known as *pradakṣinā.* It is also, however, suggestive of conquest which is often described as "surrounding" (*vaṭalāma*). The new king was treating the city both as an object of worship and an object of domination by force.

The Nāyakkars made innovations in the worship of the Tooth Relic that had implications for political solidarity and legitimacy. We already referred to one: the introduction of the Tooth Relic to the Äsala festival by Kīrti Śrī. This innovation, which proved to be a particularly successful one, was a development from a similar innovation made by his predecessor Śrī Vijaya where a spectacular Hindu rite was introduced to the Temple of the Tooth. This was the introduction of the Kārti festival at the Temple:

> now after the Lord of men had offered abundantly with all kinds of ornament, such as gold . . . he bethought himself of the great blessing inherent in a sacrifice of lamps. Hence the Lord of men issued the command that in their own town and in the cetiyas in the divers provinces on one and the same day, people should make an offering of lamps, and in that selfsame night he gathered together the people and celebrated a sacrifice of lamps with seven hundred and ninety thousand, six hundred lamps. Thus with burning lamps the Ruler of Laṅkā made the land of Laṅkā alike to the star-strewn firmament (*Cv.*, 251).

While the introduction of a spectacular festival was of credit to the king in the public eye, the king also reaped another kind of benefit. For the command was to perform the festival on "one and the same day in the diverse provinces." A potentially integrative new national ceremony was thus brought into being. Besides, the king's command was that ceremonial oil for the festival be issued from the palace. Representatives of the provincial temples came to Kandy annually to receive the ceremonial oil, providing us with another example of the familiar pattern of establishing royal tentacles in the provinces. The reality of this was reinforced by the symbolism of the venue of oil distribution, the Nātha *dēvālē*, which was also the venue of the king's consecration. Here, in the presence of the central and provincial officials, the sword of state and a forehead ornament was tied onto the king who took a new name and emerged from the ritual transformed from humanity to divinity (Davy, 1821:158-164). The ceremony also expressed the supremacy of the Temple of the Tooth over the shrines of the gods anticipating Kīrti Śrī's transformation of the Perahära. Äsala and Kārti, two of the four major festivals at the Temple of the Tooth, are thus Nāyakkar innovations. It is conceivable that the other two, New Year and New Rice, could also have been installed by them. They both exhibit the characteristic feature of island-wide participation.

III

Let us now try to specify some aspects of Nāyakkar religious and cultural policy that illustrate their attempt at idealization of themselves and the achievement of almost sacred esteem among the people. Some of these are obvious ones, while others are characterized by great subtlety. Both kinds displayed discernible patterns and had similar inner meaning. This meaning, not far to seek, consisted in the fulfilment of the fundamental prerequisite of being a Buddhist, namely honoring the primary constituents of the religion, the Buddha, the Dhamma and the Sangha; in the display of adherence to certain other commonly held religious values; and in explicit or implicit emulation of the hero-kings of the past idealized in the chronicles and celebrated in the popular imagination.

In honoring the Buddha, Dhamma and Sangha, the Nāyakkars largely followed traditional ways while making some innovations. The worship of the Buddha is traditionally through the worship of the relics. Such relics could be *Sārīrika*, or Bodily Relics such as the Tooth Relic; *Pāribhōgika*, or Relics that have been the objects of use by the Buddha such as the Bowl Relic; and *Uddēsika*, or Relics that are symbols of the Buddha such as the Wheel or Footprint. We will note that the Nāyakkars were eager to worship and display their religious esteem of all three types of relics or representations of the Buddha.

The Nāyakkars, particularly Kīrti Śrī Rājasiṃha, pursued a large-scale policy of rebuilding old religious structures or building them anew. It is not necessary to enumerate them, but it is of some interest to note their locations and their religious and political symbolism. One location is Anurādhapura, studded with sacred sites such as the Bodhi Tree, Ruvanvälisāya and Thūpārāma – the greatest religious city of Ceylon and the height of achievement of the Sinhalese kings and Buddhism. Polonnaruva, another location of Kīrti Śrī's rebuilding activity, is second only to Anurādhapura in the spheres of religious and cultural achievement. It also represents the political unification of Ceylon under King Parākramabāhu I (1153-1186). Of similar significance are many other locations: Mahiyaṅgaṇa, the site of the legendary first visit of the Buddha to Ceylon where the original *yakkha* inhabitants offered the island to him (*Mv.*, 3-4) and the site of the stūpa that enshrines two primary relics, the Hair and Collar Bone; Samantakūṭa, the site of the second visit of the Buddha and the Sacred Footprint, one of the finest symbols of the Buddha's dominion over Ceylon; Ridī Vihāra, said to have been first built by the Sinhalese Buddhist hero Duṭṭhagāmaṇī (*Cv.*, 293); and Kälaṇiya, the site of the Buddha's third visit to Ceylon. Śrī Vijaya Rājasiṃha erected statues at the Aluvihāra (*Cv.*, 251) where the Tripiṭaka was committed to writing in the first century B.C. (*Mv.*, 237).

The Nāyakkars took over from Narēndrasiṃha the support of the Buddhist Order and increased it manifold. One expression of this was the support given to the monk Saraṇaṃkara who strived to revive the study of the texts and the ascetic tradition which had then been compromised in favor of an order of semi-monks known as *ganinnānsē*. As the *Cūlavaṃsa* states, "the king was minded to further the Order which had fallen into decay" (278). The Buddhist Order, with Saraṇaṃkara as head, received a high degree of royally backed organization, which was emphasized by the establishment of an ordination center in Kandy where all monks desiring ordination had to sojourn for the purpose.

Perhaps the most fruitful of all efforts to display interest in the Buddhism that the Nāyakkars had was the establishment of *Upasampadā*, the Buddhist higher ordination. This was the result of the work of several rulers, but its political benefits were largely reaped by Kīrti Śrī Rājasiṃha during whose reign the missions to Thailand finally succeeded. According to Ceylonese belief, Ceylon is the land where Buddhism would shine. Hence the re-establishment of Upasampadā would clearly credit its architect with perpetuating the status of Ceylon as Dhammadīpa, the Island of the Dhamma.

Kīrti Śrī Rājasiṃha also organized festivals for the worship of the Dhamma, explicitly recognized as such, by the term *Dhamma Pūjā* (*Cv.*, 297). Along with large crowds he participated in special ceremonies to listen to the Dhamma. In one festival he is mentioned as having invited monks who were particularly known to be good preachers and had the *Mahāmaṅgala Sutta* and other texts recited (*Cv.*, 297). The king arranged for other and regular preachings of the doctrine (*Cv.*, 297); he also listened to the Siamese monks chant the *Dīgha* and *Saṁyutta Nikāya, Saddhammasaṁghaha*, and other texts (*Cv.*, 284).

These descriptions of the *Cūlavaṃsa* strongly suggest a conscious effort to conform to an ideal which at the broadest level can be expressed as the worship of the Buddha, Dhamma and Sangha. The *Cūlavaṃsa* mentions that the king "believed firmly in the three sacred things" (288). Again we have reference to the king holding "full of reverence for the Triad of Jewels" (291), a sacrificial festival for the Buddha and at the same time sacrificing to the chapter of bhikkhus (291). Worship of the Dhamma is only implicit here, but we noted above ceremonies where the object of worship (*pūjāvattu*) is the Dhamma itself. The ceremonial arrival of the Siamese delegation afforded an excellent opportunity for Kīrti Śrī to display his esteem of the three sacred objects: in the train of envoys there was a golden figure of the Buddha, sacred books representing the Dhamma and the *bhikkhus* with Thera Upāli at the head representing the Sangha (Geiger, 1953:281).

In the *Daḷadā*, the Tooth Relic, which had been the symbol of sovereignty since the twelfth century or so, the Nāyakkars found an ideal object of conspicuous veneration in their attempt to identify with the religion and the people. The Daḷadā was considered to be of great mystical power and was always jealously guarded by the kings throughout its history in Ceylon. The Nāyakkar kings made a particular attempt to display their proximity to and custodianship of the Daḷadā. The *Cūlavaṃsa* abounds in references to ceremonies of worship of the Daḷadā and gifts and honor offered to the Temple of the Tooth. It is also conspicuous in its references to many specially arranged expositions of the Daḷadā. The idea of display is explicit. Consider the following: the kings "displayed" the Tooth Relic (251); "the ruler in his mercy thought to show the Tooth Relic" (276); the king "exhibited the Tooth Relic for the salvation, blessing and happiness of all" (284); and the king "showed it forth" (249). Restoring the Daḷadā to the Temple of the Tooth in Kandy from its safe confine during the war with the Dutch was also made a great display. The king "could not bear the pain accruing to him from his separation from the Tooth Relic" and "with retinue betook himself to the most improbable part of the province" (*Cv.*, 269). When he saw the reliquary, the king worshipped it, "his head touching the ground" to "chase away his pain" (*loc. cit.*).

The *Cūlavaṃsa* dramatizes the event in which the Nāyakkars first publicly identified themselves with the Tooth Relic:

> Since the Lord of men had heard from foolish people . . . that great evil would befall if he were to place the relic in a new relic temple, he gave orders that this should be done by other people and betook himself thence to another town. While he sojourned there the dignitaries assembled and together with the caretakers and other people, they tried with all their might to open the reliquary. But although they tried the whole night long they did not succeed. The dignitaries went thither and told the matter to the great king. When the King heard that, he came in haste to the splendid city and after the ruler had reverently made offerings with all kinds of fragrant flowers, with lamps, incense and the like and shown his reverence, he took hold of the lock and at once opened the reliquary without difficulty. Then after opening one after the other the caskets inside it, he beheld the Tooth of the Enlightened One. "It is accomplished, with success" uttering these joyful words, he assembled the inhabitants of the town, prepared a great feast and celebrated a great sacrificial festival . . . ." (248-49).

According to the *Cūlavaṃsa*, this is the first concrete event where the king displays his veneration of the Daḷadā. It seems to be the launching point of their religio-cultural campaign.

The Nāyakkar kings held public ceremonies in connection with religious activities. A particularly striking example is the restoration and extensive adornment of the Ridī Vihāra to which *Cūlavaṃsa* devotes fifty verses (pp. 295-298). A host of Buddhist symbols were sculptured or painted in the temple. The dedication of the temple attracted large crowds who were thus treated to royal piety. One of the temple wall-paintings was that of Duṭṭhagāmaṇī, who is said to have originally built the temple. The temple was particularly appealing to the popular imagination because of the variety of colorful but serene representations pleasing to the eye evoking sentiment traditionally described as the happiness of seeing the Buddha (*Buddhālambana prīti*), the counterpart of *bhakti* in Hinduism. At the Dhammapūja festival at this temple, listening to the doctrine and seeing the images "filled . . . (the participants) . . . with the highest joy and ecstacy, as if by a sermon of the living sage" making manifest both "the beauty of his form and the charm of his sermon" (*Cv.*, 297). The sight of the golden images filled their hearts with joy, "as if they saw the enlightened one at the miracle of the double appearances" (*yamakaṁ pā tihāraṁ*) (*Cv.*, 297). The dedication of the newly built or restored temples usually took place on an auspicious day astrologically selected for the ceremony of painting the Eyes of the Images (*nētra maṅgallaya*)[6] (*Cv.*, 296). During such ceremonial occasions the Nāyakkar kings "made themselves one with the religion and the people." We have a detailed record of a *nētra* ceremony which illustrates this point. It was the dedication of the Alut Vihāra at Asgiriya by the young Śrī Vikrama Rājasiṃha, the last Nāyakkar and last king of Ceylon, before he was driven to atrocities by the intrigues of his courtiers. As Coomaraswamy notes, this was "perhaps the last of the many occasions . . . when ruler and people met together united by a common religion and common culture, in sympathy and mutual respect" (1908: 13-14). On this occasion the king, accompanied by his mother and sister, came to the *vihāra* just after sunrise and worshipped the Buddha and asked Ähälapola to read the ola leaf manuscript dedicating the villages to the new temple. One of the villages, Udasgiriya, belonged to his mother, who joined in the ceremonial offering. Then the king walked round to see the vihāra and, noticing the bare surface of the rock that formed the outer wall of the temple, ordered the land grant to be more indelibly inscribed on it. After about two months the king returned to the site and asking Ähälapola to read the land grant again checked the rock inscription against the ola manuscript. Then, pleased with the endeavor of the stone masons, the king made land grants to them (Lawrie, 1896: 74).

In a monarchy there is no better way the king can honor a person, institution, or valued object than by treating these on equal terms with royalty. The king can suffuse things outside himself with the glow of his royalty and transform them with the richness of his alchemy. Treating religious persons, institutions and objects as royalty is a subtle but intensely effective way of publicly conferring honor on them. In Buddhism there is a long and richly elaborated tradition of treating the Buddha as king (*sarvagña rāja*). The Tooth Relic, ever since its arrival in Ceylon, was treated with the utmost veneration and in all likelihood treated with royal honors. The *Kaňdavuru Sirita* describes the daily routine of King Parākramabāhu II (1224-1266) which is strikingly similar to the daily ritual of the Tooth Relic performed today. There can be little doubt that the Nāyakkar kings proliferated the idiom of the royal ritual in the daily official worship of the Tooth Relic.

We have seen that Nāyakkars made innovations in the worship of the Tooth Relic by adding new festivals or giving the Temple of the Tooth a prominent place in ritual. Śrī Vijaya Rājasiṃha, the first Nāyakkar king, "placed the Tooth Relic on a silver throne" (*Cv.*, 249), thus giving it royal honor and symbolically sharing the realm with the Relic. It is reasonable to assume that this act was followed by giving the Relic honors accorded to the occupant of a throne. Indeed, the Temple was an exact replication of the palace in other ways too, such as the naming and allocation of space and the hierarchy of officials employed in Temple service. For example, terms such as *vädasiṭina māligāva* (sacred sanctuary), *multän gē* (kitchen), *halu maṇḍape* (clothes pavillion) and *maha aramudala* (treasury) are as true of the palace as they are of the Temple. The Temple, indeed, is called the palace by the Sinhalese even today. According to some informants from Kandy, the king (Kīrti Śrī) sometimes gave up his royalty as when he honored the Tooth Relic by personally carrying the *hēmakada* or the "golden pingo" of food offerings. In an extreme instance, the king had made, out of his hair, a brush to sweep the floor of the inner sanctum of the Temple. An exquisite sweeping brush, never publicly displayed, nor even mentioned but reverently called "Its Lordship the Sweeping Brush" (*musun vahanse*), is identified by the officiating monks today as the sweeping brush made out of the king's hair.

The religious revival and the establishment of the Upasampadā afforded an excellent opportunity for Kīrti Śrī to treat the Sangha as royalty and sometimes he symbolically abdicated in favor of the Sangha. The position of *Saṅgharāja* (monk in king) he created is one example. It is not relevant whether the title was borrowed from Thailand or elsewhere. The king's act displayed to the society his high esteem for the Sangha. Further, the symbolic transference of royalty to the Sangha is perfectly in keeping with numerous other acts we have already mentioned, which also had the familiar inner meaning of tempering royal power by associating it with spiritual authority.

The transference of royalty to the Sangha was reinforced by its annual enactment in another ceremony, that of Upasampadā.[7] Of the monks ordained during the annual ordination season the king selected some each year for the title *vāhala nāga* or Nāga (neophyte) of the Court. The ceremony was held once a week for the duration of the four-week season. Two neophytes each week, judiciously selected one from each of the two great monasteries Asgiriya and Malvatta, were conducted with royal honors to the Temple of the Tooth where the king ceremonially placed crowns on the two neophytes dressed as princes. Afterwards they were entertained in the traditional manner of royal entertainment by singers and dancers. This is very likely a Thai custom, but what is relevant here is that it fits into the pattern of religious legitimation of power woven by the Nāyakkars.

The pattern of symbolic abdication and, at times, the exchange of the kingly role for another is of considerable antiquity in Ceylonese history and could have been provided by the king's examination of the past as a store of symbols for the display of religiosity. It should not surprise us, if this is the case, that he would look at similar historical occasions. The bringing of the Bodhi Tree to Ceylon was one such occasion. The families who brought the Bodhi Tree (*bōdhāhārakula*) were given royal treatment by King Devānaṁpiyatissa (250-210 B.C.). When the Tree was brought to the capital on the fourth day of its arrival in the country and when it was planted there, the king entrusted the government to the members of the *bōdhāhārakula* and they appeared in royal attire while the king acted as door keeper (*dōvārika*) to the Bodhi Tree. The handing over of the government to these families was clearly a symbolic act. In this context it is interesting to recall the legend that Yasalālaka Tissa (112-120 A.D.) exchanged kingship with his *dōvārika* in equally fictive behavior and lost his life when the now-enthroned *dōvārika* asked that the king be executed (*Mv.*, 250). One is tempted to see a shadow of this same confusion of symbol and reality in the case of Saraṇaṃkara who plotted to assassinate Kīrti Śrī when he was "monk-king," appointed by the king himself.[8]

The Nāyakkars also tried to imitate the kings of old glorified in the chronicles. The *Cūlavaṃsa* is explicit in this: "When he (Kīrti Śrī) heard the doings of former kings of Parākramabāhu and others, he recognized it as right and imitated their doings" (262). In re-building the Ridī Vihāra, originally built by the hero-king Duṭṭhagāmaṇī, Kīrti Śrī also had made a representation of the former, thus displaying his emulation of the hero. Further, the Nāyakkars tried to display their conformity to the traditional model of the virtuous king. "He (Kīrti Śrī) learned the duties of a king, was filled with reverence for kingly duties, shunned the false paths, schooled himself in the four heart-winning qualities, showed his brother and others all favor by befitting action, made them contented and won their hearts by caring for them in the right way" (*Cv.*, 262). The *Cūlavaṃsa* is numerous in its references to the "four heart-winning qualities" to be practiced by a king and "duties of a king." Kīrti Śrī's order to update the *Mahāvaṃsa* was also an attempt to link himself with the long line of Sinhalese Buddhist kings (262-263). He further displayed his desire to be a righteous king in traditional terms in such acts as public listening to the Rājovāda ("an admonishing of the king") (*Cv.*, 270).[9] The acceptance of Kīrti Śrī by the people is charmingly expressed in the *Cūlavaṃsa* author's reference to him as "our Sinhalese king" (*amhakaṁ Sīhalindo*) (*Cv.*, 292). Soon after the lines strongly disapproving of the destructive work of Rājasiṃha, we find reference to Kīrti Śrī as "our happy, sublime Sīhala ruler" (*Cv.*, 292). The unmistakable suggestion is that Rājasiṃha, by birth a Sinhalese is only nominally so, whereas Kīrti Śrī is a true Sinhalese by virtue of his conformity to the ideal of a Buddhist king. This is an ingeniously subtle recollection of the Buddhist attitude that it is work and not birth that determines a person's worth, the attitude expressed in the well-known verse "not by birth but by act is one a Brahmin or a Vasala."

Notes

For the purposes of this paper I use Geiger's chronology of Sinhalese kings (1953: IX-XV). Existing disagreements in this matter are largely irrelevant for this paper. Since the usage of the English plural marker -s to indicate the plural of Pāli and Sinhalese words seems awkward to me, I avoid this except in the case of terms that are well-known in English (for example, *bhikkhu*); instead, I use the singular consistently. I use Geiger's translation of the *Mahāvaṃsa* (1960) and *Cūlavaṃsa* (1953) and for convenience refer to the work by page number rather than by chapter and verse. Instead of the new name Sri Lanka I use the old name Ceylon.

1. Rājasiṃha II (1635-1687) did the same (*Cv.*, 235).
2. The reference is to a paper read at the meetings of the American Academy of Religion in Chicago in 1975. Tambiah's paper is currently being published in a collection of essays edited by Bardwell L. Smith entitled *Religion and Legitimation of Power in Thailand, Laos, and Burma* (Chambersburg, Pa.: Anima Books, 1978). The contents of this paper are extensively elaborated in Tambiah (1976). The Buddhist notion of the union of religion and polity, familiar to me from the work of Gokhale (*op. cit.*), Rāhula (1956) and others, and my own studies, was never more forcefully conveyed to me than by Professor Tambiah's eloquent paper. I wish to record my indebtedness to him.
3. "The Alien King: Nāyakkars on the Throne of Kandy." *The Ceylon Journal of Historical and Social Studies*, New Series, VI, 1 (1977).
4. The mythological and ritual expressions of the blending of temporal power and spiritual authority are discussed in Coomaraswamy's exemplary work (1942).
5. If this is a customary act upon accession of a new king, we do not hear of it. Even if it is so, it does not make any less likely that the performance could be manipulated by the king for his advantage. The march of the new king described here could also be interpreted as an enactment of the *digvijaya* ceremony or the inauguration of the *cakkavatti* king whose wheel travels in the four directions. In both cases the king would be using powerful traditional symbols of ideal kings. Both, it may be noted, are acts of conquest.
6. For accounts of the *nētra* ceremony, see Coomaraswamy (1908: 70-75; Gombrich, 1966).
7. Some details of this ceremony are given in Seneviratne (1969, 1973).
8. Some further examples of symbolic abdication could be cited. King Devānaṁpiyatissa wanted the city to be included within the boundaries of the Mahāvihāra so that he might abide under the command of the Buddha (*Mv.*, 110). This king also bestowed kingship on the Bodhi Tree itself (*Mv.*, 129). The *Mahāvaṃsa* states that emperor Asoka also bestowed kingship upon the Bodhi Tree (126, 127). Duṭṭhagāmaṇī offered kingship to the Dhamma five times, each time for seven days (*Mv.*, 223). He also thrice conferred on the relics of the Buddha kingship over Ceylon (*Mv.*, 216). Mahādāthikamahānāga offered himself and his wife and children, and the state elephant and horse to the Sangha who refused them and "with knowledge of the custom," the king redeemed all by giving gifts to the Sangha (*Mv.*, 244-245).
9. "Perhaps the same as Rājavagga of Aṅguttara, III, 147 ff." (Geiger, 1953: 270 n. 1).

References

1. Coomaraswamy, A. K.
1908 *Mediaeval Sinhalese Art, Being a Monograph on Mediaeval Sinhalese Arts and Crafts, Mainly as Surviving in the Eighteenth Century, with an Account*

of the Structure of Society and Status of the Craftsman. Gloucestershire: Essex House Press. 2nd edition, New York: Pantheon.

1942 *Spiritual Power and Temporal Authority in the Indian Theory of Government.* American Oriental Series, Vol. 22. New Haven: American Oriental Society. 2nd edition, New York: Kraus Reprint Corporation, 1967.

2. *Cv.* *Cūlavaṃsa, being the more recent part of the Mahāvaṃsa* (Parts I and II). Tr. Wilhelm Geiger. Colombo: Government Information Department. 1953.

3. Dewaraja, L. S.
1972 *The Kandyan Kingdom of Ceylon 1707-1760.* Colombo: Lake House.
EZ *Epigraphia Zeylonica, being Lithic and other Inscriptions of Ceylon.* Ed. D. M. de S. Wickremasinghe, later by H. W. Codrington and S. Paranavitana. Colombo: Ceylon Government Press. 1910.

4. Geiger, Wilhelm
1953 *Cūlavaṃsa* (see *Cv.* above).

5. Gokhale, B. G.
1953 "Dhammiko Dhammarāja." *Indica*, pp. 161-165.
1966 "Early Buddhist Kingship." *Journal of Asian Studies*, XXVI (1), pp. 15-22.

6. Gombrich, Richard
1966 "Consecration of a Buddhist Image." *Journal of Asian Studies*, XXVI (1), pp. 23-36.

7. *Mv.* *Mahāvaṃsa, or the Great Chronicle of Ceylon.* Trans. Wilhelm Geiger. Colombo: Government Press. 1960.

8. Malagoda, K.
1976 *Buddhism in Sinhalese Society, 1750-1900.* Berkeley: University of California Press.

9. Pridham, Charles
1849 *An Historical, Political and Statistical Account of Ceylon and Its Dependencies*, 2 vols. London: T. & W. Boone.

10. Rahula, W.
1956 *History of Buddhism in Ceylon.* Colombo: M. D. Gunasena & Co.

11. Seneviratne, H. L.
1969 "The Sacred and the Profane in a Buddhist Rite," *Ceylon Studies Seminar*, 1969/70 Series, No. 7, Peradeniya.
1973 "L'ordination bouddhiste à ceylan." *Social Compass*, XX (2).

12. Tambiah, S. J.
1976 *World Conqueror and World Renouncer*, Cambridge University Press.
1978 "Sangha and Polity in Modern Thailand: An Overview," in Bardwell L. Smith (ed.), *Religion and Legitimation of Power in Thailand, Laos, and Burma* (Chambersburg, Pa.: Anima Books, 1978).

Contradictions in Sinhalese Buddhism

Heinz Bechert

A GLANCE at the history of scholarship often answers not only the question of how we have arrived at notions which prevail today, but also enables us to recognize to what historical circumstances we owe our contemporary view, and thus what we have to do to move beyond it. It seems to me that the investigation of Ceylonese Buddhism is a good example of this. In the course of time a multitude of different approaches were employed and several apparently antithetical methods of presentation were developed. However, the representatives of different schools of scholarship often took no notice of each other's work, so that a comprehensive approach could not arise. The history of the different methods is, briefly, as follows:

First is the early *ethnographic* approach. Robert Knox, in his *Historical Relation of Ceylon* (1681), gave a descriptive account of the religion of the Sinhalese which was much used and quoted until the first half of the nineteenth century. The description is not correct in all particulars, but for its time it is astonishingly unprejudiced. Buddhism and folk religion appear in their parallel existence; the more important rituals and festivals are described, as well as the different classes of gods and the magic cults of the demon ritual. Knox knew, of course, almost nothing about the teachings of Buddhism; only the doctrine of rebirth and the theory of merit are formulated, even if not very precisely. Concerning the historical side of the Buddha tradition, he says only, "Him (i.e., the Buddha) they believe once to have come upon the Earth."

The ethnographic approach was greatly refined in the nineteenth century. An important work is Edward Upham's *History and Doctrine of Buddhism ... with Notices of the Kappooism, or Demon Worship*, London 1829. In the same year there appeared the first book – for a long time the only one – which translated texts of Sinhalese folk religion: *Yakkun Nattannawa and Kolan Nattannawa* by John Callaway. The next fairly important study of this tradition treats only folk religion: Dandris de Silva Gooneratne's essay "On Demonology and Witchcraft in Ceylon" (*Journal of the Ceylon Branch of the Royal Asiatic Society*, Vol. 4, No. 13, 1865, pp. 1-117). Gooneratne recognized to what extent Ceylonese folk religion is systematized. He writes (p. 2): "And although there is scarcely a single country in the world in which this belief (i.e., belief in spirits) does not more or less prevail in some form or other, yet we do not think there is

---

Originally published in *Tradition and Change in Theravada Buddhism: Essays on Ceylon and Thailand in the 19th and 20th Centuries* (Leiden: E. J. Brill, 1973), edited by Bardwell L. Smith. This was Volume 4 of *Contributions to Asian Studies.* Reprinted with permission.

any in which it has developed itself in such gigantic proportions, or such hideous forms, as in this beautiful island. Elsewhere, it may sometimes exercise considerable influence and even command devoted votaries; but here it has been moulded into a regular religion, arranged and methodized into a system, and carefully preserved in writing; so that the amount of the influence which is exercised over the thought, the habit, the everyday life of a Sinhalese, is such as can hardly be believed by a stranger to the character of a genuine Sinhalese Buddhist."

Gooneratne gives an extensive description of the demon cult, a description which as a whole has not been replaced even today by more recent studies. Only three modern authors have offered important contributions which in a similar manner comprehend folk religion descriptively: Hugh Nevill, Paul Wirz and Otokar Pertold. It is characteristic of these studies that Buddhism appears as a kind of superstructure over the base of Sinhalese folk religion. Thus Gooneratne observes that other authors such as Sir Emerson Tennent have underestimated the significance of the demon cult.

The second approach to be mentioned is the *Buddhological.* In Europe the investigation of Buddhism seriously began with the studies of Eugène Burnouf in the middle of the nineteenth century, and soon the importance of the hitherto overlooked Pāli sources was recognized. Ceylon was the origin of most of the manuscripts of the canonical texts, and educated Ceylonese monks offered an important source of information for an understanding of the sources. We must also not forget the studies of Daniel John Gogerly (1792-1862) which later were seldom quoted but which can be described as the first detailed and basically correct accounts of the corpus of Buddhistic teaching on the basis of the Pāli sources. Rhys Davids called Gogerly the greatest expert of his time in Pāli literature. With the studies of Thomas Williams Rhys Davids, Hermann Oldenberg and other Indologists of the last quarter of the nineteenth century an historical-critical understanding of early Buddhism was created and this understanding was applied to Ceylonese Buddhism because, in Ceylon, the canonical writings were acknowledged as the authoritative source of religion and there the *Sangha* of the Theravada tradition lived on in unbroken continuity.

This identification of canonical and modern Ceylonese Buddhism was furthered still more by the fact that the beginning Buddhist reform movement had as a result the revivification of the study of the canonical texts in Ceylon itself and by the fact that the Indologists came into contact primarily with representatives of the reform movement within the *Sangha*. To be sure, the Indologists could not overlook the fact that monastic practice did not correspond to the precepts of the *Vinaya*, that is of canon law, and that the cult of the gods and the exorcism of demons had an important place in the religion of the Sinhalese.

And yet representatives of this approach tried rather precipitously to explain away such observations or simply ignored them. Whatever could not be derived from Buddhist tradition was an "adulteration" of the religion, a Hindu influence or simply popular superstition. An instructive example of this tendency is André Bareau's book on modern Ceylonese Buddhism (*La vie et l'organisation des communautés bouddhiques de Ceylan*, Pondicherry, 1957).

In this connection it must be borne in mind that for several decades Buddhistic studies gave primacy to quite different objects of interest than the investigation of Ceylonese Buddhism. As a result of newly discovered Sanskrit versions of the canonical writings and access to the Chinese and Tibetan canons, the Pāli sources became, rather than *the* main source for older Buddhism, *a* source among others. In addition, Indian Buddhistic philosophy appeared more interesting from a broad cultural point of view than the later development of Theravadin orthodoxy.

After the pioneer years at the end of the last century, while the Buddhologists turned to other areas, the Pāli tradition remained the source for the so-called *neo-Buddhistic movement.* European Buddhists, especially those who entered monastic communities in Ceylon, wrote a number of important studies on the Pāli literature. They also presented in their writings a particular picture of living Buddhism in Ceylon. This picture was, as can easily be imagined, anything but realistic. Their writings were largely conceived as missionary tracts and they themselves had found a spiritual home in a land where Buddhism predominated. A good example of a description of conditions by a representative of this trend is Nyanatiloka's "Influence of Buddhism in a People" (*The Light of the Dhamma,* Vol. 1, No. 4, July 1953, pp. 29-32.)

Primarily in the first two decades of the present century, under the influence of the interest of broader circles of the public in Buddhism, an *apologetic activity* among theologians of the two great branches of Christianity became evident. In this activity it was not a question of giving a realistic picture of conditions by a rectification of the presentation of the neo-Buddhists, but rather of damning Buddhism itself by trying to unmask it as an inferior teaching. One of the most extreme attempts in this direction is Joseph Dahlmann's *Buddha, ein Culturbild des Ostens* (1898). According to Dahlmann, in Buddhism the "destructive elements of materialism and nihilism luxuriantly flourish." Somewhat more restrained than the Jesuit Dahlmann and yet essentially with the same tendentiousness, other theologians answered the challenge of Buddhism. For example, in 1909 Theodor Simon could say that Buddhism "threatened old cultural values by its penetration into the spiritual realm of the West and shook to its foundations what centuries have built." As absurd as this may seem to us today, yet it belongs to the history of the Western view of Buddhism. It is equally certain that this controversy has not precisely made an impartial view of modern Buddhism easier.

Under these conditions, the application of modern *religio-sociological and structuralist methods* to the investigation of modern Buddhism, which began with the studies of Michael Ames, Nur Yalman and others after 1960, was without doubt a great step forward. The hitherto totally neglected question of the systematic relationship of Buddhism and folk religion was recognized as a central problem for an understanding of Sinhalese religion of the present and an attempt was made to provide an answer to it.

In the enumeration of the different ways of viewing modern Ceylonese Buddhism that of American *political scientists* must not be omitted. W. Howard Wriggins published his classic description of the internal political situation of Ceylon in the last few decades in 1960. (W. Howard Wriggins, *Ceylon, Dilemmas of a New Nation*, Princeton, N. J., 1960). Questions of the significance of religion for this development are to be sure treated rather summarily here, yet Donald Eugene Smith and others have subsequently treated the matter in detail. In this group of studies not so much emphasis is placed on the historical background and the particular ways of thinking of the Buddhist peoples, but the religious-political developments are interpreted primarily as consequences of conflicts of power politics and ideological debates in the manner known from other countries. Without doubt these studies have enriched our knowledge of important aspects of modern Buddhism to an extraordinary degree.

Even if it does not concern itself with Ceylon, in this historical methodological survey another study must be mentioned whose manner of presentation and argument is applicable quite well to Ceylonese Buddhism: Emanuel Sarkisyanz' *Buddhist Backgrounds of the Burmese Revolution* (The Hague, 1965). Sarkisyanz proceeds from the point of view that the traditions of medieval Buddhism are evident again and again in the process of the modernization of Burma. Even the most radical Marxists make use of Abhidhamma terminology, the socialist movement conjures up messianic hopes, etc. This analysis, which is diametrically opposed to the usual political approach cannot be evaluated here, but it must be mentioned that material similar to that collected by Sarkisyanz in Burma could also be found in Ceylon.

Aside from the treatises mentioned, there are naturally numerous studies which belong more in the area of *journalism*. In these, the question of whether Buddhism will be able to withstand the advance of communism almost always stands in the foreground. Well-known, for example, is the book of the religious historian Ernst Benz, *Buddhas Wiederkehr und die Zukunft Asiens* (English edition: *Buddhism or Communism: Which Holds the Future of Asia?* Garden City, 1965). Such studies are of course only of limited use to us, because they isolate a question which cannot reasonably be answered in isolation.

The first volume of my own book *Buddhismus, Staat und Gesellschaft in den Ländern des Theravāda-Buddhismus* (Frankfurt, 1966) was finished at the end of 1964; since no account of the development of political Buddhism in Ceylon and no survey of the tendencies of Buddhistic modernism useful for scholarly purposes existed at that time, sufficient documentary material had first to be collected. But the arrangement of this material demanded a certain point of view. In the process I proceeded from the following basic considerations.

Clear differences exist between original Buddhism and the forms of Buddhistic religion which we observe today. These differences can be correctly assessed only by considering their historical development. The question must therefore be posed as to which phenomena reach back into the pre-modern period and what, on the other hand, can be observed only in more recent times. Thus a division results: canonical, traditional and modern Buddhism. Now the effort to return to the sources is a characteristic of all reform movements and therefore of Buddhistic modernism as well. As with other reform movements, however, modern Buddhists could not bring about a real regeneration of original conditions or even know what they really were. From this there results a tension between, on the one hand, the still-effective forces of traditional Buddhism, with its ties to historical social conditions, legal relationships and manners of thinking of the Sinhalese, and the determined reformers on the other. This antithesis has pervaded the discussions concerning the state-Sangha relations and the laws concerning the Buddhist temporalities and the efforts to regulate them from the middle of the last century to the present. The battlelines are, however, not at all as clear as one would like to think at first, since even the reformers do not oppose the political goals of Sinhalese-Buddhist nationalism and by so doing either give up or at least circumscribe principles of the original doctrine, to wit, the conception of Buddhistic universalism and the tolerance of other religious communities. It can be seen from the history of political Buddhism in Ceylon that this problematic was evident to many Buddhists. The situation is further complicated by the continued effectiveness of the traditional Buddhist doctrine of the responsibility of the state for the reform of the Sangha, that is to say for the so-called *Sāsana* reform, which in turn excludes the concept of a strictly secular state.

It becomes clear from these observations that the difficulties we get into in the attempt to find or to work out a really adequate description and analysis of Sinhalese Buddhism – just those difficulties which can be observed in the history of scholarship – can be traced back to objective contradictions in which Sinhalese Buddhists have become involved in the course of historical development. I now intend to try to discuss the most important of these contradictions.

There is first the question of the *meaning of religious activity.* The Buddha himself appears to have answered this question for his religion quite clearly: "Just as the sea has only one taste, that of salt, so this teaching and discipline has only one taste: that of release," and, as it is said in the *Aṅguttara Nikāya*: "Of those teachings of which it is recognized that they do not lead to passionlessness, to illumination, to Nirvāṇa, of them it can be assumed with certainty: that is not the instruction of the Master." There can be no doubt that this and only this was the goal of preaching. By means of it the Buddha became the founder of a religion: he taught his supporters a new method of winning release from the circle of reincarnations, a method which he designated as the only right one because it alone leads to success. Asceticism, flight from the world, the overcoming of all ties to society, are necessary parts of this way of release.

It is evident that the early Sangha was an elite community. I cannot believe that there should have existed an early lay Buddhism, postulated by some scholars, which deviated from the teachings we know from the canonical scriptures and which is said to have come to expression later on in the literary creations of Mahayana Buddhism. Rather, in my opinion, we must in our view of early Buddhism still consider correct the main features which Hermann Oldenberg described in his classic Buddha book.

This is not to say that there was no place for the laity in early Buddhism. But, it is clear that the line of separation between monk and layman was still unclear and that the formalism which prevailed later was a more recent development. Laymen could certainly win the releasing knowledge, but only if they accomplished the casting off of all ties, just like a monk. For such laymen who were not in a position to do so, only a sort of preparatory stage in the hierarchy of the way of release was provided for. By means of the observation of general ethical rules they could attain a better reincarnation. This was not at all specifically Buddhist, but rather corresponded to the general views of the time.

The same holds true for the doctrine of merit. Merit was at first only the fruit of good deeds generally. When the monastic orders spread the doctrine it was natural to extol good deeds rendered to the monks as especially efficacious merit. By this the beginning of a development was introduced which led to a stricter differentiation of monastic tradition and lay Buddhism. While the monks strove for their release through perception and meditation and while, further, preaching was imposed as a duty on them, the religious activity of the laity was concentrated in the assembling of merits. The monks taught accordingly how the laity could attain a good existence after death, and Buddhist religion was thus, in the realm of preaching to the laity, turned into its exact opposite: instead of emphasizing the transitoriness of all things and of stressing the worthlessness of even the best incarnation, a method of temporal progress and re-embodiment in heaven was presented as the goal of lay religion. The numerous Avadāna texts belonging to the later strata of canonical literature bear witness to this development.

With that, however, an inner contradiction in the structure of the Buddhist religious community had already arisen; for generous contributions to the Sangha could not exactly further the lack of need of the monks and this material progress of the Sangha, which was made possible by the piety of the laity, endangered the real meaning of monastic life. The Sangha became embroiled in secular matters because of its material possessions; the free ascetic community became a power factor in state and society, whose material wealth had to be administered and controlled. The decline of monastic feeling in the strict sense furthered an external formalism in following monastic rules and this in turn led to the formation of sects and to schisms in the orders.

Along with the externalization of spiritual life, there preceded the development of cultic practice. The worthlessness of cult activities as taught by the Buddha was silently ignored and cultist activities of the most varied kind were built in as merit, in the sense of the merit collection theory which was becoming more and more powerful. At the same time the "Vinaya acts" (*vinayakarma* or *saṅghakarma*), originally prescribed as formal legal instruments for the regulation of internal affairs in the Sangha, were transformed into rites.

Even by the time of King Aśoka all these developments must have advanced rather far. The necessity of a Sangha reform, which the king saw as his task in the interest of Buddhist religion, bears eloquent witness to that fact. This reform has, to be sure, been unanimously assessed in a positive sense by later Buddhist tradition, but it laid the bases for a contradictory internal development which still determines the contemporary state of affairs.

According to canon law, which is codified in the Vinayapiṭaka, the Sangha regulates its affairs completely independently and absolutely without the participation of outsiders. But the king exercised superintendance over the Sangha and even installed a magistracy for that purpose. He attempted, to be sure, as the so-called Schism Edict shows quite clearly, not to tamper with the traditional forms of administration of the Sangha and to let his measures appear to be not interference in the affairs of the Sangha but rather an aid in the carrying out of legitimate decisions of the Sangha. However, it cannot be denied that the Sangha had in fact lost its original independence.[1]

The further development in India does not interest us here, since Ceylonese tradition went back directly through Mahinda to Aśoka and accepted as a model the reform measures carried out by him. Later Ceylonese kings even formally enforced laws concerning the regulation of the Sangha, the so-called *katikāvatas*, and created a hierarchical organization of the clergy.[2] In addition, there is a special feature of Ceylonese Buddhism which can only be explained by the special circumstances of the country. The Sinhalese had migrated from northern India, but quite obviously they were in the position of colonial settlers whose culture was underdeveloped when the first Buddhist missionaries reached them at the time of Aśoka. As can be observed repeatedly in comparable situations, the most conservative form of the new religion was accepted. Despite this, very soon a profound change took place, for the missionaries had to take over civilizing tasks which had not been the task of monks in the mother country and which also did not correspond at all to the original concept of the Sangha. They became the upholders of the literary and educational tradition and developed a general school system. This led to an extensive identification of the interests of the Sangha with the special interests of the country and its people, and it is here that the historical roots of Buddhist nationalism lie.

When I treated the problem of Buddhism and nationalism in the first volume of my afore-mentioned book and called Buddhist nationalism a rather recent phenomenon, the fact escaped me that it is very old in Sinhalese tradition even if with slightly different terminology. I have attempted in the meantime to prove in an article that this union of religion and national feeling among the Sinhalese can be traced back to the first century B.C. and was responsible for the beginning of Ceylonese historiography.[3] Here, therefore, a definite historical and political situation has led to a union which, viewed analytically, presents a contradiction in itself, that is to say, to "Sinhalese-Buddhist nationalism."

Since the development of Buddhism into the national religion was also bound up with its change to the religion of the whole people, the tendency to push to the fore cult forms and merit practices was strengthened. Some medieval writings, for example Vedeha's *Rasavāhinī*, show how far the accommodation in this regard had gone. Although in theory the doctrines of the canonical Theravada were maintained, in practice different views were accepted which seem difficult to reconcile. For example: 1) the *Paritta* recitation, a use of holy texts as protective charms; 2) the *anumodanā*, the transfer of merit to others, especially to the dead in the sense of an ancestor cult; 3) the popular conception that the Buddha, although he had entered Nirvāṇa, was still efficacious and that it was possible to address him in prayers; and 4) the concept that the speaking of the Buddha's name had magical effectiveness. While these developments can be explained within the frame of historical changes of Buddhism, other innovations, for example the rites connected with the consecration of Buddha statues, are clearly of Hindu origin.[4]

With that we come to an important problem, that is to the question of how the relationship of Buddhism and non-Buddhist popular religion in Ceylon is to be determined. A main difficulty consists in the fact that material for the knowledge of the earlier phases of this relationship is extremely scanty, as can be seen from the relevant chapter in Wilhelm Geiger's *Culture of Ceylon in Medieval Times* (Wiesbaden 1960). From it can be learned merely that god cults existed side by side with Buddhism from the beginning. If we may believe the literary sources, these cults were of subordinate significance. One distinguishes in general two kinds of non-Buddhist cults, those of popular religion strictly speaking and the cults of Hindu origin. In the second category were placed the gods which are identified with Indian Hindu deities. While these are spoken of extensively in a part of late medieval Sinhalese writing, especially in the Sandeśa literature, more extensive information about the popular cults in a more specific sense can only be learned from travel descriptions – begun by Robert Knox – and from the scarcely datable Sinhalese ritual literature.

Under these circumstances the division into Hinduism and "lower popular cults," which Michael Ames[5] as well as W. Geiger employed, appears defensible. And yet I cannot accept it.

First with regard to the concept "Hinduism" in this connection. It is generally acknowledged that a religious community is designated according to the high religion which it acknowledges, and this is true of the Buddhists as well. Whatever they may have taken over from Hindu tradition, it is not therefore Hinduism by a long way, that is, not the religious confession of Hindus. The definition Hinduism is also false historically; it can be shown – I tried this first with the example of the god of Kataragama[6] – that the great gods of the Sinhalese are native gods from the pre-Buddhist period and that their identification with Hindu gods occurred only later. Further, of the three ritual systems of which Ames speaks (demonism, grahism or the planet cult, and Hinduism) grahism is historically of pure Hindu origin and there is accordingly no reason to separate it from Hinduism.

Nevertheless, it seems correct to distinguish three systems of non-Buddhist popular religion with respect to cult relationships and priest groups, that is: 1) the cult of the higher divinities; 2) the planet rituals; 3) the demon cults.

Of course, the division is fluid and the classification proposed by Ames is too schematic. When one learns, for example, that Däḍimuṇḍa is the minister of the god Vishnu or Uppalavaṇṇa and the dangerous demon Hūniyam is in turn the minister of Däḍimuṇḍa, and when one finds the shrines of all three deities in the Buddhist temple district of Bellanvila, it will quickly be clear to the observer that the systems described by Ames do not exist in reality as special systems. Rather, one must characterize the description of Sinhalese religion with the help of these divisions as strongly over-simplified, delimiting planes which cannot be sharply separated one from another.

More important still than questions of the inner structure of non-Buddhist popular religion is the question of the reciprocal relationships of Buddhism and popular religion, and here there exists in fact a sharp delimitation. Ames describes this delimitation correctly when he points to the "holy" character of Buddhism in contrast to the secular character of popular religion. In native terminology it is said that things bound together with Buddhism are *lokottara*, literally, supra-worldly. This naturally does not mean that everything Buddhist has a supra-worldly orientation but rather is taken from Abhidharma terminology, where the factors of existence leading to salvation are designated as "supra-worldly," that is to say, connected with the way of salvation.

Opposed to that, popular religion, in its goal of guaranteeing protection or help in specific situations, is an institution within the world. The designation popular religion is misleading, therefore, for these cults were in part at least state cults and had a public character. The Perahära in Kandy is the most striking example. From the realm of the state cult, which developed under the influence of medieval Hindu god-king ideology, the strong Hinduization of many god-cults can be explained.

In every case – whether in the private realm or as national cult – these non-Buddhist cults are not to be conceived as religion in the sense of a tie with the supra-worldly, but as the remains of the primitive view of the world, according to which certain invisible powers and persons exercise effects within the world. The combatting of demons by means of magic has in this world somewhat the same function as the use of disinfectants against disease germs in the modern world.

Hence one can, strictly, not speak of a co-existence of Buddhism and popular cults. Strict monastic orders, such as the monks of Rāmañña-Nikāya, have always rejected any contact with these cults. If there are nonetheless often god cults in the vicinity of the Buddhist temples, this is a concession to secular activity, as we can also observe similar adaptations with the Sangha of Ceylon in the political and cultural sphere.

Circumstances are otherwise when they are regarded from the point of view of the popular cults. Here it was very important to regard the gods as servants of the Buddha, to link them by myths with official religion and to bring the system of magical thinking bound to their cult to at least a superficial correspondence with the teachings of Buddhist religion. The national cults formed the point of intersection, cults which were naturally more strongly systematized than the village cults, and whose tie with Buddhism was already accomplished by the assertion contained in the *Mahāvaṃsa* that Buddha had installed Uppalavaṇṇa as the protective god over Ceylon.

This system is far from being without its contradictions. For example, there is a belief in the effect of karma – and this explanation of fortune and misfortune is the only legitimate one for Buddhists – and at the same time in the power of the planets, in the effectiveness of magical rites, and in the revenge of insulted deities. It is asserted that the gods were converted by the Buddha and became pious and at the same time irrational anger and arbitrariness are ascribed to them. The prescription against killing living creatures is accepted, and yet animal sacrifices have maintained their place in the demon cults right down to the present. This list can be extended.

From this it becomes quite clear that there is no general system of popular religion which can be compared approximately to the system of Buddhism, but that we have to do with a multiplicity of cults, astonishing in view of the limited area, which never became canonical and therefore are subjected to continual change. An approach which seeks to systematize here is always in danger of falsifying the picture, even if we cannot forego it in order not to lose the overall view.

The question of the function of the popular cults promises significant results. Precisely because there are no religious obligations in their practice, but because their meaning lies in the quite practical necessity of warding off magically-conditioned evil or in the effort to obtain advantages for oneself, the question of the religious dimension of a cult is always out of place. Here above all a religio-psychological approach will find good examples for the resolutions of conflicts of soul and the cure of psychogenic sicknesses by means of magic.

I would like to add another example which to me appears of interest, that of the Galēbaṇḍāra cult. It serves for the solution of the conflict between Buddhist Sinhalese and Muslims who have lived together in the area of Kurnägala since the Middle Ages. Tradition reports that Sinhalese murdered a crown prince borne by a Muslim princess in order to prevent a Muslim's becoming their king. The murdered prince became a divinity, and today Buddhists and Muslims share in the cult. The most important oracle of Ceylon is also bound with the temple of Galēbaṇḍāra. Here it becomes clear how new god cults arose for the solution of social conflicts even long after the introduction of Buddhism, cults comparable to the Nat cults of Burma.

Without doubt, the god cults of Ceylon, too, belong to the heritage of the national-Sinhalese tradition as do the Nat cults to the cultural heritage of Burma. The question presented itself to Buddhists of our time as to what relationship they should have to these cults. Obeyesekere has discussed this problem in his study of the relationship of religious symbolism and political change in Ceylon.[7] He has shown that the striking advance of the cult of the god of Kataragama, who is equated with the Hindu god Skanda, can be understood as the result of the special functions of this god, since his qualities and capacity meet the problems of the urbanized Sinhalese middle class. The cult of Kataragama was even used as a means of political struggle.

Similarly, Obeyesekere explains certain striking phenomena of the modern Buddha cult as the result of socio-psychological developments. The "Buddha in the market place," that is the erection of large figures of the Buddha at intersections, important squares, etc., unknown to tradition, is a symbol of the self-affirmation of the Sinhalese middle class and an exhibition of its newly-won political power. Here the consciousness of centuries of colonial rule is compensated for.

Surely we do not go wrong if we assess the change which Buddhism and also the Sangha has experienced in its politicization in the last decades in Ceylon equally with the change from the Indian religion of release to the Sinhalese national religion in the time after Aśoka.

Let me in conclusion touch briefly on the question of whether the widespread opinion is correct that Buddhism always needed supplementing by popular cults, that it therefore is in a certain sense an incomplete religion. It is asserted that everywhere cults of different origin have associated themselves with Buddhism because the latter, as a pure religion of release, does not meet the popular need for protection and help by supernatural powers, aside from the instances in which Buddhism has integrated with itself cults of other provenience (as in Tibet). It is correct that in most Buddhist countries such a dualism can be observed and that the structure of Buddhism is prone to such a development, but it is not permissible to generalize this statement. The Buddhist group of the Baruas in East Bengal proves the opposite: here all the functions which otherwise fall to the share of popular cults are looked after by the religious institutions which Buddhism itself has developed. In this class belongs above all the Paritta ritual which can, so to speak, be universally applied. For the understanding of Ceylonese conditions this fact is important insofar as can be seen from it how very much the function and form of popular religion are to be regarded as the results of historical factors.

Notes

For the interpretation of the Aśoka inscriptions and the corresponding sections in the chronicles of Ceylon, see H. Bechert, "Asokas Schismenedikt und der Begriff Sanghabheda," in *Wiener Zeitschrift für die Kunde Süd- und Ostasiens*, vol. 5, 1961, pp. 18-52.

See Nandasena Ratnapala, *The Katikāvatas, Laws of the Buddhist Order of Ceylon from the Twelfth to the Eighteenth Century*, Munich, 1971.

3. H. Bechert, "Zum Ursprung der Geschichtsschreibung im indischen Kulturbereich," in *Nachrichten der Akademie der Wissenschaften in Göttingen*, Philhist. Kl. 1969, No. 2.
4. Cf. Richard Gombrich, "The Consecration of a Buddhist Image," in *Journal of Asian Studies*, vol. 26, 1966, pp. 23-36.
5. See Michael M. Ames, "Magical-Animism and Buddhism, a Structural Analysis of the Sinhalese Religious System," in *Journal of Asian Studies,* vol. 23, 1964, pp. 21-53.
6. H. Bechert, "Eine alte Gottesvorstellung in Südindien und Ceylon," in *Wiener Zeitschrift für die Kunde Süd- und Ostasiens*, vol. 12-12, 1968/69, pp. 33-42.
7. Gananath Obeyesekere, "Religious Symbolism and Political Change in Ceylon," in *Modern Ceylon Studies*, vol. 1, no. 1, 1970, pp. 43-64. Reprinted in *The Two Wheels of Dhamma: Essays on the Theravada Tradition in India and Ceylon*, edited by Bardwell L. Smith, published by the American Academy of Religion, Studies in Religion, Number Three, 1972.

S. W. R. D. Bandaranaike and the Legitimation of Power through Buddhist Ideals

Heinz Bechert

EARLY BUDDHISM can be described as a way to salvation from suffering and rebirth which implies dissociation from worldly life in general and from political life in particular. In accordance with the structure of ancient Indian society, followers of the Buddha were either ascetics organized in the Sangha forming the community of bhikkhus (monks) and bhikkhunīs (nuns), or lay followers who were not formally organized. A member of the Sangha was obliged to conform with the regulations of the *Vinaya*, which was codified as an ecclesiastical law-book in a very early period of the history of Buddhism. Legitimation of the Sangha as a community worthy of support from the lay community was provided by the assurance that the Sangha upholds the standards set by these vinaya regulations. The place of lay followers in the hierarchy of religious achievements was a much lower one, because a layman as a rule could not attain the higher stages of spiritual perfection, since he was still too much involved with worldly preoccupations. The Buddha did, however, not decline to give advice to rulers and he defined precepts for the social life of his lay followers.

Early Buddhist tradition also has a concept of a just ruler and a just society (e.g., in the *Kūṭadantasutta* of the *Dīghanikāya*) and a belief in cyclic occurrence of world history where periods of the rule of just world-emperors were followed by periods of decline, etc. It also presented a theory of the origins of crime (e.g., in the *Cakkavattisīhanādasutta* of the *Dīghanikāya*). One can speak of an elementary Buddhist theory of politics, but this can hardly be described as a Buddhist legitimation of power in the early period of Buddhism. Political power was considered a reality and necessity of life, and it was organized in several contending states during the time of the Buddha, but there was no effort to legitimize it in Buddhist religious terminology. The Sangha was to remain universal and unattached to any particular political power, and it had to avoid association with politics, if only for the sake of its survival in a politically troubled period. The conversion of particular kings as lay followers of Buddhism and the support granted by them to the Buddhist Sangha, therefore, was not to result in the exclusive patronage of the Buddhist community only, if the advice of the Buddha as attested in the early texts was strictly followed.

This understanding of the relation of Buddhist religious tradition and political power was still alive with the greatest political personality of Indian Buddhism, King Aśoka (Pāli: Asoka). He deliberately made a distinction between the general *dharma* and his personal conviction as a Buddhist. The historical Aśoka, as we know him from his inscriptions, which are the only reliable source on his political ideas, in this way justifies political power not in terms of his Buddhist creed, but in terms of the principles of a universal law of morality which he follows as a ruler. It is understood that the principles of morality are common to all religious communities, and, thus, the government extends equal protection to all faiths. The relation of Aśoka's dharma to Buddhism is most aptly described by Étienne Lamotte in this way (Lamotte, 1958: 255):

> En souverain impartial, Aśoka protège indistinctement toutes les sectes: il les autorise à résider partout et, pour leur rendre hommage, va à elles en personne. Bouddhiste convaincu, il nomme des surintendants de la Loi pour veiller aux intérêts particuliers de chaque secte: Saṃgha bouddhique, Brâhmanes, Ājīvika, Nirgrantha, etc. Par deux fois, et à sept ans d'intervalle, il fait don de grottes aux Ājīvika. Sans intervenir dans les doctrines et disciplines particulières, il exige de ses religieux la dignité de vie qui convient à leur état: maîtrise des sens, pureté de l'âme, reconnaissance et fermeté dans la foi. Au for externe, il souhaite vivement que les sectes, soutenues et honorées par lui, progressent dans l'essentiel (sāravṛddhi), à savoir cette retenue du langage qui fait que l'on s'abstient d'honorer sa propre secte ou de dénigrer hors de propos celles des autres: il faut même rendre honneur aux autres sectes à chaque occasion. Le Buddha, lui aussi, a condamné l'intolérance religieuse, la sottise des maîtres qui croient détenir la vérité et traitent leurs adversaires de sots et d'ignorants: 'Je n'appelle pas vérité ce que les sots ce jettent à la face: ils font de leur propre vue la vérité; c'est pourquoi ils traitent leurs adversaires de sots.'
>
> Il résulte de ce bref aperçu que le Dharma prôné par Aśoka se distingue nettement du Saddharma bouddhique: il se borne à exposer en formules indiennes traditionnelles les principes de la Loi naturelle que les bouddhistes avaient déjà essayé d'inculquer à leurs adeptes laïcs; il n'enseigne pas *ex professo* les quatre vérités saintes ni le système de la Production en dépendance constituant l'essentiel de la Parole du Buddha. Aśoka fut un souverain pieux et zélé, et non point un propagandiste sectaire. Il n'entrait point dans ses intentions de fonder un État bouddhique, mais de morigéner ses sujets et d'édifier ses voisins. Ses envoyés, ses contrôleurs, ses surintendants ne sont en aucune manière des missionnaires bouddhiques, mais des fonctionnaires préoccupés du bonheur, présent et futur, de leurs administrés.

Aśoka's Buddhist inscriptions are mostly of a more personal nature. The so-called "schism edict," however, is of particular importance for understanding the history of the relations of Sangha and state. It concerns the reform of the Buddhist Sangha which was carried out with minimum interference into the internal matters of the Sangha (Bechert, 1961: 18-52). In the copy of this edict found at Sārnāth it is recorded that the officers of religious affairs were to exercise regular control over the observance of the rulings of the edict to prevent another decline of the Sangha.[1]

Buddhism in Ceylon was established during Aśoka's reign and Aśoka occupies a very prominent place in the historical traditions of Theravada Buddhism. However, the description of Aśoka's religious policies found in the literature of Theravada Buddhism – the Ceylonese chronicles, Pāli commentaries, and later works of Theravada tradition – is quite different from the Aśoka we know through his inscriptions. In these literary works, he is depicted as a zealous follower of the Theravada school of Buddhism who had the followers of other Buddhist sects expelled from the Sangha. This "re-writing" of history by the monastic literates of the Theravada tradition in Ceylon established the prototype of a Buddhist monarch and a Buddhist state which was to become the model for the policies of Theravada Buddhist kings. I have analyzed this transformation of the traditions on Aśoka's Sangha reform elsewhere (Bechert, 1961: 40-51), and the changes to which the traditions and records on other aspects of Aśoka's rule were subject can easily be observed by a careful reader of both inscriptional and literary sources.

The evolving political ideology of traditional Theravada Buddhism in Ceylon and Southeast Asia was based on a combination of four elements: the king is identified as a "cakravartin," i.e., as a universal monarch as described in canonical Buddhist texts; he is a "bodhisattva," i.e., a Buddha-to-be; he is a promoter and protector of Buddhism like Aśoka; and, last but not least, elements of the tradition of divine kingship of mediaeval Hinduism were absorbed into the model of the ideal Buddhist ruler. In the case of Ceylon, another element was of specific importance in traditional political thinking: the unique role assigned to Ceylon and the Sinhalese people by the Buddha in the myths of the Ceylonese chronicles on which the justification of "Sinhalese Buddhist nationalism" is based (cf. Bechert, 1969: 35-58; 1970: 761 f.).

By the amalgamation of these traditions and concepts a system of political thinking emerged in Theravada countries which must be considered as the background of much of the modern political ideas in these countries. The case of Burma, where the continuity of ideas is particularly persistent and visible, has been analyzed in detail by E. Sarkisyanz (Sarkisyanz, 1965; cf. also Sarkisyanz, 1972: 130-150), but this statement is basically true for other Theravada countries as well. The state is considered responsible for the material welfare of the people by Theravada tradition. The charisma of kingship thus cannot be separated from the concept of the monarch's duty to rule in accordance with the principles of dharma, lest disaster befall the country. These ideas made it easy for charismatic leaders to bring about a change of government, and resulted in an element of "populism" in the political traditions of Theravada countries, which at various times was being combined with movements of "Buddhist messianism," i.e., the expectancy of basic changes in the political and social order of the world preceding the coming of Metteyya, the next Buddha to appear in this world.

These traditions form decisive elements for the modern Buddhist political movement in Ceylon. We must add here, however, that there was an interruption in the organic development of Sinhalese-Buddhist nationalism during the colonial period. As late as the eighteenth century, the Sinhalese king renewed the understanding that support and purification of the Sangha is a responsibility of the government. The British administration of Ceylon, after initially agreeing to "maintain and protect" the religion of the Buddha in the Kandyan Convention of 1815, gradually "disestablished" Buddhism in the period from 1818 to 1853, i.e., it severed most ties between the government and the Sangha (de Silva, 1960: 91-159; Evers, 1964: 223-233; Bechert, 1966-73: 1, 230-234).

Another factor which contributed to change was the reinterpretation of traditional Buddhist values by the movement of Buddhist modernism (see Bechert, 1966-73: 1, 37-108). As a consequence of the leading role played by the new elite of the colonial period which had been intensively influenced by European education, the nationalist Buddhist movement made no attempt to restore a traditional form of monarchy in Ceylon, but aimed at the establishment of a democratic republic controlled by the Buddhist majority of the population. The ideals of democracy were searched for and found by the modernists within Buddhist tradition, e.g., in the structure of the early Buddhist Sangha (cf. Bechert, 1966-73: 1, 127-130). The particular situation which led to the most spectacular impact of religious issues on recent political developments in Ceylon, viz. the so-called "revolution of 1956," has to be understood against the background of these ideological factors and in relationship to the social changes of the period in question.

An observer of the scene in Ceylon could hardly foresee any major political change in the country when independence was achieved in 1948. D. S. Senanayake, the first Prime Minister of independent Ceylon, was successful in forming the United National Party (UNP) in 1945/46 as a political organization which united most of the leading politicians who had contributed to the constitutional development and to the negotiations for independence. The only organized opposition then was the still rather small Marxist movement in the island which had disunited into three separate political parties. S. W. R. D. Bandaranaike, who had organized a rather conservative political group named Sinhala Maha Sabha in 1937 which sounded the interests of rural Sinhalese Buddhists, now joined the UNP with all his political followers. He left the UNP to form his own party, the Sri Lanka Freedom Party, only in 1951.

There was, however, a short, though rather spectacular foreshadow of the changes that were around the corner, but these early signs were largely overlooked by observers abroad. It was a controversy concerning the political involvement of Buddhist monks that arose in 1946 and is not even mentioned in most studies dealing with the relations of religion and politics in the period in question (e.g., Smith, D. E., 1966: 453-509), although it was referred to in a short survey of modern Buddhism in Ceylon published by Sir Josiah Crosby in 1947 (Crosby, 1947: 177-179). One of the main documents of this ideological struggle is a book by Valpaḷa (Walpola) Rāhula which was published in Sinhalese in 1946 (Rāhula, 1946), but has been translated into English only very recently under the title *The Heritage of the Bhikkhu: A Short History of the Bhikkhu in Educational, Cultural, Social and Political Life* (Rāhula, 1974). I listed this book as one of the main documents of politically oriented Buddhist modernism in my survey of modern Buddhism (Bechert, 1966-73: 1, 62).

The controversy centered around the question of whether political activity was a legitimate part of the duties of the Sangha toward society as claimed by Rāhula and other "political bhikkhus," or whether involvement in politics was off-limits for bhikkhus. The canonical answer to the question is, of course, that it is off-limits, and this was the opinion of most leaders of the Buddhist resurgence until that period. (For a detailed discussion of the problem, see Bechert, 1966-73: 1, 67-79.) With the heritage of Sinhalese-Buddhist nationalism, no leader of the Buddhist movement in Ceylon had denied the necessity of adequate representation of Buddhist interests in national politics, but this representation was considered the obligation of Buddhist laymen. Political activity of the bhikkhus was seen to militate against basic principles of Buddhist monkhood.

The organization of monks which became the champion of politicization of the monks was the All-Ceylon Bhikkhu Congress (Samasta Lankā Bhikṣu Sammēlanaya) which represented the opinions of younger monks, many of them with strongly leftist leanings. On January 26, 1946, a public discussion between D. S. Senanayake, the Prime Minister of Ceylon, and the Buddhist monk V. Rāhula was held in Kotahena, a suburb of Colombo, on the subject of political activity of the bhikkhus. On February 13, 1946 an assembly of politically active monks published a declaration on "Monks and Politics" (Rāhula, 1946: 124-126; Rāhula, 1974: 131-133), and on January 6, 1947 the "Kälaṇiya Declaration of Independence" (Rāhula, 1946: 127-130; Rāhula, 1974: 134-136; cf. Bechert, 1966-73: 3, 456 f.) was passed by a mass assembly of bhikkhus in Colombo. I have given a description of the events elsewhere (Bechert, 1966-73: 1, 311-315) so that it is not necessary to go into more details here. Suffice to mention that a large part of the Sangha very strongly opposed the movement of these political monks and that the radical bhikkhus did not get much response from the general public at that time, so that the issue lost its importance during the following years.

The value of the documents just mentioned lies in the fact that they already presented most of the arguments proposed by the movement which ten years later swept S. W. R. D. Bandaranaike into power. Under Sir John Kotelawala, who became prime minister of Ceylon in 1953, contradictions sharpened between the upper class which had taken over political power from the colonial government and largely continued to monopolize it, on the one hand, and the lower middle class which demanded participation in government, on the other side. The conflict could also be described as a struggle of the Sinhalese educated classes urging for the immediate implementation of the national language policy which was theoretically accepted by the UNP government also, but in effect was delayed by the Anglicized elite which found it convenient to exclude large portions of the population from higher offices by this way. These developments coincided with an important jubilee in the Buddhist world, viz. the 2500 Buddha Jayantī in 1956/57. A number of popular traditions and expectations were connected with this event, e.g., the prophecy that a universal king would appear at that time, a tradition which can be traced back in Ceylon to a Sinhalese classical poem composed in the fifteenth century (see Bechert, 1966-73: 1, 365 f.).

The Buddhists were, no doubt, in a contradictory ideological position. On the one hand, there was a need for the reform of the institutions of the Buddhist religion, a so-called "Sāsana reform." A reformed Sangha was to be as similar to the original Sangha as possible, and this implied that it was a "supramundane" (*lokottara*) institution not entangled in worldly activities and exclusively directed toward religious goals. The Sangha of Ceylon, however, had become deeply involved in secular matters, particularly as a result of "monastic landlordism" and of the developments following the already mentioned "disestablishment" of the Buddhist institutions which made some bhikkhus practically owners of large estates. The Sangha was also divided on this matter, because there were rich and poor monasteries, and there were conservative and progressive factions in the Sangha. These divisions did not follow the traditional divisions of the "sects" (*nikāyas*) in the Sangha, but emerged on rather different lines.

S. W. R. D. Bandaranaike was the charismatic leader who succeeded in uniting the divergent forces of the Buddhist movement in an effort to bring about changes which have finally resulted in a kind of "cultural revolution" dethroning the Anglicized elite in Ceylon and opening the way for an improved social standing for the common man. He derived legitimation for his action from a variety of concepts based on the traditions of Sinhalese Buddhism, and he was able, at least for a while, to bridge the contradictions dividing mondernists and traditionalists in the Buddhist movement.

The political developments leading to the overwhelming victory of the coalition led by Bandaranaike in 1956 and his performance as a prime minister of Ceylon have been discussed in detail by D. E. Smith (Smith, D. E., 1966: 453-509) and by the present author (Bechert, 1966-73: 1, 316-345), and there is a rather detailed monograph on the elections of 1956 (Weerawardana, 1960). I may refer readers to these sources for factual information and confine myself here to the problems of ideology.

Which were the Buddhist elements in this process of political and social changes and how were traditional ideals reinterpreted in order to fit into the particular given situation? A prominent feature of the movement led by Bandaranaike consisted in the large-scale political participation of Buddhist monks in the political struggle, and there can hardly be any doubt that approval by the Sangha was a major factor in legitimizing the political actions taken by him in terms of the living Buddhist tradition of Ceylon. Many Western observers have accepted the arguments proposed by Buddhist monks active in the political field which were formulated in the above-quoted book of V. Rāhula (Rāhula, 1946) and, of course, in many later publications. The most quoted work of this literature is *The Revolt in the Temple* (Vijayavardhana, 1953). Very shortly before the elections in 1956, the "Buddhist Committee of Inquiry" (Bauddha Toraturu Parīkṣaka Sabhāva) which had been appointed by the leading Buddhist laymen's organization, the All-Ceylon Buddhist Congress, in 1953, and became popularly known as the "Buddhist Commission," published the complete Sinhalese text (*Bauddha Toraturu Parīkṣaka Sabhāva*, 1956) and an abridged English version of its report (*Buddhist Committee of Inquiry*, 1956). There are differences in emphasis and representation of facts and opinions in these sources, and these differences refer mostly to the role of the Sangha. Rāhula is, of course, a most ardent advocate of the role of the "political bhikkhus." The report of the "Buddhist Commission" is much less enthusiastic about the political role of the bhikkhus, and it stresses the need for a reform of the Sangha, but the relevant sections are left out in the English version of the report for obvious reasons. (For a discussion of the report, see Bechert, 1966-73: 1, 267-279).

Ceylon experienced in 1955/56 for the first time a large-scale political involvement of a majority of Buddhist monks, a phenomenon familiar in Burma much earlier, particularly between 1917 and 1938. In both countries, we witness a leading role played by the Sangha for the political mobilization of the masses and thereby for politicization and political modernization in general. To understand the background of this phenomenon, we shall recall the traditional system of Sangha-state relations. In precolonial times, integration of the Sangha into the political structure was effected in such a way that the Sangha should not exercise direct political influence. (For a discussion of these principles, see Bechert, 1970: 766 f.) However, state patronage of the Sangha had resulted in changing Buddhism from the religion of an elite into the religion of the broad masses of rural population. Thus, Buddhism was "democratized" by inducing persons from all classes to join the Sangha. The Sangha thereby grew into a power factor in politics with the potential of influencing the rural masses. In the mediaeval Buddhist states the system of formalized interrelations of Sangha and state enabled the state to restrain this influence by means of Sāsana reforms, i.e., by reforms of the monastic system to enforce the rules forbidding monks to participate in activities within the sphere of mundane life (see Bechert, 1970: 763-766; relevant documents from the mediaeval period of Ceylonese Buddhism were edited and translated by Ratnapala, 1971). Political activity of bhikkhus was limited to periods of crisis and change. In general, it was out of the question.

When the traditional ties of Sangha and state were cut by the colonial administration, the Sangha became a potential factor of mass politicization. But, in view of the generally well-known rules of the Sangha and its definition as an institution to achieve progressive liberation from attachment to worldly affairs, special legitimation of its political activity was needed. On the level of ideology, this was done by claiming that political involvement of the Sangha was nothing but fulfilling the traditional task of advising rulers on the basis of moral precepts and the teachings of the Buddha. This argument was supplemented by a collection of examples from the history of Ceylon to prove that political activity of the Sangha existed in the past also; this fact in itself was considered sufficient justification of such activity (e.g., Pahamuṇē Śrī Sumangala in Vijayavardhana, 1953: 15-19; Rāhula, 1974: 3-7 and 16-19). All writing done by politically interested bhikkhus had to cope with a rather basic contradiction in their argumentation. On the one hand, they still claimed to be orthodox Theravada monks, which implied they accepted the decision of the first Buddhist council not to change any of the rules of discipline, though the Buddha had permitted the Sangha to change minor rules. On the other hand, they daily violated rules of the vinaya. The argument which was supposed to solve the problem is formulated in the declaration "Monks and Politics" of 1946 in these words (quoted from Rāhula, 1974: 131-133):

> The Buddha permitted *bhikkhus* to change minor rules of the *Vinaya* if they so desire. Nevertheless, there is no historical evidence to show that the *bhikkhus* of the Theravāda school have on any occasion actually changed the rules of the *Vinaya*. Likewise, we do not say that even now they should be changed.
>
> But it has to be admitted that the political, economic, and social conditions of today are different from those of the time of the Buddha, and that consequently the life of *bhikkhus* today is also different from that of the *bhikkhus* at that time.
>
> In those days the ideal of monks generally was to realize *nirvāṇa* in their very lifetime. In later times their ideal was to exert themselves to the best of their ability in activities beneficial to themselves and others with a view to realizing *nirvāṇa* in a future life.
>
> It is clearly seen that as result of this very change, a great many other changes not known in the earlier days took place in the life of *bhikkhus* in later times.
>
> The extent to which the life of monks today has undergone change can be clearly gauged when we take into consideration the prevailing conditions of life in temples, monasteries, and *pirivenas*, the teaching and learning of Sinhala, Sanskrit and such other subjects, the present system of examinations, the editing and writing of books and journals, conferring and accepting nāyakaships and such other titles, participation in various societies and being elected as officers in them. It has to be accepted, therefore, that, although the rules of the *Vinaya* have remained unaltered, the life of monks has undergone change and that this change is inevitable.
>
> We believe that politics today embraces all fields of human activity directed towards the public weal. No one will dispute that the work for the promotion of the religion is the duty of the *bhikkhu*. It is clear that the welfare of the religion depends on the welfare of the people who profess that religion. History bears evidence to the fact that whenever the Sinhala nation – which was essentially a Buddhist nation – was prosperous, Buddhism also flourished. We, therefore, declare that it is nothing but fitting for *bhikkhus* to identify themselves with activities conducive to the welfare of our people – whether these activities be labelled politics or not – as long as they do not constitute an impediment to the religious life of a *bhikkhu*.

> We cannot forget that from the earliest days the Sinhala monks, while leading the lives of *bhikkhus*, were in the forefront of movements for the progress of their nation, their country, and their religion.
>
> Even today *bhikkhus* by being engaged actively in education, rural reconstruction, anti-crime campaigns, relief work, temperance work, social work and such other activities, are taking part in politics, whether they are aware of it or not. We do not believe that it is wrong for *bhikkhus* to participate in these activities.
>
> We believe that it is incumbent on the *bhikkhu* not only to further the efforts directed towards the welfare of the country, but also to oppose such measures as are detrimental to the common good . . . .
>
> In ancient days, according to the records of history, the welfare of the nation and the welfare of the religion were regarded as synonymous terms by the laity as well as by the *Sangha.* The divorce of religion from the nation was an idea introduced into the minds of the Sinhalese by invaders from the West, who belonged to an alien faith. It was a convenient instrument of astute policy to enable them to keep the people in subjugation in order to rule the country as they pleased.
>
> It was in their own interests, and not for the welfare of the people, that these foreign invaders attempted to create a gulf between the *bhikkhus* and the laity – a policy which they implemented with diplomatic cunning. We should not follow their example, and should not attempt to withdraw *bhikkhus* from society. Such conduct would assuredly be a deplorable act of injustice, committed against our nation, our country, and our religion . . . .

It is clear that the basic problem is evaded here in a rather simplistic way. The more educated section of the Buddhist lay community and a large percentage of the bhikkhus who disapproved of the political activity of the Sangha never accepted this argumentation as a valid one. On the contrary, they agitated for the outlawing of party politics for bhikkhus. This was one of the recommendations of the report of the "Buddha Sāsana Commission" which was appointed during Bandaranaike's premiership[2] and published in November, 1959 (see Bechert, 1966-73: 1, 280), and it was the declared policy of reformers in their efforts to implement these recommendations (Bechert, 1966-73: 1, 284 f.).

Under these circumstances, it is particularly remarkable that the large-scale political activity of bhikkhus, which was resented by considerable segments of the Buddhist population during other periods, was almost generally accepted in 1955/56 when it largely contributed to bringing Mr. Bandaranaike's government into power. The organization of the political monks was the Eksat Bhikṣu Peramuṇa (EBP) or "United Monks' Front," formed by the amalgamation of the aforementioned All-Ceylon Bhikkhu Congress with the Śrī Lankā Mahā Sanghasabhā, a monks' association formed for the preparation of the Buddha Jayantī celebrations. Its secretaries were Talpāvila Sīlavaṃsa, Māpiṭigama Buddharakkhita and Hävanpoḷa Ratanasāra. For details of the agitation, I shall quote from I. D. S. Weerawardana's description of the electoral campaign of the EBP in favor of the Mahajana Eksat Peramuṇa (MEP) which was the coalition headed by S. W. R. D. Bandaranaike, a campaign which had the declared aim to oust the ruling UNP from power (Weerawardana, 1960: 144-146):

> The first phase of this campaign began as a movement against the Government's decision to hold the general election in early 1956. The Buddha Jayanti celebrations were to begin in May 1956. The campaign was directed on the slogan "No election before the Buddha Jayanti." This was of course made possible by the fact that the Parliament was not due to be dissolved till May 1957. The campaign began in January 1956. In February it was decided to perform satyagraha if the general election were not postponed. The programme was announced at a series of public meetings. A meeting of representatives from 75 Sangha Sabhas was held in Colombo. A general election was described as Mara (Satan) from whom Buddhism had to be protected. When the

UNP went ahead with the dissolution of Parliament, the bhikkhus carried out the satyagraha in many towns and centers throughout the country. About 250 bhikkhus fasted in Colombo. They marched from the steps of the House of Representatives to Victoria Park.

The second phase consisted of open campaigning for the MEP and against the UNP. The EBP held meetings of its own criticising the Government. Each meeting was treated as a platform to place before the people the Great Petition of the Maha Sangha. EBP clergy were prominent speakers at MEP meetings. Each branch association decided to support the anti-UNP candidate (usually MEP) in the constituency of the area. Thus the Sangha Sabha at Bingiriya decided to support Mr. T. B. Subasinghe at Bingiriya; the Raigam Korale branch decided to support Mr. Sagara Palansuriya, the VLSSP-MEP candidate for Horana. Each Sangha Sabha decided to divide itself into small groups to go canvassing and to hold public meetings. Some of them published pamphlets presenting arguments as to why the UNP should be defeated.

The report of the "Buddhist Commission" was read out to show how Buddhists had been suppressed during the colonial period and to indicate how the UNP government was nothing else than a continuation of the colonial regime by its local protégés. Real independence was still to be achieved, and it had to be done now, lest it be too late and Buddhism would have suffered too much to recover again. A newspaper named *Rōdaya* ("Wheel") was published to spread this message (*Rōdaya* of February 25, 1956; quoted from Wriggins, 1960: 345):

The bhikkhus should be present in every polling booth. They should explain to the people how to use the vote correctly . . . . A Government that will work for the country, religion and its culture should be elected. The end of the Sasana will not be very long if we remain in silence . . . . We appeal to bhikkhus to visit every Buddhist home and to direct them on the right path. You may have to confront many difficulties. But be ready to sacrifice your life to restore a Buddhist Ceylon.

We can now sum up and discuss the factors and arguments which constituted the legitimation of political change through Buddhist ideals in Ceylon in 1956:

First of all, there was a gap between the religious and social ideals of the ruling upper class and those of the rural masses in a country where rural population still forms the bulk of the people. With the end of the colonial period, considerable changes in the policies of the government were expected by the people, and there was a set of ideals by which the performance of the government of free Ceylon was measured. This was the ideal description of glorified precolonial Ceylon under the rule of Buddhist kings which was derived from several sources: from the chronicles, particularly from the *Mahāvaṃsa* (see Smith, B. L., 1972a), from the writings of the authors of the movement of Buddhist resurgence and from popular Sinhalese tracts on old Ceylon and its culture. The liberal and Westernized leaders of the movement for home-rule widely made use of these ideals in their pre-independence agitation for the mobilization of support for their cause, but now, when their goal was achieved, they did not even include the famous fifth article of the Kandyan Convention of 1815, by which the British Crown had agreed to maintain and protect Buddhism and its rites, ministers and places of worship, into the new constitution of Ceylon, because they subscribed to the concept of a strictly secular state.

The resulting frustration revived the strength of "Sinhala-Buddhist nationalism," which was a deeply imbibed ideology in Sinhalese Buddhists from a very early period (see above, p. 2). This again served as a justification for agitation not only against the direct "survivals of the colonial period" in all spheres of life, but also against the strong hold of the Tamil minority over many spheres of the economy which had originated during the colonial period. Fear of Tamil domination, intensified by rumors that India might be planning to annex Ceylon on the instigation of the propagandists of a united Tamil state, could well activate a population which had lived with the tradition that the Tamils were the arch-enemies of Sinhalese Buddhists for so many centuries. Duṭṭhagāmaṇī, who liberated the island from Tamil domination in the second century B.C., had become the national hero of the Sinhalese soon after the tradition to write down history was initiated in Ceylon, and there was a deep change of values connected with this concept. Rāhula describes this in these words in a book which was published also in 1956 (Rāhula, 1956: 79-80):

> The entire Sinhalese race was united under the banner of the young Gāmaṇī. This was the beginning of nationalism among the Sinhalese. It was a new race with healthy young blood, organized under the new order of Buddhism. A kind of religio-nationalism, which almost amounted to fanaticism, roused the whole Sinhalese people. A non-Buddhist was not regarded as a human being. Evidently, all Sinhalese without exception were Buddhists.
>
> After the defeat of Eḷāra, the victorious Duṭṭha-Gāmaṇī repented of the destruction of many thousands of human lives. Eight arahants from Piyaṅgudīpa are reported to have assured the king that there was no cause for repentance, that only one and a half human beings had been slain – one who had taken refuge in the Buddha, Dhamma and Saṅgha, and the other who had observed the five precepts – and that the rest who were wrong-believers and men of evil life were equal to animals . . . . Thus orthodox religious opinions encouraged Buddhist nationalism.

This quotation is from a work written for the use of scholars. It is not surprising that the argument was proposed in an even stronger way in the same author's propagandistic *Heritage of the Bhikkhu* (Rāhula, 1974: 20-22). For Rāhula, the fact that the utterance made by eight arahants from Piyangudīpa "is diametrically opposed to the teaching of the Buddha" (Rāhula, 1974: 22) does not in any way seem to diminish the validity of his argument in favor of a violent struggle for the goals of "religio-nationalism."

The next complex to be mentioned is the ideal of a just ruler who follows the example of Aśoka (as described in the chronicles) in establishing a welfare-state where Buddhist ideals come true. The traditional idea of the responsibility of the state was reformulated in terms of modern concepts of socialism. Bandaranaike's MEP, indeed, included a leftist wing which followed this line of arguing.

Last but not least, the widespread expectations of a great Buddhist revival on the eve of the Buddha Jayantī jubilee, a strong element of populism in the effort to revive traditional culture, and the language issue were decisive forces in the process of ideological change. Traditional culture was seen as deprived of its legitimate status by the impact of modern Western civilization; and the lower middle class, which was the upholder of the educational tradition in the Sinhalese language, pressed for more recognition of āyurveda (traditional medicine), of astrology, and of the cults of the popular gods of the Sinhalese. The crucial importance of the language issue, which has been dealt with in many publications (in a most detailed way by Kearney, 1967), was, of course, linked to the fact that Sinhalese had remained the language of higher education in the monastic seats of learning, whereas secular higher education was almost exclusively available through the medium of English only before 1956.

We have seen that the legitimation of power through Buddhist ideals which underlies the political changes in Ceylon in 1956 is based on a rather broad variety of traditions ranging from elements of canonical Buddhism to popular beliefs and notions which contradict the teachings of original Buddhism, but nevertheless were included in the totality of traditions forming the complex of traditional Buddhism in Ceylon.

Under these conditions, some observers are inclined to conclude that contradictions in this traditional system were of no relevance for the analysis of the history of ideas in modern Buddhism. That this is, however, a basic misconception is shown by the dilemmas of reinterpretation (see Smith, B. L. 1972b). Buddhist resurgence and modernism have resulted in a renaissance of the study of the original sources of Buddhism, and have led to a counter-movement against the kind of presentation of political Buddhism and the justification of political involvement of bhikkhus that implicitly denies the validity of the Sangha's ideal, exclusive orientation toward "supra-mundane," i.e., religious goals. Many of those who accepted the participation of bhikkhus in the agitation of 1955/56 expected that the monks would return to their secluded religious life after they had helped to bring a just ruler (i.e., S. W. R. D. Bandaranaike) into power, but they soon were to realize that the Eksat Bhikṣu Peramuṇa was acting as a kind of supra-government imposing its will on the political leaders and reminding them every day that it was only with the assistance of the bhikkhus that they had come into power. (For details, see Bechert, 1966-73: 1, 325-340). Many Buddhist leaders, including the majority of responsibly thinking bhikkhus, therefore, subscribed to the recommendation of the Buddha Sāsana Commission to ban participation in party politics for monks, but opposition against its implementation from the side of political monks and opportunistic politicians was always strong enough to prevent the enforcement of this rule. (See Bechert, 1966-73: 1, 282-288 on the debates over Sāsana reform proposals after 1958.)

On September 25, 1959, S. W. R. D. Bandaranaike was assassinated in his home. Talduvē Somārāma, a bhikkhu who acted on the instigation of Māpiṭigama Buddharakkhita, a secretary of the EBP, who had contributed so much to bring Bandaranaike into power, was indicted and sentenced for the crime (for details, see Bechert, 1969-73: 1, 343-345). A report on the case was published in book form by the lawyer who defended Somārāma in the trial (Weeramantry, 1969); he argues that not all questions concerning the assassination have been satisfactorily answered yet.

S. W. R. D. Bandaranaike was not a theoretician of political science. We do not have detailed statements on his political ideas apart from his speeches (see Bandaranaike, 1959, and Bandaranaike, 1961), but he took the proper cause into his hands at the right time. And his political ideas have not died with him. He is still being venerated as a national hero and as a martyr for the cause of the resurrection of the Sinhalese nation. Traditionalists have raised him into the pantheon of Sinhalese popular religion as Horagollē devatā baṇḍāra, the god of Horagolla, the place of his family home.[3] Others consider him an incarnation of a Bodhisattva, a "Buddha-to-be." His wife, Mrs. Sirimavo Bandaranaike, was to become the first woman prime minister in the world and her husband's political successor. The change of government which took place in Ceylon in 1956 was the most important single event in the history of the island since the British take-over of the Kandyan kingdom. It has replaced the values of the colonial period by new values based upon the revival of traditions of the past. The development of political ideas in Ceylon since 1956 can largely be described as an effort to deal with the inherent problems of the cultural heritage of Sinhalese Buddhism and as a struggle for readjusting the traditional values and concepts to the needs of our times, and for amalgamating them with the new ideas that came from the West.

Notes

1. This part of the edict is not correctly interpreted in the standard editions and translations of Aśoka's inscriptions. It is found only in the Sārnāth copy of the edict. A correct English rendering runs as follows: "And these lay followers should go to the *uposatha* ceremony on every *uposatha* day to ensure that confidence is given to this edict (of the king), and the competent officer should go to the regular *uposatha* ceremony to ensure confidence and observance for the edict." For details, see Bechert, 1961: 24-27.
2. In his postscript to the translation of *Bhiksuvagē urumaya*, Rāhula makes mention of the Buddha Sāsana Commission Report (Rāhula, 1974: 107), but he suppresses information on the opposition to the political activity of bhikkhus expressed in this report, where a difference is made between legitimate action of monks in the field of social welfare, education, etc. and the involvement in party politics which is seen as not befitting for a bhikkhu.
3. See my contribution "Mythologie der singhalesischen Volksreligion" for the "Wörterbuch der Mythologie" (ed. H. W. Haussig and published by E. Klett Verlag, Stuttgart), s.v. Horagollē devatā baṇḍāra.

References

1. Bauddha Toraturu Parīkṣaka Sabhāva (Buddhist Committee of Inquiry, popularly known as "Buddhist Commission")
   1956 *Bauddha toraturu parīkṣaka sabhāvē vārtāva.* Balangoḍa. (Sinhalese version; for the English version, see Buddhist Committee of Inquiry).
2. Bandaranaike, Solomon West Ridgeway Dias
   1959 *The Government and the People, A Collection of Speeches made by the Prime Minister of Ceylon.* Colombo: Government Press.
   1961 *Towards a New Era, Selected Speeches of S. W. R. D. Bandaranaike.* Made in the Legislature of Ceylon, compiled by G. E. P. de S. Wickramaratne. Colombo: Government Press.
3. Bechert, Heinz
   1961 "Aśokas 'Schismenedikt' und der Begriff Sanghabheda." *Wiener Zeitschrift für die Kunde Süd- und Ostasiens*, V:18-52.
   1966-73 *Buddhismus, Staat und Gesellschaft in den Ländern des Theravāda-Buddhismus.* 3 vols. Frankfurt: A. Metzner (Vol. 1) and Wiesbaden: O. Harrassowitz (Vols. 2-3). (Schriften des Instituts für Asienkunde in Hamburg XVII/1-3).
   1969 "Zum Ursprung der Geschichtsschreibung im indischen Kulturbereich." *Nachrichten der Akademie der Wissenschaften in Göttingen*, I. Philologisch-historische Klasse 1969, No. 2:35-38.
   1970 "Theravāda Buddhist Sangha: Some General Observations on Historical and Political Factors in Its Development." *Journal of Asian Studies*, XXIX (1969/70):761-778.
   1973a "Contradictions in Sinhalese Buddhism," pp. 7-17 in Bardwell L. Smith (ed.), *Tradition and Change in Theravada Buddhism: Essays on Ceylon and Thailand in the 19th and 20th Centuries.* Leiden: E. J. Brill. (*Contributions to Asian Studies*, 4.) Reprinted in this volume.
   1973b "Sangha, State, Society, 'Nation': Persistence of Traditions in 'Post-traditional' Buddhist Societies." *Daedalus*, Journal of the American Academy of Arts and Sciences, Proceedings of the American Academy of Arts and Sciences, CII, No. 1 (Winter 1973):85-95.
   1973c "Buddhistische Sozialethik und Kulturwandel in Ceylon und Südostasien." *Le Muséon, Revue d'études orientales*, LXXXVI:499-519.

4. Buddhist Committee of Inquiry (Bauddha Toraturu Parīkṣaka Sabhāva)
1956 *The Betrayal of Buddhism, An Abridged Version of the Report of the Buddhist Committee of Inquiry.* Balangoda. (For the Sinhalese version, see Bauddha Toraturu Parīkṣaka Sabhāva.)

5. Crosby, Sir Josiah
1947 "Buddhism in Ceylon," *Journal of the Royal Asiatic Society of Great Britain and Ireland*, 1947:41-52 and 166-183.

6. de Silva, Kingsley Muthumani
1960 "Buddhism and the British Government in Ceylon, 1840-1855." *Ceylon Historical Journal*, X (1960/61):91-159.

7. Evers, Hans-Dieter
1964 "Buddhism and British Colonial Policy in Ceylon, 1815-1875." *Asian Studies*, II:223-233.

8. Kearney, Robert M.
1967 *Communalism and Language in the Politics of Ceylon.* Durham, N.C.: Duke University Press (Program in Comparative Studies in Southern Asia, Publication, 2).

9. Lamotte, Étienne
1958 *Histoire du bouddhisme indien, des origines à l'ére śaka.* Louvain: Publications Universitaires (Bibliothèque du Muséon, Vol. 43).

10. Rāhula, Valpaḷa (Walpola)
1946 *Bhikṣuvagē urumaya.* Colombo: Svastika yantrālaya.
1956 *History of Buddhism in Ceylon: The Anurādhapura Period.* Colombo: M. D. Gunasena.
1974 *The Heritage of the Bhikkhu.* New York: Grove Press.

11. Ratnapala, Nandasena
1971 *The Katikāvatas, Laws of the Buddhist Order of Ceylon from the 12th to the 18th Century.* München: J. Kitzinger. (Münchener Studien zur Sprachwissenschaft, Beiheft N.)

12. Sarkisyanz, Emanuel (Manuel)
1965 *Buddhist Backgrounds of the Burmese Revolution.* The Hague: M. Nijhoff.
1972 "Social Ethics of Theravada Buddhism in Relation to Socio-economic Development Problems in Southeast Asia," pp. 130-150 in B. Grossmann (ed.): *Southeast Asia in the Modern World.* Wiesbaden: O. Harrassowitz. (Schriften des Instituts für Asienkunde in Hamburg, XXXIII.)

13. Smith, Bardwell L.
1972a "The Ideal Social Order as Portrayed in the Chronicles of Ceylon," pp. 31-57 in Bardwell L. Smith (ed.): *The Two Wheels of Dhamma: Essays on the Theravada Tradition in India and Ceylon.* Chambersburg, Pa. (AAR Studies in Religion, 3.) Reprinted in this volume.
1972b "Sinhalese Buddhism and the Dilemmas of Reinterpretation," pp. 79-106, *ibid.*

14. Smith, Donald Eugene
1966 *South Asian Politics and Religion.* Princeton, N. J.: Princeton University Press.

15. Vijayavardhana, D. C.
1953 *Dharma-Vijaya, Triumph of Righteousness, or the Revolt in the Temple, Composed to Commemorate 2500 Years of the Land, the Race and the Faith.* Colombo: Sinha Publications.

16. Weeramantry, Lucian G.
1969 *Assassination of a Prime Minister, The Bandaranaike Murder Case.* Geneva: L. G. Weeramantry.

17. Weerawardana, I. D. S.
1960 *Ceylon General Election, 1956.* Colombo: M. D. Gunasena.

18. Wriggins, William Howard
1960 *Ceylon: Dilemmas of a New Nation.* Princeton, N. J.: Princeton University Press.

Buddhism without Bhikkhus: The Sri Lanka Vinaya Vardena Society

Steven E. G. Kemper

IN ITS Theravada form Buddhism has a two thousand five hundred year history in Sri Lanka, Burma, and Thailand of only minor dissension over the interpretation of Dhamma (doctrine). Sri Lanka is the paradigm case. Rhys Davids writes, "Ceylon Buddhism, so far as the philosophy, the ethics, and the psychology on which the ethics are based, remains much the same as the Buddhism of the Indian Pāli texts,"[1] and Bishop Copleston commends the study of Sinhalese Buddhism because ". . . it is confessedly among those which have least diverged from the primitive stock, and it has a far longer continuous history than any other."[2] Other readings of the religion, however, have found it "corrupt," not doctrinally so because the doctrine has survived, but with regards to the popular religion's backsliding accommodation with animism and Hinduism. "Pure" Buddhism, wherever one might choose to locate it, was rational and atheistic; popular Buddhism is an amalgam of that doctrine and a tangle of extraneous beliefs. It is thus "corrupt," but it is also "orthodox" because of the integrity of that doctrinal core.[3]

This intriguing formulation has been scrutinized recently by Richard Gombrich, an Indologist like Rhys Davids able to exploit his textual skills by comparing the early Buddhism of the Pāli texts to the traditional Buddhism which he found Sinhalese peasants and *bhikkhus* (monks) understanding and practicing in a Kandyan village in which he took up residence.[4] His conclusions echo those of earlier Buddhologists: the changes that have occurred in Sinhalese Buddhism (with the palpable exceptions of an elaborate monastic system based on caste and a decline in the standards of monastic life [chs. 7 and 8]) do not violate the spirit of the Buddhism described in the Sinhalese commentaries.[5] The Kandyan Sinhalese continue to hold beliefs about the Buddha's sacred biography, as well as about the supernatural, causation, responsibility, and intentionality which ". . . would have been approved by Buddhaghosa, [and indeed] most of their religious practices would have been familiar to him and his contemporaries."[6]

The orthodoxy which Gombrich finds is a circumscribed one, one depending upon a number of distinctions.[7] The most pervasive one is drawn between "cognitive" religion (what people say they believe and say they do) and "affective" religion (how people behave and what the analyst can infer from such behavior).[8] Although villagers may "affectively" treat a Buddha image as alive, we cannot infer that the Buddha image is generally so conceived. Elsewhere, for instance, laypeople and monks say ("cognitive" religion) that images are inanimate and such ceremonies meaningless. Gombrich's argument thus is not that other Sinhalese act "affectively" in another more consistent way, but rather that traditional Sinhalese hold abstract beliefs which may contradict their own behavior but are in themselves orthodox. "Orthodoxy" is just that, it is not orthopraxy.

In the end Gombrich's stance is an "outside" one. What finally interests him is an Indological question: can current precepts be judged to be consistent with commentatorial Buddhism and thus be called orthodox. Most can. But there are problems of method here. The Indological comparison he presents in favor of orthodoxy, for one example, is inconsistent with his definition of orthodoxy. Contrary to his fine example of an Englishman who eats with his bare hand in an Indian restaurant being considered an "orthodox" Englishman by other Englishmen, he appraises orthodoxy not in terms of his informants' sense of the religion but in terms of his own acute knowledge of the Pāli texts. Thus, while in the name of Karl Popper's renunciation of essentialist definitions, Gombrich writes, "I am for my part content to leave the definition of religion to the practitioners themselves,"[9] when it comes to the evaluation of orthodoxy Gombrich returns to a perspective more congenial to positive science.

What remains fugitive in considering orthodoxy in "outside" terms, however much it may tell us about the endurance of doctrine, is how the notion of "orthodoxy" itself weighs upon the Sinhalese and how they construe their own historical and existential positions as Buddhists. It is true, to be sure, that there never was a "pure" Buddhism. It is also true, nonetheless, that the Sinhalese draw a line between what they take to be Buddhism and what, whether scholars call it heterodoxy, magical animism, or part of an inter-connected system of belief, they take to be otherwise. Gombrich's informants make this distinction when they refer to a practice as "contrary to Buddhism" (*Buddhāgamaṭa viruddhayi*), to certain ideas as "heretical" (*vaituli adahas*) or (*mithyā ḍṛṣṭiya*), or to a belief in gods as being "not a matter of religion" (*āgama vaśayen adhanne nä*).[10] The emphasis on the similarity between early Buddhist precepts and present ones naturally neglects the phenomenological "feel" of the religion as it is experienced by the Sinhalese. The problem is not lost upon Gombrich. He concedes that the Sinhalese affectively believe, contrary to the orthodox doctrine of *karma* which they otherwise espouse, in the power of *prārthanāva* (religious aspiration) to compel events, but "cognitive congruence is achieved by a rather subtle argument which can bear little relation to the feelings of most participants."[11] That distinction leaves the explanation of Sinhalese religious awareness somewhat disjointed.

What also remains fugitive in Gombrich's Indological construction of Sinhalese experience is a sense of how the religion orients one man to another. My quibbling over what Hildred Geertz has called Indological "daisy picking" is not gratuitous. If we are to gain any anthropological purchase on religious ideologies, and Gombrich has made a beginning, then we must also locate the social provenience of those ideas. Ideas are not cut flowers. Towards finding their social origins, it might be useful to consider how the Sinhalese look at orthodoxy *tout ensemble* and how that perception in turn creates tension in Sinhalese society. I should like to do so with the case of the Sri Lanka Eka Abadda Vinaya Vardena Sangamaya (United Society for the Protection of Vinaya), a group of reformers who are themselves trying to uncover "orthodox" Buddhism.[12] I do not intend to contradict Gombrich by suggesting that the

Society has wide influence or represents the emerging shape of Sinhalese religion. To the contrary, the great bulk of the Buddhist population of Sri Lanka is unaffected by the movement, and many Sinhalese are scandalized by its very existence. That friction is all the more valuable, for it illustrates the social context of "orthodoxy." And, although the movement is in several ways revolutionary, and thus instructive, the short history of the Vinaya Vardena Society demonstrates what weight social relationships have exerted on religious institutions and ideas and perhaps can suggest why Sinhalese Buddhism has been impervious to change.

The Sociology of Patronage and Custodianship

King Asoka's son Mahinda and a coterie of four other bhikkhus arrived in Sri Lanka sometime around 243 B.C. and established Buddhism in the island by the act of tracing an emblematic boundary (*sīmā*) entirely around the Sinhalese capital Anurādhapura. The drawing of the sīmā is significant in two ways: one, it legitimated first the *saṅgha* (monkhood) and, then, by extension, Buddhism in general, and, two, it incorporated not a small plot of land (as with most sīmās) but the pre-eminent city of the realm.[13] The implication is a large one. From the first a relationship was struck between the Sinhalese nation and the full-time virtuosos of a religious tradition, not first with that tradition and certainly not with the tradition alone.[14]

In Anurādhapura, Mahinda was given land on which to found the Mahāvihāra (great monastery). Over the following one thousand years it was the Mahāvihāra which functioned as the source of Theravada conservatism. To this day Sinhalese bhikkhus of the Siyam *Nikāya* (monastic group) locate themselves in this tradition. But the Mahāvihāra was not an untested arbiter of Buddhist doctrine. In the third century of the Christian era, Mahayana monks came to the island and were eventually settled in Anurādhapura at the Abhayagirivihāra. Buddhist Tantric (Vajiravāda) monks, likewise, gained a place in Sinhalese society in the ninth century.[15]

The fortunes of the three principal vihāras, the Mahāvihāra espousing Theravada, Abhayagiri Mahayana, and Jetavana periodically shifting between the two schools, rose and fell according to royal favor. Much doctrinal dispute was all but explicitly political: for a ruler to endorse a doctrinal position implied, or perhaps depended upon his prior endorsement of a particular group of bhikkhus. Often rulers found it expedient to support all groups including brahmins. In straining for royal support, the Mahāvihāra bhikkhus exploited their descent from Mahinda. Their claims of orthodoxy based upon historical priority and apostolic succession seem to have been a compelling argument in their favor.[16] By the tenth century Theravada and the Mahāvihāra prevailed, and the Buddhism which commentators like Rhys Davids and Gombrich find the Sinhalese currently practicing derives from this conservative tradition.

The importance of orthodoxy for the Sinhalese grows out of more than the felt value of historical continuity. After the fourth century Sinhalese bhikkhus took upon themselves the burden not only of preserving the sacred books by recitation and rote learning but also of translating that doctrine into Pāli.[17] Committing the Buddha's teachings to writing protected orthodox doctrines from contamination with and subversion by heterodox ones. But because Pāli was a literary language and a difficult medium for the expression of fine points of doctrine for speakers of Sinhalese, elaborate commentaries were required. These commentaries were distinguished from the canonical literature itself which was inviolable. Many South Asianists would no longer accept Rhys Davids' curious praise of Buddhaghosa, the chief of those commentators, for his intellectual limitations, namely, his lack of independence of thought.[18] Nonetheless, the argument that the Sinhalese have taken something of a custodial role towards Theravada is supportable and useful. Such meticulousness with the Dhamma is integral to the stability of Sinhalese Buddhism.

Moreover, in the historical development of the religion there developed interlocked traditions of high caste exclusivity and monastic landlordism. When King Parākramabāhu II (c. 1236-1270) issued the Daṁbadeṇi *katikāvata* (royal decree) as an instrument of monastic reform, the document excluded from the sangha all men who were not born to the Goyigama (cultivator) caste.[19] Even before the Daṁbadeṇi *katikāvata*, monasteries had been royally endowed with paddy fields. And although the right of a bhikkhu incumbent to name his successor was legitimated only by a series of nineteenth century judicial decisions, the propriety of high caste bhikkhus exercising virtual control over monastic temporalities appears not to have been previously challenged by Sinhalese laypeople, regardless of caste. The paradoxical prospect of renouncing the world to become in turn a monastic landlord came to be a high caste prerogative. In point of fact, the incumbencies of important Kandyan monasteries became the preserve of a far smaller number of even more aristocratic Radaḷa (the highest Goyigama subcaste) families.

These trends too are related to the doctrinal stability of Theravada. Not only have the Sinhalese felt that because of the arcane and literary nature of the Dhamma, were the succession of teachers and pupils broken, the Dhamma would be absolutely lost. They also have seen the custodial care of the Dhamma devolve upon an elite group of culturally impeccable individuals who have been as well a wealthy and landed aristocracy by virtue of natal inheritances or succession to monastic incumbencies. In such a climate doctrinal disputation and independence of thought have not run riot.

Sinhalese kings who have exercised their right and responsibility to direct, reform and protect the sangha have done just that, expelling wrongdoing bhikkhus, passing judgements upon disputes over incumbencies, and making appointments to high office. Ideally, they have responsibilities to the Dhamma as well, but historically they have chosen to meet that responsibility indirectly. When they have tried to act directly, kings have found the propagation and interpretation of the Dhamma a heavy burden. The case of the Sinhalese king Duṭṭhagāmaṇī is apt.[20]

> He seated himself in the preacher's chair . . . and made ready to give the august assembly a discourse on some religious topic from the *Maṅgala Sutta*. But, although he was quite familiar with the Sacred Scriptures, he could not proceed; he descended from the pulpit, "perspiring profusely"; he had realized how difficult was the task of the teachers and his munificence towards them was made greater.

Because kings have been unequal to the task of interpreting doctrine, the powers of *rāja* and sangha have been equilibrating ones. When the British Crown replaced the Sinhalese rāja, for a time the rāja's disciplinary, judicial, and appointive prerogatives *vis-a-vis* the monkhood were met. By the 1840s, however, Christian opposition exerted through the Home Office caused the British to back away from active patronage. In place of the intervention of rāja or British Resident, the Crown gave the monkhood a set of monastic laws with which to govern itself. The sangha thus grew more independent, now not just of local lay control for that had long been the case, but also of governmental influence.[21] When the British reneged on their pledge of active support for the "religion of the Boodoo," they in turn forfeited much of their right to hold bhikkhus accountable for their actions.[22] As the example of Vinaya Vardena Society will show, the consequences for laity-sangha relationships of this lapsing of accountability are still at work.

Tradition has it that the Lord Buddha visited Sri Lanka three times in his lifetime. The island was also the first country to which his message, still relatively fresh and true, spread. For the Buddhists of Southeast and East Asia as well as for the Sinhalese, Sri Lanka thus has a special relationship to Theravada orthodoxy. It is the Dhammadīpa, the island of the Dhamma. The World Buddhist Fellowship and the Mahābodhi Society have their headquarters not in Bodhgayā or Sārnāth, but in Colombo. The countless *dagäbas* (relic mounds) which one sees all over the island carry this same custodial implication. In most of these *dagäbas* not only is a putative relic of the Buddha enshrined, but also a set of Dhamma books. The intention is explicit: beneath tons of brick and soil the doctrine which the Sinhalese have preserved elsewhere in more accessible ways is secure, not only for themselves, but for the entire Buddhist *sāsana.*[23]

The Reformative Tradition

Pictured against this background of great stability the Vinaya Vardena Society is utterly revolutionary. To be fair, however, Sinhalese Buddhism has experienced a passing amount of dissension and experimentation, especially so in the twentieth century. Many of these experiments have been explicit efforts to rethink the nature of relations between bhikkhus and their supporters. The Vinaya Vardena Society is heir in several ways to these experiments. A leading example is the role assumed by Don David Hewavitarana, a Buddhist layman who not only founded the Mahābodhi Society, but also devised an altogether new religious *cum* social role. Calling himself the Anagārika Dharmapala ("homeless guardian of the doctrine," a name which suggests another solution to a standing obligation), he adopted a style of life which drew upon that of both monk and layman. Dharmapala followed a life of celibacy, affected monkish, but distinctively white robes, and attempted to use his asceticism for worldly ends. While in his later years he was to become a full-fledged bhikkhu, his place in Buddhist history is as paradigm for what has become known eponymously as the "anagārika" role.[24]

Another form of experimentation took shape in the 1950s, a time which Sinhalese sometimes refer to as the *tāpas kāle* (austerity time). Men who assumed the dress of bhikkhus without formal initiation into the sangha, that is, in any of the several Nikāyas, began to practice austerities (*dhūtanga*) which were entirely alien to the regimen of orthodox bhikkhus in Sri Lanka.[25] These austerities included walking with knees tightly bound with rope, mixing alms with water to render it tasteless, and sleeping wherever nightfall happened to find the monks. After a period of enthusiastic support, lay interest cooled and the *tāpasa* monks disappeared altogether. The appearance of such extraordinary austerity itself made laypeople suspicious of the group's true intentions. This suspicion was compounded by the monks' not being tied to any single monastery and thus known and responsible to the local community. This suspicion is the paradox of the lay perception of the monkhood: *gamavāsi* monks in their custodial roles are known and potentially accountable, more austere monks who choose to wander "lonely as a rhinoceros" are potentially dangerous.

More successful has been a middle solution to the same problem, the creation of a number of forest hermitages, located usually in remote areas of the Southern and Eastern Provinces, where monks are both ascetic and stationary.[26] Laypeople continue to support these āraññavāsi (forest dwelling) bhikkhus, although their remoteness makes support often a matter of giving only an annual *dāna* (alms-giving) for a particular group of monks. Forest hermitages like those of the Paṃsukūlins and Vantajivakas have been heard of before in Sinhalese history. Here they assume new proportions, such as attracting support from afar. Moreover, religiously-minded laypeople come to such hermitages on retreat, spending a solitary weekend or so following the life of an *āraññavāsi* bhikkhu. Much of the support that such bhikkhus receive comes as an explicit rejection of local *gamavāsi* monks, the very ones which in the past the householder supported. Thus, the discretionary giving of alms constitutes an indirect attempt to reform the monkhood.

The Vinaya Vardena Society was formed in 1932 as a direct and collective attempt at the same end.[27] It began in a Buddhist monastery in Hunuwela, a village in Sabaragamuva Province, a mountainous and isolated part of the central highlands. The founding impulse is plain enough in the founder, G. V. S. Jayasundera's argument that ten precepts are absolutely basic to good Buddhist behavior. These included the traditional five precepts which weigh upon all Buddhist laypeople as well as five more precepts which were to be followed by the laity in dealing with the monkhood:

6. No monetary transactions between *bhikkhus* and laity.
7. Total avoidance of *bhikkhus* who do not live up to their precepts.
8. Except during calamitous times, offering food only to the alms-bowl, not to porcelain plates.
9. No reimbursement to healthy *bhikkhus* for travel expenses incurred in attending *dānas* (alms-givings).
10. Likewise, no reimbursement to healthy *bhikkhus* for travel expenses incurred in attending *baṇas* (Buddhist sermons).

Its origin in a Buddhist monastery rightly suggests that the group had the support of certain reform-minded bhikkhus. It claimed as its chief adviser, for instance, the Ven. Balangoda Ananda Maitreya, a distinguished monk who in 1969 was to become the *mahānāyaka* (chief monk) of most sections of the Amarapura Nikāya. Its program was appropriately moderate, formulated, and tentatively so at that, to bring monkly behavior into line with Vinaya (the monastic discipline), and certainly not to abolish the monkhood altogether. The thrust was to remove money, and thus its corrupting influence, from the relationship between those who have left the social world and those who remain in it.

Local monks who were asked to meet with the group hotly disagreed with the Society's interpretation and application of Vinaya. Their opposition increased disunity within the group and the movement collapsed in its first year.

Six years later Jayasundera, who by then was managing a tea *kade* (shop) in Pelmadulla, became friends with A. Sumanaratne, a local astrologer. Together they decided to publish some three thousand copies of a tract that Sumanaratne had written, *Vibhajjavādaya hevat Buddhāgama* (The Way of the *Vajjīs* or Buddhism), including in that publication Jayasundera's ten precepts.[28] Encouraged by the response to this publication and to their monthly magazine, the pair renewed the Vinaya Vardena Society on August 31, 1939, in a village close by Pelmadulla. This time bhikkhus of the three Nikāyas were excluded from membership and the veneration of Buddha images banned as a sensuous digression from the Buddha's message. Opposition meetings of monks, chiefly of the Amarapura and Siyam Nikāyas, and laypeople began in 1939.[29] On the seventh of August, 1939, a building in which two hundred members of the Society were observing *aṭa sīl* (the eight precepts which pious Buddhists take on certain days of the lunar month) was set ablaze, the first incident in a pattern of violent opposition between the reformers and the mainstream community. Such violence has been so chronic that the Society's fifty-page history devotes some seventeen pages to describing similar incidents province by province.

By the 1950s, conflict again divided the group. Jayasundera left the Society because of his opposition to the group's own financial entanglements, its collection of dues. As Jayasundera was going, James Soysa was coming, a significant change in personnel for Jayasundera had wanted only to reform the sangha.[30] After Jayasundera's departure, Sumanaratne appears to have been freer to reformulate accepted beliefs. Soysa became something of a publicist, opening a number of *daham pāsalas* (Dhamma schools) in the Colombo area, organizing the printing of the numerous publications through which the Society expressed its views, and delivering sermons at publicized times near bo tree enclosures in what the Society called *vajjī* temples.[31] Sumanaratne continued to play the role of chief ideologue, publisher of a monthly magazine, *Vibajjavādi Dharma Sanghdhaya*, and elder spokesman, but in some sense the organizational center of the organization shifted from Sabaragamuva to the Low Country.

Propaganda work took a form reminiscent of the turbulent Low Country debates of the last half of the nineteenth century between Christian spokesmen and Buddhist monks.[32] With the established monkhood the Society had numerous grievances, the reciting of supernatural curses (*vaskavi kiyanavā*), casting mantras (*yantra mantra karanavā*), inspecting horoscopes (*kēndra balanavā*), doing ayurvedic doctoring (*veda kam karanavā*), organizing fire-walking ceremonies (*gini pā gavanavā*), and allowing dancing and drumming to be performed in temple compounds. All these the Society regarded as improper for *bhikkhus* (*hāmuduruvarungē väradi kriyā*), and especially so because the Society suspected that these activities were motivated by the bhikkhus' desire to turn a profit from them. The motive need not be crass, however, to be objectionable. The Society objected to monks who choose to live in towns, who look at their appearance in mirrors, and who not only do not shave their heads but these days also affect sideburns. Throughout the 1940s Soysa engaged *vajjī* bhikkhus in debates. A bhikkhu named Karagampitiya Jinaratana, for example, met Soysa in a public debate and argued that the sangha was not defiled by the violation of any of the Vinaya rules but for the most important prohibitions, the four *pārājika* rules against sexual intercourse, stealing, murder, and claiming advanced spiritual status. According to the Society, a large gathering endorsed Soysa's position that bhikkhus must uphold all of the Vinaya rules. As a result, some thirteen supporters of the bhikkhu came over to the side of the Vinaya Vardena Society. Other debates had similar conclusions.

Vinaya Vardena proponents castigated not only the improper conduct of the *trinikāyaka saṅgha* (the monkhood of the three major Nikāyas), but also its false interpretation of Dhamma. Although Dhamma and Vinaya are usually considered radically different parts of the Buddhist religion, for the Society they are of a single piece.[33] Vinaya, they argue, is the preservation of Dhamma.[34] A bhikkhu does as much damage to Buddhism by using modern black umbrellas, footwear if not ill, and porcelain plates in place of the traditional alms bowl, as he does by misleading the Dhamma, by denying, for one example, that nibbāna is possible at this very moment.

On that point of doctrine the Society has been adamant: it is possible to attain nibbāna now. Such optimism contradicts the popular Sinhalese notion that the deterioration of the sāsana brings with it the possibility of attaining nibbāna only after a multiple number of rebirths or until the Maitreya Buddha appears.[35] This notion is so widely accepted that the Vinaya Vardena Society appears to many Sinhalese to be wildly innovative. The Society sees itself as quite the opposite. As this transcription of a Vinaya Vardena debate in Matara indicates, Sumanaratne and his followers have attacked the monkhood not only for being impious (*dussīla*) but also misled (*mulā kalā*) about what constitutes orthodox Theravada belief in this regard:[36]

Vinaya: "Do you say that it is impossible to attain *nibbāna* now?"

Bhikkhu: "I say so because of the difference in opinion as seen in the commentaries."

Vinaya: "There may be certain differences of opinion in the commentaries in elucidating difficult doctrinal points. Commentaries are written by *achāryas.* We should go by the Suttas which we hold in high esteem, not by following *achāryas* and their ideas in the commentaries. Do you say that in the Suttas which contain the real Dhamma there is disorder or unclear doctrine?"

Bhikkhu: (No answer, the *bhikkhu* turns for advice to the elders who are seated behind him.)

Vinaya: "Do you say that the essential doctrines in the Suttas are not clear on this matter?"

Bhikkhu: (No answer).

Vinaya: "Venerable Sir, all advice for the attainment of *nibbāna* is given in the three Piṭakas. If you guide yourself according to the Buddha, Dhamma, and Saṅgha, you gain the four stages of *Sotāpanna, Sakadāgāmī, Anāgāmī,* and *Arhat* which you call *Adigamaya* or *Nibbāna.*[37] Do you say that the teachings are not clear?"

Bhikkhu: (Relaying advice from the elders seated behind him) "It is clear."

Vinaya: "If so, why can't you attain *nibbāna* today?"

Bhikkhu: (No answer).

Vinaya: "If so, don't you think that it is we who don't have clear understanding?"

At this turn the bhikkhu, perspiring heavily, called for a glass of water, drank it off, and left the stage, a spectacle quite the reverse of Duṭṭhagāmaṇī's inability to preach or interpret the Dhamma.

In another debate between a spokesman for the Society and Mirissa Gunasiri, a scholarly monk of the Southern Province, the topic of the correct relationship between Buddhism and art was broached. The Society argued that artful diversions, drumming, dancing, incantations, songs, paintings, statues, poetry, and drama, when undertaken as part of Buddhist activities, were responsible for the deterioration of Buddhism. The Ven. Gunasiri conceded that art was not part of the Buddhist religion. It was, however, essential for its survival. Buddha relics, for one example, would not be respected or safeguarded if they were not kept in a silk draped relic casket. Art has thus preserved Buddhism for centuries. The Society was not persuaded by the expediency argument, countering that the religion was now buried beneath ruffles and flourishes. When the Society elsewhere charged that the Lord Buddha never in fact visited Sri Lanka, that his footprint on Sri Pada is spurious, and consequently that the island's historical relation to the Lord Buddha is factitious, the sangha has responded with a similar argument. Whether the Lord Buddha visited the island or not, the belief that he did has maintained mass religiosity and is thus more important than historical fact.

To the besetting question of what to make of its relationship to a monkhood it did not respect, the Society tried several solutions. Early on Sumanaratne experimented with offering *dāna* not to genuine bhikkhus, but to eighty pillows emblematic of the original sangha (*asumahā srāvaka dānaya*). Although it supported the *tāpasa* monks who appeared in the 1950s, the Society also ordained its own monks. As opposed to establishment bhikkhus who necessarily receive initiation from one of the three Nikāyas, the Society regarded as properly ordained bhikkhus who took the robes on their own or under the direction of a teacher who himself had not received initiation. This form of ordination was conceived of as a stopgap measure, not a final solution to the reformation of the monkhood. The number of bhikkhus thus inducted appears to be quite small, perhaps as few as ten. Another solution has been to encourage pious laypeople to assume the *anagārika* role, but the number of *anagārikas* appears to be equally small.

The happiest innovation has been the attempt on the part of the Society's membership to take on the role of religious virtuosos themselves, but in a temporary way much like a layman assumes additional precepts on *poya* days. Dressing themselves in clean white national dress, male and female members file into an assembly hall, in this case a preaching hall at an abandoned monastery early on the morning of pre-*poya* day (the day before the four quarter days of the lunar month), and observe a severe schedule of religious activities:

Figure 1: A Vinaya Vardena Society Retreat and Service

Pre-Poya Day

5:45-7:00 A.M.	Giving of *aṭa sīl* (8 precepts) followed by sermon by guest lecturer supplied by the national society. Offering of flowers, lamps, and joss sticks at empty altar.
7:30 A.M.	Morning meal (*hīl dānaya*)
9:00-10:00 A.M.	Group meditation (*samuha bhāvanāva*)
10:00-11:00 A.M.	Individual meditation

11:00 A.M.	Noon meal (*dahaval dāna*) taken as *bhikkhus* do before noon as the last meal of the day. Distribution of merit acquired by the giving of *dāna* to gods and those who have financed the ceremony.
12:00-2:00 P.M.	Rest period (*dakvā vivēkaya*)
2:00-4:00 P.M.	*Karmastāna vädīma.* Chanting of the Satipattanaya with explanatory responses in Sinhalese. A discussion about *baṇa* follows (*baṇa sākatchā karanavā*)
4:00 P.M.	Tea and Sweets (*gilanpasa*)
5:00-6:00 P.M.	Group meditation (*samuha bhāvanāva*)
7:00 P.M.	Flower offering (*mal pahan pujāva*)[38]
8:00 P.M.	Sermon (*baṇa kiyanavā*)
10:00 P.M.	Chanting of Metta Sutraya and the giving of merit

Poya Day

12:00-3:00 A.M.	Sleep for those who wish
3:30-4:30 A.M.	Pirit chanting (*pirit desuma*)
4:30-5:15 A.M.	Meditation (*samuha bhāvanāva*)
5:15-6:15 A.M.	*Mal pahan pujāva*

The schedule is properly regarded as a strenuous and important undertaking (*loku vädak*), one modelled upon the dietary and meditative regimen of the sangha itself. The *anagārika himivaru* (members) spend the day before taking the precepts leisurely and are instructed at that time in the meaning of the activity and in the proper nature of meditation, eating, and doing *pūjās.* During the entire activity no one is expected to leave the assembly hall unless on an errand for the sāsana. The aura of the ceremony is somber. The crackling loudspeakers which are a part of many Buddhist *pinkamas* (group activities like this at which merit is generated) are conspicuously missing. This demystification of the Pāli verses, of meditation, and of the Dhamma itself is an attempt not only to make accessible what the Society understands to be the Lord Buddha's message, but also to ground the Society's members in the Dhamma so that they will be at no disadvantage in arguing about correct Buddhist belief with bhikkhus and laypeople. Performance and propaganda are attempted on the same occasion: in Clifford Geertz's terms, the ritual serves both as a model "of" what the Society believes and a model "for" how such belief may be reasonably entertained.

At death the Society assumes an apparently radical role. At the one life cycle ritual at which the monkhood's presence is essential laypeople fully replace the bhikkhu-sangha. In Vinaya Vardena villages and towns, the deceased's relatives have a choice, to go to the local monastery and ask for a certain number of bhikkhus to attend the rite, or to go to the secretary of the Society and ask for an equivalent number of laypeople to assume the same role.[39] When invited, the Society's members accept the veneration of other laypeople, say *pirit*, perform the *matakavastra pūjā* for the deceased, and finally take *dāna.* On ordinary *poya* days, too, householders give *dāna* to invited members of the Society and gloat over their superior *sīla.*

Another activity, this one lighter in tone but hardly frivolous, is the annual ceremony at which students of one of the Society's Dhamma schools are given awards. The tone of the ceremony as well as its content implies a shift of responsibility from monkhood to laity. On a Sunday afternoon the meeting begins with the Society's secretary explaining word for word what the Society takes to be the meaning of the *Tun Saraṇa* (Three Refuges). Schoolgirls dressed in white mount the stage and arrange themselves in two oblique rows. Jointly they repeat Pāli stanzas from the canon, followed by the first girl in one of the rows explaining the verse in Sinhalese. A presidential address follows. The speaker says that his intention as president of the local Vinaya Vardena Society is to bring the group up to the level of any of the three Nikāyas. Our students, he asserts, must be clever enough to argue with bhikkhus. He ends with a flourish: he has warned the monks of the *trinikāyaka saṅgha* to speak the truth as it appears in the canon or else he himself will broadcast over the CBC airwaves and reveal the true shape of the Dhamma. Cries of "*sādhu, sādhu, sāāā,*" a response usually reserved for the end of monkly disquisitions, follow his remarks.

An undergraduate who has gone on from the Dhamma school to the university takes over and reviews common misunderstandings about Buddhist history in the island, raising the point that books now considered factual may have been written by bhikkhus merely to reward the patronage of Sinhalese kings. He adds that if true Theravada were practiced in Sri Lanka, there would have been no need for the Vinaya Vardena Society. But it is not. The Buddhism of the sangha is closer to Mahayana, which represents for the Society, as it does for many Sinhalese, heterodoxy and backsliding.

Next comes more Pāli reading and Sinhalese exegesis. An Ayurvedic physician from the Southern Province speaks. He wears his hair to his shoulders, affects national dress like most ayurvedic doctors, and speaks in a rhetorical way that has the avuncular quality of the most popular monkly discourse. He was a gold medal student at his *pirivena* (Buddhist school), he says, but because he learned the truth about the Vinaya, he has joined the Society. In the Southern Province, the movement has grown so that devil dancing, for which the area is notorious, is on the wane. Laypeople now prefer the powerful pirit chanting which the local Society provides. After a young girl explains the difference between Theravada and Mahayana and an intermission at which orange barley soda is served to dignitaries, James Soysa speaks on Vinaya and its abuse by the *trinikāyaka saṅgha.* Preteenage boys in national dress and girls in white cloth and jackets form on the stage. The lead girl asks a question about Dhamma and the lead boy explains. Finally prizes are given out. Soap, powder, ink, paper, and towels, gifts identical to those offered to young *sāmaṇeras*, (Buddhist novices) are given to students who have begun to decide for themselves, not by way of monkly interpretation, what is the true Dhamma.[40]

The Dhamma according to the Vinaya Vardena Society

It is difficult to explain in a discursive way the conceptual organization and the evolution of the Society's doctrine. The difficulty derives from the contingent quality which many of the Society's beliefs have: does a belief represent a free-standing reformulation of orthodoxy, or is it a political instrument for monastic reform; does this movement like the several heresies of the early centuries of the Christian religion grow out of hatred for the Church or deep doctrinal misgivings?[41] Although Sumanaratne's assault on the establishment monkhood draws heavily on the monks' violation of Vinaya, from the first he sought to correct them doctrinally as well. However tempting it may be to portray the Society as attempting to reform the sangha by scheming to reveal weakness in what the lay public considers to be the sangha's strength, its knowledge of Dhamma, the point is arguable. The Society does contend that there is no advantage in supporting curators who are carefully preserving false views, but it has always done so. Sumanaratne seems to have felt from the first the sangha to be in error, and he argues that his reformulation of orthodoxy is an objective distinct from monastic reform. Its effect is not.

The group shares many beliefs with other Sinhalese Buddhists. The Society sees Buddhism as the path to nibbāna, its realization contingent upon comprehending the Four Noble Truths. To understand those truths, one must approach them as the Buddha did by contemplating upon the fleeting nature of the five aggregates and the non-existence of the soul. A latent understanding of those truths exists in man, beast, and *deva* (god) alike but is only fully realized upon enlightenment, *bodhi*. The virtues necessary to achieve *bodhi* are *sīla* (morality), *samādhi* (concentration), and *paññā* (wisdom). The exercise of these virtues taken together is known as the Noble Eightfold Path. As one perseveres along this path towards nibbāna, one passes through four stages of increasingly higher spiritual status, *sotāpanna* or *sovan, sakadāgāmī, anāgāmi,* and *arhat.*

With these beliefs most Sinhalese Buddhists would have no trouble. Beyond this point, however, Vinaya Vardena doctrine begins to extol the laity and its spiritual potential. At the same time it conflates the distinction between monk and layman. The common presumption is that not only is nibbāna now unattainable but also that there are no living individuals who have achieved even the lowest of these four spiritual stages, *sotāpanna.* The proof is in the looking: no one appears to have special religious standing, and certainly no one dares make such a claim. To this argument the Society replies that anyone aspiring to these stages which end in bodhi can be called a *Bodhisattva.*[42] There is no Buddhist who does not strive to attain the path (*sotāpanna* and onwards) in this sāsana.[43] Enlightenment is an attainable objective, not to say a fully public one. What pleases the Lord Buddha is not homage, not offerings of flowers and food, but Buddhists who practice his teachings. In this effort no one can intercede, not the Lord Buddha and not the sangha. As the Society warns, individual moral responsibility is indispensable:

> Many believe in the Buddha as a great Teacher, who can still somehow help them in person, because of his great merits accumulated through long aeons. Helping to support an army of bhikkhus, or building innumerable temples will not help one to attain *nibbana* if he considers the lofty moral code of Buddhism as impracticable.[44]

Admitting that all Buddhists are on the path to enlightenment, and perhaps even to Buddhahood, the collectivity of these seekers can be defined according to their progress as the sangha. There is a sangha of *sotāpannas*, a sangha of *sakadāgāmis*, and so on. In these terms the sangha is a state of mind (*tatvaya*), not a corporate group.[45] Anyone in fact who sees the suffering of the world is a bhikkhu (*duka däkka minihaṭa biku*). Moreover, as the responsibility to attend to one's own destiny becomes radically personal and pervasive, so does the responsibility of protecting Buddhism itself.[46] To accept the Society's doctrine, then, is to be obligated to implement its reformative program.

One enters the Buddhist way of life, and one periodically recommits himself to it before taking *sīl*, by saying the *Tun Saraṇa*, repeating with a bhikkhu the verse that identifies the religion's most important institutions and ideological elements:

> I take refuge in the Buddha,
> I take refuge in the Dhamma,
> I take refuge in the Sangha.

In the eyes of the Society, Buddhism is now so degenerate that laymen have come to understand the verse in a vulgar, simpleheaded way:

> May the Buddha in the idol house be my refuge.
> May the Dhamma in the almirah be my refuge.
> May the *bhikkhu-sangha* of the three caste-bound *nikayas* be my refuge.[47]

For the Society, however, the purpose of observing the Triple Refuge is to fix oneself on that goal which is incumbent upon every Buddhist, nibbāna:

> I will attain Bodhi or Buddhahood.
> I will soak in the Eightfold Path of Doctrine
> I will merge in the sangha.[48]

The language itself is apt. One virtually fuses oneself in thought to the Buddhist way of life. What pre-eminently one does not do is think about these categories of experience in corporeal terms.

The point is not as rhetorical as it sounds, and the literature of the Society is at pains to explain why. One does not actually "go" to the Buddha, the Dhamma, or the sangha when one takes the *Tun Saraṇa* (*yanṇa tänak nähä*). To think in such terms entails trafficking in very gross images indeed. The Buddha is not a statue (*pilimayak*), the Dhamma is not a book (*potak*), and the sangha is not a bald pate (*mudu mahanek*). The Buddha, to the contrary, is incomparable and, therefore, incapable of being captured in a statue. What is captured in such statues is not the message of the Buddha, but the worshipper's sensuous attention. He is led astray by art (*kalāva*) and ends up not meditating on right action (*sammāditthi nähä*) but saying to himself "How lovely!" (*mēka kochchara lakshanāda*). Likewise, if bald heads identified the sangha, the Society reasons, then South Asian Muslims, because they too often shave their heads, deserve to be treated like Buddhist monks. If laymen rationalize their support of impious bhikkhus in similarly sophistic terms, by worshipping the robes and what they represent, not the fallible wearers of those robes, they might as well resort to the boutiques which sell those robes in the first place. There one can venerate robes unsullied by even pious wear!

The Society's rejection of the special reverence reserved for certain places and objects in Sri Lanka which are associated with the Buddha follows similar reasoning. Only two *bo* (*bo-bodhi*) trees, one at Bodhgayā and the other at Anurādhapura, are accepted by the Society as actually related to the Buddha's enlightenment. All the other trees which Buddhists consider to be holy are *äsatu gas* (*ficus religiosa*, merely the same species of tree under which the Buddha sat when he received enlightenment). To regard all *äsatu gas* as worthy of veneration is to confuse the one and the many, the real and the derivative. This punctiliousness has larger implications: all monks are not pious, and all "truths" which they utter need not be true. One must depend upon his own critical faculties, just as the Lord Buddha advised, and the way one sharpens those faculties for passing judgment on higher truths is by straightening out simpler ones. In doing so one realizes that it is extremely unlikely that the Lord Buddha visited Sri Lanka three times and that he left massive footprints at historically important shrines. If he had, King Devānaṁpiyatissa and his subjects would have known about the religion before Mahinda's subsequent arrival. When their material origins are exposed, such beliefs are revealed to be deceptions cultivated by monkly entrepreneurs who want to fill up merit boxes (*pin pattiya*) with coins offered by pilgrims.

Parallels to this emphasis on actions and not persons, on the spiritual as opposed to the material and the personal (*puggalika*) are not hard to find. In South Asia, the *bhakti* movement and Sufism come to mind; in the West, the Sabbatian movement and eighteenth century German Pietism are intriguing cases for comparison. In the present case, ideology and political reform are consistent and mutually supportive dimensions. If the Buddha image which one finds in every Buddhist vihāra is not worthy of veneration, then the merit boxes just alongside the image will remain empty. If one interprets the Dhamma for oneself, then the monkhood loses both intellectual privilege and financial independence. At that point, the Society envisions, monks will stop struggling over monastic prebends, indulging themselves in luxuries, the moneylenders will leave the temple and real bhikkhus will turn to the task at hand, nibbāna. So will laymen, if in a more casual way. When monk and layman alike learn that nibbāna is possible now, worldly attractions will seem absolutely trivial. Monastic landlordism and a caste-based Nikāya system will be recognized as entanglements. Monks will return to their begging rounds and the relationship between sangha and the lay community will be set right.

Reform, then, depends upon making a number of distinctions. What is special about the Buddha are the qualities which led to his enlightenment (*Budu guna*) and which can be emulated by living Buddhists, not his personal characteristics (*pautgalikathvaya*). For that matter, there never lived a man named "Buddha" (*Budun kiyā kenek nähä*). "Buddha" is only an epithet applied to a man, admittedly the first man and a very special one altogether, who achieved nibbāna. The term for present purposes is merely a vehicle for understanding the four truths, just as Dhamma is a symbol for thinking about *pragnāva* (knowledge acquired from the book of the same name), and sangha a mnemonic for the collectivity of impurity (*rāga, dosa, moha*) avoiding Buddhists (*keles handīti sangho*). With these distinctions in hand, the Society radically changes the thrust of the *Tun Saraṇa* from a profession of faith to an optative assertion.

> I am going to gain knowledge of Buddhahood.
> I am going to understand the nine otherworldly steps.
> Let me achieve the *ariya*-ship which is free of passions.[49]

The program is directly put. Although the possibility of achieving nibbāna (or, a knowledge of Buddhahood, as it is referred to here) is a public one, the prospect is not gnostic. Rather all Buddhists proceed by stages (*māgapala*), nine in number and consisting in two parts. The way (*māga*) itself consists of the four spiritual conditions, *sotāpanna, sakadāgāmī, anāgāmi,* and *arhat*, and the fruits (*pala*) of the way are those same conditions, *sotāpanna, sakadāgāmī, anāgāmī, arhat*, this time culminating in the ninth and final stage, nibbāna. In other words, the means to nibbāna is also an end in itself.

Upon joining the Society one begins this struggle in earnest by subscribing to the six basic principles of the Vinaya Vardena Society.[50]

1. Having understood the Four Noble Truths, I come to the nine otherworldly *Dhammas* (steps, in this usage), I come to the "sangha"-hood and according to these ideas I accept the *Tun Saraṇa.*
2. I will avoid the divided *nikāyas*, individuals who violate the Lord Buddha's teachings, and ordinary *bhikkhus.*
3. I will avoid ideas and methods which cannot be shown to be orthodox.
4. I accept the Five precepts (*pan sīl*).
5. Having taken this ordination, I will be calm (*tänpot*).
6. Having received a piece of Dhamma (*karmastanaya*), I will meditate upon it until I receive *māgapala*. I accept your organization and its principles and, having signed below, I accept your rules and regulations.

Some forty years after its founding, the Society continues to believe that nibbāna is within reach. If one protects his *sīl*, abandons ambition (*āsava*), the notion of the self (*ātmaya*) and all doubt (*säkaya*), release is possible in this very life (*mē atmē*). In fact, if one meets these requirements, getting nibbāna is automatic. But who can meet the requirements; that is the snag. At all events one can achieve *sotāpanna* in this life, and nibbāna can follow in, let us say, three or four or seven lifetimes. The number is not and need not be precise, for the promise is still proximate and compelling. In fact, the Vinaya Vardena Society's doctrine in general is compelling. Its grievances against the sangha are genuine, its program is internally consistent, cleverly put, and couched in terms not of innovation but the rediscovery of orthodoxy, and its members are well schooled in Dhamma and utterly sincere. There is only one problem. The great majority of the Buddhist population of Sri Lanka regard the movement, if at all, as either mildly daft or subversive.[51] Why the movement has met such hostility and why the larger Buddhist community has not questioned the legitimacy of the sangha are matters which illuminate the issue at question here, the stability of Sinhalese Buddhism.

The Sociology of Reform

From the first the Vinaya Vardena Society had a reservoir of Buddhist laypeople unhappy with the behavior of local bhikkhus. It is not difficult in Sri Lanka to detect vibrations, usually subtle, surprisingly often not, of hostility towards the sangha. What the Society, however, did not have was a reservoir of laypeople willing to commit themselves to the Society and at the same time break their relations with the monkhood. Diffuse sympathy is one thing; active and exclusive support, quite another.

Between 1939 when Sumanaratne first asserted that there was not a single Theravada bhikkhu in the three Nikāyas and 1955 when the national organization was registered with the government, the Society enjoyed steady growth. Members of the central society admit that the membership of the Society reached a peak in the late fifties. That expansion is not hard to place historically knowing the great lay antagonism which the sangha experienced in the fifties culminating in Prime Minister Bandaranaike's assassination by a bhikkhu's hand. Since the early sixties membership has declined, although members of the central society insist that the Society has again begun to expand.[52] These perceptions of recent shrinkage are supported by the contrast between the total number of local societies in 1959, 168, and the present number, 143. The Society now has a membership of 1,200 members, a number that fairly blanches when compared to a total Buddhist population in the island of some eight million.

A summary of the geographical distribution of these 143 *samitiyas* gives some sense of the group's spread and its strongholds.

Figure 2: The Distribution of Vinaya Vardena Local Societies (*Samitiyas*)

Province or District	*Number*
North Western Province	28
Kurunegala District	28
Central Province	21
Matara District	18
Colombo District	12
Kalutara District	12
Ratnapura District	10
Galle District	7
Badulla District	3
Amparai District	2
Polonnaruwa District	1
North Central Province	1
	143

It is plain that the Vinaya Vardena Society is found throughout the island, in the more traditional Central Province and in the Low Country, in the heavily Sinhalese southwestern quadrant of the island, and in the settlement schemes of the North Central and Eastern Provinces. The relative scarcity of *samitiyas* in the Ratnapura District (where Sumanaratne started the movement) and in Colombo District (where Soysa, the group's most effective proselytizer, lives) is hard to explain. The sequential establishing of local groups shows some larger pattern of priority and eastward diffusion. Groups were founded in Matara in 1938, Galkissa, 1939, followed by Ratmalana, 1947, Angoda, 1948, Akuressa, 1950, Badulla, 1951, Ambalantota, 1954, and Polonnaruwa, 1956.

A better impression of the kinds of people who make up the Vinaya Vardena Society can be gotten by considering the membership roles of two of these *samitiyas.*[53]

Figure 3: Membership Roles of Two Selected Local Societies

Mahavella *Samitiya*

Member	*Age*	*Caste*	*Profession*	*English Speaker*
R. P. Rajakaruna	55	Goyigama	landlord/planter	no
Martin Nanayakara	52	Goyigama	ayurvedic doctor	no
C. M. Wikramapala	73	Durāva	porcelain shop owner	no
L. M. S. Abhayawickrama	58	Durāva	primary school principal, homeopathic doctor	yes

Member	*Age*	*Caste*	*Profession*	*English Speaker*
Philip Samarasekera	70	Durāva	landlord	no
H. L. James Silva	50	Karāva	clerk at district court	yes
L. P. Somaratana	52	Goyigama	rice and curry stuff shop owner	no
P. K. J. Wilson	51	Goyigama	ayurvedic doctor	no
E. Siriwardena	45	Karāva	unemployed laborer	no
S. David	35	Karāva	farmer	no
P. Jemis Appuhamy	35	Goyigama	landlord/planter	no
H. Weerasingha	40	Goyigama	co-operative manager	no
T. P. Kalansuriya	45	Goyigama	landlord/planter	no
M. N. Geris Appuhamy	75	Goyigama	landlord/village headman	no
Somapala	28	Karāva	postal peon	no
H. E. W. Jayasiri	75	Goyigama	irrigation dept. clerk, retired	yes
B. B. Baron Singho	52	Durāva	ayurvedic doctor	no
Polpitiya *Samitiya*				
Eddie Mendis	67	Karāva	moneylender	no
Saderis Mendis	62	Karāva	wholesale business	yes
P. M. Perlis Appuhamy	80	Goyigama	large shop owner	no
D. G. Davith	75	Goyigama	farmer	no
D. Charles Silva	52	Salāgama	mason bas	no
H. A. D. Rupasingha	45	Goyigama	municipal van driver	no
K. Jeris	35	Goyigama	scavenger	no
G. P. Weerakoon	73	Goyigama	retired ambulance driver	no
M. K. Kalyanaratana	78	Salāgama	kerosene agent	no
Somadasa Gunasekera	33	Goyigama	stevedore	no
K. H. Paulis Appuhamy	55	Goyigama	building contractor	no
K. V. Sirinihal	65	Goyigama	curry stuff shop owner	no
L. D. Weeramanne	50	Navandannā	mechanic	no
S. P. Punchi Singho	50	Rada	Colombo harbor overseer	no
B. B. Jamis Appuhamy	56	Navandannā	municipal health van driver	no
P. S. Singhohamy	84	Navandannā	goldsmith	no
H. P. Chandrasena	72	Goyigama	farmer	no
B. Rajasuriya	38	Goyigama	CTB driver	no
A. B. Davulis Silva	45	Goyigama	harbor mechanic	no
G. P. G. Gunawathie	40	Goyigama	weaving school teacher	yes
P. D. Somapala	46	Karāva	retired teacher	yes

Together Figures 2 and 3 make it clear that the lack of growth of the Vinaya Vardena Society cannot be attributed to many of the explanations that come into mind. One is soon struck by what the movement is not: it is not geographically isolated, nor is it caste-bound, exclusively urban or rural, upper class or lower class, or English-educated. It is neither limited to people of the same surname, nor geographically clustered. Its members do not fall into elitist occupations which might alienate the group from the rest of the Sinhalese population. In fact, there are only four "trousered gentlemen" in both local societies. To the contrary, Figure 3 seems to be a fair cross section of the Buddhist population of the island. If anything, the two rosters suggest the interpenetration of categories like traditional and modern. All that seem to be missing are women. In the two groups there are only two female members. The *samitiya* explains this disproportion in thoroughly sexist terms. Women have no initiative (*yunanuyak nähä*).

That initiative is necessary for any Sinhalese to join the Society becomes obvious in reviewing the history of the Society in Dikkumbure, a Goyigama village to the interior of Weligama. What also comes into view is the strength of social relationships among people of the same family, of the same caste, and of the same village. Dikkumbure is the only Vinaya Vardena Society village in the area, and its villagers are split into two factions by the presence of the Society. Of the three Buddhist temples in the village, one belongs to the Vinaya Vardena Society. It is the smallest of the three. The temple was built in the 1950s to accommodate a wandering tāpasa monk who had settled on the temple site in a makeshift hut. He drew immediate support because many villagers felt that the other incumbent bhikkhus were *dussīla* (impious).[54] Many villages disagreed, some for differences of opinion, others because they were related to the other village monks, but support was sufficient to build a modest dwelling place for the ascetic new bhikkhu. In 1958 he left against growing suspicion about his behavior and great national suspicion about the sangha in general.

When a group of Rāmañña monks later came to stay in the abandoned monastery, they found a constituency waiting for them. But the constituency was one with standards of probity even the austere Rāmañña monks could not match. They sat on high chairs, used medicine, travelled by bus, and like the *tāpasa* monk, they were not native to the village. After Vinaya Vardena literature was distributed locally by a member of the Matara samitiya and interest in the movement began to grow, the Rāmañña monks sensed a change in the winds and left the village. Soon the Vinaya Vardena group took over the vihāra, draped cloths in front of Buddha images (here because they objected to artistic diversions and magical implications but were still chary of removing or breaking an image of the Buddha), and began to hold their own *poya* activities in the preaching hall. To this day the village remains split between a core of Vinaya Vardena people and the supporters of the establishment monks. A smaller number of people tries to support both factions. When a death occurs in this third group, the family arranges for two *paṃsukūla* rituals, one to be performed by the bhikkhus, the other by the Vinaya Vardena Society.

Hedging one's bets is not unreasonable. If *paṃsukūla* is not done, the deceased goes to hell (*paṃsukūlaya nu dunnot apāye yanavā*). If a son does not offer two yards of cloth to the bhikkhu-sangha in the name of the deceased, his kinsmen feel great shame (*vililajjavak*). If one eschews the Vinaya Vardena contingent, one risks losing friends and supporters, and that risk is a great one because people who feel strongly enough about the Society to join publicly want to win converts.[55] If one eschews the bhikkhus, one risks a less militant but larger network of relationships. It is the recognition that the village monks are men of the village (*gamērатē minissu*) that accounts for continuing support, often even when the monks are known to be *dussīla*.[56] They too are tied to networks of laypeople and other bhikkhus. They have legal rights. In the two other monasteries in Dikkumbure, wrongdoing monks have not been reprimanded. Who would do so? The rāja? The national government? The monks' kinsmen are too loyal; their other supporters, too weak.

One does not have to see a world in every grain of sand to recognize in the Vinaya Vardena Society and in its history in Dikkumbure social forces that have shaped Sinhalese Buddhism over the last 2,000 years. Sinhalese religion is acted out by people living in society. It is stabilized by social relationships. That is not exceptional. What perhaps is more characteristically Sinhalese is that in dealing with bhikkhus, the layman interacts with individuals who are kinsmen, who have economic holdings, who walk the same pathways and eat the same food as other villagers. But they are also part of the *Tun Saraṇa*, (if not for the Society's version certainly for everyone else's) the central ideological structure of the Buddhist religion. Lay relations with such polysemantic characters cannot be simple. But the tension is even greater: bhikkhus, I have argued, are seen not only as worthy of veneration while they act out the Buddha's sacred biography, but also as custodians of orthodoxy and stewards of Sri Lanka's traditional relationship with Theravada.

On the whole, the nobility and weight of this burden, given its connection with ethnic legitimacy, high caste exclusivity, and monastic landlordism, has put the sangha above reproach. The collapse of the Sinhalese monarchy increased this autonomy. On the other hand, it has contrarily increased the laity's sense of the monkhood's accountability.[57] Certainly that is Sumanaratne's case. He has not only called to account monkly behavior, but he has also called into doubt their formulation of doctrine. For his followers, however, Vinaya has been more important than Dhamma. For them, the Vinaya Vardena Society is just what it says it is, the society which protects the Vinaya which in turn protects the Dhamma. The offer of proximate nibbāna, the reformulation of correct belief, is a serendipity.

As for the bulk of the Sinhalese population, assaulting the monkhood at its strength, its knowledge of Dhamma, is altogether too much. Violations of Vinaya can be handled in other ways. One can worship the robes but not their wearer; one can transfer support to other local monks, to *tāpasa* monks, or to faraway *āraññavāsi* monks; or one can simply overlook monkly failings. The Dhamma at least is intact. Any of these choices preserves the network of social ties within which Sinhalese Buddhism has endured. When Max Weber characterized Buddhism by pointing to its commitment to dispassionate intellectual discourse, its appeal to bourgeois values and the privileged strata of society, and its teaching that a layman can do his best towards salvation by supporting the monkhood, he suggested that the character of the religion had more potential for legitimating authority than for overthrowing it. Of course those characteristics work equally well towards the legitimation of monkly authority. The Vinaya Vardena Society, in any case, tests that characterization.

Notes

1. "Ceylon," *The Encyclopedia of Religion and Ethics*, edited by James Hastings, (New York: Charles Scribner's Sons, 1911), vol. 11, p. 334.
2. Copleston, Reginald Stephen, *Buddhism, Primitive and Present Magadha and Ceylon* (London: Longmans, Green, 1892), p. 4.
3. This dichotomy has been understood both historically and social structurally: some scholars have relegated "pure" Buddhism to an early period; others have argued for the continued existence of two levels of Buddhist thought and practice, one, atheistic and pure, the other, idolatrous. This latter view distinguishes contemporary Buddhists according to those who follow a "higher" law and a "lower" one. See Guy Welbon, *The Buddhist Nirvana and its Western Interpreters* (Chicago: University of Chicago Press, 1968), p. 18.
4. *Precept and Practice* (Oxford: Clarendon Press, 1971). Gombrich looks for evidence which might bear upon the orthodoxy question only in the context of "traditional" Buddhism, which can be found in a small number of Kandyan villages. The ponderous majority of Sinhalese Buddhists fall into the category "modern."

5. Gombrich's argument for the stability of the doctrinal understanding of the religion has been persuasively challenged by Kitsiri Malalgoda in his review of Gombrich's work, "Sinhalese Buddhism: Orthodox and Syncretistic, Traditional and Modern," *Ceylon Journal of Historical and Social Sciences*, New Series, Vol. II, No. 2, July-Dec. 1972, pp. 156-169. Malalgoda takes Gombrich to task for ignoring possible changes worked when the Pāli canon was mediated through Sinhalese sources which Gombrich surprisingly dismisses, as well as for drawing a distinction between traditional and modern Buddhism and then ignoring the interpenetration of these categories.

6. *Precept and Practice*, p. 45.

7. One helpful distinction is inherent: "The Tathāgatha has no theories," *Majjhima-Nikāya* I, p. 486. Since the Buddha himself was opposed to metaphysical inquiry, apparently inconsistent beliefs are not so. They are merely beside the point, e.g., a belief in gods is not evidence for heterodoxy because the existence of gods and their worship are in principle irrelevant to the circumscribed nature of Buddhist dogma.

8. *Precept and Practice*, pp. 4-8.

9. *Precept and Practice*, p. 9.

0. See p. 175 (twice), p. 46, p. 145, and p. 176.

1. *Precept and Practice*, p. 223. See also his pp. 241 and 243 for similar examples.

2. My knowledge of the Vinaya Vardena Movement comes from two periods of fieldwork in Sri Lanka, September 1969-July 1971, and summer 1974. The first stay was supported by a dissertation research grant from the National Institutes of Mental Health, the second by a Bates College Faculty Research Grant.

3. *Precept and Practice*, p. 28, ftn. 42. Gombrich's point that the prior relationship is between laity and monkhood, not laity and the religion is a fine one and the stuff of academic discourse, but it is to the point that Sinhalese laypeople, and it is with them that my interest lies, voice similar opinions. It is likewise significant that the sangha is part of the *Tun Saraṇa* (Triple Gems or Refuges) and thus worthy like the Lord Buddha and his Dhamma of veneration. This again is a doctrinal point and a native view of things.

4. In a controversial book on the notion of religion, W. C. Smith has argued that until the Enlightenment, the Latin root *religio* and its English derivative were used to denote neither a set of doctrines nor a religious establishment, but piety or religiosity, *The Meaning and End of Religion* (Basic Books, 1962), *passim.* If the important pre-Enlightenment relationship was seen to lie between man and God, not man and dogma, and *mutatis mutandis* for Islam and Hinduism, then the Buddhist contrast is patent. In Sri Lanka men very quickly made Buddhism a social relationship between the state and a group of renouncers.

5. Alternative views of what such groups amounted to and what relations obtained between them are found in R. A. L. H. Gunawardena, "Buddhist Nikayas in Medieval Ceylon," *Ceylon Journal of Historical and Social Studies*, Peradeniya, Vol. IX, No. 1, 1966, pp. 55-66, and D. J. Kalupahana, "Schools of Buddhism in Early Ceylon," *Ceylon Journal of the Humanities* (Peradeniya: University of Ceylon Press), July 1970.

6. The Sinhalese have recently drawn a similar connection between Buddhism and Sinhalese nationalism. The founding of the nation, for instance, has been equated in the popular imagination with the historically subsequent coming of Mahinda and the Theravada monkhood. Bardwell Smith has suggested that Sri Lanka's present quest for identity has reinforced her vocation as maintaining the purity of Dhamma with "a comparable insistence upon national purity," namely the rejection of Christian, Tamil, and Western elements from their culture, "Sinhalese Buddhism and the Dilemmas of Reinterpretation," in *The Two Wheels of Dhamma*, edited by Bardwell Smith (Chambersburg, Pa.: American Academy of Religion, 1972), p. 89. Exactly what relations obtained in early Sinhalese history between Theravada orthodoxy and Sinhalese ethnicity is an open question and one with importance for the study of political legitimacy throughout South Asia.

7. The notion of custodial care is implicit in the distinction between two monkish life styles open to renouncers in Sri Lanka. Most become *gamavāsi* (village dwelling) monks, a few, *āraññavāsi* (hermitage dwelling) monks. Gamavāsi monks are not only logistically closer to the secular world, they also bear the "yoke" of teaching and preserving the Dhamma (*ganthadhura*). *Āraññavāsi* monks bear the "yoke" of meditation (*vipassanādhura*).

18. "Buddhaghosa's greatest value to the modern historian is due largely to the limitation of his mental powers. Of his talent there can be no doubt; it was equalled only by his extraordinary industry. But of originality, of independence of thought, there is at present no evidence. He had mastered so thoroughly and accepted so completely the Buddhist way of life, that there was no need for him to occupy time with any discussion of ultimate questions," T. W. Rhys Davids, "Buddhaghosa," *Encyclopaedia of Religion and Ethics*, edited by James Hastings (New York: Charles Scribner's Sons, 1910), Vol. II, p. 887.
19. The possibility of joining the same Siyam Nikāya which claims descent from the Mahāvihāra tradition remains to this day a Goyigama prerogative. Why only high caste individuals make suitable bhikkhus is discussed in my doctoral dissertation, "The Social Order or the Sinhalese Buddhist *Sangha*," (Chicago: 1973). The prescribed transactional relations between sangha and laity are confounded in a caste society, and Sri Lanka remains the single case of a Theravada Buddhist society organized according to caste principles. As renouncers, bhikkhus are chronic "receivers," of alms, robes, and other requisites, but in a caste society where to receive is to admit inferiority, or, at least, equality, "receiving" is incompatible with Goyigama status. Endowing monasteries with temporalities is a happy, if not an intended solution, for such monks are self-sufficient and need not receive at all. Indeed, that constitutes one of the Vinaya Vardena Society's grievances. Heinz Bechert has almost inadvertently suggested the outlines of an "ethnicity" explanation of Goyigama exclusiveness in the Siyam Nikāya. "Most of the lower castes of the Sinhalese originate from the assimilation of minority ethnic groups; in the coastal areas, the larger minority castes can be traced back to immigrated Dravidian populations which have been assimilated. . . . Historically speaking, the Goyigama caste can be largely identified with the Sinhalese peasant population in the larger sense of the word," "Theravada Buddhist Sangha: Some General Observations of Historical and Political Factors in its Development," *Journal of Asian Studies*, Vol. 29, No. 4, August 1970, p. 769, ftn. 29. Thus to be a bhikkhu, it could be argued, one must be Goyigama for two cognate reasons: to be Goyigama is to be sufficiently high status to control monastic temporalities, and it is also to be truly Sinhalese. Again the question of the relationship between Sinhalese ethnicity, religion and political legitimacy is one which invites scrutiny. See ftn. 16.
20. G. P. Malalasekera, *The Pāli Literature of Ceylon* (London: Royal Asiatic Society of Great Britain and Ireland, 1928), p. 38.
21. The founding of the two reform Nikāyas was an effort not only to extend the monkhood to non-Goyigama monks but also to restore some control over the monkhood to lay hands.
22. The British came to justify their interference in monastic affairs on the grounds that the *bhikkhu-saṅgha* was a landholder and, like other landholders, legally accountable to the Crown.
23. That the Buddhist sāsana is a historical phenomenon, with a precisely dated beginning and end, some 5,000 years later, increases the apparent fragility of the religion. For the Theravada tradition what is at stake is not the *sanātana dharma* (ongoing, endless religious truth) of Hinduism, but the Dhamma of the Lord Buddha, a circumscribed technique for achieving *nibbāna* discovered by a fully historical character.

    Perhaps even more cogently, Sinhalese laypeople tell the story of Kasava Kantakaya, the last bhikkhu in the Buddhist sāsana who will wear as a symbol of his "going forth" not a yellow robe but only a yellow thread tied around his arm. The implication is plain. If the monkhood were depopulated, Buddhism itself would die. As long as a single bhikkhu practices and preserves the religion, even if his commitment is reduced to a single thread, the sāsana continues.
24. A fuller discussion of the "anagārika" role in a decidedly untraditional context can be found in Gananath Obeyesekere, "Religious Symbolism and Political Change in Ceylon," in Bardwell Smith, ed., *The Two Wheels of Dhamma*, pp. 58-79.
25. The tāpasa movement is treated briefly by Heinz Bechert in his monumental *Buddhismus, Staat und Gesellschaft in den Landern des Theravada-Buddhismus* (Berlin: Alfred Metzner Verlag, 1966), p. 258.
26. See Nur Yalman, "The Ascetic Buddhist Monks of Ceylon," *Ethnology*, 1(3), pp. 315-328.
27. Much of the account that follows comes from a Sinhalese history of the movement. *Sri*

Lankā Vinaya Vardena Itihāsaya (Colombo: Oriental Yantralaya, 1959), which has been translated with the extraordinarily gracious help of Mr. G. B. A. de Silva of Minuwangoda. The balance of the information comes from conversations with the Society's leadership, chiefly A. Sumanaratne and James Soysa.

28. *Vinaya Vardena Itihāsaya*, pp. 3-4.

29. Although the monkhood is dominated in Sabaragamuva by these two Nikāyas, there are more than demographic factors at work here. The Vinaya Vardena Society has had less of an argument with the Rāmañña Nikāya because of its reputation for austerity and its attempt to eschew the use of money. Eventually, however, the Rāmañña monks joined the other Nikāyas in opposing the movement.

30. Jayasundera subsequently wrote two leaflets, "Bodhayo nagitithva" and "Bodhayo nagitithva!" (Pelmadulla: Saparagamu Yantralaya, no date) which bitterly criticize Sumanaratne and the organization he inherited. The attack is alternately etymological and *ad hominem.* Sumanaratne is criticized for not recognizing that there can be no role midway between *anagārika* (monk) and *agārika* (layman) – one might as well propose the existence of a *del-kos*, a vegetable which combines the qualities of *del* (breadfruit) and *kos* (*jak*) - for misunderstanding the *Tun Saraṇa*, and for being inconsistent in looking for orthodoxy. Such criticism is typical of the tone used both by the movement and against it.

31. The word *vajjī* suggests "heretical" and derives from an early branch of Buddhism, Vajjiputra, which was considered heretical by Theravada monks for its advocacy of the idea that an element of the *person* transmigrates from one life to the next. The irony of now applying the term back upon present-day Theravada monks whom the Society criticizes for being too entangled as *persons* with the secular world is hard to escape.

32. Kitsiri Malalgoda has argued in his D. Phil. thesis, "Sociological Aspects of Revival and Change in Buddhism in Nineteenth-century Ceylon," (Oxford, 1970), that these debates are evidence of the revival of Buddhism among the Sinhalese as well as the origin of nationalist feeling, here couched in Buddhist pride and anti-Christian feeling. In the present case, I see little evidence for the Society's having national political implications. The implications I see are local ones.

33. Dhamma, it is usually said, concerns the inner life of the Buddha's followers, above all their spiritual progress. Vinaya, on the other hand, regulates the outward life. Herman Oldenberg in his edition of the *Vinayapiṭaka* suggests that Dhamma may be said to be all that Vinaya is not. It is also noteworthy that nibbāna is mentioned only twice in the Vinaya rules.

34. This argument is not without textual support. In the *Samantapāsādikā*, Buddhaghosa's commentary to the *Vinayapiṭaka*, one finds this account of the first great convocation:

> When the Venerable One was thus seated the Elder Mahākassapa addressed the monks, "Friends, what shall we rehearse first, the Dhamma or the Vinaya?" The monks replied, "Sir, Mahākassapa, the Vinaya is the very life of the Dispensation of the Enlightened One: so long as the Vinaya endures, the Dispensation endures, therefore let us rehearse the Vinaya first."

The Inception of the Discipline and the Vinaya Nidana, trans. by N. A. Jayawickrama (London: Luzac and Co., Ltd., 1962), p. 11.

35. Gombrich aptly describes general attitudes about nibbāna. See especially p. 221 and pp. 284-286.

36. *Vinaya Vardena Itihāsaya*, pp. 24-25.

37. These four stages of increasing spiritual growth are referred to collectively as *māgapala.* See the discussion that follows on pp. 31-33.

38. The Society prefers the expression *mal pahan pujāva* (flower and light offering) to *āmisha pujāva* which connotes the giving of rice to images of the Buddha. Buddhist attitudes as to whether the Buddha image is in any way alive and thus able to partake of the rice are inconsistent. Gombrich illustrates this uncertainty, pp. 119-122, 139-140, and 142. In any case when the Society performs *mal pahan pujāva*, the *pūjā* is done in front of the *dagaba*, not before a Buddha image, thus stressing the rite's purely commemorative intention.

39. The Society says that until the time of the Sinhalese king Weligamba monks did not attend the funerals of laymen. Now they come only to ingratiate themselves (*labha satkara ganimata*) with the deceased's family. Thus the Society's assumption of the otherwise

monkly role at funerals is not only a political action, it is also a return to orthodoxy.

40. Sumanaratne makes a similarly ironic point in his *Vibbajjavadaya hevat Buddhagama* (Colombo: Munagama Mudranalaya, 1960), p. ii. Before the Lord Buddha taught his Dhamma to others, people were misled by brahmins to believe in the possibility of relieving suffering through brahminical rituals. Deliverance from suffering can be achieved only by one's own efforts. Likewise, Buddhist laypeople are now misled by bhikkhus who foist upon them false interpretations of Dhamma. One can know religious truth only by making oneself directly responsible for it.
41. What is at stake here is whether the symbols of religious controversy are arbitrary political vehicles or ideologically significant ones. In his *Essay on the Development of Christian Doctrine* (Middlesex, England: Penguin, 1973), for instance, John Henry Newman plainly takes the former position with regard to early Christianity pp. 272-7. The present case is less clear, as are the hair-splitting disputes that figure prominently in the fissiparous history of the Siyam and Amarapura Nikāyas in Sri Lanka.
42. In the Society's lone English publication, *Quintessence of Buddhism*, Martin Wengapulli, (Matara: Matara Merchants, 1957), p. 2, the argument is made that what one attains in following the path is Buddhahood itself (Pāli, *Bujjita saccani ti buddha*, He who realizes the Four Noble Truths is Buddha). The publication goes on to distinguish different types of Buddhas, namely, *Sruta* Buddha, *Arahanta* Buddha, *Pachcheka* Buddha, and *Sammasam* Buddha. *Sruta* Buddha is "one who is well instructed in the Four Noble Truths by hearing or studying the Dhamma, and then strives to get an empirical knowledge of the Four Noble Truths." That formulation makes most Buddhists at least *Sruta* Buddhas, but this point is not commonly taught. Claiming to be a Buddha of any kind has a blasphemous sound even to the Society.
43. *Quintessence*, p. 7.
44. *Ibid.*
45. *Ibid.*, p. iv.
46. The political implication of this belief, for instance, is illustrative of the contingency of many doctrinal beliefs of the Society. If the laity belongs to the sangha, then the organized sangha is not essential for the survival of the religion, and the sangha can be rightly subjected to lay criticism and reform. This is a twist on the conventional distinction between the *sammutisaṅgha* and the *ariyasaṅgha.* By this logic, all Buddhists might be said to belong to the *ariyasaṅgha.*
47. *Quintessence*, pp. 23-24.
48. *Ibid.*, p. 11.
49. In Sinhalese: *Mama Budu wēmi,*
Mama nava lovturu dahama avaboda karami,
Mama kelasun näsu ariyakama paminēmi.
50. *Sri Lanka Baudha Vinaya Vardena Paksha Pratipattiya* (Colombo: Oriental Yantralaya, 1963), p. 2.
51. The opposition of the establishment sangha is perhaps the strongest. Most monks seem to be content to dismiss the movement as lunatic fringe. Others choose to bathe the movement in abuse. The testimony of a prominent bhikkhu before the Buddhist Sasana Reform Committee in 1956 is a good example of monkly reaction to tāpasa monks and by extension to *anagārika-yogis* and the Vinaya Vardena Society. The monk calls them "the most dangerous heretics since the time of Asoka" and "communists," quoted by Bechert, *Buddhismus . . .*, p. 258.
52. Several members, half facetiously, compared the Society's lack of a popular base to the LSSP, the island's first leftist party, until recently an important part of a coalition government and best known for its unwillingness to bend its principles. Nor will the Society compromise its values. "Perhaps someday the Society will also have a chance to run the country!"
53. The personal and place names which follow are pseudonymous. Not all of these *samitiyas* are corporate or entirely local. Since the recent shrinkage in membership, some *samitiyas*, especially the first one of the two surveyed here, include members who have been incorporated after the collapse of other groups.
54. If there is any one regularity which might explain the distribution of Vinaya Vardena local societies, I would speculate that groups tend to arise in communities where an incumbent

bhikkhu has demonstrably violated the *pārājika* rule against sexual intercourse. Numerous members of the Society seem formerly to have been intimately involved in the routine of life of a local monastery and thus privy to such scandal.

5. In another coastal village I have seen a Vinaya Vardena proponent spontaneously and unsolicitedly rise to speak after a local bhikkhu delivered the scheduled funeral oration. The Vinaya Vardena speaker spoke not of the dead, but of the local monks' violation of *sīl.* Naturally, the attack caused considerable embarrassment to the audience which found itself in the middle. Elsewhere fisticuffs have erupted in a village where a deceased man's son wished to employ a Vinaya Vardena Society contingent at the funeral and other relatives with no Vinaya Vardena connections insisted that local bhikkhus participate.
6. I am reminded of an election jingle, *ūt kupāḍiyā, mūt kupāḍiyā, gamē kupāḍiyata chande denna* (Their man is a cad, our man is a cad, vote for the cad from [your own] village). The jingle would be less amusing if it were less true of Sinhalese feelings.
7. A bhikkhu is taught to reflect every day: "My life is dependent upon others – this should be reflected upon by one gone forth" (Discourse on the Ten Conditions, *Aṅguttara Nikāya,* X). The examples of the Amarapura and Rāmañña reformations suggest this same attempt to restore the monkhood's dependence.

Contributors

HEINZ BECHERT has been Professor and Director of the Seminar fuer Indologie und Buddhismuskunde at the University of Goettingen since 1965. He is also Chairman of the Committee for Buddhist Studies of the Akademie der Wissenschaften in Goettingen and Associate Member of the Académie Royale de Belgique in Brussels. His Ph.D. is from the University of Muenchen (1956), and his dissertation on Buddhist Sanskrit texts from Central Asia was published in an enlarged form: *Bruchstuecke buddhistischer Verssammlungen* (Berlin: Deutsche Akademie der Wissenschaften, 1961). He also edited *The Bhāgavata Purāṇa, from the Birch Bark Manuscript in Goettingen* (New Delhi: International Academy of Indian Culture, 1976) and Central Asian fragments of Saddharmapuṇḍarīka (*Über die Marburger Fragmente des Saddharmapuṇḍarīka*, Goettingen: Akademie der Wissenschaften, 1972). In the field of the history and culture of Sri Lanka, he is the editor of Wilhelm Geiger's posthumous work *Culture of Ceylon in Mediaeval Times* (Wiesbaden: Harrassowitz, 1960), as well as of *Buddhism in Ceylon and Studies on Religious Syncretism in Buddhist Countries: Report of a Symposium in Goettingen* (Goettingen: Akademie der Wissenschaften, 1977), and the author of a catalogue of Sinhala manuscripts in Germany (*Singhalesische Handschriften*, Wiesbaden: Steiner, 1969), of a mythological dictionary of the folk religion of the Sinhalese (*Mythologie der singhalesischen Volksreligion*, in: *Wörterbuch der Mythologie*, Stuttgart: Klett, 1976), and of many articles. The results of his studies on modern Theravāda Buddhism are formulated in *Buddhismus, Staat und Gesellschaft* (3 vols., Frankfurt and Wiesbaden: Institut fuer Asienkunde in Hamburg, 1966-73) and in numerous contributions to journals. In 1958-59 he was a research fellow in Sri Lanka, and in 1969-70 and 1974-75 he taught as a visiting professor for Buddhist studies at Yale University.

REGINA T. CLIFFORD is an NDEA Title VI Fellow studying Thai and working toward her doctorate in the History of Religions at the University of Chicago. She received her M.A. from the University of Chicago in 1975 and her B.A. from The Western College, Oxford, Ohio in 1974. In 1973 she studied in Sri Lanka.

ALICE M. GREENWALD is Curator of the Hebrew Union College Skirball Museum in Los Angeles where she has taught courses in Biblical history/literature and Jewish ceremonial art. She holds a B.A. from Sarah Lawrence College (1973) and an M.A. degree in the History of Religions, with candidacy toward the Ph.D. recommended, from the University of Chicago Divinity School (1975). A Danforth Fellow, Ms. Greenwald assisted in a course on scriptural formation in Western religious traditions at Chicago. She specializes in comparative religious studies, Judaism and Judaica, religious literature and exegesis, primitive religions, and ritual and mythology in culture.

R. A. L. H. GUNAWARDANA is Associate Professor of History at the Peradeniya Campus of the University of Sri Lanka where he has been teaching since 1960. He holds a B.A. in History from the University of Sri Lanka (1960) and a Ph.D. from the University of London (1965). In the academic year 1972-73 he was Commonwealth Fellow at Gonville and Caius College, Cambridge, and, later, Visiting Fellow at Corpus Christi College, Oxford. His academic interests include history of religion, history of technology, historiography and anthropological theory. He has published several articles in *Past and Present, Indian*

Historical Review, and academic journals in Sri Lanka. He has edited three symposia, and completed a book on the history of the Buddhist *saṅgha* in early medieval Sri Lanka. He is currently doing research on the history of irrigation in South Asia.

STEVEN E. G. KEMPER is Assistant Professor of Anthropology and a member of the Committee on Cultural Studies at Bates College, Lewiston, Maine. He took a B.A. in Anthropology from Dartmouth College and a Ph.D. from the University of Chicago (1973) where he spent one year teaching in the Indian Civilization program. The title of his dissertation is "The Social Order of the Sinhalese Buddhist *Sangha*." His more recent research has focused on astrology, marriage as a cultural institution, and social change.

SIRIMA KIRIBAMUNE is Associate Professor of History at the Peradeniya Campus of the University of Sri Lanka. She holds a B.A. (1954) and an M.A. (1956) in History from the same University. Her Ph.D. (1959) is from the University of London, the subject of her dissertation being *The Age of Parākramabāhu I (1153-1186)*. She has been teaching at the University of Sri Lanka (Peradeniya) since 1954. Her research has been mainly on the ancient and medieval history of Sri Lanka.

GANANATH OBEYESEKERE is Professor of Anthropology at the University of California, San Diego. His undergraduate training was in literature at the University of Ceylon and his Ph.D. in anthropology from the University of Washington (Seattle). He has also done post-doctoral research in Cambridge, England. He has taught at the University of Washington and until 1971 was Chairman, Department of Sociology, University of Ceylon (Peradeniya). His publications include *Land Tenure in Village Ceylon* (Cambridge, 1967) and numerous scholarly papers on Sri Lankan ethnography, culture, history and the sociology of Buddhism.

H. L. SENEVIRATNE is Assistant Professor of Anthropology at the University of Virginia, Charlottesville. He holds a B.A. in Sociology from the University of Sri Lanka, Peradeniya, and an M.A. and Ph.D. (1972) from the University of Rochester in Anthropology. Besides his current position he has also taught at the University of Sri Lanka. He has published several articles on religion and society in Ceylon and his doctoral research was on Kandyan ritual. His primary academic interests are religion and society, sociological theory, politics, and economic development. He has recently taught a course on the sociology of Theravada Buddhism.

BARDWELL L. SMITH is the John W. Nason Professor of Asian Studies at Carleton College, Northfield, Minnesota. He also served as Dean of the College, 1967-72. He has received his B.A., B.D., M.A., and Ph.D. from Yale University and was a member of the Yale University Council, 1969-74. During 1972-73 he did research at the School of Oriental and African Studies, University of London, on a grant from the American Council of Learned Societies. He has edited a number of books, among them: *The Two Wheels of Dhamma: Essays on the Theravada Tradition in India and Ceylon* (American Academy of Religion, 1972); *Tradition and Change in Theravada Buddhism: Essays on Ceylon and Thailand in the 19th and 20th Centuries* (Leiden: E. J. Brill, 1973); *Unsui: A Diary of Zen Monastic Life* (Honolulu: University Press of Hawaii,

1973); *Hinduism: New Essays in the History of Religions* (Leiden: E. J. Brill, 1976); *Religion and Social Conflict in South Asia* (Leiden: E. J. Brill, 1976); and *Essays on T'ang Society: The Interplay of Social, Political and Economic Forces* (Leiden: E. J. Brill, 1976), co-edited with John Curtis Perry.

Index